An Introduction to
Critical Social Psychology

An Introduction to
Critical Social Psychology

Alexa Hepburn

 **SAGE** Publications

London • Thousand Oaks • New Delhi

in association with

The Open
University

SAGE Publications Ltd
6 Bonhill Street
London EC2A 4PU

SAGE Publications Inc
2455 Teller Road
Thousand Oaks, California 91320

SAGE Publications India Pvt Ltd
32, M-Block Market
Greater Kailash – I
New Delhi 110 048

British Library Cataloguing in Publication data

A catalogue record for this book is available from the British Library

ISBN 0 7619 6209 3
ISBN 0 7619 6210 7 (pbk) ✓

Library of Congress Control Number: 2002101991

Typeset by Mayhew Typesetting, Rhayader, Powys
Printed and bound in Great Britain by The Cromwell Press Ltd,
Trowbridge, Wiltshire

Contents

List of boxes   vii
Acknowledgements   viii

1 The Critical Context   1

What is critical social psychology criticizing?   1
Stories of class and privilege   3
Society, knowledge and subjectivity   5
What's in this book?   11

Part I Mind and Society   17

2 Social Cognition Critics   19

Early critical work in social psychology   20
The crisis in social psychology   24
Contemporary social cognition   32
Application   42
Conclusion   43

3 Marxist Critics   46

Marxist theory: basic ideas and recent developments   47
Ideology and discursive, critical and rhetorical psychology   55
Foucault's theoretical development and critique of Marx   61
Application   66
Conclusion   67

4 Psychoanalytic Critics   70

Freud's psychoanalysis and Klein's object relations theory   71
Hollway: object relations in critical work   74
Parker and Billig's psychoanalytic cultures   79
Post-structuralism and psychoanalysis: Lacan and others   87

Application   93
Conclusion   95

5   Feminist Critics   98

What is feminist psychology?   99
Sexism and the legitimation of gender inequalities   103
Heterosexism and lesbian and gay psychology   107
Eating disorders and the body   111
Postmodern feminists: contemporary debates   117
Feminism and relativism   122
Application   128
Conclusion   128

Part II   Resolutions and Dilemmas   131

6   Subjectivity Critics   133

Some philosophical explorations of subjectivity   135
Critical psychology and subjectivity   148
Application and intervention   162
Conclusion   163

7   Discourse Critics   166

Discourse, psychology and the individual   167
Discourse and construction   174
Rhetoric and ideological dilemmas   183
Applications   193
Conclusion   194

8   Postmodern Critics   198

Postmodern theories   199
Postmodernism, deconstruction and critical social psychology   210
Postmodern knowledge and the realism/relativism debate   215
Application   223
Conclusion   224

9   Integration and Subversions   228

Critical assumptions   228
Critical practice   235
Critical evaluations   237
Conclusion: looking to the future   246

References   249
Index   269

List of boxes

Issues

1.1	Who are the readers?	2
2.1	Sociology of scientific knowledge	26
2.2	Social representations	31
2.3	Crowds	38
3.1	Actor network theory	64
4.1	Bakhtin and the diagnostic	85
5.1	Patriarchy	102
5.2	Queer theory	120
6.1	Voices of the mind	157
7.1	Foucault and discursive psychology	167
7.2	The context debate	172
7.3	Greenspeak	188
8.1	Metaphysics	207
8.2	Textuality and tectonics	213
9.1	Reflexivity	232

People

Rom Harré	28
Martha Augoustinos	35
Michael Billig	41
Ian Parker	47
Dennis Fox	57
Corinne Squire	94
Kum Kum Bhavnani	101
Sue Wilkinson	102
Celia Kitzinger	109
Tod Sloan	154
Valerie Walkerdine	159
John Shotter	176
Jonathan Potter	178
Carla Willig	193
Ken Gergen	201
Tomás Ibáñez	215
Lupicinio Íñiguez	216
Ros Gill	222
Malcolm Ashmore	233

Acknowledgements

Numerous people have inspired me to write this book. Ian Parker and Harriette Marshall are the most obvious. I have always admired Ian's enthusiasm and commitment, and aspire to his ability to not hold a grudge even though I keep arguing with him! I taught critical social psychology with Harriette at Staffordshire University for three years. It was a major learning experience on so many levels – the baltis, the pints of Guinness – it was fantastic.

Nick Hopkins was also an inspiration in his own inimitable way. If it weren't for him I'd probably be a philosopher by now. I am also grateful to Clare MacMartin for her dynamic intellectual support and feedback on subjectivity and feminism. And a big thank you goes to all the person box contributors – many of the great and good of critical social psychology – who have livened things up considerably.

I'd like to thank all my students from Staffordshire University and Nottingham Trent University, who have cheerfully endured my rants about critical social psychology. Thanks particularly to Steven Stanley for his comments on an early version of the Marxism chapter.

Sage editor Michael Carmichael has been a model of patience and professionalism, and has provided his own intellectual input. He made the whole process seem easy!

As this is my first book I must thank my parents Jean and Alex. I am grateful for the early encouragement to reject 'normal' practices, and for leading me (unwittingly, I'm sure!) to question and doubt just about everything. Moving swiftly down the psychodynamic chain I must thank my brother Duncan for preventing some truly unhappy contortions of the English language from appearing in this book (except this one). I'm also grateful to my daughter Marian, who provided important feedback on the Marxism and feminism chapters and generally cheered me up a lot when there seemed to be too much critical social psychology and not enough time. Andrew, my son, has prevented a few embarrassing misreadings (yes, misreadings!) of Derrida and was the inspiration for a box on metaphysics. I've learned a lot from his patient and scholarly approach.

Last, and the opposite of least, I'd like to thank my fabulous partner Jonathan Potter, for all his encouragement and support: for always having my tea ready on the table after I've had a hard day thinking, and for generally keeping my life running smoothly by performing myriad humdrum domestic duties – washing, ironing, vacuuming, dusting – the sort of stuff that he seems to find important . . .

A.H.

Chapter 1

The Critical Context

What is critical social psychology? If this were an easy question there would be no need for a whole book to try to answer it. After all, virtually any piece of social psychology is critical of something, even if it is just another piece of research or another researcher. What is distinctive about critical social psychology is the breadth of its critical concerns. For critical social psychology, research is locked in with issues of politics, morality and social change. It starts from fundamental concerns with oppression, exploitation and human well-being. These are precisely the issues that bring many people into psychology, and particularly social psychology, in the first place; but they often seem a long way away from the everyday reality of social psychology research.

So critical social psychology is critical of society or at least some basic elements of its institutions, organizations or practices. But critical social psychology (sometimes shortened to CSP) is critical in another basic sense: it is critical of psychology itself. It asks questions about *its* assumptions, *its* practices and *its* broader influences. For many critical social psychologists the discipline of social psychology *itself* is one of the biggest problems to be addressed, and in the course of this book we will explore a range of attacks on psychology and suggestions for its transformation, or even, in its extreme forms, for its wholesale closure.

This dual task of criticizing society and criticizing the discipline will be a theme that reappears throughout the book. These two features often seem to work against one another; yet, far from being a problem, the tension between the two directions of criticism has been productive, and has provided critical social psychology with much of its current character. If at times it seems to be an approach chasing its own tail while shooting at its own feet, it is all the more lively and vigorous for it.

What is critical social psychology criticizing?

In the course of this book we will see the way critical social psychology has drawn on broad systems for understanding the nature of the person and the nature of society. In the past, the most important of these have been Marxism and psycho-analysis, which have both provided resources for fundamental criticism. But more

BOX 1.1   Who are the readers?

Books are written *for* readers. The most obvious way this is the case is that they are written in a particular language. They also presuppose a particular linguistic competence and a particular vocabulary. More than that, literary theorists suggest that books 'imply' particular readers. That is to say, they implicitly speak to persons with particular characteristics – knowledge of the world, views of morality, social backgrounds, and so on. Some of these things may be rather obvious – a critical social psychologist reading the editorial of a right-wing newspaper such as the *Daily Telegraph* is likely to feel deeply queasy at being addressed as someone who takes for granted the importance of tradition, the fecklessness of the working class, and the unjustified hysteria of feminists. But others are much more subtle. The use of certain categories and the enrolment of teachers into a 'we' that takes certain things for granted can be almost unnoticed. I will use 'we' a lot in this book, but as Michael Billig shows in his work on nationalism (1995), little words like this are far from innocent; their very banality allows them to carry an unnoticed politics with them.

recently these systems have been supplemented and sometimes replaced by post-modernism, feminism, social constructionism and discursive psychology. Each of these systems of ideas provides a purchase on the issues of how the person and society can be made sense of, and each system therefore provides a way of under-standing what the object of criticism is.

This introductory chapter aims to provide insights into the book as a whole. The following three sections aspire to do this in different ways. This may make the chapter seem rather repetitive, but I hope that this will assist its clarity: part of the difficulty many people have with critical social psychology is in seeing the big picture – how does it all hang together? By discussing the contents of different chapters, both here and in a more developed and in-depth way in Chapter 9, I hope to make things more accessible.

1   Section one aims to read critical social psychology through the newspapers. Surely if the discipline is to have any merit it must be able to tell us something about everyday life?

2   Section two takes a different route, aiming to lay out three broad sets of assumptions about the nature of society, subjectivity and knowledge often relied on by critical work, but seldom specified explicitly.

3   Section three aims to describe more explicitly the contents of the book, providing both a rationale for the two-part structure and a discussion of the contents of each chapter.

So let's imagine that we are sitting down to breakfast on Wednesday 31 May 2000. This is a day like any other. The new millennium is still pretty new and the papergirl has delivered (oh no!) *The Times* instead of the *Guardian*. It would be a little bit like getting the *National Enquirer* instead of the *New York Times*. Can we read critical social psychology through the papers?

Stories of class and privilege

Our aim is to track the relevance of perspectives like Marxism, psychoanalysis, feminism, discursive psychology and postmodernism. We do not have to look far to see the significance of Marxism, as *The Times* leads with a story about class and inequality and higher education. An Oxford college has turned down a gifted comprehensive school student from a northern city where she wanted to read Medicine. Members of the (slightly) left-of-centre government criticize the college, and the paper describes ministerial criticisms as preparing the public for a policy change whereby students from middle class backgrounds would be charged more to take degrees on the grounds that such degrees allow them access to highly paid and rewarding jobs.

    Not all discussions of social class are Marxist, but the broad framework for conceptualizing society in terms of competing classes with different interests has had a profound impact on most thinking of this kind. This framework will be introduced in Chapter 3. What else may be relevant to critical social psychologists here? From a more traditional perspective we may be interested in how prejudices might come into play in situations such as interviews. When the student was rejected the interviewers wrote in their notes that she was 'low in confidence, as with other comprehensive school pupils'. Does this display a prejudice against comprehensive pupils? Or does it record faithfully an actual lack of confidence? And, if so, where does that lack of confidence come from? Are there systematic inequalities of expectation that are stratified through different classes? How are such inequalities perpetuated? Some of these issues will be discussed in Chapter 2, on social cognition.

    Alternatively, could it be that the interaction itself generated an apparent confidence deficit? Being faced by the arrogance and accent of the Oxford interviewers the girl froze in a way that a private-school pupil, who would have found it more familiar, would not. Again, this is an issue for critical research into language, power and interaction. Some of these issues will be discussed in Chapter 7, on discursive critics.

    These questions are important, but by no means the only ones that critical social psychologists ask. This is a story about a *girl* pupil. That is, it is not just a matter of class, but is also about gender. And it is not just any course – Medicine is a degree that has been notoriously hard for female pupils to get into. Perhaps the prejudice was as much rooted in sexism, and perhaps the crucial aspects of the interaction that caused her problems were about gender. This will be the focus of Chapter 5. Issues of class, gender and interaction have been understood in very different ways in critical psychology. Psychoanalysis provides an individualized perspective that some feminists and other social theorists find useful, and will be discussed in Chapter 4. Here the pupil's subjective states would be the focus of attention, a move that many critical social psychologists would reject outright. The debates and theories that go with using features of subjectivity in explanatory ways will be the focus of Chapter 6.

There is a very different perspective available for understanding this story. Rather than investigate the events as they are depicted, or the inner subjective features of the pupil, we can ask how these things are constructed and what they are constructed to do. Stories can be assembled in different ways, using different sorts of description, and stories are used to make points, to offer moral tales, to criticize and celebrate. In this case the girl's headmaster, perhaps to put pressure on the Oxford college and other elite institutions to accept more of his pupils, released the story to a local newspaper. The story was widely publicized by the Labour Chancellor of the Exchequer, as an example of the kind of elite privilege the Labour Party was concerned to do away with. The theme here is how the world is manufactured to make arguments – how it is fashioned for rhetorical purposes. Issues of the construction of versions and their involvement in practices will be the topic of Chapter 7 on discourse.

The story of class and privilege is in a newspaper that has traditionally supported right-wing parties at election times. It is also in a newspaper that sells several hundred thousand copies a day to make money directly and through advertising. The story is linked with other stories about education and political problems. Various other stories highlight the way this story has been fashioned, and how it may be motivated; they report what may have been the reasons why the Chancellor used it, and what the headmaster may have got out of it. This 'intertextual' weave of stories is one of the characteristics of postmodernism. There is no secure basis, external to stories, from which truth can be assessed in a neutral manner. Right here I am putting together another story about stories to make a point, to highlight the nature of critical social psychology: and this story could *itself* be studied for how it works and what it is doing. This theme is explored in Chapter 8 on postmodernism.

Finally, critical social psychologists are, inevitably, concerned with social change. To paraphrase Marx, the point of critical social psychology is not merely to describe the world in a disinterested manner, but to change it. How to do this is a far from simple question. Some social psychologists advocate action research, which directly intervenes in settings. For others the aim is to increase people's understanding so they can change things, or to generate resources for change and criticism. The various perspectives explored in the course of the book understand change in very different ways and each chapter will explore issues of application and practice. The different perspectives on application are systematized and developed in Chapter 9, along with other ideas about future directions of CSP.

Writing a book about critical social psychology is inevitably both a descriptive and a critical exercise. In describing studies and perspectives that make up critical work in social psychology it necessarily makes a series of choices about what counts. Where should the boundaries be drawn between what is critical and what is not? Where does social psychology end and some other social science start? How will perspectives be linked together? Will it suggest a coherent front or emphasize diversity? Will it be inside one of its perspectives? These choices are part of the politics of textbook writing. If the book is doing its job then readers should be able to turn their critical understanding on to the book itself.

Society, knowledge and subjectivity

One of the aims of this book is to highlight the way critical work is dependent on a range of assumptions that are not always made explicit. Three groups of assumptions are most fundamental.

1   The first concerns the nature of society: how it works and how it can be changed.
2   The second concerns knowledge: how it changes, how it is justified, how 'solid' it is.
3   The third concerns the person: how personhood and subjectivity are understood.

Let me try and lay out these concerns in a way that will allow us to understand better the material that comes in later chapters.

Writing society

There are many different ways of understanding society, and I will try to indicate some of the things that separate one view from another. However, first it is important to emphasize that the very decision to start with ways of understanding *society* brings baggage with it. Critical social psychologists need to be on the alert for assumptions that can slip into their work unnoticed, particularly at such a fundamental level. We think of society as an obvious thing, something that we are part of and that exists 'out there'. But society is a relatively recent term; it is a theorized way of understanding . . . (um, now I am struggling for a more neutral term – and of course there isn't one) how people collect together. 'Society' is connected with an assortment of ideas and practices: social and political institutions, the economy, social groups and classes, political procedures and so on. We can 'see' these things with the aid of a developed set of notions from social and political science that have become part of our everyday currency. But we do not want to forget their status as constructions that come out of social science disciplines at particular points in history.

One major alternative we could consider would be culture. This notion, developed from the discipline of anthropology, would emphasize the symbolic and ritual side of . . . human life. (Note the way I am again caught trying to use a neutral word to describe a thing while highlighting the absence of such a neutral word.) For a critical social psychologist the problem with the notion of culture is its organic, timeless connotations. Society, with its associated thesaurus of notions, is a way of constructing . . . er . . . stuff that makes it more malleable, makes it something that can be transformed or overturned.

There are very different ways of theorizing society. Political science, political philosophy and sociology texts cover a range of competing classifications of types of society or ways of understanding society in general. Rather than go into the technicalities of these, and thereby get very far away from our critical topic, I am going to draw a rather simple distinction between three ways of viewing society. The reason for choosing this is that it helps us pick out assumptions in critical work. It provides a simple and convenient way into our topic. The three ways are, roughly, Liberal, Marxist and Postmodern. Let me take them very briefly in turn.

Liberal view of society

One of the crucial things marking out different views of society is how they view individuals. Liberal models of society tend to take the individual as logically prior to society. Thus society will be fair if it allows people the freedom to pursue their own goals. From a critical perspective, adopting a liberal view will lead to emphasis on tackling problems at an individual level rather than focusing on political structures and institutions. The critical aim is the emancipation of the individual. As we shall discover in Chapter 2, in most traditional forms social cognition sees group processes as independent of broader political structures and institutions. A cursory flick through the more traditional social psychology textbooks such as Myers (1993) displays the caring, thoughtful (very well written) yet liberal view of society that permeates social psychology. However, there are intergroup (and more Marxist-inspired) theorists who emphasize broader group processes such as nationhood and class (e.g. Reicher and Hopkins, 2001), and there has been a deliberate decision to deal more with this latter version of social cognition research: critical social psychology is usually suspicious of the liberal individualist view of society.

Marxist view of society

As we shall discover in Chapter 3, many of Karl Marx's insights are still useful in making sense of early twenty-first-century capitalism, and have been inspirational for the development of both European social cognition and critical social psychology. Marxist theories of society emphasize the importance of historical change, and the centrality of class conflict. In particular, social class is seen as a fundamental factor in making sense of social structures – power relations are often understood in terms of class relations. From a Marxist perspective, to be critical and political necessarily involves particular ways of making sense of social structures and institutions. The institutionally supported structures of power are often viewed as pre-discursive – they exist as part of the 'real' – so we can start to see how a theory of knowledge (e.g. realist versus relativist) impacts on our understanding of society and social change. Also, if social structures can simply exist outside our ways of making sense of them, we are forced into thinking about personhood in particular ways. These tensions between what is individual and social, what is real and discursive, provide a great deal of dynamism and debate for critical social psychologists, and will be returned to and clarified throughout the book.

Postmodern views of society/ies

A postmodern theory of society has been developed by social scientists such as David Harvey (1989) and Scott Lash and John Urry (1987). It is a way of characterizing contemporary society and the degeneration of capitalism and modernity. This emphasizes the importance of the move away from mass industrial production towards new information-based technology in which control of communication is paramount. State control is increasingly diversified, and transient social movements prevent an easy characterization of what the 'political' may be. Critical work from a postmodern perspective therefore focuses on language and communication. Unlike Marxism, critical analysis presupposes no primary political structures; unlike liberalism, the individual is not assumed to be prior to social and institutional structures.

These three ways of understanding society are a major simplification. My point in highlighting them here is that the tasks of critical social psychology are strongly related to the assumed view of society. What we take to be knowledge and how we think it proceeds is also highly consequential for how we think we ought to do critical social psychology.

Writing knowledge

At first glance knowledge seems like an obvious category. In everyday situations such as university courses we assume that we accumulate knowledge in a range of ways, including reading books, being taught, and so on. We have familiar ways of testing the amount of knowledge that has accumulated ('Personality is an ideological construction. Discuss'). The fact that people are usually tested in isolation reflects the basic assumption that knowledge exists within the individual. However, the nature of knowledge has been a preoccupation with philosophers and social theorists and there now exists a striking variety of different ways of making sense of it. I will focus on four ways of considering knowledge that have been important in recent social psychology: 'positivist', 'realist', 'relativist' and 'postmodern' theories of knowledge.

Positivism

The term 'positivism' was first used by Auguste Comte (1798-1857) to refer to humanity's intellectual stage of scientific or, as he called it, *positive* understanding. This was based only on observable facts and the laws that could be discovered by considering the relations between them. Comte was the first person to use the term 'sociology', and positivism is typically understood to involve the application of scientific methods to the understanding of human societies.

These days there are different types of positivism, but one emphasis has been the verification of laws of human nature. This means that theories are formulated and tested with reference only to empirical observations. Experiments and surveys form the bedrock of such social science research, with theorizing having a much less significant role. Facts are thought of as existing in the world to be discovered, and can be isolated by inductively considering a large number of cases. As facts accumulate, so knowledge accumulates.

As we shall see in the next chapter, many critics of the mainstream social psychology of the 1960s and 1970s have accused it of adopting a positivist approach to knowledge. The complaint from figures such as Rom Harré and Ken Gergen was that the discovery of regularities in observations was insufficient to get a deep understanding of human behaviour and action.

Realism

What distinguishes a realist approach to knowledge from a positivist one is what happens under the surface. Both place a major importance on the use of empirical methods. However, realist approaches to knowledge place equal importance on the production of underlying mechanisms that account for the observable regularities. Although these mechanisms are studied empirically, it requires theory to generate models of the mechanisms. So realists do not expect research to develop through the accumulation of more and more facts; instead, facts need to be ordered through the development of increasingly powerful theories.

Most modern experimental social psychology in the social cognition tradition (Chapter 2) falls somewhere between positivism and realism. It makes some attempts at theorizing underlying mechanisms, but critics argue that these are often small-scale and unambitious and that full-scale models of human action are lacking.

In critical social psychology there is a dilemma. A central feature of critical research has been an attack on traditional social psychology and the assumptions that drive it. But realism has also been reasserted and refined in ways that produce some fascinating tensions. For example, a major tension in critical research often lies between just finding things out and making theoretical claims. A reassessment of this theory of knowledge has therefore provided critical social psychology with one of its central elements.

A version of realism popular with critical psychologists is *critical realism* (Bhaskar, 1989; Parker, 1992). Here, as with the standard realist philosophical position, external realities are thought to exist outside our perceptions of the world. However, there is also an acceptance of the complexity and unpredictability of human behaviour (Parker, 1997a), and an understanding of the social context in which cognitions and emotions occur, as well as some recognition of the fallibility of traditional forms of knowledge generation.

Critical realism has been popular among some critical researchers, as it seems to provide a way of reconciling a broadly Marxist analysis of society with the sorts of epistemological critiques that have been developed by sociologists and post-modernists. Whether it does this has been a topic of vigorous debate (see Parker, 1998, and the debate between Parker, 1999, and Potter et al., 1999). As we will discover throughout the course of this book, having particular notions of reality implies corresponding versions of subjectivity.

Relativism

Relativism is not a direct theory of knowledge equal and opposite to realism, although supporters of alternative positions sometimes treat it like that. Relativism is better conceived as an approach of pervasive doubt about the absolute basis of knowledge. This takes the form of an interest in the rhetorical devices and techniques through which knowledge is constructed as absolute and timeless. Its aim is the rigorous exposure of the basis of all claims, including its own (Smith, 1988, 1997). It is not against realism as such; realism is treated as one potentially good story among others, with no special or absolute basis.

A common criticism of this approach in critical work is that it means that 'anything goes'. However, these arguments gloss over the complexities of this approach (e.g. see Edwards et al., 1995; Potter, 1998). Proponents of relativism argue that doubting the possibility of absolute, objective or foundational knowledge does not require the acceptance of a timeless general idea such as 'anything goes'. These are complex arguments, and they resonate through many aspects of critical social psychology. Chapter 5 discusses the relation between relativism and feminism, while Chapter 8 discusses the debates between realism and relativism in more detail.

Postmodernism

Postmodernism poses a challenge to traditional 'modernist' ways of knowing. In some ways it parallels and overlaps relativist critique. However, it takes more of a sociological perspective that emphasizes the local nature of knowledge claims. Postmodernists also doubt the modernist story (or metanarrative) that the self is an individual knowing entity, capable of rationally reflecting on reality in the pursuit of timeless truths capable of advancing human progress. In addition, they doubt the idea that human practices and features can be scientifically (neutrally and objectively) analysed.

As we shall discover in Chapter 8, one of the key figures of postmodernism, Jean-François Lyotard (1984) argued that the postmodern condition is characterized by incredulity towards 'metanarratives' – the self-referential organizing stories and principles of modernism. He also claimed that there is a crisis of representation. This means a rejection of the metanarrative of scientific rationality (central in both positivism and realism) as a progressive accumulation of knowledge that can *represent* reality. It is replaced by little narratives – multiple wisdoms and cultures. Knowledge becomes localized and relativized.

There is a range of complexities surrounding the way truth and evidence is understood in traditional and critical social psychology. There is no neat one-to-one parallel between particular theories of knowledge and particular approaches to research. Nevertheless, such theories are consequential and are implicated in important disagreements over the role of empirical research and the possibility of social critique. It is true that critical social psychology has tended to be critical of positivism, and often critical of the central role that quantification has in positivism. As we shall see in Chapter 2, the crisis in social psychology was partly a crisis

of method motivated by doubts about the success of experiments for understanding human behaviour and broader philosophical doubts about scientific
method (see Chalmers, 1992). However, as critical social psychology has matured
some key figures have argued that positivism can provide an important pathway to
social critique. For example, Celia Kitzinger (1997) argues strongly for the *strategic
value* of positivist empiricism in pressing lesbian and gay issues in mainstream
psychology. Its critical effectiveness comes not from the sophisticated basis of its
knowledge but from the rhetorical effectiveness of numbers and easily understood
differences. This issue will be discussed in the final section of Chapter 5.

The stance we adopt on knowledge therefore has big implications for what
we think we ought to be doing, or 'discovering', as critical social psychologists. This
in turn relates to what kind of place we think society is, which itself has
implications for what we take to be the 'subject' of our research.

Writing the subject

As we shall discover in Chapter 6, what seem like the most private, 'inner' features
of our 'selves' can be understood as historical, social and cultural. Does that make
them feel any less real to us? This is a big question for critical social psychologists.
Some want to retain aspects of subjectivity that just exist – we know things about
ourselves, things that cannot be put into words, but which are crucially important
for understanding what it means to be a person. Others suggest that, whatever may
or may not exist inside an 'individual' (another dangerous description), it is not
knowable outside our systems of making sense of it. As with 'society', it will
be useful to set out three theories of subjectivity as the most salient for critical
social psychology: social cognitive, psychoanalytical and discursive postmodern
dissolution.

Social cognitive theory

Social cognition, especially as it is practised in North America, relies heavily on
cognitive psychology, seeing aspects of information processing such as encoding
and retrieval as key mediators in our social judgements. Two of the most prominent views of the person here are the *cognitive miser*, suggesting that social
perceivers' processing capacities are limited, and the *motivated tactician* (Fiske and
Taylor, 1991). This more recent position places greater emphasis on the goal-
directed nature of information processing as a means of simplifying complex
stimuli.

Why do (mainly European) critical social psychologists adopt social cognition? Sometimes they are concerned with some basic issues related to oppression,
discrimination and inequality. For example, questions about why we tend to exaggerate differences between groups, or what criteria for judgement and evaluation of
others we employ, and why, have been tackled using a model of the person of this
kind. Chapter 2 traces the development of social cognition research from its early
beginnings through to current attempts to forge connections with more critical
discursive and social constructionist perspectives.

Psychoanalytic theory

Many social theorists over the years have been preoccupied with tackling questions about why people participate in their own oppression. As we shall see in Chapter 3, this has been a particular theme of those working with Marxist theory. Many have turned to psychoanalysis for an answer. Psychoanalysis is founded on the idea that exploring the interior of the self and dealing with our unconscious fantasies leads to self-improvement. The focus is often on the ways in which the 'rational' subject, popular with traditional psychology, is constantly subverted by our 'desires'. There is also concern with the historical development of the person, of the past implicated in the present. The person is viewed as full of irrationalities, contradictions and unpredictability; but through psychoanalysis it becomes possible to trace some of the 'causes' of these features historically, applying psychoanalytical notions of the development of the psyche.

Not surprisingly there are many difficulties with importing psychoanalysis wholesale into critical social psychology. Chapter 3 will review and explore the tensions in three areas of recent psychoanalytic work in critical psychology: Ian Parker and colleagues' recent work in *Psychoanalytic Culture* (1997a) and *Deconstructing Psychopathology* (1995), Wendy Hollway's work around Melanie Klein and Jacques Lacan, and Michael Billig's latest work on Sigmund Freud. Each of these areas will be interrogated for what it assumes about subjectivity.

Discursive and postmodern dissolution

A discursive take on subjectivity moves us away from any centred focus on the subject to consider *interactions and practices* instead. These can be characterized as part of the broader postmodern fragmentation but, as we shall see in Chapter 7, discursive psychology sees psychology and the 'inner' world as something that is produced out of particular actions. Subjectivity is a *consequence* rather than a cause of human action.

Similarly, the postmodern declaration of 'the death of the subject' appears to eliminate completely the autonomous intentional agent that has traditionally been the defining feature of psychology. Popular in critical work are postmodern philosophers who see power (Michel Foucault), narrative (Jean-Françoise Lyotard) or writing (Jacques Derrida) as constituting subjectivity. This style of philosophy will be explicated in more detail in Chapters 6 and 8.

We have here three broad sets of assumptions organizing critical work: assumptions regarding theories of society, knowledge and the subject. The assumptions provide us with a clear set of tools that will be useful for understanding the different types of research that come under the broad heading of critical social psychology. They will also be used to develop some themes in the final chapter.

What's in this book?

In Malcolm Bradbury's novel *The History Man* (1975), the central character is a sociologist who incites conflict on a university campus focused on the visit of a well known psychologist who is publicizing his theory of racial differences in IQs. The psychologist's visit becomes an occasion for stirring up revolutionary ferment. Throughout the book the sociologist has a mantra that he recites to support radical politics. Forget the big complicated stuff; to be radical and critical all you need is a little bit of Marx, a little bit of Freud and a little bit of social history.

It is certainly possible to criticize the superficiality of Bradbury's central character, and the liberal message that is being offered. But the novel can be reread in a way that is more sympathetic to some of his ways of promoting critical practice. The idea of providing just enough Marxism and social history to inform our critical endeavours has been one of the aims of this book, although the hope is that it will inspire the reader to study these areas in a more scholarly way! One of the disappointments of work in criticial social psychology has been the rather superficial treatment of more complex philosophical positions and theoretical developments and broader interdisciplinary engagement. Often it is done without any investigation outside the disciplinary boundaries of psychology. My aim throughout has been to provide just enough detail for the reader to grasp some of the complexities of different theoretical positions. The hope is that this will high-light the need for further study in order to actually engage with the arguments.

So the book as a whole provides the reader with a bit of history (and geography!), including some of the things that paved the way to CSP – the crisis in social psychology, academic Marxism and psychoanalysis, the experiences of World War II, sociology, feminism, discursive psychology, postmodernism and post-structuralist philosophy. The following section provides a brief breakdown of the contents of the book, and the first thing to note is that it is organized in two parts.

Chapter contents and a tale of two parts

The first part of the book – 'Mind and Society' – includes Chapters 2–5. The focus is on the different ways that critical research has grappled with the problem of the relation between 'the mind' and 'society'. For example, for the social cognition critics in Chapter 2, society is the 'outside' that needs to be processed in order to get 'inside'. This outside is usually divided into social groups of various types that somehow trigger subjective psychological processes. In Chapter 3, Marxist critics see society's conflicts and inequalities as providing the setting for understanding the possibility of social psychological processes.

However, in Chapter 4, classic psychoanalysts such as Melanie Klein argue that we need to take subjective processes into account if we want to understand broader social relationships. Psychoanalytical critics attempt to draw upon these psychoanalytical ideas without buying into some of the more problematic assumptions of the classic research. Feminist critics in Chapter 5 belong in both sections – some are happiest with the 'mind and society' problems in Chapters 2–4, while others would want to line up with discursive and postmodern critics in Chapters 7 and 8, trying to resolve or dissolve these issues.

Let me outline the chapters in Part I in more detail. *Chapter 2* begins with a historical review of some of the landmarks of social psychological research. This early research is distinctive in its critical zeal in addressing the social problems of the day, and also in its reliance on more qualitative field-based studies. In general the move in social cognition research has been towards the laboratory and away from the messiness of people's everyday practices. Chapter 2 also documents the 'crisis in social psychology' that emerged in the late 1960s and lasted throughout the 1970s. These critiques revolve around three central areas: theory, method and individualism.

Most of the social cognition research covered in Chapter 2 has been deliberately selected for its more critical focus. Although theory and method are still underdeveloped in this type of research, in general there has been a move towards more sophisticated ways of understanding the 'individual'. Consequently one of the themes that develops throughout the chapter is an exploration of the split between the 'individual' and the 'social' that social cognition forces us into, which is rather like the split between psychology (the individual) and sociology (the social) in Bradbury's novel.

Part of the reason why the individual has been such a thorny issue for critical researchers has been the influence of the strongly anti-individualist perspectives of Marxism, covered in *Chapter 3*. Marx would have suggested that an easy way of maintaining inequalities and controlling a population is to make sure people do not see their impoverished circumstances as arising from changeable social structures, but rather from their own unchangeable individual features. From this perspective, psychology is part of the oppressive bourgeois system, as Bradbury's sociologist would have confirmed, because it usually assumes there are identifiable individual causes at the root of people's problems. Chapter 3 provides the required 'little bit of Marx' needed to think through these radical and highly influential ideas.

Chapter 3 also assesses work by researchers in psychology who adopt an explicitly Marxist perspective, and in doing so develops critical discussion of other themes central to critical social psychology: power and ideology. The discussion of power will assess Marx from a Foucauldian perspective. Michel Foucault argues that power is more about relations built into everyday life than the Marxist version of power as authoritarian top-down imposition. Foucault's work suggests that we need to rethink the idea of a struggle between the working classes and those who own and control the means of production: we need to develop a new type of critical analysis to account for new kinds of social fragmentation and the absence of some unified 'base' of social existence giving rise to one central contradiction in (supposedly cohesive) social class struggles.

The tensions between Foucault and Marx allow some interesting insights into why critical social psychologists are attracted by psychoanalysis, given its historical and cultural specificity, its misogynistic notion of women as secondary and less important than men, and its rampant individualism. Marx is strongly anti-individualist, yet because he sees social structures as primary, questions are left open about why people participate in their own oppression, how they become resistant to change. Psychoanalysis, with its focus on the fundamentally irrational state of the human psyche, is an attractive option for critical social psychologists inspired by Marxism.

Chapter 4 discusses classic psychoanalytical ideas, covering the work of Sigmund Freud, Melanie Klein and Jacques Lacan, and then assessing the work of critical social psychologists who have chosen to draw upon psychoanalysis in one way or another. The most prominent of these are Wendy Hollway, Michael Billig and Ian Parker. One issue that arises throughout this chapter relates to the status of language. Can we assume that what people say is evidence of underlying psychic structures, or do we focus on what people are doing with what they are saying in their specific contexts? There is an incompatibility here that provides one of the many tensions in critical social psychology.

These tensions are also apparent in *Chapter 5*, which focuses on feminist critics. Here, early feminist discourse research is examined, and this explores how participants' versions of gender relations are made to seem natural and obvious. But if gender is something that resides within us due to bodies – hormones or biology or whatever – then in terms of political organization and policy making it would seem reasonable that our social relations should be moulded around this biological difference between the sexes. It also doesn't seem unreasonable to assume that what people say – their language – reflects this inner female/maleness. But these are precisely the kinds of assumption that this early discourse work challenged.

The move away from seeing gender as something tied to people's bodies, and towards seeing it instead as being located in discursive practices, is also followed through in the discussion of research into heterosexism. Here Celia Kitzinger's research on the social construction of lesbianism is discussed, along with the post-structuralist work of Judith Butler. The debate around gendered bodies continues in section three of Chapter 5, which looks at research into embodiment generally, and women's bodies more specifically.

The final section explores the issues of postmodern and post-structuralist feminist practice in more depth. What is often at stake in these types of argument is the status of 'knowledge' that we can have about humanness, or more specifically what it is to be human and/or female: so the focus will be on the types of epistemological debates feminist psychologists have engaged in.

All of which leads us neatly to the second part of the book, 'Resolutions and Dilemmas', which includes Chapters 6–8. Here the loose category holding the chapters together is the attempt to resolve or problematize the difficulties that are a result of seeing Mind and Society as separable categories. For example, some of the subjectivity critics in Chapter 6 theorize ways that society can be put into the mind, while others develop a notion of subjectivity that is socially constructed. The discursive critics of Chapter 7 take this one step further; dispersing whatever 'mind' is into society. In a similar way, postmodern critics in Chapter 8 generally question the whole notion of whether we should resolve anything once and for all, and whether categories such as 'mind' and 'society' are 'knowable' in an either/or kind of way.

These debates require some philosophical exploration, and the first section, on subjectivity critics, in *Chapter 6* provides it, with a discussion of the problems associated with seeing mental terms as representations of mental states. This leads to a discussion of Foucauldian perspectives on subjectivity – how people are made into subjects of a particular type through the discursive operation of various paradoxes and oppositions.

Chapter 6 also explores some of the themes that crop up in critical psychological research around gender, textuality and subjectivity, with links to psychoanalysis, 'bodies' or 'others'. In the third section we review a set of critical work that focuses on subjectivity, including debates about whether critical psychology needs a 'theory of the subject'. We also cover critical research on personality, and some more postmodern versions of subjectivity from the contributors to the classic *Texts of Identity* collection.

Chapter 7 continues the themes of textuality and subjectivity but moves the focus of discussion on to discursive critics. The first section takes memory and emotion as two of the ways in which discourse researchers have sought to put the 'mind' back into 'society'. The second section looks at constructionism, especially in relation to ideological views of the world, and how reality is made into something solid. The third section looks at rhetoric and ideological dilemmas, drawing on an initial discussion of ideology in Chapter 3. The attempt with discursive work is to look at psychology and criticize it, and also to look at society and criticize that.

Chapter 8 covers postmodern critics, beginning with a discussion of Frederic Jameson, Jean-François Lyotard and Jacques Derrida, allowing some insights into the complexities of their work, but also aiming to be relevant to the concerns of critical and discursive psychologists. The focus in this first section is postmodernism itself, and the difficulties associated with defining what it 'is'. The second section looks at critical social psychological work that has situated itself with respect to postmodernism, and Derrida's post-structuralist notion of deconstruction. This leads to a discussion of the relation between broad epistemological arguments about realism and relativism and different kinds of critical practice in the third section.

Chapter 9 brings us full circle, back to some of the initial themes presented in this chapter. In the first section critical assumptions about subjectivity, knowledge and society and their relation to one another are discussed. In the second section critical practice is discussed, with a view to the further development of critical social psychology as a discipline along more practical lines. The third section provides some critical evaluation of the state of critical social psychology. A concluding section discusses prospects for the future. Where should critical social psychology go next? What is the best case/worst case scenario for the future?

Overview

Critical social psychology is not all theory. There is now a huge body of work that is done under the title critical social psychology, or can sensibly be included in that category. My coverage is necessarily highly selective and it is certainly idiosyncratic. I have focused on covering and clarifying the theoretical issues and perspectives that underlie critical work. Specific studies have been included as they fit in with this broader scheme. I have chosen studies and writing that I find important and interesting. The book is not an encyclopaedia, nor a definitive guide! In the course of it particular topic areas will be dealt with in detail:

1   There will be a focus on racism and nationalism, sexism and heterosexism. It is not surprising that these topics recur, as they reflect a central agenda of critical work – the way conflicts and inequalities are both generated and obscured.

2   Another focus will be the production of particular notions of the psychological subject and the way this relates to issues of reality, power and knowledge.

3   A third focus will be on critical possibilities of resistance and change, and the development of practical interventions aimed at challenging established psychological and social practices. Each chapter ends with a section on application in order to assess these possibilities for the individual subject areas.

Features

To help the reader the chapters will also incorporate a number of features.

1   *Boxes*. These will be used for important topics or issues that have only a loose connection with the theme of individual chapters.

2   *Persons*. These boxes are intended to bring the contributors to this field alive. A range of key figures in critical social psychology have written a few sentences on their involvement with critical work and their hopes for its future. Again, this is just a selection of possible figures, certainly not a definitive list.

3   *Critical dilemmas*. These are ways of highlighting particular debates between different positions. They are designed to help the reader to think through particular issues.

4   *Discussion questions*. These provide ideas for discussion. They could be used in a class or tutorial, or just treated as some important questions to think about.

5   *Practical exercises*. These are designed to help the reader think through relevant issues and concepts in practical circumstances – watching television, reading the papers, questioning friends, working or studying. Some of these exercises are quite brief, and could be done in a few minutes; others could be used for practicals or even mini-projects.

6   *Applications*. Each chapter will discuss the way the ideas lead to particular interventions or practical results.

7   *The best thing and the worst thing*. I have tried to suggest what is best and worst about each of the perspectives discussed. Again, these are my personal 'stick your neck on the block' views and are given in the spirit of promoting discussion, rather than advocating any closure of debate.

8   *Suggested reading*. I suggest different types of reading that will be useful for each chapter. Often there is no one reference that covers everything. Occasionally I have commented on the reading to make the choice of what to read more straightforward.

Part I

Mind and Society

Chapter 2

Social Cognition Critics

In the United Kingdom in early 2001 there were ongoing debates about how sympathetic 'we' should be to refugees seeking asylum. The *News of the World* – a tabloid Sunday newspaper with a reputation for sexual prurience and reactionary politics – ran a campaign for tighter control over asylum seekers. To give you a flavour of this, one story reports 'social tension where a community feels they are having to support a very large number of asylum-seekers, most of whom aren't real refugees'. A poll of its readers showed that 75 per cent 'voted' against continuing to take in asylum seekers. So a national newspaper with a wide readership was conducting a campaign widely criticized from left wing and liberal groups as racist and dehumanizing. How are we to make sense of this debate and its context?

The social cognition perspective on these debates (employing varying degrees of complexity) would be that human information processing uses heuristics to make sense of things, and so when something unusual like asylum seekers is brought to our attention – partly through racist media reporting – then we use the same simple racist heuristic to make sense of it.

Yet however strenuous the efforts to hide the fact behind scientific rhetoric, it seems that psychology, including social psychology, participates in a particular socio-political and historical context. Indeed, it could be argued that social psychology emerged out of an overt attempt to address the social problems of the day. Social cognition in particular is concerned with some basic issues related to oppression, discrimination and inequality. Why do we tend to exaggerate differences between groups? What criteria for judgement and evaluation do we employ, and why?

It is worth noting at the outset that I am using the term 'social cognition' in a broader sense than is common in recent social psychology. I take the tradition of social psychology discussed here to be cognitivist in a broad sense, in that it tries to explain social behaviour with reference to individual mental processes of some kind or other. However, within social psychology there is now an identified strand of work that calls itself social cognition. This is distinctive in drawing upon the ideas and findings of cognitive psychology – memory prototypes and so on – and applying them to social psychological processes (see Fiske and Taylor's classic introduction and overview, 1991).

Looking back through the history of social psychology we can see the 1940s as a particularly significant time. At the end of World War II there was a great deal of excitement about the emancipatory potential of social psychology: many North American psychologists had been refugees from Nazi persecution, others had helped out in the war effort, and many had lived through the depression of the 1930s. Much of the classic work that has helped to shape social psychology emerged out of this social context, hence its strongly emancipatory and critical edge.

This chapter begins by reviewing this work. The early work of researchers such as Gordon Allport, Muzafer Sherif, Soloman Asch and Stanley Milgram will provide a familiar starting place: they were deeply concerned with issues of conflict, oppression and obedience, capturing fundamental themes of later critical work. We will also consider the way this early impetus was dissipated in the more recent social cognition tradition, leading to the 'crisis' in social psychology and the development of a more 'European' brand of social psychology through the work of Henri Tajfel and others.

Social identity theory will be discussed as a more recent social cognitive theory, emerging from the 'crisis' with a 'European' critical spin. Social identity theory has grown up with critical pretensions in a largely experimental arena, and has recently seen further developments through the introduction of self-categorization theory. This will be illustrated using examples from the work of John Turner, Stephen Reicher and Nicholas Hopkins.

This chapter is thus highly selective. Certain pieces of research have been selected as illustrative of the huge body of work that makes up mainstream social psychology. This work is well described elsewhere; its role here is to set up a contrast for what comes later and to help understand why these critical develop-ments take the form that they do.

Early critical work in social psychology

This section will cover early social psychology from Gordon Allport, Muzafer Sherif, Solomon Asch, Stanley Milgram and Philip Zimbardo. The focus will be on the critical potential of this early work, and on identifying the kinds of objectives and assumptions that characterize or conflict with contemporary critical social psychology.

Prejudice and group conflict

A fundamental feature of Gordon Allport's (1954) classic work on prejudice was the so-called *contact hypothesis*. In its simplified form, this is the idea that bringing existing groups into contact with one another will reduce prejudice and promote more positive intergroup relations. For example, if people from different ethnic backgrounds are housed together on the same estate, would this significantly reduce racial tension? In the strong form of this view, racism is largely a form of individual misunderstanding; if only we understood one another better we would not harbour negative feelings.

However, Allport thought things were more complex than this. He suggested that this type of contact on its own would not be enough to reduce prejudice. Other conditions would be necessary, such as the idea that people should be of equal status, and should co-operate over common goals; and there should be clear institutional support for integrationist policies. He also suggested that ethnic minorities develop 'self-hate' – low self-esteem. This was partly based on the pioneering research by the African-American couple Kenneth and Mamie Clark (1947), in which they reported that black children showed a preference for white rather than black dolls.

A central feature of this work is its emphasis on prejudice being largely a consequence of people's understanding of ethnic minorities, so that the way to tackle prejudice is to work on those individual prejudices. In terms of our political scheme in Chapter 1, the solution to prejudice is seen in the framework of a liberal view of society that emphasizes the fundamental nature of individual actions and understandings. It does not give much of a place to conflict between classes, or issues of groups with different interests and values. In many ways it illustrates what is good and what is bad about the early tradition of social psychology: it is motivated by a concern with human welfare and improvement, but it works within an individualist notion of social organization.

But there is a pattern here. Many of the most enduring early theories were responsible for debunking previous more individualistic theories. For example, Muzafer Sherif's *Realistic Conflict Theory* marked an important step away from individualistic theories of conflict such as Allport's. For Sherif the idea was that *material conditions* determine psychological processes in intergroup relations. Thus the theory predicts that hostility between groups can be explained in terms of their competition with each other for scarce and valued resources. When material gains by one group create losses for another, this maximizes group cohesiveness and solidarity, giving rise to increasingly unfavourable stereotyping and intergroup hostility. These ideas were supported by a series of field experiments conducted in boys' summer camps. In the famous Robber's Cave study, boys were split into groups, and then the environment was manipulated to generate inequality or require co-operation. In this work it is still assumed that 'individual' psychological processes are central to explaining action, though much more weight is given to broader group processes and influences.

Erving Goffman (1961) suggested that institutionalized norms also play their part in creating conflict between people who adopt the roles of the institution. He developed these ideas through studies in which he posed as a janitor in a mental hospital and observed the interactions of staff and patients. The classic experimental exploration of this idea is the Stanford prison simulation study, in which Philip Zimbardo and colleagues (1971) constructed a simulation prison and arranged for volunteer students to play the roles of prisoner and guard. Much attention was paid to building up the realism of the study. (Local police helped out by 'arresting' the prisoners in their homes!) The prisoners had to wear loose, shapeless clothes while the guards wore military style uniforms. The prisoners became progressively passive and distressed recipients of brutal treatment, and the guards seemed to spend their time finding new ways to degrade their prisoners

(Zimbardo, 1972). The hostility of the guards was such that the two-week study had to be abandoned after six days, as the researchers became increasingly concerned for the safety and sanity of all involved.

This work illustrates some of the best features of the North American tradition. It was a study of huge ambition designed to directly address a major social problem. Throughout the 1960s there had been a series of prison sieges and riots during which large numbers of inmates and guards had been killed. The conservative response was that these deaths were a natural consequence of collecting large numbers of dangerous people together, and the way of dealing with them should be more security, more punishment, more use of the death penalty, and so on. This response is an individual one that explains events in terms of the aggressive and deviant personalities of the prisoners. The brilliance of Zimbardo's study was that it highlighted the way randomly chosen and mentally healthy individuals could act in precisely the same cruel ways if the context was right. It is the *situation* – deindividuating (a key concept for Zimbardo), humiliating and full of violent cues – that is crucial. He highlighted the disturbing power of institutional identities, rules and norms on people's actions, and provided an important resource for social reform of prisons and similar institutions.

One element that is central in Zimbardo's study is the way prisoners conformed to particular norms and obediently followed orders. This has been another important critical issue that has resonated through social psychology. What is conformity, and why do people conform?

Conformity studies

Solomon Asch could be characterized as the researcher who launched a thousand conformity studies in social psychology. As a boy he recalls attending the traditional Jewish Seder at Passover, and being amazed by the idea that the invisible prophet Elijah was going to visit every Jewish home and take a sip of wine from the cup reserved for him. He recalls watching the cup intently, feeling that 'indeed something was happening at the rim of the cup, and the wine did go down a little' (quoted in Aron and Aron, 1989: 27). His later experiments dealt with this same apparent tension between seeing things for yourself, being an authentic 'individual', and being persuaded to conform to other people's way of seeing things, simply following the herd.

Asch was curious to find out whether we would conform to other people's obviously 'wrong' answers in an experimental situation. He set up the famous line lengths study, where participants were asked to say which of three different-size lines matched the standard line in length. Participants were seated sixth in a row of seven people, all of whom were coached to give wrong answers by the experimenter. Imagine yourself in a situation where you are performing what seems like a simple judgement about the length of a line, and five people call out the wrong answer before it gets to your turn. In the actual study it turned out that 37 per cent of the time participants conformed to the majority opinion. Of course this means that 63 per cent of the time they didn't, but most participants conformed at least once. Asch was concerned about the implications of his experiments that seemed to show that people who were intelligent and apparently normal in every way could be led to act in this bizarre way. It is worth highlighting a few things about this study:

1   It is a study of conformity – the participants offered a public judgment in line with what others had said – but this is not to say that they actually believed this or perceived the lines in this way.
2   By focusing in on individual features of 'freedom' and 'conformity' to explain what is happening we are forced back to an explanation that looks to individual cognitive features of participants.
3   Although the study emphasizes group processes rather than individual ones, the general image is of a rational, sensible individual being distorted by the power of the group. This image has been a central one in social psychology, and has been criticized by Stephen Reicher (1987) and others.
4   This is a study of conduct in a laboratory situation; the practical contingencies of actual situations may make actions very different.

Obedience studies

Stanley Milgram worked originally with Asch. He was particularly concerned with developing ways of making the conformity experiments more socially relevant. He wanted to build in some consequences of action. The result is one of the most controversial and influential pieces of research in social psychology. Milgram suggests that his concern with obedience and authority was:

> forced upon members of my generation, in particular upon Jews such as myself, by the atrocities of World War II. The impact of the Holocaust on my own psyche energized my interest in obedience and shaped the particular form in which it was examined.
>
> (Milgram, 1977, cited in Myers, 1993: 236)

Milgram started out with a basic question. If someone tells you to hurt another person, under what conditions will you carry out that command and under what conditions will you refuse? Imagine you are arriving at Milgram's laboratory to take part in an experiment on learning and memory. You are told that the experiment will examine the effects of punishment on learning. You discover one other participant and you each draw lots to be assigned to roles – you are the 'teacher' and the other person is the 'learner'. You're quite glad about this, as it turns out that the learner gets wired up to some scary looking apparatus, and will be receiving electric shocks from you (starting out fairly mild but going up to a dangerous 450 V). But in fact the other participant is an actor working with the experimenter and it has been fixed that you will be the teacher.

The learner then goes through a memory task and pretty soon he is making errors, which you have to punish him for. (Note that in the original study all participants were male.) You're very uncomfortable about this, but the experimenter seems quite calm about it and instructs you to carry on. As the shocks go further up the scale the learner starts to protest by screaming (in some conditions), pounding on the wall, and will ultimately fall silent if you continue further. When you ask whether all this is necessary you are simply told that you have no other choice and must continue. What do you do?

If asked to forecast what happens next, people generally predict extremely low levels of obedience (Miller, 1986). However, in Milgram's first study only fourteen out of forty participants disobeyed the experimenter by walking out before administering severe shocks, meaning 65 per cent of participants went all the way up the scale. Many other conditions were set up and all seemed to support the basic premise that participants could often go to great lengths to comply with the experimenter's wishes. This showed that, first, being placed in a situation of this kind seemed to have a powerful effect, and second, that people did not expect the effect to be so strong.

Conclusion

Much of the early research in social psychology was concerned with understanding how action was related to its social context. Research focused on big issues such as prejudice, obedience and conformity, and the aim was to move away from explanations based solely on individual features. Much of this early work used field studies and was very concerned with the direct relations between research studies and real world settings.

How and why are these studies relevant to contemporary research in critical social psychology? There are two main themes. Firstly, as the above studies show, early work in social psychology has had a deep concern with issues of conflict, genocide, oppression, pressures on the individual, the role of institutions, and so has captured fundamental themes of what we can now identify as critical work in social psychology. Despite this, many critical social psychologists would argue that social psychology has lost track of these big themes, particularly during the 1960s and 1970s when huge numbers of laboratory experiments were performed on increasingly technical and small scale phenomena. This continuing move away from the 'social' towards the 'individual' is one central feature of what has come to be termed the 'crisis in social psychology'.

The crisis in social psychology

This section will focus on the crisis in social psychology – how it developed, what the different arguments were about, and where it has led us. Running in parallel to the crisis were two particularly influential European social psychologists, Henri Tajfel and Serge Moscovici. This section will conclude by examining their contribution to the development of the crisis literature.

During the 1960s and 1970s social psychology became more routinized and seemed to move away from its earlier concerns with oppression and exploitation. It became more of a technical enterprise, concerned with scientific adequacy. The crisis in social psychology comes out of the perceived loss of this radical edge. The crisis can be most clearly understood by organizing it into three broad themes:

1   *The critique of individualism.* This was triggered by social psychology's backward move towards employing more individual cognitive explanations.

2   *The critique of method.* Generated by concern about the increasingly narrow and technical focus of social psychological research methods and their inadequacy for understanding human action.

3   *The theoretical critique.* This was generated by a concern about the loss of broader social structures from research.

Individualism

Most critical psychologists are on some level also social psychologists – they believe that psychology needs to incorporate the social, and relies too much on hypothesized features of individuals as explanations for human functioning. However, critics such as Mark Pancer (1996) have suggested that mainstream social psychology in North America has become less social. He cites Gordon Allport's definition from the 1985 edition of the *Handbook of Social Psychology* to make his point: social psychology is 'an attempt to understand and explain how the thought, feeling, and behaviour of individuals are influenced by the actual, imagined, or implied presence of others' (1985: 3, cited in Pancer, 1996: 150). The focus is very much on documenting changes to/by what is taken to be the individual's internal information processing system.

Pancer is following on from a range of influential critics in the 1970s who raged against the individualism of social psychology (e.g. Steiner, 1974; Pepitone, 1976; Sampson, 1977; Hogan and Emler, 1978). The arguments work on two levels. At a basic level of research, they highlight distortions of understanding that result in taking such a one-sided view of human action. At a broader level, they are concerned with the cultural effects of such a view of research, as it encourages an unquestioned explanatory focus on features of individuals. For any social issue the tendency will be to look for solutions in changing individuals or diagnosing individual characteristics. For example, if the topic is crime, the focus will be on individual attributes: personality, criminality, and individual moral learning, rather than on broader social phenomena: unemployment, a linking of identity with consumer goods, and a crisis in masculinity.

These issues of individualism versus social understanding are clearly related to broader ways of understanding society. The individualism in social psychology is, to some extent, a fitting accompaniment to a more liberal view of society, while the more social perspective, with its emphasis on the crucial role of conflict and inequality, fits in with a more Marxist view of society.

Methodological critique

The academic laboratory approach became dominant in North America during the 1950s and 1960s, but was not without its criticisms even then. For example, Kenneth Ring (1967) argued that social psychology was in a profound state of intellectual disarray and relied too heavily on experiments that trivialized important

BOX 2.1   Sociology of scientific knowledge

The 1970s and 1980s saw the emergence of a revolutionary set of studies of how sciences actually operate. Up till that time science had been understood primarily through various philosophical views. Although there was a lot of disagreement between them, they tended to start from a single question: how can scientific knowledge be justified? That is, the special status of scientific knowledge was the starting point of analysis. However, the work of the historian of science Thomas Kuhn (1962), alongside certain radical philosophers such as Paul Feyerabend (1975), led sociologists to ask fundamental questions about the nature of scientific knowledge.

Harry Collins (1985) performed a series of groundbreaking studies of the replication of scientific experiments. For example, he looked at the way a classic study that claimed to have identified gravity waves was repeated by other scientists. Replication is interesting because it is often treated as one of the central procedures for ensuring the objectivity of scientific knowledge. Collins showed that most of what were called replications actually differed in important ways from the original study. Most tried to modify or improve it. More significantly, there was lack of agreement over what should be seen as a competent replication. Those scientists who supported the existence of gravity waves tended to see those replications that found them as competent; disbelieving scientists found replications that failed to find them competent! Thus replications do not stand outside the gravity wave controversy, ensuring its objective outcome; rather, replications and their status become one more element in the controversy.

Work of this kind, conducted by Karin Knorr Cetina (1999), Michael Mulkay (1991) and Bruno Latour and Steve Woolgar (1986), has transformed our image of science and objectivity. Its constructionist and relativist account suggests that particular claims are supported in a range of *ad hoc* ways, that observations have theories and assumptions embedded in them, and that scientific writing provides a rhetorical and conventionalized account of scientific action.

This work is particularly relevant in psychology, and especially social psychology, where traditional positivist views of science have been regularly wheeled out as if they were the last word on the nature of science. In fact, what this work shows is that the kind of methodological fetishizing of experiments that is common in North American and much European social psychology is quite unlike the approach to method in healthy and developing natural sciences such as biochemistry. It also casts doubt on the way experimental facts are treated as a fundamental and uninterpreted bottom line in research.

For this reason I suggest it is a major historical, not to say rhetorical, error for critical psychologists to characterize themselves as anti-science. What they ought to be against is the rhetorical vision of science that social psychologists have used to keep a range of critical and innovative work out of major journals.

social issues into the fun-and-games of experimental manipulations. Even within the experimental paradigm there were critics pointing out problems related to experimenter bias (Rosenthal, 1969) and demand characteristics (Orne, 1969) – although these were often seen as technical problems that could be managed by careful design of studies.

A range of more fundamental criticisms emerged during the 1970s. These focused on the inadequacy of laboratory methods and hypothesis testing, and their failure to understand the significance of the cultural and historical context of human action (e.g. Harré & Secord, 1972; Smith, 1972; Gergen, 1973; McGuire, 1973; Armistead, 1974; Silverman, 1977; Cartwright, 1979). Some are in a more humanist vein; others simply claim that experiments are flawed science for studying human behaviour. They are by no means accepted by experimental researchers, who have fiercely disputed many of the claims. Some of the key points are:

1   *Experiments involve a mechanistic model of the person*   The claim is that the underlying model of causes and effects treats people as machines rather than agents with their own plans and possibilities. Defenders of experiments say that they can study the regular actions of sovereign agents and draw sensible conclusions. Critics doubt that experiments allow space for that sovereignty to be expressed.

2   *Experiments are artificial*   The suggestion here is that the artificial nature of experiments makes it very difficult to extrapolate to complex real situations. There are various more or less sophisticated forms of this criticism, and more or less sophisticated replies. Defenders of experiments have suggested that the extrapolation to natural contexts works via sophisticated theory. Critics suggest that however sophisticated the theory, it depends on an understanding of the context and how it is organized, which experimental work does not, and cannot, supply.

3   *Experiments predefine action possibilities*   The claim here is that experimental work is very insensitive to the varied possibilities of action, and it breaks it up into categories and patterns that are quite unlike those in less constrained situations. Experimenters claim that you need that to do experiments, and good experiments depend anyway on exploratory and observational work. Critics suggest that these constraints suspend the investment and stake in their own actions that people have in their everyday lives.

4   *Experiments wipe out history and society*   The point here is that experiments work with an idea of action driven by timeless social processes that are unaffected by historical change, and are more or less standard across different institutional contexts. Experimentalists claim that this is indeed the goal, and suggest it is a powerful one. Critics point to evidence of historical change and doubt that social processes can be understood separately from the various institutional settings in which they appear.

We will revisit some of these methodological issues in later chapters.

Theoretical critique

The critique of methodology was often supplemented by the observation that traditional social psychology often placed very little weight on theory. We have already encountered this idea in Chapter 1 in discussing positivism and its short-comings. This theoretical critique has been developed from early work by, for example, Ring (1967), Harré and Secord (1972), Smith (1972) and Gergen (1973). Their arguments often pointed to the cultural and historical contingency of empirical research and the superficiality of the traditional approach. They also attacked the view of the self and assumptions about the person incorporated in traditional work.

Often this critique drew on the linguistic philosophy of figures such as Ludwig Wittgenstein and John Austin, which provided both a more developed understanding of what a person is, and a view that gave a pre-eminent position to language and interaction (Potter, 2001). These critical resources were sometimes supplemented or supplanted by the post-structuralist philosophy of Michel Foucault (Henriques et al., 1998). We can see some of the later fruits of these critiques in the discourse work discussed in Chapter 7 and the work on subjectivity and postmodernism discussed in Chapter 6 and Chapter 8.

Rom Harré

Rom Harré began his academic career in physics and mathematics, turning to the philosophy of science in the 1950s. By chance he came across social psychology, finding its pretensions to scientific status quite untenable. Muddles about the nature of social phenomena and misunderstandings about the methods of the advanced sciences seemed endemic. In the 1970s many people were beginning to push for a more realistic social psychology, in which studies of the management of meaning and of the role of rules, customs and conventions in the creation of social order would be dominant. A genuinely scientific social psychology would have little room for the artefacts of the naive experimental method. New analytical methods of enquiry were required. Pursuing these lines led him into studies of the role of language in social interaction, of the social forces of emotional feelings and displays, and more recently into positioning theory, the study of dynamic moral orders of close encounters. The discursive psychology movement calls for ever closer liaisons between linguistics, anthropology, moral philosophy and micro-sociology. The future of the subject lies in further developments along these lines.

After retiring from Oxford Rom Harré took up work abroad. He is currently in the Psychology Department at Georgetown University in Washington, DC, and teaching short courses in various countries, including Australia.

'Crisis' as a category surfaced to describe the various dissatisfactions and critiques that emerged from the early 1970s on, as documented by Harré above. Does it make sense, thirty years later, to continue to speak of a crisis?

Continuing crisis?

Pancer (1997) provides a useful discussion of various responses to the crisis. He notes that some researchers feel that the crisis has been successfully resolved by the development of more sophisticated experimental methods and more of a focus on application (Reich, 1981). Others suggest that we should celebrate an unprecedented surge of scientific endeavour consequent on the crisis (Operario and Fiske, 1999). Some claim that there was no such thing; talk of a crisis was got up by unsophisticated critics who did not understand the nature of social psychological research (Jones, 1985). In their overview of work in social cognition, Martha Augoustinos and Ian Walker (1995) suggest that the sense of immediate crisis has faded without seriously tackling the problems it identified.

The situation is very different in continental Europe, Australia and New Zealand, and in Britain in particular. In these places the crisis was the start of a much more fundamental reassessment of the nature and value of social psychological research, and more traditional experimental social psychology continues alongside very different styles of work.

The most immediate consequence of the crisis, however, was the development of a distinctly European social psychology that emphasizes social context as opposed to the individual. This work was less concerned with the methodological critique and continued with largely experimental work. Let us consider that work now.

European critics

Serge Moscovici, writing in France in 1972, contributed to a key work of European social psychology, a volume of essays entitled *The Context of Social Psychology*. In his chapter he lamented the fact that social psychology had until then been almost exclusively North American. He disliked the implicit moral stance and the individualist values in the North American research: *'all that goes beyond individualism and all that diverges a little from a capitalist model enters by definition the domain of irrationality'* (Moscovici, 1972: 30, emphasis in original).

He is here complaining about the individualist and capitalist assumptions of traditional social psychology. In his view social psychology of this kind reinforces the political *status quo*: it starts by assuming the existing *status quo* and focuses on describing and documenting it as if it were the universal timeless norm. Moscovici suggested that the social sciences must be more creative and participate in 'the dynamics of knowledge' and the formulation of 'dangerous truths'. Along with Henri Tajfel in the same volume, he also argues that the 'scientific ideology' is an obstacle to the development of social psychology. He argues that more attention should be paid to language and ideology – suggesting even that 'man is a product of his [sic] own activity' and that 'culture is created by and through communication'

(Moscovici, 1972: 56, 57). Society is seen as a 'machine' that both socializes and individualizes – society forces us to become individuals of particular types. The essential feature of 'social behaviour' is that it is symbolic, and that this symbolism is shared.

Moscovici takes an anti-individualist line, suggesting that to reduce the symbolic to the cognitive is to misunderstand the difference between these two phenomena, resulting in research that starts and ends with the individual as the unit of analysis. Symbols only acquire their meaning relative to 'those who receive the messages and those who emit them' (Moscovici, 1972: 61) and are only possible thanks to our common history of norms and rules. In this new and dangerous era of European social psychology, the study of symbolic processes should be developed along these anti-individualist lines.

In a similar vein, Henri Tajfel (1972) discusses three kinds of reductionism – biological, psychological and sociological – which have meant that 'sociopsychological man [*sic*]' is bypassed. Again the focus is on producing a more *social* social psychology, in which the reciprocity between individual and society is acknowledged, and the individualist bias is eliminated. The difference between North American and European social psychology for these researchers, therefore, was not the methods they used but the fact that European social psychologists had a more political, critical edge. They wanted to take into account group context and conflicts, and to incorporate the Marxist-inspired notions of ideology and exploitation that might offer social critique and emancipation.

Conclusion

This section has focused on the dissatisfaction that many researchers felt with the way social psychology was developing. The dissatisfaction split into three variants, sometimes appearing together, sometimes exclusively: the critique of individualism, of methodology and of theoretical development. By the start of the 1970s these early criticisms had given rise to new ways of doing social psychology in Europe, stimulated in particular by Henri Tajfel and Serge Moscovici. It is no accident that Tajfel and Moscovici were deeply affected by their experiences of World War II. Tajfel spent much of the war in prison camp, where he risked extermination as a Polish Jew; Moscovici walked across virtually the whole of Europe at the end of the war as a refugee. More recently both were coming to grips with the turbulence of the student uprisings of Paris in 1968, which almost brought down the French state. Like other key figures in social psychology, these experiences fed into their work.

So has nearly thirty years of European social psychology fulfilled the early promise? In Chapter 6 we will discuss the subjectivity critics who are building, in part, on the disquiet and critique raised in the crisis literature. Some of the themes highlighted by the methodological critiques have come to fruition in the work of discourse critics (Chapter 7) and postmodern critics (Chapter 8). In the final part of this chapter we will consider the development of social psychology in its classic European variety which makes experimental methods fundamental, but pays particular attention to issues of group identity and social context.

BOX 2.2   Social representations

One of the most important alternatives to North American social cognitive social psychology is the theory of social representations that was developed from the work of the sociologist Emile Durkheim by Serge Moscovici (1984).

In the 1950s Moscovici carried out what is still one of the classic pieces of research on social representations (Moscovici, 1976 [1961]). He studied the way psychoanalysis was absorbed in post-war France. He looked at a wide range of materials, including women's magazines and church publications, as well as doing some surveying of people's views.

Moscovici concluded that psychoanalysis had trickled down from the analytic couch and scholarly journals into both 'high' culture and popular common sense. People would 'think' with psychoanalysis, without it seeming as if they were doing anything more than seeing things in an obvious or commonsensical manner. This version of psychoanalysis was simplified, however; some of its concepts had filtered down into everyday use while others had not travelled out of the arcane scholarly world. For example, the notion of repression had taken on wide currency yet the notion of libido – the sexual drive that Freud saw as the major motivation of behaviour – had not. People's social representation of psychoanalysis was much simpler than that used by analysts.

The theory of social representations is characteristically European in stressing the shared nature of understanding and therefore suggesting a basis for collective rather than individual action. Members of social groups share representations of society, say, or political processes, and this is one of the things that lead them to act collectively. Another difference from the North American social cognition tradition is that social representation theory is constructionist. Representations are not merely passive images of the world, rather the images construct and evaluate the world for people. More generally, social representation theory provides links with sociology, history and anthropology. While North American social cognition tends to assume the significance of universal patterns of information processing, social representations theory emphasizes the crucial consequences of the specific set of representations available to a culture.

Social representation researchers have done important work on representations of health and illness (Herzlich, 1973) and madness (Jodelet, 1991). They have also engaged in productive debate with discourse researchers over the nature of action and the status of representations. (For a recent example see the debate between Wagner et al., 1999, Markova, 2000, and Potter and Edwards, 1999.)

Contemporary social cognition

Today social cognition provides one of the main traditions in European social psychology. It draws heavily on the theory and methodology of cognitive psychology. In this section we explore this field in more detail, focusing on two of the best-known theories – social identity theory and self-categorization theory that developed out of it. We will end with an examination of the critical potential of self-categorization theory. These theories are by no means the only ones central in European social cognition work, which is lively and complex, but they convey the feel of many of the issues that are central to critical researchers.

On the surface, contemporary social cognition seems like a return to the very reductionist approach that was so heavily criticized by predecessors such as Israel, Tajfel and Moscovici. However, Neil McRae and Miles Hewstone point out three ways in which social cognition is more complex than ordinary cognition:

> First, perceivers typically go beyond the information given in any social encounter. Second, the objects of social cognition (e.g. beliefs, judgements, desires) are malleable, and can be changed by being the focus of information processing. Third, nearly all social cognition is evaluative in implication (i.e. there is an affective involvement between perceivers and persons perceived).
> (Cited in Spears, 1995: 533)

Note that the focus here is very much on individual 'perceivers' and their putative cognitive processes. Social cognition research has ambitions to explain how information about other people can be processed and stored, and how this in turn can affect the way we perceive and interact with others (Abrams and Hogg, 1999: 6). Research that attempts to explain various social problems related to prejudice and stereotyping therefore focuses on cognitive phenomena such as 'perceptual judgement effect' and 'memory'. The issue is that human information processing is cognitively biased, giving rise to things like 'illusory correlations' (Hamilton, 1981). A person may see a minority group member perform some negative behaviour. According to the theory, the infrequency of such behaviour makes it more memorable. It is then generalized to the minority group as a whole, thereby conveniently explaining prejudice as simply a feature of limited human cognitive functioning. This is known as the 'cognitive miser' view of social perception.

How does this link with a critical agenda in social psychology? Advocates would suggest that by documenting features (that is, *cognitive* features) of discrimination they are better equipped to promote programmes of change.

Q **DISCUSSION QUESTIONS**

1   What might be the consequences of seeing people as cognitive misers?

2   What would the outcomes of such research be focused on?

3   What implications would this have for solving social problems such as racism and sexism?

Social identity theory

An important recent development of social cognition research is social identity theory, in which the focus is on social groups and social change. This is probably the theory that most centrally typifies distinctively European social psychology, with its emphasis on social and intergroup aspects of relations, but its adherence to the North American experimental tradition. Social identity theory was developed by Henri Tajfel, who spent five years of his life (during the Second World War) in prisoner-of-war camps in Germany and Austria, living as a French Jew. If the authorities had discovered his real identity as a Polish Jew he would have almost certainly been executed. On his release he discovered that a whole community of Polish Jews, including his parents, brother and other members of his family, had been killed. He spent the next six years rehabilitating refugees from different countries, before embarking on his studies in social psychology. From 1967 to 1982 Tajfel led the social psychology group at Bristol, creating a major centre for the European brand of social psychology and developing his work on social categorization and social identity.

Social identity theory was supported by classic studies using the 'minimal group paradigm' (Billig and Tajfel, 1973; Tajfel et al., 1971). These studies involved experiments in which anonymous participants were arbitrarily categorized (often by the toss of a coin) as members of minimally meaningful groups, e.g. X or Y. Despite the experimenters' best efforts to show that group membership was arbitrary the members started to treat the groups as significant, for example by allocating members of their own group greater rewards than the members of alternative groups.

These findings were thought to refute theories like *realistic conflict theory* (Sherif, 1966; see p. 21 above), which attempted to explain hostility between groups in terms of conflicts of interest over scarce and valued resources. As a way of explaining these results, Tajfel, along with John Turner (Turner, 1975; Tajfel, 1978; Tajfel and Turner, 1979) developed social identity theory.

Social identity theory holds that there is a universal and fundamental human cognitive requirement for positive differentiation from others, and that this drives our antisocial behaviour. It also emphasizes the way that people's psychological processes can change when they are in group settings. This is because we define ourselves in terms of our *social* identity rather than in terms of our *personal* identity. When we define ourselves in terms of our personal identity we are displaying our identity as someone with a unique personality, a set of attitudes, preferences, skills and so on. So if we were, say, in a one-to-one conversation with a close friend, or expressing strong disagreement with other group members, our personal identity would be more likely to be salient.

When we define ourselves in terms of our social identity, however, we take on the characteristics of that particular social group. Instead of simply being a unique individual with our own preferences, we start to define ourselves in terms of say, being a woman, a lesbian, a Muslim and so on. In certain settings, then, one or more of these group identities will become salient to us; we will see ourselves, or label ourselves, in terms of this group category. This process of self-labelling changes our own and other people's views about who we are and what we are like. Tajfel and Turner (1979) see a number of implications related to the psychological changes that occur when social identities become salient:

1   Firstly, our self-esteem begins to get caught up in the fate of the group. If we can't see our own groups in a positive way, then we can't see ourselves in a positive way.

2   We become *depersonalized*. This means that we stereotype ourselves: our self-perceptions are dominated by the collection of ideas and images of what it means to be, say, a woman. This in turn affects how we think it is appropriate to behave in particular circumstances.

3   Another 'psychological' change is that members of out-groups have less influence on us: we pay less attention to their points of view.

The key thing about a social identity is thus that it involves a cognitive process through which we can be socially defined. From a critical perspective, what it hopes to offer is an explanation for *how ideology determines our actions*. We will consider ideology in more detail in the next chapter on Marxist critics; for the moment, ideology can be treated as system of concepts or ideas that hides oppression or prevents radical action. Previous explanations of group behaviour, which saw it arising through an accumulation of interpersonal bonds, were not able to deal with the fact that people join together in demonstration and mass action on the basis of common identification, whether they know each other or not. In this sense, social identity theory has been a step forward for social psychology. (Reicher and Hopkins, 2001, give a useful discussion of ideology, social identity and collective action.)

Criticisms of social identity theory

There have been a number of different criticisms of social identity theory. Some have come from within the social cognition tradition, and are concerned with the design and interpretation of experiments. Others come from outside the tradition, and ask more radical questions.

From within the tradition, Rabbie and Horowitz (1988) argue that the minimal group paradigm, upon which social identity theory is based, is flawed in the sense that the categories created by the experiment are not necessarily minimal. For example, it could be that participants decide that the experimenter must have some reason for allocating them into groups. Also Rabbie and Horowitz (1988) report that, if participants believe that the amount of money allocated to them at the end of the experiment depends only on allocations made by the out-group, they favour the out-group.

Reicher and Hopkins (2001) extend this critique, suggesting that the experiments are 'maximal' as well as minimal, in the sense that they exclude all the factors that might modify the process of differentiation outside of the laboratory. If all we know about a person is their group affiliation, this will be the aspect of them that we select in making our judgements concerning them. Outside the laboratory, where we interact with people more directly, there may be many different dimensions along which we can achieve positive distinctiveness if we are so inclined.

Augoustinos and Walker (1995) point out that there is no firm evidence supporting the hypotheses that (1) those with low self-esteem ought to display greater in-group bias than those with higher self-esteem and (2) that those who display in-group bias have raised levels of self-esteem. In defence of the theory, Turner (1995) argues that failing to find a relation between self-esteem and differentiation does not challenge the theory, because it depends on the contextual relationships that a group member finds her/himself in. However, Augoustinos and Walker (1995) argue that the proper focus of the theory ought to be 'group esteem' rather than self-esteem.

Martha Augoustinos

Martha Augoustinos is Associate Professor in the Department of Psychology, Adelaide University, Australia. Her major contribution has been the introduction of critical approaches to mainstream social psychology, and, in particular, the development of discursive psychology as a significant research tradition in Australia. She is co-author of Social Cognition: An integrated introduction *(1995) with Iain Walker (Murdoch University) and co-editor of* Understanding Prejudice, Racism, and Social Conflict *(2001) with Kate Reynolds (Australian National University). Her recent work adopts a critical discursive approach to analyse the local particulars of racist discourse in Australia. This has involved mapping the trajectory of the 'race debate' that has dominated Australian public discourse over the last decade, including debates over native title, reconciliation and apologizing to the 'stolen generations'.*

Brown (1996) questions social identity theory's crucial analytical distinction between personal identity and social identity. She suggests that in practice actions result from a complex mixture of personal, group, situational and even idiosyncratic contextual influences, past and present. It therefore becomes very difficult to assert where 'personal' ends and 'social' begins. Brown also suggests that the social groups that people identify with do not always supply us with a clear collective image. Groups may form in *ad hoc* and arbitrary ways, where there is no apparent reason for people being together, and it is perhaps over-generalizing to suggest that a social identity will always develop for those group members.

From a rather different methodological tradition, more associated with discourse analysis, Marshall and Wetherell criticized social identity theory's assumption that 'one "true" representative process can be hypothesized and discovered by the analyst' (1989: 125). A group of female and male law students who were about to become solicitors and advocates were interviewed. The aim was to explore how they constructed their identity in relation to their gender, in their talk about becoming lawyers. It was concluded that participants displayed a 'variable, inconsistent and highly negotiable image of the group' as well as group strategies and identities (Marshall and Wetherell, 1989: 126). We shall encounter more critiques of this kind later in the book.

Self-categorization theory

Social identity theory has been extremely influential, particularly in European social psychology. However, in the face of criticisms of this kind, John Turner (1985) developed a modified version he termed self-categorization theory. Self-categorization theory aims to tackle some of the difficulties with social identity theory, where social and personal identities are no longer seen as qualitatively different forms of identity but rather as representing different forms of self-categorization. The focus is on the factors that lead people to make particular self-categorizations, and the consequences that those categorizations have. The aim is to understand how the change of self-categorizations from personal characteristics to broad social identities can explain 'emergent, higher-order processes of group behaviour' (Turner, 1995: 502). Thus if I stop categorizing myself as a fussy eater and start categorizing myself as an oppressed and underprivileged worker I will start to act in line with my understanding or, more precisely, my stereotype of this group. Perhaps my dislike of the food in the works canteen is initially understood in terms of personal likes, but as other workers raise issues about the firm's lack of funding of the canteen, the relevant category changes, and I start to understand my dislike as a legitimate aversion shared with other exploited workers. My subsequent actions will thus be more likely to be a collective protest than an expression of personal dislike. As other group members categorize themselves using the same stereotype of our shared group, my actions will become part of collective actions. I will thus become *depersonalized* as I act on this stereotype.

Self-categorization theory is therefore primarily a cognitive theory, as opposed to social identity theory's motivational focus. I act as a group member because I carry around inside me a stereotypic representation of the group category. Self-categorization theory provides a model of how the individual acts as a societal member. The existing stock of category stereotypes provides the material for collective action. Cognitive processing, and in particular self-stereotyping, provides the motor. And the shared nature of category stereotypes ensures that collective action will be, broadly, collective. Self-categorization theory has explanatory ambitions similar to those of traditional social psychologists – to understand and work with stereotyping, group polarization, social judgement and cohesion – but provides a strong emphasis on the importance of group categories and intergroup behaviour (see Turner et al., 1987).

Self-categorization theory provides a novel understanding of one of the basic concerns of social psychology; that is, social influence (Turner, 1991). Firstly, self-categorization theory provides us with insights into what influences people. I will be influenced most by things that confirm my characterization as a category member. For example, the bad canteen food may be just the kind of thing that confirms me as one of the downtrodden workers. Second, it provides insights into who will be influential – other members of our group, other workers who start to complain and agitate about the food. Third, self-categorization theory explains who is influenced – those who identify with the category of group membership. All the people who self-categorize as workers will potentially be influenced. As Reicher and Hopkins (2001) point out, this gives us a clear picture of the nature of all collective human action – it all depends on how group categories are defined. The broader the category boundaries 'the more people are liable to be influenced together, and act together.

One of the aims of the research into self-categorization theory has been to refute theories that assume a central role for personal self-interest in their explanations of group phenomena (Turner 1995). Self-categorization is always context-dependent. There is always a range of possible categorizations available, and the one that is actually used will be dependent on what Turner calls the 'meta-contrast ratio'. This is the ratio of differences within a category to the differences between categories. When differences *within* categories are large and differences *between* categories are small we are likely to understand our actions using idiosyncratic or personal self-stereotypes.

Thus when there is a lot of variety among shopfloor workers and their response to the poor canteen food, and there is not a lot of difference between them and the managers, who occasionally dislike their food, then the individual worker is likely to use a personal self-stereotype such as fussy eater. However, when there is a lot of similarity between the shopfloor workers, and they all dislike their food, and the managers all seem the same, and eat in some fancy white restaurant, then the individual worker is likely to use a group self-stereotype as a downtrodden worker, and maybe act accordingly.

The emphasis in this theory moves away from the perceiver and her or his cognitive abilities, and on to 'relative, varying, context-dependent properties' (Turner, 1995: 503). Society has a major significance in this theory, as it provides both an existing organization of social groups and also a set of group stereotypes that guide interaction. It is this version of society, combined with the constraints of human information processing, which is crucial for collective action. Moreover, how we categorize ourselves depends on the particular social context that we are in. Our discussion of self-categorization theory has become technical at times, but it is worth persevering with because self-categorization theory represents one of the most ambitious attempts to develop a theory, using the methods and assumptions of traditional social cognition, that can address critical concerns with group relations and collective action.

Criticisms of self-categorization theory

One of the virtues of self-categorization theory is its stress on the significance of the context of action. Stereotypes and categories do not simply work as fixed objects within a system of information processing. Rather, they are flexibly modified according to relevant contrasts and diversity. However, Reicher and Hopkins

BOX 2.3   Crowds

Crowds and their actions have been a central topic of social psychological explanation. The classic account of crowd action comes from Gustav LeBon, who observed the revolutionary crowds involved in the Paris commune of 1871. His view of crowds as primitive and guided by violent and animal instincts has been refined in more recent social psychology, but is still highly influential. For example, its residue can be seen in the influential deindividuation theory, which treats crowd violence as a product of the loss of social restraints on individuals and allows them to revert to a baser animal nature that is violent, selfish and cruel.

Steve Reicher (1996) has argued that crowds have been implicitly viewed from an establishment, pro-*status quo* position which treats them as a threat to order. This despite the involvement of collective action in important social change. He suggests that the US riots of the 1960s and 1970s were at least as important as boycotts and sit-ins in generating black advancement. Moreover, studies of deaths in crowd action show that members of the crowd are much more likely to be killed than members of the security services or passers by. He argues that many studies of crowd conflicts fail to see them as (often highly one-sided) intergroup conflicts where the crowd is often in conflict with agents of the state such as the police or army.

Reicher conducted a classic study of the so-called 'St Paul's riot' of 1980 in Bristol (Reicher, 1984). This involved several hours of conflict with the police, who were driven out of the local area. Police cars were set alight and police officers stoned. There was also a period of looting. Reicher interviewed people who had been members of the crowd. Using a social identity theory perspective he found that, rather than losing their identity for some kind of animalistic deindividuated state, crowd members acted in terms of a shared social identity that suggested particular values and understandings of the situation. Reicher suggests that the pattern of the violence, and the looting, as well as the order of events, support a social identity account. More generally, it is important to understand crowd actions in terms of the understandings of the crowd members themselves rather than taking the outsiders' perspective.

(1996a, b, 2001) suggest that this strength is also a source of weakness. While much effort has gone into relating stereotypes to their contextual determinants, little thought has gone into the nature of context itself. Indeed participants are usually supplied with ready-made vignettes about context, which bear little relevance to conditions outside the laboratory (e.g. Oakes, 1987; Oakes et al., 1991; Reicher and Hopkins, 2001). Because self-categorization theory treats category definitions as merely the cognitive reflection of social reality, it misses the sense in which participants can re/create different contexts. Reicher and Hopkins (2001) argue that this extends the lopsidedness of social identity theory, discussed above, in which the route from context to the person is well documented, but the route from person to context is largely ignored. As it stands self-categorization theory has very little to say about how people go about actively defining and making their worlds – indeed, this possibility is all but denied.

Reicher and Hopkins (2001) have themselves attempted the ambitious task of developing a version of self-categorization theory that allows for this creative process of reality construction. A central part of this is trying to add the insights of a discursive psychological approach (discussed in Chapter 7) with some of the explanatory power of self-categorization theory. In a study of nationalist political discourse in Scotland they attempt to combine an emphasis on the active construction and reconstruction of society in interviews and political speeches with elements of information processing and category effects. The problem they never completely solve is how to reconcile the *activity* of practices of construction with the automatic nature of the cognitive processing. For example, how can identity be both a precondition (as in self-categorization theory) and *also* something that can be managed and constituted (as in discursive psychology)?

General critiques of social cognition work

When critical social psychologists have discussed social cognition they have tended to be concerned about the enormous explanatory force given to cognitive processes. Put simply, whatever existing social resources (stereotypes or whatever) are drawn on in the processing it is the processing itself that governs outcomes. Things going on in the heads of individuals are made paramount. Moreover, some have suggested that the move within social cognition research has been from more social to more individual cognition. For example, taking studies from the early 1990s, Ian Parker (1997a) laments a trend towards individual cognitive processes in European social psychology journals. For instance, Hewstone et al. (1992) replace notions of group identity with cognitive models of stereotype change; Ellemers et al. (1992) represent minority group status as the backdrop for individual action; Bruins and Wilke (1993) study individual power bids through the 'power-distance reduction' framework. Simon (1993) explains in-group bias in terms of 'egocentric' social categorization, and Evans (1993) conceptualizes class as if it were 'simply a collection of individual cognitive processes' (Parker, 1997a: 47).

Michael Billig (1996) highlights a tension between Tajfel's (1972) early work, discussed above, and his later work on social identity. This later work attempts to provide generic explanations for group processes, and hence social action, despite the earlier insistence on the need to understand the particularity of such phenomena in their social context. The more generic the processes the more they are treated as automatic and driven by cognitive processes and the less space is devoted to the construction of group categories and the management of their effects.

This critique is an extension of his earlier influential critique of social cognition in general and social categorization theory in particular (Billig, 1985). Billig highlights the centrality of perception to traditional social cognition and its emphasis on categorization as natural and even adaptive. This underplays the role of talk and especially rhetoric. After all, although much of the time racism is produced by individuals about people in groups they have rarely or never seen, they are likely to spend time talking to others and producing racist views in conversation. So to understand prejudice, say, researchers need to understand more about talk and rhetoric. In making this argument Billig is starting to put together a position that we can now see as a form of discursive or rhetorical psychology.

Billig suggests that categorization and an opposite process of particularization – splitting categories into parts or specific instances – are *both* important in racism. By focusing purely on categorization, as social identity theory does, and by treating it as a perceptual and cognitive phenomenon, as social identity theory does, a vital part of the development of racism is missed. Indeed, Billig is critical of the whole model of thought that underlies social cognition approaches of this kind. He calls it the bureaucratic model. In this model:

> much of thinking is seen as a process of locking the unfamiliar into safe, familiar categories . . . the image of the person to emerge from this approach resembles that of a bureaucrat sensibly ordering the messy stimulus world . . . so [social cognition researchers] talk of organization, order, management, efficiency, etc.
>
> (1985: 87–8)

By introducing particularization Billig was able to reject the social cognitive view of prejudice as an outcome of the way thinking gets done and thus an inevitable feature of social life. What makes racism and other forms of prejudice work in practical arguments, as we shall see with Wetherell and Potter's (1992) work on racism in Chapter 7, is an extraordinary flexibility of arguing.

Take anti-capitalism protestors on television. When in the course of a mealtime conversation a father dismisses them as misguided and intent on mindless violence this involves a fairly gross categorization, an expression of prejudice. However, what happens when the television news comes on? (This family always watches the news over tea.) There is an interview with an articulate middle class white protester who is neatly turned out. She criticizes the violence but makes the case for Third World countries suffering from the power of multinationals. It is at this point, when family members are starting to say, 'Hey, Dad, *she's* not an extremist nutter,' that the skilled practical rhetorician (Dad) will start to particularize to save the general categorization. 'Some clever people are involved . . . she's unusual . . . she's probably a dupe of the really violent organizers . . .' The simple bureaucrat is not the most effective in the world of prejudice.

In a similar way to Billig (1985), Julian Henriques criticized the cognitivism of Tajfel's approach, arguing that the premise of an individual–society dichotomy entails 'the reduction of prejudice and intergroup perceptions to effects occasioned by failures in the mechanism of cognition itself' (1984: 61). It is therefore 'severely limited' in its explanations of social phenomena.

Derek Edwards (1991) provides an effective critique of cognitivist ways of thinking about categorization that starts to go beyond a mere playing down of 'cognition' in favour of the 'social'. He suggests that categories should not be

Michael Billig

'I have mixed feelings towards the growth of critical psychology. On the one hand I am delighted that in the past fifteen years psychology has been opened up to wider influences than hitherto. It has been good to see the boundaries between social psychology and other social sciences becoming increasingly permeable. In my own work, I've tried to cross disciplinary boundaries. On the other hand, every approach that becomes successful carries the potential to become an orthodoxy. Critical social psychology, when established as a discipline to be taught to undergraduates, will be in danger of becoming an uncritical orthodoxy. Then it will be time to return to experiments. After all, Solomon Asch was both a great experimentalist and great critical social scientist.'

explained in perceptual and cognitive terms; rather, 'categories are for talking'. This approach starts to problematize the way that 'social' and 'cognition' have been assumed to be two separable and identifiable interacting entities. We will consider this classic discursive psychological move of respecifying what have hitherto been assumed to be cognitive phenomena as discursive practices in Chapter 7.

Antaki and Widdecombe (1998) make a similar discursive move with the notion of identity. Because the discursive move means that identity becomes something that we 'do', rather than something that we simply 'be', if we want to study 'identities in action' we should be looking at records of everyday interaction. This type of work renders most of the debates that occur from within the social cognition paradigm redundant, as it rejects the basic assumptions about what 'social' and 'cognition' and thus 'identity' are. Again this is discussed in more detail in Chapter 7.

Conclusion

This section has focused on the development of one of the classic theories of social cognition that has been treated as a critical counter to more mainstream, often US, social cognition. It considered Tajfel's social identity theory, its modification by Turner into self-categorization theory, and briefly the attempt to merge this with more constructionist and discursive positions by Reicher and Hopkins. What all these approaches have in common is a willingness to accept that what is 'social' and what is 'cognition' influence each other greatly. What they are less willing to consider are the dangers of basing theories on two pre-defined categories in this way.

More broadly, many of the problems with this approach can be traced to its development out of the crisis in social psychology. In effect, it developed out of the political and ideological crisis, and the loss of society and intergroup relations in social psychology. So that half the crisis was fundamental to this kind of European social psychology. Yet it missed the half of the crisis that was devoted to high-lighting the problems with traditional methods. The challenge for this work is to show that it can genuinely address the broader social and contextual issues that were there in the core of Moscovici and Tajfel's work while staying true to a world of austere empiricism and experimental manipulation. I have already noted sugges-tions that this work has drifted toward a more individual cognitive position. Reicher and Hopkins have tried a mix of experimental social cognition and constructionism. As we continue our tour of critical approaches we shall see that most of them follow the lead of the methodological crisis and eschew experimentation.

Application

How might social cognition research be applied? It may be the case that researchers in this area develop robust findings that relate to cognitive functioning of certain 'types' of people – e.g. those who are more or less likely to 'stereotype' others. How can such findings be applied to real world contexts? The overall goal appears to be the development of well supported theories through rigorous scientific testing. Once a good social psychological theory is proved and refined we are then justified in using it to tackle problems such as group hostility.

However, in practice people of a specific type (students) are mainly studied in laboratory conditions – Sears (1986) found that 85 per cent of all articles appearing in three major social psychology journals were done on undergraduate students in laboratory settings. People are mainly studied using hypothesis testing through the manipulation of a limited set of independent variables. How far can such work be applicable when it seems that the focus is very much on individual features of people, with the assumption that these isolated findings will simply build up into a theory that will transfer and map on to the complex environments within which people interact on a day-to-day basis? Moscovici emphasized the importance of a full understanding of a social context before a social psychology theory could be applied in that context. You ought to have a thorough understanding of the existing group relations in a classroom, say, before applying a theory of prejudice to try to alleviate racism. Yet social psychology in this tradition simply does not have the analytical apparatus for such an analysis of 'context'. And the researchers who do have such an apparatus – some discourse analysts, for example – have not found added value to come from bolting social cognition theories on to their analysis of interaction. This may change, but at the moment a lot of application of this kind relies more on promissory notes than well attested change arising from theor-etically guided interventions.

Social psychology and the three worlds

Fathali Moghaddam (1987, 1990) surveyed the global scene in psychology and described North America – the United States and Canada – as the psychological

First World, the superpower of academic psychology, particularly social psychology. Other industrialized regions such as Europe and the former Soviet Union form social psychology's Second World. For example, the former Soviet Union has a similar population to the United States, but only a tenth as many psychologists (Kolominsky, 1991). The developing nations such as Nigeria, Bangladesh and Cuba form social psychology's Third World. The point is that psychology is culturally biased, and that different styles of psychology are appropriate to different cultures, so that different ways of applying psychology will also be appropriate for different worlds. Moghaddam's observations offer a fundamental challenge to the idea of a universally applicable social cognition by emphasizing the very different cultural contexts that psychology will be practised in.

Conclusion

Overall I have traced the development of social cognition research from its early beginnings to current attempts to forge connections with more critical discursive and social constructionist perspectives. The focus on individuals and their identities has been a running theme – each perspective seeks to provide a more sophisticated solution to the problem of focusing on the individual in social psychology. But why is the individual such a problem? Surely that is what psychologists must be most interested in? If we are not focused on the individual aren't we simply turning into sociologists? Part of the reason why the individual has been such a thorny issue for critical researchers has been the reliance on the strongly anti-individualist perspectives of Marxism. One way of maintaining inequalities and controlling a population is to make sure they do not see their impoverished circumstances as arising from changeable social structures, but rather from unchangeable individual features. These are important and inspiring ideas, and so we begin the next chapter by taking a step even further back from current practices in critical social psychology to examine the influence of Marx.

B The best thing about social cognition

Social cognition researchers have been concerned to tackle social problems involving inequalities and oppression in a systematic way. The hope of many researchers has been to find a scientific basis for the alleviation of problems such as racism.

W The worst thing about social cognition

First, is the focus on the individual. Baumeister's review of the field led to the conclusion that 'most social psychologists think of people as largely self-contained units . . .' (1995: 75). And Augoustinos and Walker suggest that 'the only thing social about social cognition is that it is about social objects – people, groups, events' (1995: 3). The second thing is the assumption that 'individual' and 'social' are separable identifiable categories that can be experimentally manipulated, rather than useful categories for getting things done in everyday interactions.

Where next?

On the one hand it seems like a good idea to advocate the wholesale closure of social cognition owing to its pervasive problematic assumptions about both cognition and social reality. On the other hand perhaps the critical developments brought about by the work of Augoustinos, Hopkins, Reicher and Wetherell will be its salvation! The jury is still out. There is a lot of argument to be done. US social psychologists still take remarkably little notice of two decades of non-experimental critical work.

Practical exercises

1   Choose one of the classic experiments in social psychology – Sherif, Asch or Milgram. Read though the summary and imagine yourself a participant who has turned up to take part, and has acted in the manner of the typical participants. Try to think of the experience. What reasons might you give someone who asked you why you acted like this? Are any justifications possible? Or do you end up saying that these studies highlight flaws in human nature?

2   List the various problems with experimental research highlighted in the crisis literature. Take a social psychology journal such as the *British Journal of Social Psychology* or the *Journal of Personality and Social Psychology*. Take the problems in turn and try to apply them to the article. Do they hit home? How might the authors of the study respond to defend it?

3   List ten different social categories that you fall into (female, British, student, etc.). Consider how many of these categories are significant for how you act. Can you imagine situations where categories start to take on more importance for your actions? Try to think in terms of social identity theory and its account of self-stereotyping and group actions.

Reading

If you read only one thing, read:

Reicher, S. and Hopkins, N. (2001) *Self and Nation*, London: Sage. **This provides a good discussion and critique of social identity theory and some interesting developments of self-categorization theory. It provides a useful bridge to other areas of critical social psychology.**

Classics

Billig, M. (1985) Prejudice, categorization and particularization: From a perceptual to a rhetorical approach, *European Journal of Social Psychology*, 15, 79–103.

This is a classic paper that undermines the whole focus on categorization that is central to the social cognition approach.

Billig, M. (1978) *Fascists: A Social Psychological View of the National Front*. London: Academic Press.

Clark, K.B. and Clark, M.P. (1947) Racial identification and preference in Negro children, in T.M. Newcombe and E.L. Hartley (eds), *Readings in Social Psychology* (pp. 169–178). New York: Holt.

Moscovici, S. (1972) Society and theory in social psychology, in J. Israel and H. Tajfel (eds), *The Context of Social Psychology* (pp. 17–68). London: Academic Press.

Robinson, P. (ed.) (1996) *Social Groups and Identities: Developing the Legacy of Henri Tajfel*. London: Butterworth Heinemann. *An interesting set of papers showing the variety of critical perspectives that intersect on the terrain of social identity theory.*

Sherif, M. (1966) *In Common Predicament: Social Psychology of Intergroup Conflict and Cooperation*. Boston, MA: Houghton Mifflin.

Tajfel, H. (1972) Experiments in a vacuum, in J. Israel and H. Tajfel (eds), *The Context of Social Psychology* (pp. 69–119). London: Academic Press.

Other useful texts

Augoustinos, M. and Walker, I. (1995) *Social Cognition: An Integrated Introduction*. London: Sage. *An excellent overview of social cognition from a sympathetic but critical direction.*

Difficult but worth it

Wetherell, M. (1996a) Constructing social identities: The individual/social binary in Henri Tajfel's social psychology, in P. Robinson (ed.), *Social Groups and Identities* (pp. 269–285). Oxford: Butterworth Heinemann.

Chapter 3

Marxist Critics

Most people are familiar with Karl Marx's claim that philosophers have only interpreted the world in various ways; the point is to change it. There is a wonderful irony here, given the endless debate among Marxist theorists and philosophers about how we should interpret the world. And after all Marx (1818–83) was himself a German philosopher whose influence on the philosophical development of the social sciences has been colossal.

But Marx was also a revolutionary – he was a man with a vision. He saw the possibility that working people might control their own destiny, and his mission was to make it happen through communism. He saw more clearly than anyone of his time that there were features of people's *social context* and *economic status* that were causing them misery and suffering, and he sought to change things. The way to change things was to emancipate working people from the alienation caused by nineteenth century capitalist society, and from the divisive relations of production and reproduction that emerged from it.

Although there are many problems in adopting Marxism wholesale, or even of producing it as a coherent and agreed-upon set of principles, many of his insights are still useful in making sense of late twentieth century capitalism. In particular, the Marxist critique of inequalities and oppression has been a major source of inspiration for many critical social psychologists.

As Parker (see box) suggests, from a Marxist perspective we can see psychology as an ideology (see below for a discussion of ideology) that prevents people from recognizing the oppression of class position by encouraging them to focus on themselves and other 'individuals' as the source of any problems that arise. The 'scientific' training produces 'objective' psychologists, who can nevertheless view themselves as creative individuals, the primary source of their own brilliant psychological insights. This objectivity allows psychologists to detach from their 'subjects' and so not be affected by their alienation and suffering. The role of a thoroughgoing Marxist psychologist would instead be to work towards the abolition of class society through the empowerment of the working classes. It's not hard to see how some social cognition researchers who are interested in moving away from the individual and towards group processes (e.g. Reicher) and minority groups (e.g. Moscovici) could also be inspired by or sympathetic to a Marxist perspective.

Ian Parker

'I was a Marxist before I was a psychologist, and have always viewed psychology as a fascinating ideological system and horrible coercive apparatus for normalizing and pathologizing behaviour and experience. That is precisely why it is worth taking seriously. All the elements of alienation and reification that characterize capitalism are condensed in the discipline of psychology, and the task of critical psychology is to expose and combat the witting and unwitting abuse of power that psychologists enjoy, and to include the analysis of discourse in our writing and unwriting. This is "practical deconstruction", and it can become part of radical politics in groupings like Psychology Politics Resistance. The study of the formation of psychoanalytic subjectivity is also useful here, for it reaches into aspects of our lives that mainstream psychology detests. However, to do this in the name of any notion of "true" underlying psychological processes, whether theorized from psychoanalysis, deconstruction, discourse analysis or Marxism, is also a mistake that any critical psychology should beware of.'

But what does it mean to adopt a Marxist perspective? There are many different types of Marxism. This chapter begins with a simplified characterization of key aspects of Marxist theory, followed by a discussion of the reinvention of Marx's critical method as 'critical theory' by the Frankfurt school.

We then explore how Marxist ideas have been picked up and transformed in recent discourse and rhetorical work, with further exploration of the notion of 'ideology' and 'ideological dilemmas'. The notion of ideology as a unitary set of ideas that sustain false consciousness has been replaced by the image of a fragmented pattern of discourses that sustain practices and legitimate patterns of social relations.

This leads to Foucault's elaboration and critique of aspects of Marxist theory, in particular its notions of power, ideology and subjectivity. This discussion identifies some arguments that will be followed through in subsequent chapters.

Marxist theory: basic ideas and recent developments

This section has four parts:

1   *Key terms and distinctions*, in which the philosophical, historical and economic features of some of Marx's key ideas are outlined.

2   *Power, ideology and subjectivity*, which draws upon some of the key terms explained in the first section, and uses them to develop Marxist notions of power, ideology and subjectivity, concepts close to many critical social psychologists' hearts.

3   The third section will discuss some *preliminary problems* with Marxism.

4   Section four examines the work of the *Frankfurt school* in trying to address some of those problems.

Key terms and distinctions

This section will outline some of Marx's key terms and distinctions. It is simplistic but helpful to split Marxist theory into three components: philosophical, historical and economic.

Philosophy: dialectical materialism

Marx's philosophical developments are drawn from an assortment of German philosophers such as Hegel and Feuerbach, and like theirs his work is organized by the philosophical distinction between materialism and idealism. Materialist philosophy (influenced by Feuerbach) is based on empiricism, seeking an understanding of how the human mind perceives reality via the senses, and in particular how we come to 'know' things 'objectively'. Questions from a materialist perspective revolve around how we can know whether something is real or whether it is a product of our 'subjective' mental processes.

The 'dialectical' part of Marx's philosophy comes from Hegel, who suggested that ideas or social formations are never fixed, but occur in particular patterns of motion or flux, which he called 'dialectic'. An original idea or 'thesis' always stands in opposition to another idea or position – the 'antithesis'. The struggle between these two opposed positions, thesis and antithesis, results in a third set of ideas or practices – the 'synthesis' – which eventually itself becomes a thesis, and so on. Change happens, according to Hegel, through this continual movement.

Historical materialism

Marx also gives us a way of understanding history. Historical materialism is materialist in the sense that it sees historical change and social organization occurring through people and their tools, rather than any kind of (idealist) mystical destiny or the 'hand of god'. Tools, and the workers available to use them, are seen as the *forces of production*; the organization that shapes how people use those tools forms the *relations of production*. Together the forces and relations of production form a *mode of production*.

Everything that happens in society is determined by the mode of production, or *economic base*. The economic base – the form of ownership and control of the means of production – generates other social formations, known as the *ideological superstructure*. The superstructure embodies social arenas of ideology, such as religion, politics and law.

According to Marx, under capitalism, the economic base is capable of much more rapid progress and change than the ideological superstructure. Because the superstructure embodies all our ideological assumptions, our capability for thought and problem solving will always lag behind our capability for material production. Hence material conditions (the economic base) determine ideas (the ideological superstructure) and types of consciousness. *Problems arise for us to solve only when the material conditions for their solution already exist.*

Marx identifies five basic historical changes in the mode of production: the primitive community, the slave state, the feudal state, capitalism, and socialism. Each evolves into the other through the processes of thesis, antithesis and synthesis.

Capitalism

Marx developed his ideas about capitalism in contrast to the enthusiastic adoption of 'commercial society' by Adam Smith (1723–90) and his followers. Smith suggested that people naturally pursue their own self-interest, yet by doing so they inadvertently pursue the ultimate advantage of all by increasing the wealth of the nation. Every individual 'is led by an invisible hand to promote an end which was no part of his [*sic*] intention' (Smith, 1776: 456, cited in West, 1996: 47). Marx wanted to abolish this capitalist system of production and the ownership of private property, and much of his work provides us with various kinds of critique of capitalism.

However, for Marx and his collaborator and financial supporter Friedrich Engels (1820–95), it was necessary to bring capitalism's economic development to completion before communism could be effective. Although capitalism is exploitative, it is necessary to develop its dynamic productivity in order to ensure maximum resources, enabling adherence to the communist principle 'From each according to his [*sic*] ability, to each according to his need!' (Marx, 1972: 17, cited in West, 1996: 51).

Marx therefore set about exploring the internal contradictions of capitalism, the conditions that would eventually lead to its demise and to the evolution of socialism and communism. This leads us to the third area of Marxism.

Marxist economic theory

One of the contradictory aspects of capitalism that Marx predicted would lead to its demise is articulated in his 'labour theory of value' (Read, 1996). This in essence suggests that workers' wages will always tend towards subsistence level so that producers can maximize profit. This occurs owing to the existence of a 'reserve army' of unemployed labour living below the subsistence level. In order to compete with other capitalists, the introduction of new labour-saving machinery increases the output per labourer, and ensures that the reserve army remains in place. The drive to compete also ensures that the strong will either crush or absorb the weak, resulting in the concentration of wealth in the hands of increasingly few capitalists. Various other factors were predicted by Marx to reduce profits, increase the concentration of capital, and so increase exploitation. Eventually life under capitalism would become so bleak that the workers would organize a revolution, and replace the capitalist system with a fairer socialist economy.

This section has provided a brief overview of the philosophical, historical and economic aspects of Marxist theory. This gives us some basic notions with which to understand some more relevant topics for critical social psychology – power, ideology and subjectivity.

Power, ideology and subjectivity

This section draws upon some of the key terms explained in the last section, and uses them to develop Marxist notions of power, ideology and subjectivity.

Power and class struggle

One of the central features of Marxism is the notion that class position will determine the social consciousness, or ways of understanding, of its members. This is translated into the familiar terms of *bourgeoisie* – those who support the capitalists, the owners and controllers of the means of production, and *proletariat* – those who produce the goods through their labour. They are divided by their differing material interests, which ultimately leads to class struggle, which in turn inevitably leads to the proletariat living under a dictatorship (Marx, 1852, from Read, 1996). The distinctive twist that marked out Marx's brand of historical materialism was the notion that as capitalism developed it would inevitably give rise to revolution, in which the proletariat would take over the means of production. Power for Marx resides in class relations – money, capital and commodities are merely tokens of it.

Alienation and human nature

Marx suggested that work under capitalism is alienating. What does he mean by this? Let us consider two features of alienation:

1   *Economic alienation.* The idea here is that the labour power that produces surplus value for the benefit of the capitalists' profit is alienated labour – it no longer belongs to the labourer.
2   *Self-alienation.* Because labourers have to sell their labour power they become commodities – something to be bought and sold – and thus less than human, lacking the free will to determine their own actions. (Note the humanist/modernist notions of the person in operation here.)

Marx saw capitalism not simply as a source of economic exploitation of the proletariat, but also as a source of alienation from our true being – what he calls 'species being' (West, 1996: 48). Species being is realized through labour – the way we have of expressing ourselves creatively – which of course the proletariat have no control over. The creative abilities of the workers – for Marx their very essence –

become the capital of the privileged few. In order to earn money and accumulate possessions we must 'sell ourselves', little realizing that the more we accumulate the more of our 'selves' we must lose. We define ourselves in terms of our accumulated possessions, which become worth fighting and dying to defend.

How is it that such mass exploitation has been allowed to continue? Marx offered the notion of false consciousness as a way into answering this question.

False consciousness

For Marxist theory the likelihood is that people will not have a clear understanding of the ways that their motives, intentions and actions are conditioned by objective structural causes imposed by those in authority. If people do not see that their consciousness is dominated by bourgeois ideology, that 'the ruling ideas of any era are the ideas of the ruling class' (Marx and Engels, 1965: 60), they are suffering from false consciousness.

Antonio Gramsci provides an addition to Marxist notions of false consciousness in his development of the notion of *hegemony*. Hegemony refers to the proletariat's internalization of the ideologies of the ruling classes. This allows the ruling classes to maintain their favoured social order without having to try – it just seems like the natural order of things, rather than something tied to the institutional practices and agenda of the dominant group.

Ideology

The Marxist theory of ideology would predict that ideas gain their force or usefulness solely in so far as they support existing social relations or promote appropriate class interests: so power relations that derive from the mode of production will determine the development of ideas. It follows that any new philosophical or sociological ideas, or political groups, will have no impact upon society in terms of social change. Such change will come about only if the modes of production are changed, which for Marx will be likely to occur only when the proletariat organize a revolution – 'not criticism but revolution is the driving force of history' (Marx & Engels, 1964: 58). Further implications of Marx's view of ideology are that theory, philosophy, ideas generally are secondary to the more useful and down-to-earth pursuits of science and politics (West, 1996: 53). We can hear echoes of the old 'idealism versus materialism' philosophical debate here.

Historically ideology has signified beliefs that political elites impose on the masses in order to maintain the *status quo*.

> For instance, beliefs that people always get what they deserve, that the government only goes to war for good reasons, and that people are poor because they don't work hard are examples of ideological beliefs that blunt criticism of the *status quo*.
>
> (Fox and Prilleltensky, 1997: 13)

Marxism and subjectivity

The Marxist theory of ideology gives us a clear insight into subjectivity – it depends on class. Our values and ideas are simply a reflection of bourgeois self-interest, projections of capitalism. We cannot therefore presume to have access to rationality, knowledge or truth as individuals. As a group, however – the proletariat – we can expect to achieve true consciousness through subordinating our alienated selves to the collective consciousness of our class, and by overthrowing capitalism. Once all this happens, our ideological distortions will end, and subjectivity will be unimpeded.

Preliminary problems

This section draws upon the developments in the last two sections and begins to outline some problems commonly found in Marxist thought.

Mechanistic

After Marx's death in 1883 it was left to Engels to revise and disseminate his work. Nineteenth century thought at that time leaned heavily towards positivism (see p. 7), which Engels had sympathies with. Scientific thought was seen as the most advanced form of human knowledge. At the same time, Marx's ideas were beginning to take shape as 'the official doctrine of a mass political movement' (McLellan, 1975: 75). West (1996) suggests that these factors – the simplification of his ideas for mass consumption, and the assimilation of his thought with positivistic principles – tended to divert attention away from the complexities and contradictions in Marx's work. Historical materialism became a 'rigidly mechanistic model of social change' (West, 1996: 54).

Social class

Contemporary struggles are not (or are no longer) confined to class – there are various gender, sexuality, race and ecology struggles that are mixed up with issues of class. Though many are still living in abject poverty there are also many more in the West who are wealthy to varying degrees, which starts to make the division into separate classes a difficult job. Can we just define ourselves as proletarian or are we automatically part of the bourgeoisie if we earn above a certain amount?

Base/superstructure

Capitalism's traditional base of 'heavy' industries is shifting towards 'knowledge'-based forms of production – computing, education, information systems and media (McHoul and Grace, 1993). It no longer makes sense to impose a distinction between an economic base involving production and an ideological superstructure involving ideas and information.

Changes in science and technology since the 1960s have demonstrated that economic factors often depend on technical developments, which in turn depend on scientific ideas. This suggests that the one-way movement from economic base to ideological superstructure is at best simplistic.

Failed predictions

Marxist theory predicts that, as capitalism advances, the conditions by which a proletarian revolution will develop increase. Such conditions include predictions about the falling rate of profit, and the increased impoverishment of the working classes. But for the most part this has not happened, and where it has, the results have been disappointing, and often attacked by Western powers. Žižek (1998) suggests that this is why psychoanalysis (see Chapter 4) has played a strategic role in 'closing the gap' in contemporary Marxist theory by attempting to explain why individuals participate in their own oppression.

Collapse of the Eastern bloc

On top of this, the fall from power of the communist parties of the Soviet Union and Eastern Europe would suggest that Marxism has little contemporary political significance. However, 'Western Marxism' assumes a range of different forms (West, 1996: 55), for example, Althusser's (1971) structuralist Marxism (see Elliott, 1987, 1994), or Sartre's more existential approach (see Poster, 1979). But perhaps the most influential body of Marxist-inspired research, as well as some important insights into the limitations of Marxism, have come from the Frankfurt school.

The Frankfurt school

The Frankfurt school began as the Frankfurt Institute of Social Research, which was founded in 1923. From there it developed, first as a school examining the roots of Marxism, and subsequently as pioneer of the dialectical and critical approach for which it is known best. It boasted many famous names such as Max Horkheimer, who was director from 1930 onwards, Erich Fromm, Herbert Marcuse, Walter Benjamin and Theodor Adorno.

Most of the members of the school were Jewish Marxist radicals, and anti-fascist, and so were forced to flee first to Geneva and then to the United States after Hitler's ascent to power in the 1930s. Hitler's fascism must have been an especially disappointing indicator for the members that the predicted transition to communism was a long way off. In particular the degree of popular support for fascism among the working classes cast doubt on the Marxist claim that the proletariat were the agents of emancipation (West, 1996: 56).

Critical theory

In practical terms, the Marxism of Stalinism in the East, and of the communist parties loyal to Stalin in the West, paved the way for the 'bureaucratic authoritarianism of Soviet Marxism' (West, 1996: 59). Here Marxist thought became iron law, and this meant that important decisions about everyday politics and morals became questions to be answered only by those with sufficient knowledge of Marxist theory, rather than by the workers themselves. In the light of the many difficulties arising from wholesale adoption of Marx's theories and predictions, the Frankfurt school opted instead to reinvent Marx's critical method as 'critical theory'. We will trace aspects of critical theory by examining some of the key members of the Frankfurt school.

Adorno and authoritarianism

Most social psychologists will recognize Adorno as the person who brought us the 'authoritarian personality' (Adorno et al., 1950). However, his work developed from the wider focus on authoritarianism in the Frankfurt school. This involved an extension of Marx and Engel's original idea of false consciousness, in the sense that as capitalism became more advanced, psychological and cultural factors became more influential. This helped Adorno to 'explain' why the predicted revolution of the working classes never happened – these psychological and cultural factors were reducing the effectiveness of working class resistance.

The authoritarian state does not simply control the economic base: it also controls the ideological superstructure, which in turn becomes more influential as capitalism becomes more advanced. Thus late capitalism gave rise to 'an authoritarian state, an authoritarian culture and an authoritarian personality' (Roiser and Willig, 1996: 54). The Frankfurt school was beginning to introduce the more troubling notion of personality, as opposed to economic and social factors, as the source of the explanation for the problem of fascism. The following quotation illustrates one of these strands of thought:

> In every revolution, there seems to have been a historical moment when the struggle against domination might have been victorious – but the moment passed. An element of self-defeat seems to be involved in this dynamic.
>
> (Marcuse, 1955: 82)

Marcuse goes on to suggest that Freud's notion of the death instinct reveals 'the unconscious tie which binds the oppressed to their oppressors, the soldiers to their generals, the individuals to their masters' (1955: 247). Thus Freud's psychoanalysis (see Chapter 4) sheds light on that age-old problem of why the working classes continue to participate in their own oppression. The answer is that their darkest instincts keep getting in the way.

These and other integrations of psychological ideas led to empirical investigations of the working classes such as Fromm and Weiss's study of workers in Weimar, Germany (Horkheimer et al., 1936). The study was questionnaire-based, and participants were rated on a scale from 'radical' to 'authoritarian'. This study has been described as a central work for the development of ideas in the Frankfurt school (Bonss, 1984: 3, cited in Roiser and Willig, 1996: 56).

In the United States the school was affiliated with Columbia University, and here they conducted a study similar to the one in Weimar, which came to be the most well known analysis of authoritarianism among social psychologists (Adorno et al., 1950). The characteristic features of this research are the focus on harsh disciplinary parenting producing particular patterns of childhood socialization, along with psychoanalytic notions of the child's repression of hostility towards her or his parent, leading to later displacement on to 'safe' targets such as Jews.

Although there have been many studies criticizing the authoritarian personality, Michael Billig (1978: 36) suggests that it deserves praise as 'the single most important contribution to the psychology of fascism'. Billig's own study of fascists (1978) developed from this, and he courageously speaks out against members of the National Front, keen to represent themselves as patriotic Britons. His study suggested instead that members included 'men of violence' and 'classic authoritarians'. It is worth noting that within three years of the publication of Billig's book the electoral base of the National Front was effectively destroyed. Billig (1978, 1982) also suggests that members of the Frankfurt school tended to conceal their more radical work for fear of being imprisoned or deported. These refugees would have seen social psychological questionnaire studies on prejudice as a safe enterprise. Roiser and Willig (1996) are more critical of studies by the Frankfurt school, suggesting that, by focusing increasingly on individual psychology, they abandoned their Marxist roots.

However, they praise them for remaining independent from the destructive influences of Stalinism and social democracy.

Conclusion

This section began with an overview of the philosophical, historical and economic aspects of Marxist theory. This led us into notions of power, ideology and subjectivity, and then to the identification of a number of problems with Marxism: the mechanistic nature of aspects of Marxism such as the simple causal relations between base and superstructure and the primacy of social class alone as an explanation of how inequalities are perpetuated. Some of these problems were addressed by the development of critical theory by the Frankfurt school, but to understand how Marxist ideas have been picked up and transformed in recent discourse and rhetorical work, we need to explore further the notion of 'ideology'.

Ideology and discursive, critical and rhetorical psychology

A traditional social scientific view of ideology might be that it describes a coherent set of political beliefs and values associated with particular political parties. But critics such as Thompson (1984) and McLellan (1986) argue that restricting ideology to a set of formal political beliefs ignores the relations between ideology and everyday life. This strips ideology of its critical component, in which it becomes a vehicle for the maintenance and preservation of relations of power and control. As Thompson has argued, 'to study ideology is to study the ways in which *meaning (signification) serves to sustain relations of domination'* (1984: 131, emphasis in original). In particular the work of Foucault, discussed below, has been instrumental in identifying ideologies – or what Foucault would respecify as discourses – as the central way of re/producing power relations.

Some of the classic work in critical social psychology (e.g. Billig, 1987, 1991; Billig et al., 1988; Potter and Wetherell, 1987) has replaced the Marxist notion of ideology as a unitary set of ideas that make up a false consciousness. These developments were set out in Billig et al. (1988). Their argument is that the common sense of everyday talking and arguing is organized around dilemmas. These dilemmas are often ideological in the sense that they relate to broader societal concerns with authority, legitimation and social organization.

For example, they discuss the way classroom teaching is organized around a dichotomy between, on the one hand, student self-discovery and, on the other, teacher control over learning outcomes. (For a more developed study of these educational discourses see Edwards and Mercer, 1987.) The point they make is that these dilemmas are not a problem that has to be resolved; rather their tensions structure social settings and provide contradictory sets of resources that sustain current practices.

CRITICAL DILEMMA

What might be the problems involved in simply accepting dilemmas as irresolvable? Surely that's what a dilemma is most fundamentally – something that needs to be resolved? Is it OK simply to accept that there are irresolvable dilemmas?

The traditional Marxist notion of ideology has been replaced by the notion of a fragmented pattern of discourses that sustain practices and legitimize patterns of social relations and inequalities. This mirrors Foucault's treatment of ideology. Within this perspective, discourse is viewed as having an essential and inescapable 'action orientation' (Heritage, 1984). Discourse is also viewed as a social practice rather than as a neutral transmitter of information. There is more on the notion of discourse in Chapter 7, on discursive critics.

Critical psychology and ideology

In contrast to this discursive respecification of ideology, we have the view espoused by Fox and Prilleltensky (1996), as one fairly representative example of how ideology is taken up by critical psychologists. (See also the discussion of Tod Sloan's work in Chapter 6.) Fox and Prilleltensky assert that false consciousness exists, and that, because political elites impose their ideas on the masses in order to maintain the *status quo*, broadening the notion of ideology to include discourse waters down our ability to criticize this. They therefore criticize the broader use

Dennis Fox

'Especially in the United States, mainstream psychology marginalizes critics who insist that, to create a fundamentally better society, we must reject many academic, professional and societal norms. My responses to this situation reflect my interests within critical psychology as well as my own strengths and weaknesses. Trying to expand psychology's limited space for radical critique, I've emphasized in mainstream journals justice, anarchism, utopia and other topics that challenge basic assumptions of psychology in general and of the psychology/ law interface in particular. Hoping to make critical approaches understandable to curious students, I co-edited Critical Psychology: An Introduction, *the first basic critical psychology text. And, seeking to foster interaction among critical psychologists isolated by those whose power derives from things as they are, I proposed, co-founded, and help maintain "RadPsyNet: The Radical Psychology Network". Join us at www.uis.edu/~radpsy!'*

of ideology as a 'depoliticized version of the term' in which 'everyone has an ideology' (Fox and Prilleltensky, 1996: 13, emphasis in original).

Fox and Prilleltensky (1996) draw heavily on Marxist theory, aligning themselves with critical psychologists who suggest that:

> false consciousness is a common phenomenon. We believe that traditional institutions such as schools, religious bodies, courts, political parties, and the media very successfully direct public opinion away from fundamental criticism of the *status quo* by teaching that problems are inherently individual in nature rather than societal or political.
>
> (1996: 13)

They then complain that this brings charges of their being ideological from mainstream camps who don't realize that their own individualist position is equally ideological. Adopting an individualist stance blots out any recognition of social factors.

However, it could be argued that the critique by mainstream psychologists arises from the same (Marxist) tendency to see ideology as a particular political rather than a (more Foucauldian) pervasive phenomenon. In later chapters (particularly 6 and 8) we shall see how this more traditional understanding of ideology ties researchers into espousing forms of realism and more standard epistemological paths, particularly with regard to notions of subjectivity.

Critical social psychology

So how has Marxism been taken up by critical social psychologists? One edited collection devoted to this question is Ian Parker and Russell Spears' *Psychology and Society: Radical theory and practice* (1996). Parker and Spears say that they do not seek a Marxist psychology, but they do believe that some varieties of psychology are compatible with Marxism. They see Marxism as both a theoretical research programme and a political movement, which allows 'attention to underlying structures of economic exploitation, and to revolutionising social relations through the praxis of the oppressed and their allies' (1996: 2). Although they accept the basic Marxist centrality of class, they also want to include 'structures of patriarchal and racist domination' (1996: 2) in their analyses.

Marxist resources

Parker and Spears suggest that useful resources for Marxists in psychology come in the shape of 'Radical personality theories, Psychoanalysis, the Soviet Developmental Psychology tradition, Feminist Psychology and Social Constructionism' (1996: 8).

Radical personality theories

The development of 'radical' personality theories is traced back to Sève's (1974) work, where there is an attempt to specify a notion of 'man' [*sic*] that fits in with historical materialism. As Parker and Spears suggest, the dangers of this sort of approach are that 'The very employment of the concept of personality can be interpreted as a way to crystallise and compound these structuralist leanings, rather than a way out of them' (1996: 9). Paradoxically they do applaud the attempt to see 'concrete people instantiated in specific social relations' (1996: 9). (See the discussion of Sloan's work on critical approaches to personality in Chapter 6.)

CRITICAL DILEMMA

What may be the difference between specifying, on the one hand, a notion of the person from within historical materialism, and on the other hand specifying 'concrete people instantiated in specific social relations'?

Psychoanalysis

As with Parker's later work (see Chapter 4), there is a sense of nostalgia for psychoanalysis in Parker and Spears' discussion here. They suggest that psychology is repressing its past psychoanalytic allegiances. Oddly, they also assert that it is the 'political quietism' of post-structuralism (see Chapter 8) that has led to increased interest in psychoanalysis (although most strands are critical or hostile to Marxism) – e.g. the development of feminist psychoanalytic theories, the Kleinian Marxist work of Hinshelwood (e.g. 1983) and Langer (1989).

DISCUSSION QUESTIONS

1   What do you think is meant by 'political quietism'?
2   Whose version of 'politics' are we dealing with here?
3   How might postmodernism lead us into this political quietism?
4   How might psychoanalysis lead us away from it?

Soviet developmental psychology

Vygotsky (1962) is gaining credibility in the West as an important alternative to Piaget. However, Parker and Spears suggest that Marxist aspects of Vygotsky's work are suppressed, and that his notion of the 'zone of proximal development' is 'a progressive Marxist theory' (1996: 11). This is mainly due to Vygotsky's idea that human development should not be seen in isolation from cultural development, and that the potential for growth and transformation was always present.

Feminism and radical psychology

Although Marxism has provided key tools allowing the subsequent politicization and theorization of gender, women, as the postmodern feminist Haraway (1991a) suggests, 'existed unstably at the boundary of the natural and social in the seminal writings of Marx and Engels' (p. 131). She suggests that the reasons for this relate to unexamined heterosexuality implicit in the idea of a 'natural sexual division of labour', as well as the notion that women's subordination was examined only in terms of capitalist class relations, rather than in terms of sexual politics between men and women. Despite an approving reference to Haraway's pioneering work, Parker and Spears feel that the danger for feminists lies in the move towards 'social constructionist anti-realism'. This type of misplaced concern is discussed in Chapters 5 and 8.

Social constructionism and discourse

Parker and Spears' misunderstanding of the radical potential of social constructionist and discursive work is replicated further in their discussion here. They return to Burman's (1990) claim that the radical relativism of such a perspective:

> removes any foundation for critique or change . . . the social constructionist position that we cannot aim for the truth but must only rely on rhetorical

skills to persuade others of a version of reality necessarily ignores the differences in power and resources which may make voices more or less heard.

(Parker and Spears, 1996: 12)

This criticism is based on the idea that social constructionist and discourse researchers are simply presuming that all those in interaction are in some pre-discursive sense equal. This is simply a misunderstanding and misreading of these perspectives. See Chapters 7–8 where this is argued in more detail.

We will now explore some other Marxist themes in critical social psychology, both in Parker and Spears and in other related works.

Utopia

Mike Michael picks up on the notion that Marx and Engels shared a utopian vision, which incorporates 'a decentred self, but one based in labour and practical activity' (1996: 143). Michael argues for a reintroduction of utopias for critical social psychology. He suggests that even post-structuralist, anti-foundationalist perspectives in critical social psychology incorporate some implicit utopian view of the 'happy person' or the 'free society'. For example, Michael suggests that Sampson's deconstruction of the self (1983, 1989) incorporates the same utopian vision – 'a dispersed awareness, a fragmented self and a dissipated and multiply populated identity' (Michael, 1996: 145). Also, in Sampson's more recent work (1993), there is an appeal to a 'dialogic Utopia'. Sampson speculates that if it is true that we can 'know' our 'self' only through dialogue with others then we can be only as free as the people around us. This necessitates equality and democracy in order to foster positive dialogues.

Commodity fetishism

Marx argued that in capitalist societies we routinely forget the productive origins of commodities. Billig (1999) argues that awareness of the origins of consumer goods would diminish the pleasures of consumerism, and so 'the routines of consumerism contain a collective forgetfulness, which can be understood psychologically as a form of social repression' (p. 313). Billig is not referring to the classic Freudian notion of repression, however; rather he wants to situate repression dialogically, because he feels repression is situated within the routines of everyday life and constituted in dialogue. (See Chapter 4 for further discussion of this.)

Cognitivism in psychology

Reicher (1996) argues that the cognitive paradigm in psychology assumes the existence of a lone, passive, information-processing individual. This ignores the role of the researcher in setting up the context and terms in which their interaction with participants takes place. Participants' behaviour is then abstracted from the experimental interaction with the researcher, and is seen as emerging from internal processes. This is a similar type of argument to that which was pitted against various types of social cognition research in the previous chapter.

From a Marxist perspective this adoption of individualist explanations is exactly the kind of thing one would expect the bourgeoisie to engage in as a way of maintaining their social power, as it encourages everyone in society to see their problems as emanating from themselves and their individual processes, so discouraging explanations that might lead to social unrest – for example, that resources are unfairly allocated, leaving some in poverty, which in turn creates the conditions for problems to arise.

False consciousness

Martha Augoustinos (1999) has argued that the general tendency in mainstream social cognition has been to relate false consciousness to false cognitions, locating it in the mind. She argues instead that false consciousness be reappropriated as a socially emergent product of capitalism – contemporary social life creates the mystifications and distortions that prevent social change from taking place, and as such false consciousness is a useful theoretical construct.

Conclusion

This section began with an exploration of ideology as one way in which traditional Marxist notions of ideology have been picked up and transformed by recent critical social psychologists. The more recent developments of the notion of a fragmented pattern of discourses that sustain practices and legitimize patterns of social relations and inequalities has replaced the traditional Marxist treatments of ideology. As we shall see in the following section, this discursive move draws upon Foucault's treatment of ideology. We also examined how critical social psychologists have drawn upon Marx in a more straightforward way, accepting the basic Marxist centrality of class, along with a consideration of commodity fetishism and utopias.

Foucault's theoretical development and critique of Marx

The French social theorist Michel Foucault, who died of AIDS in 1984, has been one of the most influential thinkers of the last thirty years. He has had, and continues to have, an enormous influence on critical social psychology. This section will focus mainly on Foucault's notion of power, aiming to trace the implications of the differences between Foucault and Marx. We will also briefly explore Derrida's work on Marx as a way of extending post-structuralist (see Chapter 8) developments of Marxist thought.

Marx sees the person as ideologically produced by class and history. In a similar way Foucault (1972) – respecifying ideology as discourse – suggests that discourses *produce* people. For Foucault, institutional practices and forms of speaking relate closely to the construction of subjectivities. In order to understand the differences between Marx and Foucault, we need to explore the differences in the way that they view power and ideology/discourse.

On a simple view of Marx, society can be divided into ruling and subjected classes. The ruling class are those who own and control the means of production. This economic base drives all possible change in a society. It follows that whether or not one is powerful will depend on whether or not one owns and controls the means of production. Marx holds that the subjected and powerless class produces most of the wealth through their labour, and because they have to stand by and see that wealth appropriated by the ruling class, there emerges a conflict of interests. Power on a Marxist analysis is therefore inextricably linked with class struggle and conflict. Class relations become characterized in terms of power relations – one class achieves its interests at the expense of another, and is therefore more powerful.

Foucault's view of power is quite different from Marx's. We can begin by looking at what Foucault (1979) does *not* mean by 'power' in his own words:

1   I do not mean 'Power' as a group of institutions and mechanisms that ensure the subservience of the citizens of a given state . . .

2   I do not mean, either, a mode of subjugation which, in contrast to violence, has the form of rule.

3   Finally I do not have in mind a general system of domination exerted by one group over another, a system whose effects, through successive derivations, pervade the entire social body.

(1979: 92, numbering added)

We can see that Foucault's view of power is radically different from Marx's. It is not simply about the oppression of one group by another, nor even simply about social structures that oppress us. So what is power for Foucault? He goes on to set out a list of propositions:

1   Power is not something that is acquired, seized, or shared . . . power is exercised from innumerable points . . .

2   Relations of power are not in a position of exteriority with respect to other types of relationships (economic processes, knowledge relation-ships, sexual relations), but are immanent in the latter . . .

From these first two points it is clear that Foucault does not regard power as a thing that can exist in its own right. On the contrary:

3   Power comes from below; that is, there is no binary and all-encompassing opposition between rulers and ruled at the root of power relations . . . One must suppose rather that the manifold relations of force that take shape and come into play in the machinery of production, in families, limited groups and institutions, are the basis of wide-ranging effects of cleavage that run through the social body as a

whole . . . Major dominations are the hegemonic effects that are sustained by all these confrontations.

In contrast with Marx, who sees power as something that emerges through class relations from the top down – from the ruling classes to the proletariat – Foucault wants to alert us to power relations that emerge from and run through a variety of social settings. If we are feeling oppressed we should think about the whole spectrum of relations that we engage in, not simply look to those in power as the source of our oppression.

4   Power relations are both intentional and non-subjective . . . there is no power that is exercised without a series of aims and objectives. But this does not mean that it results from the choice or decision of an individual subject . . .

This is an interesting point for psychologists. On the one hand Foucault is saying that power cannot be extricated from the notion of intention – whatever it is, it is bound up with doing things. However, we should not see intention as something emerging from individual choices and decisions, in the way that Marx would with his notion of false consciousness. Rather, intentions are respecified as discursive practices. This alternative notion of intention is something that discursive psychologists follow up (see Chapter 7).

5   Where there is power there is resistance . . . points of resistance are present everywhere in the power network. Hence there is no single locus of great Refusal, no soul of revolt, source of all rebellions, or pure law of the revolutionary.

(1979: 94–96, numbering added)

This highlights a major difference between Marx and Foucault. For Marx, the end result of the problems with capitalism is revolution – resistance by the working people to the power of those in authority. Foucault sees resistance as a more diffuse thing, which occurs in different ways in different contexts, and is paradoxically produced by power.

For Foucault the Marxist notions of power are insufficient, and we should therefore:

1   Avoid identifying some single locus of power, such as 'the ruling classes' or 'the state'. Instead we need to examine more local and provisional con-figurations of power relations, for example organizations with their own procedures, such as families or classrooms.
2   Avoid trying to explain power in terms of the motives, interests and inten-tions of individuals or groups. We are all the vehicles of power, rather than its point of application.
3   Understand that power does not operate from the top down: class domi-nation alone is not an effective guide to understanding power relations.

4   Understand the historical conditions of possibility of our knowledge, the
procedures that produce it, rather than simply focusing on its effects, such as
subjectivity and ideology.

Nicholas Rose (1989) illustrates these points in his Foucauldian study of
psychology. Rose argues that as psychology has developed it has produced
successive 'regimes of truth', which have entered new areas of peoples' lives. These
truth regimes have constructed particular psychological objects – for example, the
motivation of workers, the attachment of parents and children. The 'new ways of
saying plausible things about other human beings and ourselves' (Rose, 1989: 4)
that result from this illustrate the twin processes of producing objects and subjects.
We have psychological discourses generating new identities, new ways of
understanding ourselves, new positions from which to speak, and new rights and
obligations (Potter, 1996a: 86).

BOX 3.1   Actor network theory

One of the radical perspectives that came out of the new sociology of scientific
knowledge is known as actor network theory. Actor network theory was
developed by the French sociologists of science Michel Callon and Bruno
Latour (1981). In some ways it is a development of and application of Michel
Foucault's perspective on power. The radical move in actor network theory is
to massively broaden the notion of agency. In this theory anything can have
agency – a text, a person, money, an object, an idea and so on.

Let's see how it works with a science example. Callon and Latour ask this
question: If there is a dispute between two scientific theories which one will be
successful? Their answer is that the most powerful theory will be the one that
connects together ('enrols') the largest or densest network of powerful actors
(hence the name). These actors may be scientific grants, support from government organizations, particular findings, rhetorically artful texts, and (contro-
versially) the natural objects that are being studied themselves. The art of
successful science, then, is partly to enrol these different actors, align their
interests, and mobilize them in action.

This is a radical approach with important potential for social psychology.
Mike Michael (1996a) has started to develop some of this potential in a series
of studies which combine discourse ideas with actor network thinking on the
topic of environmental risk.

In *Discipline and Punish* (1977) Foucault historically reconstructs the development of the penal and disciplinary systems, revealing how, just as with psychology's production of subjects and psychological objects, humanitarian action in
prisons has the opposite effect of its intention, producing the criminal discursively.
Simply by setting up an institution that is designed to 'deal with' the criminal, we

are discursively producing the criminal at the same time. This also relates to the notion of resistance as something that emerges from power. So power produces things and people, but in a paradoxical way, in the sense that in creating institutions as a way of tackling social problems we end up producing the very thing we seek to deal with. The French philosopher Jacques Derrida has, like Foucault, explored the progress of precisely this type of irony and duplicity in the logic of Western culture, and has, conveniently for us, applied his thought to Marx.

Derrida on Marx

In his complex work *Specters of Marx*, Derrida (1994a) suggests that he developed deconstruction (see Chapter 8) as an extension of a 'certain spirit of Marx'. Note Derrida's characteristic play on the word 'spirit': it can mean both 'in the spirit of' and 'spectre', which picks up on Marx's own use of the metaphor in its ghostly sense. Derrida's admiration of Marx shines through his text:

> few texts have shed so much light on law, international law, and nationalism. It will always be a fault not to read and reread and discuss Marx . . . There will be . . . no future without Marx, without the memory and the inheritance of Marx: in any case of a certain Marx, of his genius, of at least one of his spirits.
>
> (1994a: 13)

Derrida develops his arguments about Marx in response to the claims made by the US political theorist Francis Fukuyama (1992) about the end of history. Fukuyama writes about the 'remarkable consensus' that has developed across the world, a consensus of liberal democracy as a legitimate system of government. For Fukuyama the ideal of human history is free market capitalism and liberal democracy: he asserts that liberal democracy has 'conquered rival ideologies' such as communism, and also therefore Marxism.

In *Specters of Marx* Derrida opposes both Marxist communism and the New Right neo-liberal democracies of the West, offering as he does so a strong indictment of global capitalism. However, deconstruction does not strive for a revolutionary inversion of hierarchies, in the manner of Marxist thought. Marx is metaphorically buried, but then resurrected in ghostly form. Through this process there is a disengagement with some Marxist reality knowable without the 'spectres' or traces of its own making – any attempt to write Marx out of history will only result in his returning to haunt us in ghostly form. Derrida suggests that our duty must be 'fidelity to the inheritance of a certain Marxist spirit' (1994a: 87): our critiques of liberal democracy need to include the spirit of Marx. Derrida accuses Fukuyama of evangelizing in the name of the ideal of liberal democracy, while 'violence, inequality, exclusion, famine, and thus economic oppression' (1994a: 85) are affecting more human beings than ever before.

So while Derrida wants to make Marxism more anti-foundational, he also wants to reject the problems created by global capitalism. This involves retaining some aspects of Marxism, but what does it leave us with? Derrida's work is highly complex, and he appears to give no clear guidance for any alternatives to liberal democracies. As I have argued elsewhere (Hepburn, 1999a), while most modern democratic theories stress the *necessity* of judgement, e.g. the will of the majority, Derrida has redefined the political as the *impossibility* of judgement, by emphasizing the fundamental undecidability and paradoxical nature ('aporia') of questions of law and politics. But this is not as pessimistic as it sounds. Derrida's point is not that democracy should be countered by some other political system in which judgement is impossible; judgements are never final and certain, although there are plenty of ways of constructing them as such. Instead, recognizing the tensions and revisability of our judgements and choices will be *central* to developing a richer, more sensitive democracy. And I believe this is where the political strength of deconstruction lies.

This incorporation of Derrida's notion of deconstruction is in contrast to Parker's development of 'practical deconstruction' (see Ian Parker's box above), which moves away from the original philosophical sense of deconstruction by characterizing it in terms of simply dismantling, or taking apart. Without a more sophisticated version of deconstruction Parker's theorizing slips into the realm of realism and subjectivity, hence perhaps his focus on Marxism and psychoanalysis. We shall return to these types of debate around deconstruction, realism and relativism in Chapter 8.

Conclusion

This section has traced Foucault's view of power and compared it with a more traditional Marxist version. For Foucault the Marxist notions of power are insufficient, as they focus on single entities such as 'the ruling classes' or 'the state' at the expense of more local and provisional configurations of power relations. Power does not operate from the top down, and so class domination alone is not an effective guide to understanding power relations. From Derrida we learnt the importance of keeping the spirit of Marx, but of introducing a more sophisticated understanding of not just power, but also democracy, politics and law. Recognizing the tensions and revisability of our judgements and choices becomes fundamental to developing a richer, more sensitive democracy, which is why we need deconstruction.

Application

Marxism encourages thought about potential application in terms of the broader structural system. There is an emphasis on two styles of social change: on the one hand, we have revolution, where social change is brought about by the organization of social conflicts rather than by, say, changing people's attitudes. On the other hand, there is an emphasis on ideology, where social change is brought about through looking at the role of ideas in making particular (e.g. capitalist) types of social organization legitimate, and in hiding social conflicts. For example, we examined Billig et al.'s (1988) argument that the common sense of everyday talking and arguing is organized around *dilemmas*, which are *ideological* in the sense that they relate to broader societal concerns with authority, legitimation and social organization. The traditional Marxist notion of ideology, as something driven by economic conditions and structures (the ruling classes), has therefore been replaced by the notion of a fragmented pattern of discourses that sustain practices and legitimate patterns of social relations and inequalities. This mirrors Foucault's treatment of ideology. Within this perspective, discourse is viewed as having an essential and inescapable 'action orientation' – words *do things* for us. They are not secondary referents to something more primary. One way into application then is to analyse discourse – what are the everyday practices sustainable through discourse?

There is an interesting tension here, as the spotlight on ideology (the super-structure in traditional Marxist theory) as a focus on social change contradicts the Marxist analysis of the centrality of the economic base. We may hypothesize that the social cognition approaches reviewed in the previous chapter would prefer to focus on the traditional notion of Marxism, which would not see a study of ideology as of particular significance. Rather the important thing would be to see social change as emerging through basic conflicts. The important task must then be to discover social psychological truths about group influence, so that post-revolution, when the blinkers of ideology are stripped, the new social order will have the techniques of social psychology to help stop the bourgeoisie fighting back.

Conclusion

What is needed from a Marxist perspective is some idea of why and how people participate in their own oppression. If we take Foucault's criticisms of Marxist notions of power seriously then what we need is a new type of critical analysis to account for new kinds of social fragmentation, and the absence of some unified 'base' of social existence giving rise to one central contradiction in (supposedly cohesive) social class struggles. A rethink of the struggle of a particular class against domination by another class is also necessary. As Foucault argues, power is more about relations built into everyday life than top-down imposition.

Also for Foucault it is important that we don't try to explain power in terms of the motives, interests and intentions of individuals or groups. Issues such as subjectivity and ideology are simply the *effects* of the historical conditions of possibility of our knowledge and the procedures that produce it, so we should be seeking to understand how we are situated by the theories and procedures for producing knowledge that we have. This is why a particular focus of this book has been to highlight the different theories that make up what we historically have come to term critical social psychology. But the questions for Marxists remain: why do people participate in their own oppression? Why can't they see the chains that bind them? To answer these types of question, many critical psychologists have turned to psychoanalysis, and it is to this topic that we now turn.

B The best thing about Marxism

Marx was committed to ending the oppression of the poverty-stricken workers, and his sense of how their personal suffering was linked with their social positions was inspirational. His sense of outrage that some people should have so much more than others, and that people's economic relations re/create their interpersonal relations is a crucial insight for critical social psychology. Moreover, Marxist thinking encourages us to be aware of both the importance of conflict, and the possibility that conflict is being hidden.

W The worst thing about Marxism

Most of the problems with Marx relate to the clumsiness of his materialist philosophy. This has led to the notion of the economic base as a causal force, and a view of power as a self-existent thing that can be wielded by the few, rather than something built into the flows and everyday discursive practices of social life.

Where next?

There will probably be a continued engagement with the collapse of the Eastern bloc, and the political crisis in Marxism that it has given rise to. Another challenge for Marxism is how to retheorize class and power in a more global economy. Will there be something that can capture the radical emancipatory vision of Marx, and integrate it with new notions of subjectivity, action and criticality?

Practical exercises

1   Go to a library and choose two or three social psychology textbooks written by North American authors. Marxist critics of social psychology often argue that their work emphasizes individual processes at the expense of institutions, and avoids considering real conflicts of interests, particularly between workers and owners. Look at the broad coverage of topics and themes to see if this criticism is fair. Consider the way conflict is understood. Is it treated as embedded in structures or individuals? Of the different social groups mentioned, how many times is social class referred to?

2   Take a copy of a broadsheet newspaper. One common kind of article is about problems or breakdowns (the exam system, the Northern Ireland peace process, etc.). It is quite likely that you will find some in any issue. Now consider how responsibility is attributed. Marxist social psychologists claim that there is a tendency to see problems as a result of individual actions or cognitions rather than as a product of structures or genuine conflict of interest. How far is this true? Look for the possibility that issues of class conflict have been overlooked. Where might they be relevant?

3   Read again the section on Mike Michael's notion of utopias. Choose a current political party that is either in power or in opposition. Using your under-standing of its claims or official information (from the Web site, say), try to get beyond the immediate set of arguments (typically against competing parties)

to identify its utopia. What is its ideal state of living for people? How will they be organized? How will they be satisfied? What kinds of family and community groups will there be?

Reading

If you read only one thing, read:

Billig, M. (1982) *Ideology and Social Psychology*. Oxford: Blackwell. **As well as covering some basic features of Marxist theory and its relevance to social psychology it provides some early indications of the value of a rhetorical approach.**

Classics

Marx, K. and Engels, F. (1964) *The German Ideology*. Moscow: Progress.
Marx, K. and Engels, F. (1965) *Selected Correspondence*. Moscow: Progress. **Marx is not easy to read, but the letters to and from Engels provide a striking and illuminating way into his thinking.**

Also useful

Augoustinos, M. (1999) Ideology, false consciousness and psychology. Special issue of *Theory and Psychology*, 9, 295–312.
Billig, M. (1991) *Ideologies and Beliefs*. London: Sage.
Billig, M. (1999) Commodity fetishism. Special issue of *Theory and Psychology*, 9, 313–330.
Billig, M., Condor, S., Edwards, D., Gane, M., Middleton, D.J. and Radley, A.R. (1988) *Ideological Dilemmas: A social psychology of everyday thinking*. London: Sage.
Michael, M. (1996) Pick a utopia, any utopia: How to be critical in critical social psychology, in I. Parker and R. Spears (eds), *Psychology and Society: Radical theory and practice*. London: Pluto Press.
Parker, I. and Spears, R. (eds) (1996) *Psychology and Society: Radical theory and practice*. London: Pluto Press.
Roiser, M. and Willig, C. (1996) Marxism, the Frankfurt school, and working-class psychology, in I. Parker and R. Spears (eds), *Psychology and Society: Radical theory and practice*. London: Pluto Press.
Theory and Psychology (special issue on Marxism and Psychology).

Difficult but worth it

Derrida, J. (1994) *Specters of Marx: The state of the debt, the work of mourning and the new international*. London and New York: Routledge.
Thompson, J.B. (1990) *Ideology and Modern Culture*. Cambridge: Polity Press.

Chapter 4

Psychoanalytic Critics

In summer 2000 a child in the English country of West Sussex was abducted and killed. One newspaper, the *News of the World*, launched a campaign that involved publishing pictures and details of dozens of convicted sex offenders. This sparked off a flurry of public debate and a number of crowd protests against paedophiles, particularly on the Paulsgrove estate in Portsmouth, where, for seven evenings running, crowds marched upon a number of houses of alleged paedophiles.

These crowds were mostly concerned and angry parents, who often brought their children with them. But why do paedophiles evoke such strong reactions for many people? In comparison with the vast number of children who will be murdered or abused in other ways by family and friends, or who will be killed by motorists, poverty and suchlike, this kind of collective action seems out of proportion.

One thing psychoanalysis is really good at is explaining such extreme and apparently out-of-perspective reactions. For example, in psychoanalytic terms, we could propose that individual members of the crowd were able to 'project' their own inner problems and hostilities out on to paedophiles and treat them as the object of their condemnation and punishment. Members of the crowd gained some 'inner' satisfaction by establishing paedophiles as 'the problem', rather than, say, motor cars or even their own abusive impulses – statistically much more 'rational' sources of threat to children's lives.

This gives us an insight into the fascination that psychoanalysis has for some critical psychologists. From what we have covered so far, it would seem that the individualism of psychoanalysis opposes the general thrust of critical social psychology. But particularly for those who follow Marx's materialist leanings, psychoanalysis offers a 'theory of the subject' that fills the gaps left by Marxist theory: as we saw in Chapter 3, the question of why people participate in their own oppression became salient for those working with Marxist theory. In order to explore this fascination, this chapter will review and explore the tensions in recent psychoanalytic work in critical psychology in three areas: Ian Parker and colleagues' recent work in *Psychoanalytic Culture* and *Deconstructing Psychopathology* (the latter being a more critical take on psychoanalytic practices); Wendy Hollway's work around Melanie Klein and Jacques Lacan, and Michael Billig's latest work on Sigmund Freud.

Hollway presents a Foucault-informed, Lacanian take in her later work, which draws heavily on the work of Klein. Billig and Parker lean towards something more discursive and rhetorical, in that both offer different ways to treat psychoanalysis as a cultural phenomenon that throws up political and ideological issues. For example, Billig wants to highlight the repression of antisemitism in Freud's analysis of Dora, while Parker wants to use psychoanalytic ideas such as projection and repression as metaphors to understand such things as the disciplinary power of the British Psychological Society.

The chapter will conclude with some discussion of post-structuralist develop-ments and critiques of psychoanalysis by explicating the work of Lacan, Butler and Derrida. Before we start all this, though, it will be important to establish some key ideas and terms in both Freud and Klein's work, so we can develop a feel for some of the important psychoanalytic issues and concerns.

Freud's psychoanalysis and Klein's object relations theory

Psychoanalysis derives from Freud's research into the causes of 'hysteria' – a term used commonly in the nineteenth century to describe (or produce, cf. Foucault in Chapter 6) most kinds of mental disturbance. The central idea at this early stage was that all mental disturbances arose from the unconscious, so if we want to be cured, we need help in exploring our own unconscious thoughts and feelings and in bringing them to consciousness.

Initially (e.g. see Freud, 1955: vol. II) Freud thought that pathological symp-toms came about when morbid thoughts occurred in dissociated states, and got blocked from their normal expression by altered states of consciousness. Bringing these repressed thoughts to consciousness would prevent further blockage of them and cure pathological symptoms.

Freud developed this initial hypothesis further through closer attention to his patients (surely a radical move for many of today's psychologists!). He moved from simply seeking to discharge morbid thoughts stored in the psyche to trying to discover the meaning of the symptoms, and their role in the unconscious, via 'free association'. If patients find it difficult simply to lie on a couch and free-associate (and they invariably do) this is evidence of *resistance* caused by barriers between conscious and unconscious. Symptoms can be seen as a result of this intrapsychic conflict. This research and treatment method has become known as psycho-analysis.

One of the main sources of conflict, and therefore of noxious symptoms, occurs between our desires (what we are supposed to want) and morality (what we know we are not supposed to have). Often our pathological symptoms allow a certain amount of gratification of our desires, and therefore represent some kind of compromise for us.

Freud hypothesized that our psychic structure is made up of three parts: *id*, generating desire, arising from sexual and aggressive impulses; *superego*, generating moral imperatives and ideals; and *ego*, providing mediation between id and superego with respect to 'reality'. According to Zaleznik (1996), these are not meant to represent the 'real' structure of the mind, as is often assumed; rather they are abstract concepts designed to organize the theory of intrapsychic conflict.

But why are we in intrapsychic conflict? Freud suggests that our human instincts create pressure to obtain different kinds of gratification. We are driven by this pressure to act in ways that will produce gratification. Life instincts relate to hunger, thirst and sex. Death instincts relate to aggression and hostility. Our social settings provide the controlling influences through laws, rules and regulations, as well as authorities and peers. We internalize these controlling influences, thereby learning to control our instincts, hence the conflict, and the requirement for the id, ego and superego notions of the mind (see Freud, 1927 and also 1936, especially Chapter 8 on superego).

We control our inner conflict through the ego, which can be divided up into conscious and unconscious. The ego has a number of defence processes for keeping things under control, such as repression, denial, displacement, sublimation, projection and rationalization. They are largely unconscious, though expressed in conscious behaviour. Our uniqueness of personality for Freud arises through the unique combination of defence mechanisms and processes, most of which we are unaware of.

So is everyone caught in such a conflict/control dynamic? And if so, is there any way out? Freud would say yes and no respectively. The idea is that as children we all start life in the same way – rather as we imagine animals to be, driven by strong desires and instincts that are tempered by our environment. He suggests that the conflict and psychic structure that we experience has been established during the Oedipal stage (Freud, 1955: vol. VII), the final stage of infant development occurring at around age five. In this stage we generate a need to repress our illicit desire for our opposite-sex parent, and are provided with the basis for experiencing guilt and anxiety over such desire. Not surprisingly, this classical version of psychoanalysis has been a source of controversy both within and outside the psychoanalytic profession, and Freud's patriarchal, male-centred view of sexuality has been heavily criticized.

However, Freudian ideas are still very influential in psychoanalysis. Psychoanalysis continues today not just through variants of psychoanalytic psychotherapy, but also through its application to disciplines such as philosophy, literary criticism, politics and social sciences (Ricoeur, 1970). As Parker, below, argues, it has informed our cultural perspectives, particularly on personhood, and as such needs to be taken seriously by critical social psychologists.

Of particular relevance is the outgrowth and contemporary manifestation of Freud's work – the 'object relations' school of psychoanalysis pioneered by Melanie Klein, whose work we now turn to. Parker (1997a) and Hollway focus in different ways on object relations theory, so we need to understand it before we can make sense of their work.

Object relations theory

This theory suggests a marginally less traumatic start to human life than Freud's, with less focus on human instincts and strong drives that have to be struggled with by infants and growing children, and more focus on interpersonal dynamics, particularly from object relations theorists such as Winnicott and Fairbairn. Object relations theorists (apart from Winnicott) believe that a rudimentary ego capable of relating to objects is present in the infant from birth. Klein (1932) worked mostly with children through play, and her use of toys allowed children to display objects (people) in relation to one another. Family members or their substitutes still occupy a central role in the formation of an individual's sense of self: it is here that an 'interpersonal field' is built. These early relationships provide the mental residues that help to structure the unconscious for us. Thus any problems we may have in later life relate strongly to the quality of relationships that we have encountered in our earlier years (Frosh, 1987). There is a kind of innocence about the infant – it is dependent on a nurturing environment to develop a healthy internal world. With Freud, in contrast, the infant starts out in an objectless world as a narcissistic pleasure seeker.

Klein's work with children led her to believe that they are subject to various anxieties from an early age, and that various defence mechanisms are produced by the infant's budding ego. Object relations theorist Donald Winnicott suggests that our sense of self is 'undifferentiated' when we are babies, because we experience extremely close relations with our primary care takers (usually termed 'mothers' in this type of text). We then experience a gradual process of separation and 'individualization', and it is this axis of 'separation/engulfment' that haunts us, to a greater or lesser extent, throughout our lives.

Klein's conception of the internal world was complex. It comprised internal objects, which we identify with and which create an important basis for our relationship with our 'self'. As infants we come to have feelings for our internal objects, and this decreases our egocentrism. Transferring an object from outside to inside is called 'introjection', and conversely transferring an internal object from inside to outside is called 'projection'. As we saw in the paedophile example above, establishing an object (something or someone) as 'the problem' allows us to treat it as the object of our condemnation and punishment. For example, our inner concerns or worries can be projected out on to, say, bacteria, which then become the source of our concerns and worries. This allows our inner concerns to be successfully avoided by attention to outer ones, perhaps resulting in excessive cleaning or hand washing to get rid of the bacteria.

Similarly the classic defence mechanism of 'splitting' is applied when we start to see our objects in an 'either/or' kind of way – as either all good or all bad. A typically Kleinian example is the mother's breast. Klein noticed that sometimes babies turn away from their mother's breast when they are most in need of it – i.e. when they have been crying through hunger. This is because the hungry baby has produced a 'bad' internal object of its mother's breast (through splitting, which tears at the ego and the object), so that when mother finally turns up, baby needs to project this bad internal image out on to her. She thus temporarily becomes the source of badness. This is because, for Klein, infants are born with two conflicting *instinctual* impulses – to love and to hate.

Objects – things or people – can therefore be used for the purpose of *projective identification* (Klein, 1946). The infant's hate towards the bad internal object is got rid of by projecting on to the external world, so that bad feelings seem to be coming from the outside world. But those feelings can then rebound to haunt the infant, and the resulting persecutory anxiety that the infant feels takes shape as an early mental state that Klein dubbed the *paranoid schizoid position*. If the infant has a sufficiently strong relationship with its mother – the internalized good mother – it will be able to repair the damage done by its own frustration and hate. The guilt that arises from this conflict between love and hate results in the *depressive position* – characterized by sadness and withdrawal. Once this position is achieved the child can enter the 'real' social world. Alternation between these two positions remains a feature of our adult experience.

Q	**DISCUSSION QUESTIONS**
1	Think again about the strong reactions that paedophiles evoke. How would you explain these reactions in object relations terms?
2	What are the costs and benefits of adopting this form of explanation?

Conclusion

This section has covered some of the classic areas of psychoanalytic work, focusing on Freud and Klein. There are various persuasive features of these explanations for human action, especially if we think in the context of the Western individualist culture that most of us are born and raised in. These psychoanalytic ideas of conscious, unconscious and defence mechanisms will form the basis for understanding the attraction that psychoanalytic theory has for critical social psychologists in the subsequent sections.

Hollway: object relations in critical work

Wendy Hollway has been a major figure in introducing psychoanalytic notions to critical psychologists. This section will cover aspects of her earlier and later work, and we will encounter more of Hollway's work in the subsequent section on Lacan and post-structuralism below.

In her earlier work (1983, 1984, 1989) Hollway conducted a classic set of studies in which British couples talk about their relationships, in particular making love without contraception. This work is also covered in Chapter 5 in relation to feminist research. Hollway links various 'discourses', evident in participants' talk, with various unconscious mechanisms, such as 'splitting' and 'projection'. By discourses Hollway means 'the organised way in which meanings cohere around a central proposition, which gives them their value and significance' (Hollway and Jefferson, 2000: 14). The argument is that, despite men and women having similar basic needs – e.g. for love, sex, security – they are socialized along different lines through gendered discourses that can operate to protect male power and gendered ways of relating, but at the cost of *repressing* basic needs.

How does this work in practice? Hollway argues that an examination of talk about relationships will reveal several common 'discourses'. First, the 'male sex drive discourse', in which male sexuality is distinguished from female, characterized as a matter of responding to physiology and female attraction. This allows men to present themselves as motivated not by a need for their partner, or for women in general (which would dredge up feelings of vulnerability) but by biological forces.

Hollway also suggested the 'have and hold' discourse, which emphasizes love, romance and commitment. This was most commonly linked with women: women saw sex as an indication of love and commitment, whereas men saw themselves in terms of being the objects of this kind of discourse – the focus of women's attempts to obtain commitment.

Similarly the 'permissive discourse' coheres around the central proposition that sex with many partners is harmless and pleasurable, as well as separable from marriage and commitment. The basic point is that these types of discourse provide a social context through which we come to understand ourselves and our gender and sexuality.

Where does psychoanalysis fit into all this? Well, these discourses organize a set of feelings and desires that may not be appropriate, and so will be repressed. As any good psychoanalyst knows, when things are repressed they don't just disappear, but leak out on to the 'surface' in the form of some kind of pathological symptom. For example, men may display 'projection', which involves characterizing emotions (like dependence, vulnerability) that have been repressed as belonging to the other person (e.g. female partner). For a man in a heterosexual relationship this would presumably manifest itself through thoughts/utterances such as 'I'm the strong one, I have to look after her' or 'She needs me more than I need her' and so on. This will in turn have implications for how this person relates to his partner (and for how long his partner is prepared to put up with him!). On hearing this type of utterance in this type of context in an interview setting, the analyst would suggest that it arises through initial repression of negative emotions, and subsequent projection of same on to partner: they therefore feel able to say a lot about their participants and their 'subjectivities'.

DISCUSSION POINT

In what practical ways would it be helpful to be told that you are projecting or introjecting various emotions? How might it be counterproductive? In what theoretical ways would it help you as an analyst of people's talk? How might it be unhelpful analytically?

In summing up her analysis of gendered subjectivity in the talk of a couple, Will and Beverley, Hollway states that 'Repressed desires do not go away' (1998: 258). Instead they are 'projected' by Will and 'introjected' by Beverley. 'Will suppresses his feelings because of his vulnerability' and Beverley introjects them 'because discourses have already conferred upon her a position of doing the feelings' (1998: 259).

In order to understand interaction between Will and Beverley, Hollway wants to trace their talk back to putative inner structures of their unconscious minds. This is obviously at odds with the post-structuralist discursive insights into language (see Chapter 8), which see it as constructive of subjectivity rather than reflective, and this is a point of contention between different critical psychologists that we will be returning to, particularly in Chapter 6, on subjectivity critics.

Hollway and Jefferson's defended subjects

In her later work with Tony Jefferson, Hollway expands on this earlier work (Hollway and Jefferson 2000). The call is for a method that represents the complexity of human subjectivity. Here the research context itself provides a focus, and we learn that people protect themselves against their anxieties in the interview context because they are 'defended subjects'. In order to understand the stories that these defended subjects tell of their lives, it is suggested that we need a method in which narratives play a central role. This reflects the growing interest in narrative research in the social sciences, and the general move away from scientific 'objectivity'. Hollway and Jefferson's work is based in Kleinian notions of subjects being forged out of unconscious defences against anxiety. And because we need to explore the unconscious of our participants, we also need 'free association' to be more important than narrative coherence. It is suggested that free association enables us to elicit hidden meanings, and to incorporate a notion of the defended subject within the interpretation of biographical narratives.

What we have, then, is a qualitative method that attempts to capture the complexity of participants' inner worlds by doing a kind of psychoanalysis on what they say in an interview context. The task is to show that we can access the 'psychosocial' through this method – that people's words can be treated as a reliable indicator of their experiences and their inner life.

Hollway and Jefferson's choice of methodological tools draws heavily upon psychoanalysis: for example, they discuss the unconscious intersubjective dynamics of the interview relationship and therapeutic concepts such as countertransference, recognition and containment. They support these tools through their discussion of individuals' responses to crime and fear of crime, in which largely unconscious ways of coping with external threats to safety are examined (2000: 138–9).

Let's look a little more closely at what the claims are here. Below is one of the extracts that Hollway and Jefferson work with:

Tony   What was it like growing up in such a large family with

Tommy [interrupting]   It were great . . . You know wi' us being a big family, and everybody, and all at school . . . We, we always used to race 'ome for cow pie . . . big meat potato pie – that's when we 'ad coal fires as well . . . They were the best fires that we've ever 'ad, and we all used to race 'ome at teatime, to see who got [*laugh*] biggest plate and everything. We used to 'ave some right arguments, to see who got [*laugh*] biggest plate! And 'Is there, any more, is there, is there any more?' It were brilliant. And sleeping arrangement – 'cos it . . . were a three-bedroom 'ouse, between ten of us . . . Well it were brilliant. [*Tony: laugh.*] There were – one, one, two, there were six of us. Three in one double bed, no, two, two in each double bed. [*Tony:* Yeah.] And in, well, you know then, we were skint. [*Tony:* Yeah.] In the 60s we were skint. [*Tony:* Yeah.] And to get a, to get a blanket to get covered up were unbelievable. To get big, big, big overcoats.

[*Tony:* Yeah, yeah.] What me mother used to do, you, you know plates in oven – she used to put some bricks in. Get bricks out – t' warm bottom, warm bottom of the bed. And get plate out of oven, wrap it up in a er, a, a, a sheet and put it in bottom of bed, so stretch your feet out. And it were, it were, it were 'orrible in the morning 'cos it were, it were freezing cold. [*Tony:* Yeah.] Y'know, plate and brick. There were no double glazing, no central 'eating or anything. All we, all we lived for were coal fire. [*Tony:* Yeah.] And me dad used to get up every morning, make s-sticks out of paper. [*Tony:* Yeah.] About six o'clock. Used to *get fire* blaring out before we get up . . . Always used to run down for a cup of tea, run at side of fire . . . They were tremendous years. (Hollway and Jefferson, 2000: 55–6)

Hollway and Jefferson note that at face value this would be taken as a story about being poor but happy. They suggest that this assumption is belied by attention to the detail and the contradictions present in the talk. For example, at the beginning Tommy interrupts the interviewer, as if to pre-empt some potential negative evalu-ations that the interviewer might have. They suggest that 'the subsequent chorus of how "brilliant" it all was begins to feel a little forced' (2000: 57). This justifies a reading that gives more weight to the negative aspects of how life was.

Hollway and Jefferson suggest that if we take evidence from the whole interview and from interviews with Tommy's mother and sister it is possible to see that Tommy is unable to acknowledge the 'emotional reality' – the 'pain' – of his memories. In classic object relations speak we learn that Tommy 'splits the bad from the good in order to protect his present self' (2000: 59). The good is located in his ideal version of childhood, while the bad is projected on to his sister, who, he says three times throughout the interview, he hates. This splitting allows his continued investment in his happy family story. In order to ascertain whether Tommy's professed hatred of his sister is warranted, Hollway and Jefferson examine his statements about her and suggest that his accounts coincide more with his mother's than his sister's. Also he doesn't grant the same tolerance to his sister as he does to his other siblings. He hates her for having distanced herself from her family and from the estate they were brought up in.

Problems with Hollway and Jefferson

Hollway and Jefferson point out that 'If you, the reader, wish to offer a different interpretation of our data, you are welcome to do so' (2000: 80). However, the level of transcription prevents us from doing this. For example, much is made of Tommy's interruption of the interviewer, in that the subsequent analysis builds upon this interruption as evidence of Tommy's 'defended' status with respect to his childhood. But given the lack of detail in the transcript, it is not possible for us to tell whether the interviewer asked the question in an encouraging way, already projecting (in a textual rather than psychoanalytic sense!) a positive second assessment, or in a neutral way, or in a challenging way. Much is made of 'using all the available evidence' with this new method of analysis, yet not enough detail is given.

There is a disturbing sense in which we are almost encouraged to take sides in a family dispute in order to ascertain whether Tommy's version is accurate or not: mother and sisters are enrolled to check the veracity of Tommy's account. To be led analytically and theoretically into decisions about whose version should be prioritized, and to make judgements about the people on the basis of those decisions, somehow seems to replicate what critical psychologists find so troubling about psychoanalytic thought in the first place – namely the focus on individual pathology as an explanation for why people talk and act (a problematic distinction for some, see Chapter 7) as they do.

Hollway and Jefferson seem to replicate the same rather basic notion of language that we saw in Hollway's earlier work, despite the claim to be drawing on the work of Foucault. Attention to people's language gives us access to the nature of their 'defended subject' status, rather than seeing people's accounts in their interactional context, analysing the interviewer's own contributions as well as the interviewee's, and seeing the account, along with its constructions of subjectivity, as action-oriented – produced by and for this particular context.

CRITICAL DILEMMA

On the one hand, Hollway and Jefferson are trying something creative – they are bringing together different analytical perspectives to produce a method that can develop practical ways of helping people. On the other hand, as we have seen, there are theoretical and analytical difficulties with this project. Do you think that the practical usefulness of being able to identify the problems that arise from Tommy's 'defended subject' status outweighs the difficulties we have identified? Does it matter what view of the person/knowledge/reality we adopt, if we are able to provide some practical help?

Conclusion

This section has covered Wendy Hollway's work, and her concern has been to put subjectivity into centre stage in critical psychological research. However, in doing so it has been argued that strong critical insights and analytical tools are lost: the action-orientated nature of talk, and the indexical or the context-dependent feature of talk. This means that language must not be taken as some simple representation of inner states, but that people's talk should be treated as action-orientated – it has a particular function in particular contexts. This point will be developed more thoroughly in Chapter 7. It is possible to see Ian Parker and Michael Billig as theorists who attempt to import a more sophisticated notion of language into their theorizing about psychoanalysis.

Parker and Billig's psychoanalytic cultures

Ian Parker and his colleagues have written a number of papers and books on the topic of psychoanalysis and critical psychology. Parker's (1997a) central argument is that psychoanalytic discourses structure both cultural practices and the subjectivities of those who employ them, and that psychoanalysis wrongly reduces the effects of the economic constraints of capitalism to individual personality problems. Like Billig (see below) Parker seeks to ground Freud's unconscious in culture rather than in individuals. He accuses psychoanalysis of reducing societal phenomena, such as the alienation and commodification created by capitalism (see Chapter 3), to individual pathology.

Following Marx, Parker sees capitalism as the source of human problems: 'Capitalism constructs a place for people to experience their economic distress as a *psychological* problem and to look into themselves as if *they* were the cause of social ills' (Parker, 1997a: 27, emphasis in original). Similarly for Parker et al. (1995) Marxist notions of alienation, commodification and reification are seen as the cause of patients' personal distress and 'psychopathology'. One of the aims of Parker's work is therefore to highlight how psychoanalysis reduces what are essentially capitalist economic phenomena to the inner world of the individual's mind.

Parker's work has a stronger critical-psychological focus than Hollway's, pinpointing as it does the individualism of psychoanalysis, and the products of that individualism, as the problematic feature. In his earlier work Billig (1976) also criticizes this aspect of psychoanalytic explanation for reducing social conflict to inner unconscious conflict. Parker criticizes the accounts of individual and group behaviour that have emerged from object relations theory, and, drawing upon Marxist terminology, suggests that they 'run smoothly along the tracks of bourgeois humanism and empiricism' (1997a: 28). Bourgeois humanism is explained in terms of the assumed division between individual and society, which organizes the idea that the 'perceptions and preferences at the heart of the self' are the proper focus for psychoanalysis. Empiricism is linked to the notion that internal conflicts are capable of being studied through observations of infant behaviour. Although in contrast to Parker's view, perhaps it is not so much the notion that infants are observable and studiable that is the problem as the (humanist/cognitivist/individualist) notion that those observations provide evidence of internal conflicts.

Despite his condemnation of these aspects of psychoanalytic discourse, Parker does not comprehensively integrate this critique of individualism. He suggests that as well as circulating fantasies and notions of self that are oppressive,

Kleinian psychoanalytic discourses hold up some kind of mirror in which to view our own 'helplessness, fantasies of parentage, projective identification and reality testing' (1997a: 106). This seems to buy into many of the explanatory notions and binaries that themselves rely on the very system of humanism and individualism that is being rejected; a common pitfall for those attracted by psychoanalytic notions.

Parker also discusses the Frankfurt school (particularly the work of Erich Fromm and Herbert Marcuse) in terms of the psychologizing of Enlightenment culture and its general impetus to engage in ideology critique, and strip away the false consciousness of the masses. Parker seems to accept this project as the proper direction for psychoanalytic and critical interpretation, suggesting that Western consumer culture is the evil that we must fight, with its 'deadly virus of cynicism and self-destruction' (1997a: 109; see Chapter 3 for a critique of this view).

Despite Parker's acceptance of certain aspects of Marxist theory, he also draws upon the Foucauldian insight that both psychology and psychoanalysis *produce* the very thing that they attempt to illuminate. This generates some important tensions in Parker's work, and it is not clear that these have been, or can be, resolved (Potter et al., 1999). For example, Parker does not seem to integrate those aspects of Foucault's work that provide a strong critique of Marx. He uses the term *psy-complex* (Ingleby, 1985; Rose, 1985; for a discussion of Nikolas Rose see Chapter 6) to describe the network of assumptions and pronouncements about the behaviour and cognitions of individuals, which itself drew heavily on the Foucauldian notion that the disciplinary 'expertise' of psychology and psychiatry organizes the construction of self-regulating subjects (Parker, 1997a, c).

Parker's relationship with psychoanalysis is therefore not straightforwardly negative, and this may relate to his acceptance of certain aspects of Marxist theory. Drawing upon Burman's (1994) work, he suggests psychoanalysis is the 'repressed other' of the positivist experimental aspects of psychology, which themselves draw upon it. Parker also suggests that because we experience ourselves as isolated from others, our relations with people become hostile and fearful, a tendency that is magnified when relating to those in authority. 'The beliefs that we have deep down about our own nature and about those lesser and greater than ourselves are forms of ideology' (Parker, 1997a: 135). These 'beliefs' prevent us from being able to change our oppression, but help is at hand – 'Psychoanalysis can help us interpret ideology and reveal its power' (1997a: 135). Again there is reliance on the same individualist and cognitivist explanatory notions that Parker claims to reject.

Let us take an example to illustrate the way Parker (1997a) blends an impressive (and potentially creative) mix of Marxist, Foucauldian and Lacanian psychoanalytic theory. He discusses Robert Bly's *Iron John* in order to display the authoritarian function of ideology – a classic Marxist move. Bly suggests that 'When a contemporary man looks down into his psyche, he may, if conditions are right, find under the water of his soul, lying in an area no one has visited for a long time, an ancient hairy man' (1990: 6). Bly therefore constructs getting in touch with this inner hairy old man as a liberating experience for men, who are downtrodden by women with too much power. (Try a refreshing dip into Chapter 5, on feminism, if this is getting too much!)

Parker traces psychoanalytic themes operating in Bly's text, such as the Jungian idea of the self, emerging through the archetypal forms of King and Warrior and also through mythical themes from European fairy tales. He also suggests that 'the figure of the wild man carries some authoritarian prescriptions for male subjectivity' (Parker, 1997a: 158). Psychoanalytic knowledge is therefore embroiled in the re/production of different forms of masculinity. This does not entail some unchanging 'nature' of masculinity, however; rather, like Edley and Wetherell (1997), Parker aims to highlight aspects of the discursive field that men need to negotiate in order to be men.

I agree with one of Parker's positions on psychoanalysis, which suggests that we need to be aware of psychoanalytic notions in order to make sense of the potentially oppressive, individualizing and authoritarian aspects of discourses that surround and construct us. This theme was developed from earlier more applied work with various colleagues, such as *Deconstructing Psychotherapy*, which aimed to identify taken-for-granted assumptions about what passes for therapeutic practice. As the title suggests, Parker draws upon the post-structuralist notion of deconstruction, which he has a rather uneasy relationship with (see Chapter 8). Perhaps we can further unravel some of the tensions in Parker's work by exploring this theme of psychoanalysis and postmodernism further.

Psychoanalysis and postmodernism

According to many contemporary theorists (e.g. Lyotard, 1984, see Chapter 8) we are living in the 'postmodern condition'. For many (e.g. Gergen, 1991) this provides a way of seeing both realities and selves as local, provisional and political, and has been both the spur and the touchstone for much critical and discursive work in psychology. Parker discusses the relation between psychoanalysis and postmodernism in two ways, both of which reflect his dislike (and rather partial view) of the term 'postmodern'. Although many people have problems with the vagueness of the term 'postmodern', for Parker the problems seem to stem from seeing it as referring to rather narrowly defined things. On the one hand he claims to use psychoanalysis as a way into understanding the development of a 'new postmodern culture, which is breeding forms of narcissistic pathology' (1997a: 184). On the other he claims to use 'postmodern ideas to rework psychoanalysis to make it compatible with the changed state of things' (1997a: 184). Despite his desire to 'use postmodernism' in this way, Parker can't help producing a set of rather wild, speculative and seemingly unsupported (certainly by him) claims about postmodernism and 'postmodernists':

> The postmodernists are dangerous because they encourage people to follow through to an extreme end-point the options which modernism opens up but which modernists always utilised carefully and critically, and they risk romanticising psychosis as an escape from the social . . . 'postmodern' forms of psychoanalysis scorn the possibility of changing things for the better . . . they tend to describe political activity as symptomatic of psychopathology.
>
> (1997a: 184–5)

All in all, postmodernists seem pretty scary people (or, following a Marxist account, simply the unfortunate dupes of those in power). But help is at hand: what we need to develop is a 'critical progressive account of society and subjectivity against the postmodernists' (1997a: 185). This helps us to make more sense of Parker's statement in the previous chapter – that the 'political quietism' of post-structuralism (see Chapter 8) leads to increased interest in psychoanalysis (see Discussion questions p. 59).

Parker suggests that the onset of the postmodern condition spells trouble for psychoanalysis, which is based on the premise that intense self-reflection leads to progressive self-knowledge, and that 'a rational, even scientific understanding of mental development' is necessary (1997a: 237). The problem is that:

> a thorough postmodernist will distrust metaphors of depth; there is no self or internal experience to be recovered from the patient's past, there is no path forward to be taken for self-understanding, and there is no narrative, scientific or otherwise, that could be privileged over any other.
>
> (1997a: 237)

Citing Burman (1997), Parker suggests that the postmodern condition is 'a world of surfaces', unable to take claims about the past seriously.

Problems with Parker

Parker largely adopts Jameson's version of postmodernism in which Marxist theory is heavily drawn upon. As we see in Chapter 8, Jameson's version of postmodernism is by no means the prevailing version, and is at odds with some of the basic tenets of contemporary postmodern theory. By contrast, Foucault (1984) contemplates the term 'postmodern', suggesting that we think of it as a general 'ethos' – a set of discourses and practices – rather than a historical era.

Although Parker frequently claims to be adopting a more Foucauldian perspective (e.g. in 1997b) he assumes a Marxist notion of how power operates, overlooking the Foucauldian perspective (see Foucault's critique of Marx in Chapter 3). In highlighting what he sees as the authoritarian function of ideology (e.g. in his discussion of *Iron John* above), the complexity of Foucault's work on how knowledge/power gets done, and in particular Foucault's notion of how subjects are produced through the operation of power/knowledge, is bypassed. Without this insight we are forced back on to traditional Marxist notions of power as authoritarian and the subject as the unfortunate dupe of the repressive ideologies produced by those in power.

As we have seen, Parker tends to legislate about the horrors of various things, without providing much explanation or theorizing about why. For example, there are certain things that we must all accept as wrong – Western consumer culture, and its 'deadly virus of cynicism and self-destruction'; postmodernism (see Chapter 8), which risks 'romanticising psychosis as an escape from the social' and is 'a world of surfaces', unable to 'take claims about the past seriously'. These are all bad things from a standard Marxist perspective. By providing the reader with a range of different and often competing theoretical perspectives it is hoped that this book will provide the type of resources needed to evaluate this type of critical work.

Parker explores Jacques Lacan's work, precisely because he considers him to be the psychoanalyst whose work is most congenial with postmodernism, and therefore someone who can show us how postmodernism and psychoanalysis could most fruitfully come together. Parker claims that Lacan's use of structuralism allows him to develop suspicions about the possibility of extra-discursive phenomena. However, his use of phenomenology entails a focus on 'the subject finding itself in the gaps of discourse, where it does not think' (1997a: 236). This is a troubling focus, assuming a division between discourse and subjectivity that ossifies both into separable things, a strangely anti-Foucauldian position for one who claims to adopt a more sophisticated Foucauldian perspective on discursive analysis than most. (See Parker, 1997b – these complex arguments around subjectivity are spelled out in more detail in Chapter 6.) Parker suggests that 'Lacanian postmodern fragmentation operates as a romantic alternative to capitalist society' (1997a: 213; we examine Lacan's work in more detail below). This all seems rather confusing – it is not clear where Parker stands here: is he adopting a Lacanian psychoanalytic or a Foucauldian perspective on subjectivity? They are certainly not compatible, as we see in Chapter 6.

Postmodernism, therapy and counselling

For those interested in this area, Fee (2000) has edited a collection bringing together a number of researchers concerned to make links with pathology and postmodernism. For example, Viv Burr and Trevor Butt (2000) discuss the implications of postmodernism for therapy and counselling. They suggest that:

1   The notion that the therapist is in possession of 'expert' knowledge is questioned, subverting the traditional power relationships between therapist and client.
2   Practitioners are encouraged to question taken-for-granted notions of normal and deviant, sane and insane, and offer their clients new and more liberating ways of constructing their experiences.
3   Practitioners need to help their clients to understand the situated and relational nature of selfhood, to allow them to understand their different voices.
4   A more thoroughgoing understanding of the constructive role of language needs to be developed, such that we learn that there is nothing internal that can be isolated from language and social practice. How we construct our histories and ourselves is therefore of prime importance. It follows that finding new ways to articulate these things will be empowering, and this is something that a postmodern psychology can help us to develop.

5   Postmodern psychology suggests that our interactions with others (rather than our intrapsychic processes) are a key site for understanding why we act the way we do. Building strategies for resisting the way that we can be positioned to adopt particular identities is therefore a key focus for postmodern work in the various forms of therapeutic psychology.

This gives us more positive ways of thinking through how postmodernism can influence psychoanalysis and therapeutic psychology. We will discuss the implications of postmodernism for critical work in more detail in Chapter 8.

The politics of madness

Another area of critical psychology focused on psychiatry and its fall-out via forms of therapy is exemplified by the work of Hare-Mustin and Maracek (1997), whose aim is to help us to see the connection between a lack of political power and problems conventionally defined as psychological. They suggest that 'abnormal' and clinical psychology today reflect the norms and values of our time and place, and they use the framework of social constructionism (see Chapter 7 for a discussion of social constructionism) to criticize them. They argue that the dominant meanings of 'normal and abnormal' constrain everyone's behaviour. However, alternative accounts are available, and are often used by marginalized groups. These alternative accounts are the key resources for the development of critical psychology, and so the role of the critical psychologist is to bring these accounts to the attention of colleagues and students.

    The decision to regard sets of behaviours as a psychological disorder, rather than as responses to a difficult environment, a criminal act or a medical problem, is a *political and moral* decision rather than a value-free scientific one (Hare-Mustin and Maracek, 1997: 109). The effect of this type of decision is that more and more of our behaviour is brought under scrutiny by our 'self' and by others, and that the causes of problems are located within individuals. It is therefore important that marginalized groups are well represented in clinical work, and that self-help and other lay groups are allowed a voice. This is an area that Erica Burman, Ian Parker and their colleagues have been concerned to develop (see 'Application' below).

Billig and the dialogic unconscious

In developing a notion of the 'dialogic unconscious' (see Billig 1997b, 1999a, for further reading), Billig situates the unconscious dialogically (borrowing the term from Bakhtin, see box 4.1, opposite), repressed from conversational attention by 'what is habitually spoken about' (1997a: 32).

    Billig (1999a) develops these arguments in more detail. Using a rhetorical reworking of the notion of repression as his main analytical tool, he suggests that Freud missed out, or 'repressed', certain features of repression. Billig's notion of this repressed repression is that it occurs through everyday conversational practice, in which speakers readily repress conversational topics from their talk, perhaps just out of the social requirement of politeness.

BOX 4.1   Bakhtin and the dialogic

Mikhail Bakhtin was a Russian literary critic and social theorist. His theories focus on the notion of *dialogue*, which consists of three elements: (1) a speaker, (2) a listener/respondent and a relation between the two. What language is, and what it says, is therefore the product of interactions between at least two people. Bakhtin contrasts this notion of dialogue with monologue, or the monologic, meaning utterances that seem to come from only one person or source.

Bakhtin (in *The Dialogic Imagination*) suggests that monologic language (*monologia*) is produced by the polarity between language as a system and language as emerging from the individual. He opposes monologia with the idea of *heteroglossia*, which could be defined as the flexible deployment of the collection of all the discourses and conversational strategies that people have access to. Monologia operates through what he terms *centripetal force* – which tends to push things towards a central point. Heteroglossia operates through *centrifugal force*, which tends to push things away from the central point. In his discussion of the dialogic (1981: 672), Bakhtin suggests that all utterances are directed towards, and inseparable from, some kind of response. We use heteroglossia – employ a variety of languages and styles – in order to make any utterance, or enter into dialogue with others.

Bakhtin suggests that both heteroglossia and monologia, the centrifugal and centripetal forces, operate simultaneously in any utterance. Hence language is seen as both shaped by the individual speaker, and by social formations beyond the individual. Critical social psychologists who have adopted Bakhtin like the way he shows that monologic texts are infused by a weave of the dialogic – he puts the social into the individual.

Billig explores some of Freud's cases to make his point. One of them is the 'Rat-man' (originally from Freud, 1955: vol. X; Billig kindly reinstates his original pseudonym, Paul) who in his attempt to ward off his inner voices devises defensive formulas that he repeats to himself. Billig suggests that Freud would see this as a battle between the ego (the civilizing effects of language) and the id (the instincts of sex and aggression). For Freud, what is to be repressed – human instinct – lies outside language and emerges from within the individual.

Billig suggests instead that we can see the objects of repression – Paul's complicated set of expressed desires – as themselves forged in and through language. This means that 'the battleground may be within language – between what is permissible to be said (and to be thought) and what is impermissible' (1999a: 71). Billig suggests that in order to participate in conversation, we need to practise the social codes of politeness, to comply with our culture's moral restrictions. The fear of shame which results from the infraction of these social and moral codes keeps the 'desire to disrupt social life' at bay – keeps it repressed. We can situate the unconscious dialogically through the built-in linguistic expression/repression of social disruption: 'Conversation demands constraints and what is forbidden becomes an object of desire' (1999a: 254).

Billig applies his thesis on a wider level, suggesting that contemporary Western capitalism represses the images of production, and the feelings of shame and guilt that those images might provoke, in its celebration of consumption. (See Billig's views on 'commodity fetishism' in Chapter 3.)

Freud's antisemitic repression

Billig (1997a) points out that there have been many feminist analyses that have rightly highlighted the masculinist assumptions of Freud's work (for example, Mitchell, 1974; Gallop, 1982; Brennan, 1989; Hollway, 1989; Sayers, 1990; Frosh, 1994). This is particularly so in Freud's studies of Dora (e.g. see Gallop, 1986; Moi, 1986). However, Billig makes the point that this feminist 'politicizing' of psycho-analysis misses an important issue – the politics of race. Both Freud and Dora were Jewish, living in Vienna at a time when antisemitic parties controlled the city. In his analysis of Freud's (1955: vol. VIII) early accounts of psychoanalytic dialogue, Billig suggests that Freud and Dora 'can be heard collaborating to avoid the sort of Jewish themes which Freud overtly excludes from his published text' (Billig, 1997a: 32). This type of dialogic repression is replicated in the writings of today's critics.

Billig shows that while Freud's work could be seen as the biggest exposé of self-deception in Western culture, Freud himself mirrored the same self-deception – he chose to read a newspaper that did not report antisemitism, and he refused to discuss it with his children. These small private irrationalities involved ignoring wider public irrationalities.

Problems with Billig

There are times in Billig's work when it is unclear where the unconscious (or in earlier work 'thinking', see Chapter 7) is situated. Billig claims to be developing a discursive psychological perspective (see Chapter 7), which entails respecifying psychological phenomena as discursively situated. Yet he still wants to retain 'feelings of shame' and the 'desire to disrupt social life' as part of his explanatory resource in showing how language can operate repressively. As with Parker's work, there is a (less overt) tendency to slide back into traditional psychological notions of subjectivity, in the forms of 'feelings', 'fears' and 'desires' that can be used as *explanatory resources*, rather than seen in terms of their interactional currency. So both Parker and Billig claim to adopt a discursive perspective, yet both employ more traditional aspects of subjectivity as explanatory resources. Perhaps the engagement with psychoanalysis is part of this – is it possible to do something called psychoanalysis without adopting some bottom-line causal role for some aspect of subjectivity?

Another problem is that Billig does not engage with Lacan, who in his own way has forged a link (albeit a rather tortuous and convoluted one, as Billig points out) between language and the unconscious. Lacan has been a popular choice for critical and discursive work that, on the one hand, recognizes the importance of the insight that reality and subjectivity are discursively constructed, but on the other wants to retain some notion of the subject, or desire, or the unconscious.

Conclusion

Ian Parker has been an inspiration for many critical social psychologists. His work spans Marxist, Foucauldian and psychoanalytic theory. However, this eclectic mix of different styles of work does not always gel into something capable of providing a strong critique of current practices in psychology. Some would argue that Michael Billig provides a more thorough integration of contemporary notions of language, rhetoric, power and discourse with psychoanalysis, yet even here there are problems with the status of what Billig takes to be the unconscious – is it something lodged inside our heads, or a thoroughly discursive phenomenon? Billig does not seem clear on this. One person who does seem definitive (though perhaps not clear!) on the relation between language and the unconscious is Lacan.

Post-structuralism and psychoanalysis: Lacan and others

Jacques Lacan

Peter Greenaway's fascinating film *The Pillow Book* opens with heroine Nagiko's birthday ritual. We see her father gently painting a birthday greeting on her face. These images indicate how influential Lacan's ideas about our initiation into language, the symbolic and the law of the father have become. Lacanian notions of subjectivity and textuality are further invoked when Nagiko sees her own written-upon reflection in a mirror – for Lacan an important moment of self-recognition, of acceptance of ourselves as both selves and 'others', as possessors of authored subjectivity. Like Freud, Lacan's psychoanalytic discourses are filtering through into everyday life.

Jacques Lacan was a French psychoanalyst who developed his own version of psychoanalysis based on cross-fertilization with structuralist linguistics and anthropology (see Lacan, 1977, 1989, 1992). Lacan applied Saussure's semiology (see Chapter 8) to some of Freud's ideas about the mind. This involved a move away from humanism and the notion of a stable self, capable of free will and autonomy, and instead resulted in Lacan's position statement – 'the unconscious is structured like a language'. This involved the replacement of Freud's id, ego and superego with structures of the *imaginary*, the *symbolic* and the *real*, which portray the stages of psychic maturation. Whereas the Freudian goal of psychoanalysis is to strengthen the rational ego in order to minimize repression and neurosis, for Lacan this is impossible, because the ego or self is itself illusory – a product of the unconscious, which in turn is a product of language. We need the symbolic structures of language in order to develop an unconscious. So how do we develop this illusion that we call a 'self'?

The *imaginary*, or 'mirror', stage (Lacan, 1949) refers to the way we develop a sense of self from our own external reflection. Between the ages of six to eighteen months the developing person will see itself in the mirror, providing a vision of the self as similar to others, and as whole and integrated. This first *pre-linguistic* signification of a self stays with us as an ideal ego throughout our lives. We (mis)identify with this visual perception, or what Lacan calls specular imaging.

Q   DISCUSSION QUESTIONS

1   How do we know when something is pre-linguistic?
2   What form of evidence may be gathered?
3   How will it be presented and argued for?
4   What purpose would be served by doing so?

The *symbolic order* refers to the existing social structures that we are born into, e.g. social class, gender, family and so on. The pre-linguistic identity gained at the imaginary stage is constructed within this symbolic order. While Freud invoked 'penis envy' as central to the development of femaleness, Lacan replaces this with the notion of the *phallus*, which is not so much a thing as a symbol of that which is not the mother (simply assumed as the primary care taker). The phallus provides the child with its first inkling that it is separate from its mother, that there is a whole world of not-mother separated selves. To become a proper 'person' inevitably entails a tragic loss of unity and security. This original sense of unity is what Lacan terms the (psychic) realm of the *real*. It is something that we long to return to, but once we enter into language and knowledge of the 'other' it is irretrievably lost.

With the phallus we gain our original perceptions of difference, and it thereby becomes the ultimate signifying mechanism (see Minsky, 1992: 190–2, for further discussion of this). We develop our 'selves' through the operation of this masculine regulatory principle. Lacan reads the symbolic order, and 'civilization' itself, as the 'law of the father', or sometimes just the law. To become a speaking subject, we must submit to the laws and rules of language, the 'centre' of the whole system. Through this we all develop desire, which can never be satisfied, as it is a desire for the impossible – to control the system, to be the centre.

Because the phallus supplies symbolic and hence patriarchal order, the same Oedipal relations are set up as with Freud, in which the father prohibits any mother–child 'incest' relationship. The male child identifies with Phallic power, which itself imposes the symbolic order. As a result men may feel that they are more likely to occupy the position of centre – to be in a place where there is no lack. The problem for women is that they cannot escape from the imaginary into the symbolic as they obviously lack a penis, which signifies the phallus. They therefore are forever cast in the role of 'other', but then every subject in language – male, female or otherwise – is constituted in the same way.

Because Lacan acknowledges that the subject is produced through the system of meanings available to us – and that identity is a construction – he has been interesting for critical psychologists adopting a social constructionist perspective who are nevertheless concerned about how to theorize subjectivity and the 'self'.

Hollway, Lacan and the discursive production of selves

Wendy Hollway was a central figure in the production of *Changing the Subject* (Henriques et al., 1984 [1998]), a key text for early critical social psychologists. In her chapter she suggested that psychoanalysis provides ways of dealing with some of traditional psychology's most pressing problems:

1   Traditional psychology is based on the notion of a rational subject. Psycho-analysis offers a solution to this problem, as it recognizes 'our fundamental irrationality' (1984: 205).
2   Traditional psychology assumes a unitary subject, but psychoanalysis under-cuts this through its focus on unconscious processes.
3   Traditional psychology wrongly separates cognition from affect, but psychoanalysis acknowledges their dependence on each other.
4   Traditional psychology provides oversimplified views of the subject, which draw on either social or biological determinism. By contrast psychoanalysis provides an account of the continuity of the subject, because a person's historical life events are implicated in their present ways of behaving. Psychoanalysis thus challenges the traditional individual/social split that organizes most areas of psychology.

Henriques et al. recognize the classic critiques of psychoanalysis – its his-torical and cultural specificity, its perpetuation of women as secondary and less important than men, and its exclusivity to the bourgeoisie. They also take on board Foucault's points about the role of psychoanalysis in the regulation of sexual norms (see below) and Donzelot's (1980) critiques about the regulation of familial roles and responsibilities. But they think that psychoanalysis nevertheless offers us 'an account of subjective processes and their production which we cannot afford to ignore' (Hollway, 1984: 207). It does this in two ways:

1   Psychoanalysis shows us how we come to repeat behaviours that have nega-tive outcomes, and hence how we become resistant to change.
2   Psychoanalysis links sexuality with the unconscious, and will therefore be useful in understanding 'the forms and possibilities of change in personal life' (ibid.).

How this comes about is best shown in terms of Hollway's critique of aspects of Lacan's work, which in turn highlights what is distinctive about her own work.

Hollway's problems with Lacan. Hollway argues that although Lacan focuses on the production of subjectivity via signification, his reliance on Lévi-Strauss's 'law of the father' means that the privileging of the phallus does not offer us any way out of our gendered subjectification. We are just as stuck with our gendered 'natures' as if they had been Freud's biological instincts.

Hollway also criticizes Lacan for using a structuralist paradigm, which involves the construction of a universal and dehistoricized subject, bound by existing structures of language. Again this leaves little room for change.

What Hollway proposes is a replacement of Lacan's 'universal and timeless symbolic order with an emphasis on discursive relations . . . using the concept of 'positioning' within discursive practices' (Hollway, 1984: 217). This allows them to specify 'motivational dynamics through which people are positioned in discourses, which is not addressed in the post-structuralist work' (1984: 218). The basic insight that people are discursively constituted is 'supplemented' by the further question about why they are motivated to 'choose' the discourses that they do. We can see that Hollway's work, although in many ways sophisticated and thought-provoking, again relies on a notion of language as the medium of expression of the motivated, choosing individual. This is a theoretical position on subjectivity that can be criticized from a postmodern, discursive and/or Foucauldian position – positions developed throughout Part II of this book.

Feminists changing the psychoanalytic subject

There has been a lot of activity in feminist theory around the issue of psycho-analysis and subjectivity. Two much discussed figures are Hélène Cixous and Luce Irigaray, who have explored the politics of these processes of signifying selves. The result has been a fusion of Derrida's term *logocentrism* (see Chapter 8), with Lacan's notion of the Phallic, to produce the term *phallogocentrism*. Derrida's insight that Western metaphysics is rooted in the philosophy of presence manifested in the *logos*, which can mean some central reality such as the word, God and so on, means that what we need to *deconstruct* is logocentric thought; and now, as poststruc-turalist feminists, also *phallogocentric* thought, centred on the primacy of the phallus. Derrida's deconstructive work may thus allow us to escape what seems to be the pessimism and inevitability of Lacan's view of the development of gender and the self. As we shall see in the next chapter, Butler (who also draws heavily on Derrida's work) proposed the *lesbian phallus* as a way of disrupting the patriarchal connotations of the Lacanian phallus.

One of the consequences of theorizing within and against the Lacanian version of self-development is that the priority for women is to seek our own ways of writing, signifying, our own language, in order to escape being forever defined as secondary to the masculine order of things. Cixous (1986: 314) suggests that the least we can do is to define female identity in more positive terms. 'We have no womanly reason to pledge allegiance to the negative'. Ideally this should involve writing about our own experiences, our own bodies and our own sexualities from our own perspectives – developing new signifiers in a new signifying system – with the aim of freeing us from our negative relation to the phallus. Cixous calls this new system *l'écriture féminine* or feminine writing, a way of getting ourselves back to the pure experience of the real.

Cixous develops the term 'sexts' to illustrate the gendered text and its implications (1986: 315). Feminine sexts need to embrace *jouissance*, a French term for orgasm, to claim women's sexuality and enjoyment as something positive and fundamental, rather than essentially lacking.

Irigaray also stresses the importance of a new signifying system for female sexuality. Irigaray (1985: 28) explores multiple erogenous zones that constitute female sexuality. The inevitability of being defined in terms of lack through participating in the masculinist system of signification entails that women must learn to take their sexuality into their own hands (literally and metaphorically). We must therefore form lesbian relations in order to establish the positive self-sufficiency of women's sexuality, and wait for the day when there will be equality between the sexes.

On the positive side, this psychoanalytically-inspired feminist theory encourages us not to passively accept negative versions of our sexuality. The focus is also on language as a way of addressing these problems. However, one of the problems of this line of thought is that it relies on automatic acceptance of the notion of selves developing through possession or lack of a penis. Because women lack more than men, we must make extra effort to develop our own signifying systems. Also – what does 'women's experience' mean? This presupposes that there will be a set of experiences that are peculiar to women that we can all recognize. This starts to run into the same problems that will be identified in Chapter 5 in the discussion of feminism and postmodernism.

Foucault's critique of psychoanalysis and of Lacan

For psychoanalysis, and for Hollway, a subject of desire is foundational. For Freud, similarly, sex gives us insights into the truth of the subject. By contrast, Foucault would see 'sex' and 'desire' as products of various discourses and institutions. They are produced out of the very regulative practices and regimes which seek to control them: 'one should not think that desire is repressed, for the simple reason that the law is what constituted both desire and the lack on which it is predicated' (Foucault, 1979: 81). Desire becomes the truth of the subject, who is endlessly subjected to a law that produces desire.

This is similar to Lacan's (1992) position in *The Ethics of Psychoanalysis*, where he claims that an object of desire is only that in so far as it is prohibited. However, Foucault's work can be characterized as seeking an analysis of the subject without employing psychoanalytic concepts. Foucault's project in *The History of Sexuality* is to outline genealogically – historically – how people come to recognize themselves as subjects of sexuality. This entails developing an account of 'the practices by which individuals . . . decipher, recognise and acknowledge themselves as subjects of desire' (1985: 5). Psychoanalysis fails in the sense that it denies the 'historicity of forms of experience' (see Foucault, 1985: preface, or Dreyfus and Rabinow, 1982: 334); most notably 'desire and the subject of desire' (Foucault, 1985: 4) are characterized ahistorically.

It is not enough simply to recognize that desire is constituted by what Lacan would term symbolic law, rather the whole notion of desire as the truth of the subject, as the *a priori* starting point for an analysis of subjectivity, is something Foucault argues against. (See Chapter 6 for further discussion of Foucault and subjectivity.)

Other postmodern–post-structuralist critiques of psychoanalysis

Judith Butler criticizes psychoanalysis from a feminist perspective (see Chapter 5). If we adopt a postmodern perspective (see Chapter 8) we can examine psychoanalysis as a 'metanarrative' – an overarching story which starts with no differentiation between sexes, moving through to the enforced separation and creation of gender difference in the Oedipal narrative. This metanarrative gives 'a false sense of legitimacy and universality to a culturally specific and, in some cases, culturally oppressive version of gender identity' (Butler, 1990a: 329).

For example, Freud's story assumes that we must *either* identify with one sex *or* desire it – no other relations are possible. So if you identify yourself as a woman, you must desire men. If you desire other women that means you are really identifying with men whether you know it or not. The implication of rejecting this traditional view, according to Butler, is that gender becomes a set of narrative effects and performances rather than the primary category psychoanalysts assume it to be.

Jacques Derrida's post-structuralist thought disrupts the whole notion of the inevitability of meaning arising through the symbolic order. For Derrida meaning arises through a process of hierarchical differentiation whereby meanings are shaped out of the often invisible exclusion of their 'opposite'. The privileged and positive meanings associated with 'man', for example, are constituted through the marginalized and negative meanings associated with 'woman'. The very symbolic tools at our disposal are therefore saturated with a power that is itself unrecognizable to us. Derrida develops *deconstruction* as a way of disrupting this inherited symbolic order. (See Hepburn, 1999a, and Chapter 8 for further discussion of Derrida's work and its significance for critical social psychology.) By highlighting the *constructed* nature of the hierarchical binaries constituting the symbolic order, Derrida can also be used to disrupt the taken-for-granted categories of psychoanalysis.

CRITICAL DILEMMA

Klein developed the defence mechanism of splitting and the either/or logic that results from this in her work. In what ways would Derrida's focus on either/or logic be different from Klein's? What are the implications of moving in a more Derridean, post-structuralist direction? Do you think subjectivity is being left out? If so why and how do we include it? What would be the consequences of either including or excluding subjectivity?

Conclusion

Lacan has been attractive to critical psychologists interested in psychoanalysis, as he theorizes subjectivity as the outcome of practices of signification. But for Lacan, as with Freud and Klein, one foundational aspect of personhood still remains – the subject of desire. Even though that subject is constructed through language it still makes sense to take it as the cornerstone of our theories and ways of making sense of human action. This basic assumption about where we should start in our critical theories will be examined in more detail in Chapter 6.

Application

Deconstructing Psychotherapy (Parker, 1999) is a collaborative work that aims to highlight taken-for-granted assumptions about what passes for therapeutic practice. As we learn from Parker's introduction:

> the task of the deconstructing therapist, and just as much so the deconstructing client, is to locate the problem in certain cultural practices and comprehend the role of patterns of power in setting out positions for people which serve to reinforce the idea that they can do nothing about it themselves.
>
> (p. 3)

As a deconstructive therapist (see Chapter 8 for an explanation of deconstruction) the task is to persuade one's client that their problems stem from 'cultural practices' and the positioning created by 'patterns of power', which disempower them by encouraging them to think they can't just solve their own problems. But surely part of the problem is also that people are encouraged to see their problems as 'problems' and also to see themselves as the source of those problems? Problematizing the very terms in which issues are constructed moves towards a more Derridean deconstructive and, more broadly, postmodern perspective.

Another important work in critical psychology that draws on practical and applied expertise has been *Deconstructing Psychopathology* (Parker et al., 1995). In the midst of this applied work comes a clear legislation about what is being meant by the complex term 'deconstruction' – it is referred to as 'a process of reading which unravels the way insane categories are used to suppress different perceptions and behaviours, and it overturns the opposition between, for example, illness and health' (1995: 4). It is argued, quite rightly, that the term 'deconstruction' is employed in a 'less pure' sense than Derrida, but their rationale is that the identification of conceptual oppositions is where they want to start, not where they want to finish (1995: 3). Again, this implies that for Derrida deconstruction begins and ends with the identification of conceptual oppositions, and by itself is not a useful tool for applied work.

Parker et al. propose instead what they term a 'practical deconstruction' which attends to 'politics and power' in a way that a Derridean deconstruction does

Corinne Squire

'The directions I am most interested in seeing develop within critical social psychology are those that will bring it into association with other disciplines, particularly sociology and cultural studies, at the same time as maintaining a distinctly psychological approach through its focus on subjectivity. I think such an address to subjectivity will continue to require a qualified interest in psychoanalysis. I would like critical social psychology to take an approach that is liberal about the possibilities but rigorous about the performance of qualitative methods. At the same time, I would like the field to be less theoretically and methodologically driven than it has often been – to become more like action research. I guess this is also to ask for more explicit political or micropolitical engagement in the work. My own work on narrative and culture in psychology, and its topics – HIV, talk shows, public morality – tries to tackle these concerns. In addition I am concentrating now in this work on examining popular representations of subjectivity in the West, and on analysing how psychological theory is being expressed in novel forms. I am trying, that is, to find theory in unlikely places.'

not; they are interested in 'the practices of power that hold traditional oppositions in place' (1995: 3). A common theme in the adoption of deconstruction by these critical psychologists is that Derridean deconstruction does not allow the required commitment to political endeavours. Indeed, Parker suggests that '[b]y its very nature it is hostile to any attempt to construct conceptual or political priorities . . .' (1989: 198). In Chapter 8 I will attend to these critiques, and show some of the ways in which deconstruction *can* underpin political commitment and practical application. It is interesting that a book focused on the practice of therapy should become so embroiled in rarefied notions like deconstruction. Perhaps this theory/ practice distinction isn't all it's cracked up to be? Perhaps in acting we are always relying on some form of theory, and in theorizing always engaging in some form of practice?

This is not to detract from the practical achievements of Parker et al.; once out of the minefield of Continental philosophy and into the applied arena there is some important work covered in these collections. For example, the Hearing Voices Network (see Parker et al., 1995, and Romme and Escher, 1993) aims to help people who hear voices to reconstruct their experience in ways that do not pathologize them. Similarly Harper (1995) calls on practitioners to provide their clients with alternative, less individually pathologizing constructions of their experiences. The general aim seems to be to align with oppressed and marginalized groups, or relatively powerless service users, and to help them to develop their own critiques and empower them against established psychological practices – critical social psychology *par excellence*.

Conclusion

Psychoanalysis holds a big attraction for some critical psychologists. The question is whether even flirting with it in the way Billig does, as in his invoking of the term 'unconscious' in his theorizing, is a dangerous enterprise for those working within the discipline of critical social psychology, steeped as our Western cultures are in individualism. The danger is that we will slide back into some form of individualist theorizing, in which we want to start talking about theories of subjectivity, people's inner states and so on as *explanatory theories of human action*. In this chapter we have seen the various problems and confusions that can arise, both theoretically and analytically, for critical social psychologists moving in this direction.

There can be no doubt that psychoanalysis has many problems: it is historically and culturally specific, it perpetuates misogynistic notions of women as less important than men. It assumes, and thereby re/produces, misogynist sexual norms and familial roles and responsibilities. But in doing all this it also shows us how it is that we can repeat behaviours that have negative outcomes, and hence how we become resistant to change, and it is this latter explanatory power that has been attractive, though perhaps not productive, for critical social psychologists.

B The best thing about psychoanalysis

Most theorists who employ psychoanalysis say that it provides a strong irrational and emotional – and so more 'human' – balance to the rationalist tendencies of traditional psychology. It explains why we sometimes don't act in a 'rational' way.

W The worst thing about psychoanalysis

Apart from the misogyny, the worst thing about psychoanalysis has to be the way that it focuses on individuals as the source of their own problems. Put simply, it is like saying 'the world is the way it is because people are the way they are' – or some version of this. I think this is a backward, stultifying move for critical psychology, and for humanity more generally.

Where next?

The challenge for critical social psychologists interested in psychoanalysis is to do it in a way that doesn't end up with essentialist notions of the person and gender. Can psychoanalysis be adopted without the drift into individualism and essentialism?

Practical exercises

1   Start with Judith Butler's suggestion that psychoanalysis can be viewed as a metanarrative. That is, it can be treated as a particular story about actions and events. Choose one of the psychoanalytic perspectives discussed in the chapter (Klein, say, or Lacan). Decide to spend the day thinking about all interaction (conversations with friends and family as well as television and newspapers) from this perspective. What sort of things does this story of people highlight? How does it help in taking a critical or sceptical view of everyday expectations about life? What are its dangers?

2   Think of a tendentious and self-serving version of how you were brought up. Couch it in psychoanalytic language and use it to blame your parents for everything bad. Make sure you keep all gender roles strictly in their place as you do this.

3   Familiarize yourself with Michael Billig's notion of dialogical repression. He argues that rather than seeing repression as a direct product of unconscious dynamics it is a practical concern in interaction. Take the extract from Hollway and Jefferson's interview on pages 76–77. Try to apply Billig's ideas to understand what is going on. This will involve being imaginative and rather speculative, as you have such little information. How does the interpretation differ from Hollway and Jefferson? What difference does the different approach to the unconscious make?

Reading

If you read only one thing, read:

Billig, M. (1999) *Freudian Repression: Conversation creating the unconscious.* Cambridge: Cambridge University Press. **Even though Billig takes a very particular line it provides a rich engagement with Freudian thinking.**

Classics

Freud, S. (1936) *The Problem of Anxiety.* New York: Norton. (See chapter 8, on the superego.) **It is important to read Freud in the original. He is, perhaps surprisingly, clear and unpretentious.**

Frosh, S. (1987) *The Politics of Psychoanalysis: An introduction to Freudian and post-Freudian theory.* London: Macmillan.

Parker, I. (1997) *Psychoanalytic Culture: Psychoanalytic discourse in Western society.* London: Sage.

Sayers, J. (1990) Psychoanalytic feminism: Deconstructing power in theory and therapy, in I. Parker and J. Shotter (eds), *Deconstructing Social Psychology* (pp. 196–207). London: Routledge.

Also useful

Brennan, T. (ed.) (1989) *Between Feminism and Psychoanalysis*. London: Routledge.
Squire, C. (1989) *Significant Differences: Feminism in psychology*. London: Routledge.

Difficult but worth it

Henriques, J., Hollway, W., Irwin, C., Venn, C. and Walkerdine, V. (1984, 1998) *Changing the Subject: Psychology, social regulation and subjectivity*. London: Methuen. **For psychoanalytic work see especially pp. 212–26.**

Chapter 5

Feminist Critics

What is feminism *for* in the twenty-first century? 'Surely we don't need it any more?' is a common grumble heard in pubs and newspapers. Sexual equality has been achieved. There's too much, if anything! There has been a woman Prime Minister, after all. And feminists are just stirring things up because they have trouble with men . . .

The Promise Keepers would certainly agree with this. They are a religious right wing organization, founded in 1990, which calls for 'active male Christian leadership to set things right' (Daly, 1998: 80). The basic message is that reclaiming one's manhood is a necessary and enlightening thing for the North American male. Full instructions are given:

> Sit down with your wife and say something like this, 'Honey, I've made a terrible mistake. I've given you my role. I gave up leading this family, and I forced you to take my place. Now I must reclaim that role.' I'm not suggesting that you ask for your role back, I'm urging you to *take* it back . . . There can be no compromise here. If you're going to lead, you must lead . . . Treat the lady gently and lovingly. But *lead*.
>
> (Evans, 1996: 79–80, cited in Daly, 1998: 80)

This sounds like an extremist minority group, but it has grown alarmingly. In 1996 between 40,000 and 60,000 people (mainly white Christian men) were present at Promise Keeper rallies. By the spring and summer of 1997 numbers had grown enough to pack eighteen football stadiums around the United States – 'never before in the United States have so many political mass events been staged on such a scale' (*National NOW Times*, cited in Daly, 1998: 81). All the leaders of religious right wing groups support the Promise Keepers. The Center for Democratic Studies (1996) has found their rhetoric to be a disturbing mix of religion and military terminology – the goal is 'spiritual warfare', and their beliefs are predictably anti-abortion, anti-lesbian and anti-gay.

Maybe now more than ever it is time for feminists to be vigilant. But what is a feminist, and what does feminist psychology entail? In tackling this question, this chapter will be organized into six sections. This reflects the diversity of contemporary feminist research as well as some of its key themes. The first section examines definitions of different types of feminism and feminist psychology. The second will consider the research that has studied sexism and the way gender inequalities are legitimated. This section will focus in particular on the work of Rosalind Gill and Margaret Wetherell et al. The third will focus on the important notion of heterosexism and lesbian and gay psychology more generally. This will cover Celia Kitzinger's work on the social construction of lesbianism and the debates about heterosexism and the naturalization of heterosexual sex.

The fourth section of the chapter will focus on eating disorders and the body. This is a topic where feminist social psychologists from different perspectives have explored a range of critical issues. Helen Malson's study of eating disorders will be taken as a central example. This also provides an opportunity to describe recent arguments about the female body, embodiment generally, and the role of discourse. This topic throws up some theoretical issues around subjectivity, embodiment, politics and knowledge that will need to be clarified; the final two sections of the chapter are designed with this aim in mind. The fifth is concerned with the sometimes troubled relation between feminism and postmodernism. This will be concerned with the impact of postmodern thinkers from outside psychology, notably Judith Butler and Donna Haraway. This will lead in the final section to a consideration of the relation of feminism to relativism. Recent debates around this issue will be discussed.

What is feminist psychology?

Let me start by considering the nature of feminist psychology. There is no one straightforward consensual definition. One of feminist psychology's features over the 1990s has been creative debate over assumptions, notions of the person, issues about how inequality and exploitation should be understood, as well as relations between gender, class, ethnicity and other categories.

Here are two sample definitions. Sue Wilkinson, drawing on work by Rhoda Unger and Mary Crawford (1992), defines feminism as involving two themes:

1 Feminism places a high value on women, considering us as worthy of study in our own right . . .
2 Feminism recognizes the need for social change on behalf of women: feminist psychology is avowedly political.

(Wilkinson, 1997: 247–8)

Second, Maggie Humm suggests that feminist theory shares three defining assumptions:

1 Gender is a social construction that oppresses women more than men.
2 Patriarchy (the male domination of social institutions – see Box 5.1) shapes these constructions.
3 Women's experiential knowledge best helps us to envision a future non-sexist society.

(1996: 296)

These definitions are contestable in various ways, as there are a number of different types of feminism, some well established and some emerging.

These different styles of feminist work include: (1) Marxist feminism, (2) liberal feminism and (3) radical feminism, traditionally picked out as the major traditions (Chris Beasley, 1999). However, they will here be supplemented by (4) postmodern feminism and (5) feminism engaged with issues of race and ethnicity. Marxist feminism sees women's oppression as part of the wider class structural inequality. Once the capitalist ruling class has been forced out and communist society prevails, women's oppression will disappear. Liberal feminism sees government as a neutral institution. Women have previously been excluded from it, but its potential for equal rights is certainly there. The political organization of women's groups is then required to be well structured for improving women's situation in work and the home.

In contrast to Marxist and liberal feminism, radical feminism emphasizes the concept of patriarchy (see Box 5.1). Kate Millett (1985) argues that relations between men and women are always political, because they are based on power. For Millett the power lies with men, who dominate women in all significant aspects of life. This means that, for radical feminists, everything is political (i.e. things like the family – which have traditionally been seen as non-political structures) and state power is simply part of the wider context of patriarchal power. This means that there is no reduction to an economic class as in Marxist feminism, and the fact that women have been excluded from power in the state is much more complicated than the liberal feminists believe. One reason for this is that state structures have been/are male-dominated and thus male interests dominate. Radical feminists also argue that legislation would not do as much for the real position of women as liberal feminists believe.

Postmodern feminism is a relatively new area of feminism that will be explored in the fourth section of this chapter. The focus here is on dissolving or subverting the fixed nature of categories such as 'woman'. For some feminists such as Hélène Cixous and Luce Irigaray postmodern/post-structuralism overlaps with psychoanalytic feminism, and this type of work is considered in Chapter 6, and was touched on briefly in the previous chapter. Another interesting development has been feminism focused on race and ethnicity (see Bhavnani and Phoenix, 1994). As with postmodern feminists, there is a tendency to reject a unified category of 'woman', but there is more of a focus on the operations of power and identity with respect to the particular category of race/ethnicity than is found in postmodern approaches. This dislike of universalized positions in feminism means that some feminists in this area, such as Bhavnani (1993), criticize the more traditional types of feminism.

Feminism is an important movement; but why do we need a specifically feminist psychology? According to Wilkinson (1997) psychology has asserted women's inferiority in at least four distinct theoretical traditions:

1   The history of psychology has been a history of poor science. It has mismeasured women, repeatedly taking male as norm, female as deviant.

Kum Kum Bhavnani

'I have always been attached to psychology, from when I first studied it at Bristol with some wonderful teachers to my time on that Master's course in Child Psychology at Nottingham where the Newsons facilitated my knowing the importance of child psychology, and during my time at King's College, Cambridge, a decade after my MA, where Colin Fraser supervised my completing a totally qualitative social psychology doctorate in 1988. While I have always enjoyed my ambivalent relationship to psychology and my close connection with critical psychology – where I hope I have contributed in shifting the discussion away from a "First World centrism" in some small measure – I am also aware that both my critical psychology and my critical cultural studies/development studies work remains intellectually, and at times, politically, a little too distinct from each other. Thus my desire is to work within critical psychology and critical development studies simultaneously to assist each in engaging with arguments from the other. In this way I hope that critical psychology can move towards becoming truly interdisciplinary rather than the multi-disciplinary project I consider it to be at the moment.'

2   Some psychologists suggest that the problem is not that women are actually oppressed by men or patriarchal structures, rather they have internalized fear of success because of their socialization as women. The remedy is therefore therapy to alleviate the internal fears and blocks that are holding them back and lowering their self-esteem. This apparently well motivated position leaves women as the source of their own problems.

3   Psychology has sought a different perspective by listening to women's voices. For example, the American feminist psychologist Carol Gilligan (1982) suggests that women have distinct 'voices' – moral registers and ways of knowing that need to be heard. The danger again is that this different voice draws on, and feeds back into, traditional stereotypes of women.

4   Psychology has produced a huge body of work on sex differences. How are females different, in some basic or timeless way, from males? Or how do they blend genders together, as in Sandra Bem's scale for measuring androgyny (e.g. 1974). The problem here is that the focus continues to be on the individual as the source of gendered actions, reinforcing traditional masculine/feminine stereotypes.

As a consequence of these kinds of problems, Wilkinson suggests, we should reconstruct the question of sex differences. We need to dismantle maleness and

Sue Wilkinson

Sue Wilkinson's major contribution is the establishment of feminist psychology in the United Kingdom, and its subsequent national and international development. She played a leading role in the campaign for a BPS 'Psychology of Women' Section and was its first elected chair; she is also the founding – and current – editor of Feminism and Psychology. *Her books include the classic* Feminist Social Psychology *(1986) and, with Celia Kitzinger,* Heterosexuality *(1993),* Feminism and Discourse *(1995) and* Representing the Other *(1996). The key feature of her work – which has ranged across a variety of topic areas and methodologies – has been the definition and development of an approach which is both critical and specifically feminist. Her most recent work is on breast cancer, cervical cancer and lesbian health, using focus group methodology.*

Sue Wilkinson is Professor of Feminist and Health Studies in the Department of Social Sciences at Loughborough University.

BOX 5.1   Patriarchy

Literally translated as 'the rule of the father', patriarchy has become a useful term for feminists seeking to explain and lament the condition of male superiority over women. Often the term incorporates particular assumptions about the relations between 'individual' and 'society'. For example, radical feminists of the 1970s (e.g. Millett, 1971; Daly, 1978; Dworkin, 1981) saw patriarchy as an ideology that organizes relations between the sexes on the basis of inequality. This inequality was thought to provide the framework for the production of all other social inequalities. More recent feminist approaches have argued that the prioritizing of gender differences incorporated within this view is part of the problem, as it builds in a 'natural' distinction between men and women. Hence relying on early notions of patriarchal dominance misses the complexity of issues of identity, gender and sexuality. 'Patriarchy' as a term can be recovered by integrating a more sophisticated notion of ideology within feminist theory. Patriarchy is most visible in authoritarian systems, such as the right wing Christian fundamentalism of the Promise Keepers.

femaleness as fundamental categories. We will explore this possibility in the final two sections of this chapter.

Now we have some idea about what feminism and feminist psychology are all about, but how does feminist psychology relate to critical social psychology? Feminist thought, from within as well as from outside psychology, has in recent times been one of the major stimuli for critical social psychology. As well as bringing to the fore new topic areas, feminist social psychology has highlighted a number of ways in which mainstream psychology is complicit with, and supportive of, patriarchal ideas. However, some feminist psychologists feel that to characterize feminist psychology as a 'type' of critical social psychology is 'to obliterate feminist psychology's passionate driving force: its central – and overt – political goals' (Wilkinson, 1997: 179), goals which critical social psychology may neglect. So while feminist psychology has contributed to critical social psychology, it is more than a mere facet of it.

We now have some idea about what feminist psychology is, why it is important and how it relates to critical psychology. The rest of this chapter will be devoted to examining some of the key issues that have arisen in feminist psychology, starting with some of the earliest critical social research done from a feminist perspective.

Sexism and the legitimation of gender inequalities

One way for feminist psychology to challenge the *status quo* is to examine how taken-for-granted assumptions about gender are built into people's everyday descriptions and accounts. Here we look at two classic studies of accounts of gender inequality. The interest for feminist researchers in psychology is twofold: firstly, how are particular versions of gender relations taken for granted, and made to seem natural? And secondly, how are inequalities of income and opportunity presented in a way that attends to the speakers' own accountability?

Unequal egalitarianism

Margaret Wetherell et al. (1987) studied the way university students talked about women's career opportunities when they were given the opportunity in open-ended interviews. Conversational interviews of this type have been common in discourse analytic research, as we shall see in Chapter 7, because they allow participants to provide extended descriptions, explanations and judgements in their interaction with the interviewer. Close analysis of the interviews found that people supported the *principle* of women's career opportunities and attacked discrimination based on gender.

The researchers drew on a theoretical and analytic notion called an 'interpretative repertoire'. This consists of coherent clusters of words, often organized around central metaphors. They can be thought of as little packages of ideas that people use to make sense of and evaluate the world. One of the interpretative repertoires that Wetherell and her colleagues found in the interviews emphasized equal opportunities and egalitarianism. Here are a female and a male participant drawing on the equality repertoire.

> *Female*. I would expect the father to do his equal share in bringing them up. I would take great offence to the father turning round and saying, they're your duty, you look after them.

> *Male*. It's very hard to see their point of view, because I've never been, I've never been a male chauvinist, so, I mean, I just, on the business side, women are just as good as men, I mean if not better, I mean obviously perfectly equal.

Most of the participants said things of this kind, and if you collected them all together they would seem to be overwhelmingly in favour of gender equality. However, they also offered a wide range of *practical* reasons for the actual failure of women to reach full employment equality, including references to such concerns as child care, tradition and emotional unsuitability for stressful work. So alongside the equality repertoire it was possible to trace out a second repertoire that emphasized practical considerations. Here are some illustrations.

> *Female*. I said that to some friends the other night who have got children and they said, yeah, well, that's what we thought as well, and one of them was high up in management but once her children came along that was it, she just, all these maternal urges came surging out of her and she just couldn't go back to work again.

> *Male*. I mean there are other considerations, like by and large women are probably better for bringing up children in the home, so, uh, you know, if they're all working then they are not going to be able to do that which . . . you know wouldn't be good.

This was a rather looser repertoire, with a very wide range of different explanations and ideas drawn on as practical problems with equality. Interestingly from a psychology and gender point of view, many features of this repertoire involve intrinsic, inbuilt psychological characteristics of mothers.

Note the significance of the pattern of contrasting accounts. The students involved in the study were able to present themselves as pro-equality while at the same time offering a variety of practical reasons why equality had to be limited. They were what the authors of the study called *unequal egalitarians*. In a political sense, then, the deployment of these contradictory repertoires could be said to maintain the *status quo* in which women are expected to achieve less than men in the workplace.

This is quite a simple study (although supported by many others in discursive psychology – see Chapter 7) but it has radical implications for traditional social psychological accounts of prejudice and social change. It is quite common to treat issues of inequality such as this in terms of attitude change. People need to have their attitudes to women (or old people, or people with learning difficulties) changed so equality can be promoted. The problem with this seemingly obvious idea is that the unequal egalitarians studied here have no trouble in making broad declarations about equality. If an attitude change programme was needed, it has produced this outcome. Yet the broad declarations of positive attitude are not enough to promote equality in practice, because other considerations come into play. The lesson is a monumental one for traditional social psychologists (most still haven't learnt it): *social change is not dependent on attitude change, but needs to consider arguments and their organization in talk.*

Justifying injustice

Ros Gill (1993) drew on and developed the unequal egalitarians study, showing that its implications went beyond interviews with students talking about relatively abstract dilemmas to people involved with hiring and firing in actual situations. She studied disc jockeys' and programme controllers' accounts of being on the radio. How did they explain the huge imbalance of representation of men and women in DJ jobs on the radio?

She found that inequalities were both explained and justified by a weave of contrary accounts. Again she identified a number of repertoires to organize these accounts. Here is a disc jockey explaining the inequality as due to 'audience objections':

> *DJ.* Research has proven (.) and this is not mine but it's echoed by many surveys throughout the years (.) that people prefer to listen to a man's voice on the radio rather than a woman's voice. Women like to hear men on the radio because they're used to it (.) and it's a bit strange to have a woman talking to you. And men like hearing men on the radio (.) perhaps because they're just chauvinistic. Whatever the reasons, research has borne out this fact, you know, that people like to have men on the radio (.) and we just go along with the consensus of opinion. We do have women – Marie does an admirable job on the phone-in. We've got a lot of women newscasters so you know there's certainly no prejudice.

Here inequality is justified by appealing to what other people – the audience, both 'women' and 'men' and also 'research' – have forced upon the radio station. The DJ speaker is not himself being divisive or chauvinistic, but simply going along with public opinion in the way that people involved in broadcasting have to.

Another example is an idea that women have special voices:

> *DJ.* As I said to you before (.) people are sensitive to voice (.) they pick up a lot in a voice. They can see it as exuding friendliness, sarcasm, angriness or whatever and if it happens to be (.) and if a woman's voice sounds grating or high (.) shrill, then that will switch them off. If it sounds dusky and sexy (1.0)

unfortunately that switches them on (.) now Marie has got a dusky, sexy, deep voice perfect for it (.) she's actually nothing like that when you meet her (.) she's a very sweet lady but she's not like that but people are conned totally by the voice.

Again there is an appeal to what 'people' want and like in a woman's voice, along with a rather disturbing opposition between women who are 'dusky' and 'sexy' and 'ladies' who are 'very sweet'.

Overall, Gill's study shows DJs and controllers describing and justifying their recruiting practices. Gill shows how their accounts typically treat inequalities in hiring as the responsibility of the women (they are not competent, they sound funny) or the audience (they prefer men, they don't like women's voices) rather than of the stations themselves. Accounts are constructed to portray the lack of recruitment of women as a product of external factors rather than of the speaker's own desires or motives.

As Gill (1993: 98) suggests:

The role of the radio station was made invisible in these accounts, and discussions of the employment practices and institutional sexism were conspicuous by their absence. In this way broadcasters were able to present themselves as non-sexist, whilst they simultaneously justified the lack of women at the radio station.

Wetherell and colleagues, as well as Gill, are doing research that is described as *discourse analysis*. We will discuss this in detail in Chapter 7. For the moment it should be emphasized that discourse analysis takes talk as a medium for doing things. For example, Wetherell et al.'s unequal egalitarians are presenting themselves as egalitarian (and therefore, sympathetic and modern) while using a range of ideas to construct practical limits on equality.

Ideas of this kind were developed by Michael Billig and others (1988), who suggested that we consider everyday reasoning of this kind in terms of dilemmas. We will consider this work in more detail in Chapter 7. For the moment, we can note that their argument is that the contradictory patterns seen in these studies are characteristic of everyday talking and arguing. These dilemmas are often *ideological* in the sense that they relate to broader societal concerns with authority, legitimation and social organization (see Chapter 3 for further discussion of ideology). In both the above examples it is possible to see that the tension between egalitarian values and discriminatory practice is not a problem for the stability of the institution; quite the reverse, the ability to do these contradictory things – emphasize equality, note practical reasons why it is not possible – is one of the things that *sustain* stability. The point, then, is that *political power and the* status quo *are sustained by the contradictory or rhetorical nature of ideologies or discourses*. The force of a political perspective *does not rely on its internal coherence*. This is important if we are considering what it means to have a political perspective, and what constitutes a persuasive one.

Conclusion

This section has examined some early feminist discourse research, and two main themes are evident. Firstly there has been a concern with how certain traditional versions of gender relations are made to seem natural and obvious. But why may this type of work be important? Some people have some old-fashioned ideas about gender. So what? I think the value of this type of study is that it challenges 'gender essentialism', that is, the idea that there are certain essential, biologically based or psychologically universal features of gender. If gender is something that resides within us due to bodies – because of hormones or biology or whatever – then in terms of political organization and policy making it is an easy step to arguing that our social relations *should* be moulded around these differences. If we accept an essentialist, traditional, conservative version of gender we are likely to be happier with the *status quo* and likely to be hostile to feminist calls for change.

The second theme is seen in the focus on gender in practical situations where speakers are managing the responsibility for their own actions. Gill's DJs, for example, are attending to their own responsibility for the unequal gender representation on their radio stations. The version of gender they produce is not an abstract piece of theory but a version for practical use. The research is showing how an essentialist notion of gender is produced in a particular setting to do a particular job. Essentialism does not have any problem in getting employment in this talk!

What can we take away from this style of research that studies the way people construct gender in their talk for particular purposes? One thing it does is to free the researcher from the sort of essentialism that is endemic in traditional sex differences research. It also shows that traditional arguments for equality have been effective. Almost all the people who took part in these studies made a virtue of equality, and none of them argued for a return to Victorian subservience (although there were no Promise Keepers in the sample!). Nevertheless, these studies show this is only the first step. Arguments for equality need to be blended with visions for new possibilities of change in social and gender relations, and arguments that are critical of the sorts of practical considerations used against equality.

The focus on feminism and social constructionism, the relevance of these things to real-world problems, and the dilemmas that are raised in the process, are all issues at the heart of the next section.

Heterosexism and lesbian and gay psychology

What is meant by heterosexism? Feminist psychologists have used 'heterosexism' as a way of distancing themselves from the reactionary implications of the term 'homophobia'. Homophobia implies that anti-gay and lesbian talk or actions are a result of individual pathology, rather than something embedded in existing social relations and practices that we all need to address (e.g. Kitzinger et al., 1992; Kitzinger, 1996; Speer and Potter 2000). This section will assess some of the classic work on heterosexism by Celia Kitzinger and Judith Butler.

Kitzinger and the social construction of lesbianism

In her classic work on lesbianism, Celia Kitzinger (1987) draws attention to the rhetorical nature of scientific writing as well as exposing some of the more outlandish claims thrown up by so-called objective scientific research. She criticizes the 'pathological' model of lesbianism, which sees lesbianism as arising from some kind of physical or mental disorder, claiming that this view has attracted such wide criticism that it is no longer acceptable. However, she is also critical of the movement that has been largely responsible for arguing against the view of homosexuality and lesbianism as pathologies, that is, gay affirmative research.

Gay affirmative research puts in place a notion of lesbianism as 'a normal, natural and healthy sexual preference or lifestyle' (Kitzinger, 1987: 33). However, rather than seeing lesbianism as a lifestyle choice that can be integrated into, and will contribute to, the existing social order, Kitzinger argues for a radical lesbian position, which sees lesbianism as 'the greatest threat that exists to male supremacy' (Kitzinger, 1987: 64). Indeed, Kitzinger claims that gay affirmative research is just as effective as the 'pathological model' in turning lesbianism into an individual and apolitical lifestyle choice. How does it do this?

Kitzinger suggests that the problem with gay affirmative research is that it stems from the ideological position of liberal humanism. (The implications of a liberalist view of society were discussed in Chapter 1; see also Chapter 8 for a critique of humanism.) This is because it treats lesbianism as an object that can be investigated using rational and impartial scientific methods, with the aim of revealing its 'true nature'. Although it turns out that this 'true nature' is exactly what is required by the patriarchal social order. By replicating the positivist and empiricist model of science, gay affirmative research replicates the same categories that maintain patriarchal structures, and what she describes as the same 'psychological terrorism' that characterizes other humanist endeavours. According to Kitzinger, what we need is to be committed to 'deconstructing' our everyday expectations about gender and social organization, and the way to achieve this is through using a social constructionist approach.

Kitzinger (1989) builds on these discussions of the implications of liberal humanism. Kitzinger argues that identities are not the private property of individuals; rather they are social constructions that can be promoted in line with the dominant social order. She again argues against the liberal humanist ideology that some lesbians adopt, in which personal happiness and fulfilment are valued more highly than the political goals of women's liberation. By focusing on personal fulfilment as the ultimate goal, the liberal humanist ideology encourages us to reaffirm the values of the dominant patriarchal social system.

Kitzinger bases her specific research claims on a 'Q methodological' study of lesbian identity. This involves sorting statements about lesbianism into groupings. Since then she has changed her analytic approach considerably, arguing for the benefits of conversation analysis to avoid some of the problematic assumptions about the nature of language and lesbian identities (see Chapter 7 and 'Where next?' below).

Celia Kitzinger

Celia Kitzinger is a lesbian feminist psychologist whose major contribution has been to put lesbian and gay issues on the agenda – both for critical psychology and for psychology as a discipline. She has published ten books and around a hundred articles on issues relevant to challenging sexism and heterosexism – including the now classic The Social Construction of Lesbianism *(1987) and the edited books* Heterosexuality *(with Sue Wilkinson, 1993) and* Lesbian and Gay Psychology *(with Adrian Coyle, 2002). She spearheaded the campaign for a BPS Lesbian and Gay Psychology Section (founded in 1999 after three defeated attempts) and acted as its inaugural chair, in which capacity she strove to influence BPS scientific statements on British legal issues such as the age of consent and civil unions for lesbians and gay men. She has argued for theoretical and methodological pluralism in pursuit of social and political change and her own research embraces both social constructionist and essentialist perspectives. Her most recent work uses conversation analysis to develop an understanding of how the everyday heterosexist world is produced, reproduced and resisted.*

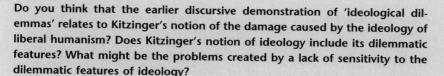

CRITICAL DILEMMA

Do you think that the earlier discursive demonstration of 'ideological dilemmas' relates to Kitzinger's notion of the damage caused by the ideology of liberal humanism? Does Kitzinger's notion of ideology include its dilemmatic features? What might be the problems created by a lack of sensitivity to the dilemmatic features of ideology?

Overall Kitzinger's work has made a major contribution to feminist psychology. It opened up debates about heterosexism, feminist politics and sexuality that still continue. Her refusal simply to accept definitions of what is 'gay affirmative' also encourages serious questioning about the role of the 'inner world' and 'subjectivity' in feminist psychological research. Her work can be usefully contrasted with a more complex and heavily theorized take on heterosexism coming from the US cultural critic Judith Butler. So, taking a deep breath, let us consider her work.

Judith Butler and the lesbian phallus

In Chapter 4 we explored Lacan's notion of the phallus. The phallus for Lacan is the ultimate signifying mechanism through which we gain our original perceptions of difference. Our 'selves' are developed through the operation of this masculine regulatory principle. Butler attempts to destabilize the heterosexist signifying chain (see the discussion of Saussure and structuralism in Chapter 8 to elucidate the notion of signs and signification) that operates in Lacan's theorizing: the idea that the phallus is still dependent on the existence of the penis. Butler claims that despite operating at a symbolic level, it is still the case that, by virtue of having a penis, men are symbolized as 'having' in a way that women are not – there is a relation of identity between phallus and penis. As a way of destabilizing this, Butler introduces the notion of the lesbian phallus. She suggests (1993: 88) that:

> The simultaneous acts of depriviling the phallus and removing it from the normative heterosexual form of exchange, and recirculating and repriviling it between women, deploys the phallus to break the signifying chain in which it conventionally operates.

Because the lesbian 'has' the phallus, while also not 'having' it in the traditional sense, there is some flexibility regarding what it means to 'have' one at all. Rather than seeing the phallus as the foundation for further signifying chains, as Lacan claims, Butler suggests that what gives the phallus its privileged status is its continual reiteration as a signifier. The phallus doesn't 'possess' this privileged status in any self-evident way, but is rather reiterated as privileged, and is therefore open to destabilization. The lesbian phallus thus opens up the possibility of resignification and depriviling in relation to anatomy – the supposed site of 'sexual difference' itself – and the masculinist assumptions that this incorporates, as well as to the heterosexism endemic in the Lacanian scheme.

CRITICAL DILEMMA

Shouldn't we be more interested in what our 'signifying systems' are supposed to be signifying – the 'things' themselves, like 'material bodies'? But how would we then make sense of 'materiality' and 'bodies' outside our signifying systems?

Heterosexist talk

Butler's work is heavily influenced by Jacques Derrida (take a few more deep breaths then see Chapter 8). In her more recent work *Excitable Speech* (1997), she uses his notion of 'iterability' (Derrida, 1976) to look at ways in which offensive heterosexist speech can be subverted. Derrida suggests that the meaning of a term is *iterable* – it can be repeated but is never exactly the same. Butler takes up this idea and suggests that if a word is resignifiable in this way then we are not entitled to say that it will always mean the same thing; words that have the power to injure (heterosexist talk) can be subverted. Terms such as 'dyke', for example, 'can be reclaimed, or "returned" to the speaker in a different form' (1997: 14, cited in Speer and Potter, 2002). This means that legislation on the use of offensive words is probably not the best way forward.

Discursive directions. Susan Speer's research adopts a discursive psychological perspective, and one of her aims has been to refine the kind of approach developed by Butler, and explore in more detail what counts as a derogatory remark. The discursive perspective displays how words do not come with their negativity built into them, but need to be worked up as such. Gay men and lesbians, for example, sometimes use terms like 'queen', 'queer' and 'dyke' in affectionate ways.

It follows that making hard-and-fast distinctions about what counts as heterosexist talk is misguided. Instead we need to pay close attention to participants' talk, and particularly its interactional context. This will allow more sophisticated insights into how hearably heterosexist, derogatory remarks are constructed and oriented to by others (Speer and Potter, 2000).

Conclusion

There has been a gradual move towards more post-structuralist, discursive positions in research concerned with heterosexism. This reflects the move away from seeing gender as something tied to people's bodies, and towards seeing it instead as being located in discursive practices. Butler asserts that we can produce a politics of change and difference by producing affirmative images, living positive alternative lifestyles, and disrupting assumptions in the practical politics of everyday life. Debates about heterosexism bring to the fore assumptions about heterosexuality as the norm in Western culture – it shows how ingrained it is both in psychology as an institution and in other social practices. Speer's work develops this by emphasizing how heterosexism is done conversationally – how it is assumed, ironized and undermined in everyday interactions.

Nevertheless, there is a historical and cultural context in which gender is easily equated with biology and bodies. Women in particular have been encouraged to evaluate themselves and each other in terms of the shape of their bodies. It is to this topic that we now turn.

Eating disorders and the body

Nawal El Saadawi is an Egyptian feminist activist, writer and physician, whose publications focus on the oppression of women in the Arab world. The Egyptian government has banned her books for the past three decades, and has shut down her women's organization and her feminist magazine, which have campaigned among other things to end female genital mutilation. Islamic fundamentalists put her on their death list in the early 1990s. In an interview (in Daly, 1998: 79) she remembers that as a medical student in the 1950s, there were no veiled women. Now 80 per cent of women in universities and schools are veiled. In Iran women are not allowed to reveal parts of their body other than their hands and their face. They are not allowed to organize themselves into interest groups. Women need sixteen reasons for getting divorced whilst men do not need any reasons. And finally, women are not allowed to go out of the country if their spouse objects. Lest we be tempted to disparage the Middle East as an extreme case, El Saadawi makes connections between different brands of fundamentalism around the world, including Christian fundamentalists in the United States, one particularly sinister example being the Promise Keepers, whom we encountered earlier.

The point here is that women's oppression is often centred on their bodies. Women's bodies become something dangerous, to be hidden, or some criterion for positive or negative evaluations. This section will focus on Helen Malson's research into anorexia, and will also cover work by Jane Ussher.

Helen Malson's book *The Thin Woman* (1998) is an exploration of the issue of gender and 'the body', in the context of the problem of anorexia nervosa. She has attempted to study anorexia in a way that does not see it as a problem emerging from the psychology of individual women and their 'pathologies'. She adopts the strong anti-individualist stance common to many critical psychologists. She also adopts a post-structuralist framework which she suggests enables acknowledgement of the complexity of anorexia's '*multiple* socio-cultural and gender-specific locations; a framework that enables us to explore its multiple discursively constituted meanings' (1998: 6, emphasis in original). In this she is influenced by work on eating and discourse by Margaret Wetherell (1996).

Because of this post-structuralist focus (see below for more on postmodern/post-structuralist feminism), the idea of producing more 'knowledge' about anorexia is seen as problematic, as if it existed as a clinical entity, a thing in itself. Instead Malson is concerned to examine the supposed 'facts, fictions and fantasises' of anorexia and femaleness. She begins with a historical look at how anorexia has moved from being thought of as a theological matter to being characterized within the emerging medical discourses of the Georgian and Victorian eras. Here the female body was constituted as 'nervous' and 'hysterical': so no further explanation, apart from the fact that one is 'female', was needed for why anorexia might be taking place.

By contrast, in contemporary thought there are now multiple 'anorexias' constituted through a wide range of clinical and academic discourses. In her exploration of interview talk with women diagnosed as 'anorexic' (a discourse analysis of 'interpretative repertoires' following the earlier style of work developed by Potter and Wetherell – see Chapter 7) Malson found that participants had multiple ways of mobilizing the thin or anorexic body. For example, the body may be constructed as attractive in a heterosexual sense – signifying romantic femininity as delicate and weak, requiring protection. On the other hand the same body could be constructed as androgynous or boyishly thin, signifying a rejection of 'traditional femininity'.

Malson explores 'the discourse of Cartesian dualism' – the pervasive idea of a mind-body split, in which the body can be seen as threatening and alien to the mind or self. This provides people with both the problem (the need to control the body) and the solution – the construction of a subjectivity that can provide some control and order. Women are thus encouraged to produce a self-governing individual such that their problems become individual ones related to socio-cultural and political factors. Malson's analysis also reveals that anorexia can be both 'self-productive' and 'self-destructive'.

Malson's analysis of participants' talk is similar to the kind of discourse analytic research we have already discussed. Readers are presented with small extracts of talk, which are not transcribed in a way that allows us to hear how things are being said – there is little indication of pauses, overlaps, intonation and so on, clues which can make a huge difference to the meaning of an utterance. Neither are readers given much of a feel for the conversational context in which the women are speaking – often what is presented is the interviewee's talk on its own, without the interviewer's question or prior turn that led them to speak in the way that they did. Although it is interesting and makes some important points, there is, as we shall see a bit later with the work of Sally Wiggins, the possibility of a more contextualised and fine-grained discursive psychology of eating and body talk.

Jane Ussher and women's bodies

Jane Ussher has written widely on women's bodies (e.g. 1989) and women's madness (e.g. 1991). In her later work she draws these threads together, and argues for a strong social constructionist perspective. This should help us understand women's madness in a way that denies 'the influence of biology or genetics, and diminishing the meaning ascribed to the body in general' (Ussher, 2000: 218). Ussher feels that madness is a phenomenon experienced by women at different levels – material, discursive and intrapsychic – and that all three need to be explored in making sense of women's madness. As with Lucy Yardley's work (1997) there is a call for 'materiality' – some experiential or physical grounding for discourses of health and illness. There are experiencing bodies behind the discourses.

CRITICAL DILEMMA

Compare Ussher's claims about the importance of the material and intrapsychic dimensions of woman's madness with Butler's focus on the lesbian phallus as a way of destabilizing these types of 'essentialist' accounts. Which do you think is most useful for understanding women and their 'problems'?

In more recent work Ussher (1997) explores the paradoxical associations between 'woman' and 'sex'. On the one hand, media representations of women are infused with sex; on the other, women face a long history of condemnation for any signs of exploration or enjoyment of their own sexual desires. Ussher bases her study on explorations of 'woman' in art, film and pornography, as well as interviews with women and men, beginning with a survey of 'fantasies of femininity' via fairy stories, where a girl gains salvation through the prince. The salvation is dependent on her being 'fair of face', of course, if she is 'ugly' then she is probably 'bad' – more body evaluations. Although most of us may feel unscathed by these early discourses, the danger, according to Ussher, quoting feminist iconoclast Andrea Dworkin, is that these fantasies are still there 'chewed but still lying in the stomach, as real identity'. So the important question for a feminist scholar becomes 'How, and why, do women take up the script of femininity, and become "woman"?' (Ussher, 1997: 11). More recently many feminists have started to ask whether this question relates to the question of how we become *embodied* as women.

Embodiment

Those focusing their theoretical energies on embodiment often wish to distinguish themselves from discursive and constructionist approaches in psychology (see Chapter 7). Indeed, the body has become something of a terrain for theoretical conflict between different camps of thinkers. There is a growing body of critical work that sees embodiment as a potential problem for discursive psychology's interactional focus (e.g. Burr, 1995, 1999; Parker, 1998; Gergen, 1999; Willig, 2000). To take one example, Ian Burkitt (1999) states:

> I am unhappy with discursive constructionism because it has difficulties in dealing with human embodiment and also, therefore, with the multi-dimensional way in which we experience reality . . . persons are not simply constructs, but are *productive bodies . . . communicative bodies . . . powerful bodies . . . thinking bodies.*
>
> (p. 2, emphasis in original)

For Burkitt the body is not 'simply' something social but is also a 'natural construction', and indeed a 'malleable organism'. Through the possession of a body we can change our 'social relations'. So although Burkitt claims to be transcending Cartesian mind–body dualism he reinstates other dualities such as natural–social and discourse–reality, in order to appeal to some realm of entities that are 'real' and 'natural' and knowable outside their discursive specificity. This kind of dualistic theorizing where ideas get lodged into either/or binary logic is something that Derrida's deconstructions encourage us to subvert (see Chapter 8).

Burkitt considers this more deconstructive area of thought when he examines feminists' – and particularly Judith Butler's – challenges to dualistic constructions around the body.

Judith Butler and bodies that matter

Butler (1990b) rejects the notion that the body has a materiality prior to its signification, and prefers to seek ways of reading the body as a *signifying practice.* Butler produces a deconstructive criticism of the 'natural' 'realities' of terms such as 'man', 'woman', 'heterosexual', 'homosexual'. The idea that there are primary essences of masculinity and femininity emerging from within the body, giving rise to particular gender identities, is challenged. Instead, masculinity and femininity arise through the performance of gender.

Butler (1993) suggests that notions of 'sex', 'gender' and 'desire' are regulated by a 'heterosexual hegemony' that re/produces discursive constructions of 'masculinity' and 'femininity'. Remember the discussion of hegemony in the previous chapter; it is a notion that refers to the internalization of assumptions so they become natural and taken for granted. The 'heterosexual hegemony' is the set of taken-for-granted assumptions that treat sexuality as heterosexual. The discursive constructions of heterosexual hegemony give rise to the 'symbolic law of sex'. These constructions include the 'homosexual taboo', which Butler sees as more problematic than the Freudian 'incest taboo' organizing the Oedipus complex.

However, Burkitt (1999) does not like Butler's formulations, and wants to retain some notion of pre-discursive materiality – 'Butler's writings submerge the bodily and the material beneath the text and autonomize language as the precondition of all being . . . of the material body itself' (1999: 95). Burkitt's basic premise then is that there is some material reality knowable independently of our ability to construct it discursively. He judges positions which want to examine this premise and hold it up for question as simply wrong, because they don't accept that premise. This inability to engage with arguments that do not accept a realist paradigm is a common problem with realist/relativist arguments in critical psychology (see Chapter 8).

Butler's interests are more Foucauldian, involving an exploration of how subjectivity is produced through the production of a fictional interior. Gender is created as a 'social temporality' (Butler, 1990b: 141) through the stylized repetition of gestures and movements: our bodies are materialized through the performance of gender. We do not act the way we do because we possess a gendered subjectivity, rather that gendered subjectivity is sustained as such by its continued performance.

As we saw in the previous section, lesbian and gay researchers aiming to 'prove' the biological underpinnings of homosexuality, or simply lesbian and gay people who have struggled hard to come out, can have difficulty with this post-structuralist notion that their sexuality is 'merely' a performance. The implication of the notion of performance in this traditional sense is that it has been a free choice to act in this way, and that the chooser is therefore morally culpable. This does not capture the sense that many of us have of our sexuality as something emerging from within us. We feel we are recognizing something that already exists rather than re/producing something. But as Foucault shows (Chapter 6), in order to 'recognize' the 'truth' about ourselves, we must employ a whole range of historically contingent discourses of sexuality. Often such discourses can be involved in the production of the 'truth' about 'sexuality' and 'subjectivity', thereby obscuring their status as discourses and making our reflexive appreciation of that status difficult.

Haraway and the cyborg manifesto

Another approach to issues of gender, subjectivity and embodiment comes in the work of Donna Haraway. Haraway has argued that the growth of technoscience, particularly in the areas of communication, computing and genetics, has implications for changes in our understanding of subjectivity and embodiment. Her example of a genetically engineered mouse – OncoMouse™ – that is guaranteed to develop cancer (Haraway, 1992) is an example of what she terms a 'cyborg': a compound of the organic, technical, mythic, textual and political. In her feminist 'Manifesto for Cyborgs' (1991a) she argues for the utility of the cyborg image for feminists, in that it can be mobilized against ideas about 'natural' femininity linked with biology and hormones. It also allows us to subvert the idea that we need universal and correct theories of gender and gender relations. Rather than treating embodiment as a limit to discourse and to what can be socially constructed, Haraway treats bodies, physiology, genetics and robotics as changing possibilities that can enter new narratives. Rather than opposing the material with the political and critical, Haraway wishes to infuse feminist concerns into objects and biology; the cyborg is the both a productive metaphor and a way of highlighting the enmeshing of persons with machines and information systems.

Haraway has taken features of postmodern culture and developed them in the service of a feminist political narrative. This is also evident in her massive study of primatology: *Primate Visions* (1989). Here the study of primates is shown to re/create myths of human origin and reactionary stories about gender and race. As Potter (1996a) suggests, in telling her own tale about these primate stories, Haraway proposes that her study should be treated as a form of science fiction. Although she is telling a story about primatology, the story inevitable draws upon, yet also resists the temptations of, four primary narratives: sociology of scientific knowledge, Marxism, the legitimating narrative of the scientists themselves, and histories of gender and race and their involvement with science. These are stories that risk taking over the account and turning it into 'fact'. Postmodernism involves living with the contradictions and tensions between different narratives rather than trying to produce the definitive version.

Discursive embodiment

One notable development in social psychology is for researchers interested in discourse to consider issues of embodiment. Part of the reason for taking up this issue, apart from its intrinsic significance, has been to show how discourse work can throw light on topics that at first sight seem to be beyond its purview. For example, Sally Wiggins's research (Wiggins et al., 2001; Wiggins, in press) illustrates how embodied practices (Wiggins focuses particularly on eating, though without an explicit gender agenda) can be constructed and used interactionally. She argues (in press) against critical work that sees embodiment as a potential problem for discursive psychology's interactional focus. As we saw above, this type of critical research argues that discursive psychology does not look beyond talk, so cannot take embodiment seriously. The 'extra-discursive' features of bodies are disregarded or overlooked (see also Sampson, 1998; Burkitt, 1999; Burr, 1999; Cromby and Nightingale, 1999).

However, Wiggins's research shows that discursive psychology *can* address issues of embodiment, through an interactional (as opposed to an individual) approach. For example, some of her research focuses on the expression of food 'pleasure', showing through her analysis how it becomes a public act, an inter-actional concern that is part of talk and accounting for actions.

Wiggins concludes that bodies and their pleasurable sensations are con-structed for local, interactional concerns. She is at pains to point out that this does not involve denying the existence of the body, suggesting instead that the actual *form* of how bodies are represented is dependent on their discursive construction (Edwards et al., 1995; Miller, 2000).

Nikki Parker (2001) develops a similar criticism of Nightingale and Cromby's (1999) research into embodiment in critical social psychology. She uses Gergen's (1999) theoretical explorations of social constructionism to show how Nightingale and Cromby are confused about exactly what social constructionism is. Showing how they mix social constructionism up with various other things, Parker suggests that they should call what they do something else rather than turn social con-structionism into a theory of the body, the subject or materiality. As Gergen points out, pre-theorized ontology is not the job of social constructionism. Chapter 7 discusses social constructionism in more detail.

Conclusion

Research into women's bodies, and embodiment generally, is mixed. Some of it seems to have slid (not surprisingly) into more essentialist notions of gender and sexuality. The pull of dominant traditions and 'scientific' ways of making sense of humanness generally, and human bodies more specifically, is a strong one. Malson's research is focused on building a more post-structuralist perspective, in which it is suggested that bodies are made into material objects through discourse. Butler argues for an anti-essentialist approach, and new researchers such as Wiggins are respecifying embodiment discursively. In order to be in a better position to make sense of these debates we need to develop a clear understanding of the issues facing post-structuralist feminist research.

Postmodern feminists: contemporary debates

This section will explore two broad areas. First it will examine some of the debates around 'modern' versus postmodern feminist practice. This sets up a number of issues that Judith Butler engages with, so her work will be explored in the second section.

Postmodernism and femininity

This section will begin by examining and clarifying the pros and cons of adopting a postmodern (incorporating a post-structuralist − see Chapter 8 for discussion of the links between postmodernism and post-structuralism) feminist approach. For the purposes of rhetorical clarity and pedagogic value, and for those unfamiliar with these debates, this involves utilizing the horrendously neat and dangerously polarized categories of 'modern' and 'postmodern'.

The artificial construction of a debate around 'modernism' versus 'postmodernism' has divided liberal emancipatory (and so 'modern') feminists from postmodern feminism. Liberal feminists seek the emancipation of women, without necessarily disrupting existing social institutions. This relates to Kitzinger's complaints about gay affirmative research that adopts a liberal humanist ideology. The dilemma within the modernist paradigm is therefore whether to *either* coexist with men in this emancipatory way *or*, more radically, to forge a separate route for women. For feminists in the modernist tradition, feminism involves 'the ideology of a female nature or female essence reappropriated by feminists themselves in an effort to revalidate undervalued female attributes' (Alcoff, 1988: 408).

By contrast, postmodern/post-structuralist feminists generally seek to problematize the category 'woman', as we saw earlier with Butler's work, and to some extent with Malson's. The choice is not simply between assimilating women to 'malestream' categories and constructing a unique voice for women. To do either of these things is to construct woman as a homogeneous category and to employ this as the baseline for further recommendations. From a postmodern perspective the way to disrupt the oppression of women is rather to recognize that any attempt to construct the meaning or truth of what 'woman' is will be exclusionary and repressive. Working with a fixed idea about what constitutes women's oppression excludes the possibility that oppression may not be the same for all women.

For the postmodern feminist, the problem with the modernist feminist response is that it misses the way oppression works discursively – it:

> does not criticize the fundamental mechanism of oppressive power used to perpetuate sexism and in fact reinvokes that mechanism in its supposed solution. The mechanism of power referred to here is the construction of the subject by a discourse that weaves knowledge and power into a coercive structure . . .
>
> (Alcoff, 1988: 415)

By seeking to mobilize around some essential feminine identity, the modernist feminist is in danger of missing out on the Foucauldian sense in which identity can be constructed through a profound, discursively organized subjection (e.g. see Foucault, 1982, and the discussion in Chapter 6). We therefore need to take a deconstructive line – to try to understand the use to which the discursive notion of an 'essential female identity' is being put, rather than simply to accept it as given. It is this structure of signification *itself* that is the focus for deconstructing potentially oppressive frameworks.

In response to this criticism, modernist feminists would point to the fact that for centuries women have been denied the position of subject, and have been defined as lacking, as 'other'. They suggest that, in order to gain a strong political voice, feminists need to steer clear of the postmodern trap that would deny us our own language and experiences. Developing a deconstructive counter to this type of argument, Peggy Kamuf has the following challenge:

if feminist theory lets itself be guided by questions such as what is women's language, literature, style or experience, from where does it get its faith . . . if not from the same central store that supplies humanism with its faith in the universal truth of man? . . . will it have done anything more than reproduce the structure of woman's exclusion in the same code which has been extended to include her?

(Kamuf, 1982: 44–5)

The fixity which keeps women's 'language, literature, style or experience' as exclusively women's is the same fixity which organizes humanist accounts – the metanarrative which extols us to seek universal truths within ourselves. The postmodern feminist would seek to replace unitary ideas about identity with the more fluid postmodern variety – 'with plural and complexly constructed conceptions of social identity, treating gender as one relevant strand among others, attending also to class, race, ethnicity, age, and sexual orientation' as Nancy Fraser and Linda Nicholson (1988: 101) suggest.

However, these easy categorizations are easily disrupted. Some would see Julia Kristeva as a postmodern feminist thinker, yet Kristeva (e.g. 1980) sees the unconscious as the preliminary to meaning – it is capable of disrupting signification. Rather than being stuck outside meaning, women are capable of both withholding and allowing meaning, and are therefore in a position to disrupt the dominant symbolic order of meaning.

Similarly for Luce Irigaray, another broadly postmodern feminist, women are 'this sex which is not one' (1985). As we saw in our survey of psychoanalysis, women have been written into theories of sexuality as imaginary, incomplete, as empty signifiers. This leaves us with two options – either there is no feminine sexuality, except as it is imagined by men, or feminine sexuality is a schizoid duality which is simultaneously subordinate to the needs and desires of men, and explorable only within a completely separated women's movement. In critical psychology, Corinne Squire's work (1989, 1995; see box, p. 94) has been post-structuralist while forging links with psychoanalysis.

CRITICAL DILEMMA

We have a choice: we could accept some aspect of our essential femaleness as the basis of our feminist theory and politics, or we can reject such a move as we would reject all attempts to 'produce' people in particular fixed ways. Which option do you prefer? On what do you base your preference?

One way to clarify what is at stake in the dilemmas produced by the cross-fertilization of psychoanalysis, postmodernism and feminism can be found by thinking our way further through the work of Judith Butler.

Judith Butler

Judith Butler has played a significant part in the development of queer theory (see box), revolutionizing our appreciation of the constructedness of sex, gender and desire. Her concern, as we saw above in the development of the lesbian phallus, is to denaturalize what it is to be a 'woman' and what is meant by 'sexuality'. Butler conceptualizes gender as a 'discursive practice', and gender identity as a 'performative' accomplishment. Performative (a term originally developed by Austin, 1962, and extended by Derrida, 1982c) acts are both constrained and enabled through repetition, or the 'iterability' of signs (see Chapter 8), and are therefore to be understood in a post-structuralist sense, and not in a realist one, where there would be an agent choosing to put on a performance of gender, implying some kind of pretence.

BOX 5.2   Queer theory

Queer theory addresses gay and lesbian topics in relation to post-structuralist theory – for example, Foucault's studies of subjectivity, power and knowledge (see Chapter 6), Butler's notion of the lesbian phallus (see above) and Derrida's deconstructions (see Chapter 8). Diana Fuss (1991) applied Derrida's notion of the 'supplement' to an analysis of the binary opposition homosexual–heterosexual. The supplement is characterized by its appearance as an *addition* to some presumed original, as homosexual is to heterosexual. Other oppositions support this state of hierarchical binary logic – Fuss (1991) warns of the dangers of 'inside–outside'. Declaring oneself 'out' as lesbian or gay may not be as liberating as it seems, as it relies on the fundamental centrality of heterosexuality as well as reinforcing the continued marginalization of those still 'in the closet'.

As Derrida would suggest, we cannot assume the possibility of simply moving outside or inverting existing oppositions. The task for queer theory would be to examine how these types of opposition have shaped our ways of understanding sexuality, and to trace the implications of different forms of understanding for the way we relate to one another. Many queer studies focus on the relations between lesbian and gay sexualities and their cultural production. The question then becomes one of explaining how we come to know ourselves as lesbian, gay, bisexual or straight. Foucault's work suggests that these sexual categories are bound up with a cultural network of discourses which re/create sexuality and gender. Judith Butler (1990b, 1993) has developed this line of thinking. She establishes the discursively constructed nature of gender and sexuality, suggesting that they are structured around a discourse of heterosexuality as the norm of human relationships.

Butler dismisses the claim that feminism needs to have any kind of grounding in materiality. She asks, 'How is it that the materiality of sex is understood as that which only bears cultural constructions and, therefore, cannot be a construction?' (1993: 28), in other words, what grounds do we have for understanding femaleness as somehow prior to its discursive construction?

To say that something is a construction does not mean it is artificial or easily dispensable. This formulation of real versus constructed would be begging the constructionists' questions about existing divisions between material and constructed worlds: divisions that are, after all, imposed by realist positions.

Butler engages in an examination of the 'scenography and topography of construction' while stressing that the 'matrix of power' that organizes this scenography cannot be articulated if we take constructedness and materiality as binary opposites. The following quotation illustrates the importance of *deconstruction* (see Chapter 8) for a postmodern feminist perspective:

> the category of women does not become useless through deconstruction . . .
> Surely it must be possible both to use the term . . . even as one is used and
> positioned by it, and also to subject the term to a critique which interrogates
> the exclusionary operations and differential power relations that construct
> and delimit feminist invocations of 'women' . . . it is a critique without
> which feminism loses its democratizing potential through refusing to engage
> – take stock of, and become transformed by – the exclusions which put it
> into play.
>
> (Butler, 1993: 29)

Here Butler struggles with the use of the category 'woman'. As we have seen, feminist debate has in some ways polarized around this issue, with the 'modernist side' insisting that feminism does not make sense without the term 'woman', while the 'postmodern side' warns against the dangers of unreflexively taking on board terms like 'woman', which have been central to our continued oppression.

Borrowing another Derridean term, Butler emphasizes the importance of a kind of *double movement*, which allows feminists to have political identification and recognition, while maintaining the constructionist necessity that this kind of identification should itself be perpetually open to examination and reinscription. She also stresses the importance of developing a multiplicity of identificatory sites, rather than advocating a single identity around which to mobilize.

Conclusion

This section has clarified arguments for and against postmodern feminist practice, serving as a considerable simplification of a large and diverse body of feminist theorizing. It is interesting to note that what is often at stake in these arguments is the status of 'knowledge' that we can have about humanness, or more specifically what it is to be human and female. The following section will go on to examine some of the implications that these epistemological debates can have for the practice of feminist psychology.

Feminism and relativism

This section will begin with a review of feminist psychologists' arguments against relativism, some of whom have argued that discourse analysis's theoretical commitment to *relativism* (see Chapter 8 for further debates about relativism in critical social psychology) gives us the critical edge we need, yet provides no grounds for 'application' in terms of a feminist politics. Here we have a rehearsal of the same arguments between modern and postmodern feminists referred to in the previous section – that in order to develop a strong feminist voice we need some kind of grounding – some kind of 'given' about femaleness. The second part of this section addresses some of these concerns.

Feminist psychologists' arguments against relativism

As I have argued elsewhere (Hepburn, 2000a), feminist critics who make claims about the incompatibility of feminism and relativism have sometimes been arguing from an explicit alternative perspective such as critical realism (e.g. Kitzinger et al., 1992) or psychoanalysis (see Chapter 4), and sometimes the connection between feminism and relativism is treated as intrinsically problematic. The following illustrate the sorts of concerns and criticisms raised:

> For feminists attempting to bring about social change, the relativism and reflexivity of constructionism, discursive and postmodern approaches poses some serious problems. If there is nothing outside the text, then there is no means to assert the existence of even the starkest material realities: war, genocide, slavery, poverty, physical and sexual abuse.
>
> (Wilkinson, 1997: 184)

> If no one set of meanings is more valid than any other, there is no basis (for example) for distinguishing between the rape victim's account of sexual coercion and the rapist's account of pleasurable seduction.
>
> (Wilkinson, 1997: 185)

> Relativists' refusal to engage with questions of value has led to political paralysis. There is no principled way in which they can intervene, choose one version over another, argue for anything.
>
> (Gill, 1995: 177)

> Relativists' refusal to engage with questions of value has also led to political paralysis.
>
> (Wilkinson, 1997: 186)

> In other words, a motivated, partisan political orientation is proscribed. Theory floats disconnected from any political position, and this is a return to a disturbingly familiar liberal pluralist position.
>
> (Parker and Burman, 1993: 167)

I think it's a kind of nihilism . . . To me it's very important to say . . . an incestuous act happened. And it wasn't just someone's interpretation . . . It is very dangerous to say, 'Oh well, there's no external reality, there's only stories, nothing really happens' . . . That's not to say that there aren't different interpretations, but it can get to a point where nothing's real, nothing happened, nothing matters, and nobody knows – and I think that's a dangerous thing for feminists to be saying.

(Gilligan, in Wilkinson, 1997: 185)

Increasingly, research from a [social constructionist] perspective points reflexively to its own socially constructed nature and thus loses the potential rhetorical impact of 'empirically verified facts'.

(Kitzinger, 1995, in Wilkinson, 1997: 185)

The fundamental claim here is that 'commitment to relativism disavows the grounds for feminist politics' (Wilkinson & Kitzinger, 1995: 6) and leads to 'depolitization' (Burman, 1990). These are important arguments, and if they are correct they make a strong case for feminist psychologists to be circumspect in using constructionist perspectives such as discursive psychology, or postmodern perspectives such as those of Butler. So are they correct?

Evaluating the arguments against relativism

Anti-relativist argument can be divided into four points, used sometimes alone and sometimes together. These are: (1) choice between versions; (2) textual idealism; (3) the researcher's feminist commitment; (4) influencing the community. We can spell each one out and indicate the kinds of counter-arguments that are available.

Choice between versions

This is the argument that constructionist perspectives do not provide the basis for choice between different accounts on two levels: (1) between moral or political perspectives, and (2) between claims made by different people (the rapist and rape victim, say). Taking (1) first, the big question here seems to be whether taking an anti-foundationalist position on knowledge, which rejects the sovereignty of the standard truth-production machinery of data, experiments, human nature, reality or God – *necessarily* entails the claim that 'anything goes', that any one position or claim is as good as another.

In defence of their perspective, the proponents of the various constructionist positions argue their cases, with examples, evidence, rhetoric, visions of solidarity and so on (e.g. Edwards et al., 1995; Potter, 1998). As Barbara Herrnstein Smith (1997) argues, living without epistemological guarantees does not downgrade choice; instead, it stresses its *centrality and necessity*. It is *not* an argument for 'anything goes'.

Tackling point (2), the issue of choosing between the claims of research participants is of a different order and presents a range of complexities. First, it is worth commenting on the rhetorical construction of the arguments about the relativist's supposed inability to properly choose between participants' versions. Take Sue Wilkinson's suggestion, quoted above, that relativist researchers have no basis for distinguishing between the rape victim's account of sexual coercion and the rapist's account of pleasurable seduction. This implies that relativism involves a perverse insensitivity to the obvious facts of abuse and suffering. Yet, as will be immediately apparent from studying the diversity of work in feminist psychology done under the rubric of post-structuralism, discursive psychology and decon-struction, this is almost the opposite of the case. A predominant concern for researchers using these perspectives has been social criticism including a range of feminist issues to do with desire, exploitation, sexism and subjectivity.

Indeed, a variety of studies have considered the way sexual violence is excused and justified, the way judicial judgements are bound up with assumptions about sexuality, and the way courtroom cross-examination assigns blame (e.g. Wowk, 1984; Drew, 1992; Matoesian, 1993; Coates et al., 1994; Wood & Rennie, 1994; Davies, 1995; Frohmann, 1998; MacMartin, 2002). These 'discourse' studies are not denying the awfulness of sexual assault; it is precisely the concern that motivates them.

At a broader level, it should be stressed that a central feature of construc-tionist perspectives is the consideration of claims (about sexual pleasure, say) as rhetorically oriented, and understood on their occasions of use as related to issues like *stake* and *interest* (Potter, 1996a; these terms are explained in Chapter 7). For this reason, the relativist's criteria for judging diverse claims are *different* from the traditional realist criteria. They move away from whether or not claims represent some reality towards *what these different claims are doing for different participants in different contexts.* How is a claim about sexual pleasure, for example, used as part of a discounting strategy on behalf of someone accused of 'date rape'? To suggest that all claims are equally valid for the relativist is to understand the arguments from within a realist paradigm, in which access to the 'real' provides criteria for making judgements. This employs circular reasoning, as well as begging the relativists' question about the status of the 'real'.

Textual idealism

The argument here is that constructionist perspectives have no way to encompass the real, material, worldly phenomena that are central to feminism. These may be such things as incestuous acts, the experiences of rape victims, and the facts of power and patriarchy.

As with the argument about choice between versions, the way this issue has been formulated presupposes a particular realist or *objectivist* orientation. 'Objec-tivist' is a term used by Barbara Herrnstein Smith (1988) to describe those who seek objective reality. The argument treats the existence of particular objects as both obvious to the anti-relativist and denied by, or inaccessible to, researchers using constructionist perspectives.

A research concern with 'incest', for example, as a category that is applied as parts of different practices and can be rhetorically worked up and undermined, is not a denial of the significance and awfulness of child sexual abuse. Yet while it is easy to condemn sexual abuse, research, understanding and prevention are much more complex. They involve dealing with descriptions embedded in practices delivered by various interested parties: children, parents, social workers, psychiatrists, social workers, outraged MPs and so on. Constructionists are not persuaded that there is a simple brute reality of 'incest' or 'child sexual abuse' outside, and separable from, those complex practices. However, to claim such things are not simple free-standing objects is not to treat them as any less important or shocking.

The way the anti-relativist arguments are developed here suggests that there is something simple being offered in asserting the existence of 'material realities' such as war and sexual abuse, and this simplicity is being weakened by the constructionist stress on the way these categories are assigned, built up, rhetorically used, embedded in discourses, undermined. However, recognizing such complexity is not a perverse celebration of the limitations of truth, but the result of a huge range of philosophical and analytic work done across the human sciences. It is perfectly appropriate to disagree with such work, but it is surely insufficient merely to legislate the existence of a class of objects that come free from epistemological trouble.

My general argument here has not been that constructionist perspectives are the only ones that enable critical research on topics of feminist interest (although I would elsewhere want to argue their virtues – Hepburn, 1997, 2000a). Instead I have been developing the more modest, but important, case against the way they have been dismissed as purveyors of textual idealism.

The researcher's feminist commitment

The point here is that relativist doubt about foundations of theories or claims makes it hard for the researcher to express commitment to a position or a set of values, and act on that commitment in a political arena.

Let us split the issue of commitment into two. The stronger form of this argument would be that there is something about constructionist perspectives that is *intrinsically* counter to the notion of the feminist researcher being committed to some set of views. The weaker form of the argument would be that it is contingently the case that researchers find it hard to commit to views when they are constructionists. The first form is epistemological; the second is psychological. Let's take the epistemological argument first.

Commitment to something is quite different from treating it as simply objectively the case. Indeed, the official rhetoric of objectivist science is that the scientist is uncommitted and disinterested, pervasively sceptical. The facts do their work by *forcing* themselves on the scientists, who are *forced* to accept their existence (Woolgar, 1988). Commitment is seen as something that is a problem, as it can distort scientific development. So it is unclear how those wanting a traditional objectivist position can claim a monopoly of commitment – indeed, it is not clear *epistemologically* that it ought to be in their position at all!

For constructionists, no position or claim is *simply* forced by the data, by the theory, or whatever. There is always contingency. In contrast to the official objectivist story, commitment may be a *necessity* for holding positions or making claims. To put it another way, *commitment is a perfectly coherent part of the constructionist account of holding positions or espousing beliefs, while for the objectivist or realist it is a potential embarrassment.*

The psychological argument is rather different. This argument has it that the scepticism about foundations, the emphasis on the constructed basis of positions, the awareness of variability and contingency, make it hard for any particular feminist psychologist to hold on to strong commitments. This argument seems to embody a patronizing and psychologically reductive view of feminists. Bronwyn Davies has noted that it also rests on rather weak evidence, making only 'vague reference to specific unnamed others who are incapable of commitment' (1998: 136). The Gilligan argument cited above is typical in its reference to unnamed feminists who '*can* get to a point' where nothing matters. In contrast to this, Davies contends that for her, and the teachers and students she has worked with, an understanding of the inherently constructive nature of self and reality has enabled rather than inhibited action and commitment.

Ultimately the psychological argument seems to depend on the view that objectivist feminists have significantly more commitment to feminist politics and critique than feminists who hold constructionist positions. Like Davies, I see no evidence for this and I feel that feminists who make this argument in the future should provide appropriate evidence.

Influencing the community

This strand of argument holds that the complex and self-referential elements of constructionist positions, combined with avowed doubt about the foundation of claims, make it hard to persuade the research community of claims, let alone the broader community which might act on feminist work.

The issue of community influence is again best treated in two parts: influencing the academic community and influencing the wider community outside academia. With respect to the academic community, it is not at all clear that constructionist perspectives have been unpersuasive. Constructionist and discursive psychological articles are well represented in *Feminism and Psychology*, and it is not uncommon for feminist psychologists to complain that one or other constructionist perspective has *too much* influence. For example, Ros Gill suggests that 'as Erica Burman (1991) points out, discourse analysis has become almost synonymous with critical and (sometimes) feminist research' (Gill, 1995: 168). Whether this is true or not, the huge influence of work by (to perhaps invidiously choose some particular names) Valerie Walkerdine, Wendy Hollway and Margaret Wetherell in Britain, Judith Butler, Mary Gergen and Donna Haraway in North America, and more French thinkers than there is space to list, suggests that objectivist credentials are far from necessary to make an effective intellectual contribution.

It may be the case that many North American feminist psychologists have yet to be convinced of the virtues of constructionist perspectives. Celia Kitzinger (1997), well known for her constructionist and, more recently, conversation analytic work, argues strongly for the *strategic value* of positivist empiricism and individualism in pressing lesbian and gay issues in mainstream psychology. Should constructionists conclude from this that we should re-adopt objectivist perspectives to gain influence with this or any other group? Or is it more intellectually honest, and more effective in the long term, to develop the general case for the contribution that constructionist methods can make in feminist arenas? After all, there is a general argument currently taking place between constructionists (in this case discursive psychologists) and cognitivists, and the outcome of core theoretical and analytic disputes such as this might transform the whole context of persuasion.

The second issue is that of influence in the 'broader' community. There are interesting convergences and differences here. Collections of feminist psychologists have argued for the selective adoption of realist narratives. For example, Corinne Squire (1995: 160) suggests 'tactical essentialism' (attributed to Nicola Gavey, 1989) and Margaret Wetherell suggests that a feminist political programme can be advanced by means of a more subtle 'arbitrary closure', which entails pretence at truth telling (1995: 142). There is nothing anti-relativist about such stances. Indeed, the flexible use of realist discourses for strategic ends has been a major theme in constructionist perspectives. Realism can be a good story. Nevertheless, I think these approaches carry a risk of underestimating and patronizing the broader community. Perhaps intellectual honesty combined with criticism of the pretensions of objectivist psychological work is the most coherent approach here too. Should we not, as feminists, value and work toward a polity that is openly forthright and epistemologically sophisticated?

The issue of persuasion is a deep one with implications for the basis of our work as feminist *academics* (rather than feminist politicians or citizens). I have certainly not wanted to imply that the issues are simple, or that there are no potential costs for those rejecting objectivist perspectives. However, I hope to have at least indicated the case against treating the persuasion argument as *necessarily* troubling to postmodern relativist perspectives.

Conclusion

I have not argued here that objectivist feminists are wrong or incoherent, or that postmodern relativist perspectives are always superior. Rather, the main objective has been to reveal the limitations of the anti-relativist arguments that have recently been developed, and which aim to show the incoherence or impossibility of relativist feminism. Some people will undoubtedly be left still feeling that they want to employ constructionist work, but that they don't want to subscribe to relativism. However, it is important to be clear that, without the relativism of a strong constructionist position, you are left as a researcher with the difficult job of arguing for, and providing evidence of, non-constructionist realities. Some may feel that this is a price worth paying in order to ground their commitment. However, as I have argued, *commitment to something is different from treating it as simply objectively true*, and indeed commitment presents all kinds of difficulties for objectivists or realists, as it obstructs the ability of 'truths' to speak for themselves through their data. In contrast, relativists are in a potentially stronger – and more intellectually honest – position to deal with the many contingencies, arguments and agendas that go with doing feminist and critical research.

Application

One thing that feminist research gives us is a questioning of the boundaries between theory and practice, between the personal and the political. Examples of 'applied' work often come with 'theoretical' notions built in. For example, Sam Warner (1996) employs the theoretical notion of 'normative heterosexuality' to show how it is prescribed for women in high-security mental hospitals. Warner found examples of women being forced to attend discos with men, wear skirts, go to knitting classes and so on. Colleen Heenan (1996) also employs theorized notions of 'the normalizing practices of conventional psychotherapy' (p. 56) in order to develop resistance to such practices in her analysis of a feminist psychotherapy group for women with eating disorders. In making sense of this applied setting, Heenan wants to explore the tensions and possible overlaps between post-structuralist and psychoanalytic discourses in therapy.

So it seems that whatever applied feminist work we carry out, we need to develop a certain vigilance that comes only from reflexive attention to our own theoretical perspectives. This is precisely the kind of thing that Butler's work has shown us – that consciousness raising, denaturalizing, encouraging fundamental changes in our common sense structures, do make a difference. Early discursive work has also shown how our interpretative repertoires can both encourage change and help to maintain the *status quo*, while later developments have urged us to look at practices in everyday settings.

Conclusion

In some ways feminism has been the paradigm of how critical work can change the world: it has helped to drive social reforms and policies. This has led to changes in labour relations and even in everyday personal relations between partners, peers and family members. What feminism has done – and hopefully can continue to do – is open doors to creative new ways of being, and close the doors to oppressive fixed identities, not just for those who will be considered (for whatever reason) 'female' (whatever that may become), but also for those who will be considered to be 'the opposite' (if it is still made sense of in that way). However, as we saw at the start of this chapter, there is no room for complacency – now more than ever is the time for positive reflexive feminist vigilance.

B The best thing about feminism

Feminism has been at the centre of theoretical and analytical practice for decades. It has had a critical focus on a range of different issues to do with selves, bodies, inequalities, oppression, emancipation and social change. Feminist work has been immensely productive and critically focused, engaging with debates of broad consequence. This makes it one of the most exciting areas of academic work today.

W The worst thing about feminism

Like many other areas of academic study, feminism has produced some confused and sloppy theorizing, which can border on the pretentious and mystifying.

Where next?

It will be interesting to see whether the different areas that are emerging around embodiment, psychoanalysis and conversation analysis will develop separately or amalgamate.

Practical exercises _____

1   Choose two or three acquaintances who would be willing to talk to you about feminism (preferably a range of different ages). First ask them what feminists believe. What kind of society do they want us to live in? What do they think about men? Second, ask them what kind of women feminists are. What do they dress like? What do they like doing? Now compare the answers with the descriptions of feminism at the start of the chapter. Consider the sorts of stereotypes of feminists that these questions reveal. Where may these stereotypes have come from?

2   Choose two or three more acquaintances who would be willing to talk to you. The same people will do if they are patient and helpful! Ask them about sexual equality and employment for, say, engineers. First, ask them about principles. Do they support the principle of equal employment? Then ask them about the practice. Do they see practical problems that interfere with equal employment? Think about the pattern of answers here. Do you find the same pattern as found by Wetherell and colleagues in their study? Is it still possible to identify 'unequal egalitarians' who support the principle but argue against equality in practice two decades later?

3   Remind yourself about the notion of 'heterosexism'. Kitzinger argues that discussions of relationships and sexuality overwhelmingly assume a heterosexist norm. Spend a bit of time looking through newspapers or television chat shows for people talking about the nature of relationships, or asking questions about sexuality. Try to imagine the descriptions applying to gay and lesbian relationships. Is it possible to do this or do the descriptions reproduce the normality of heterosexual relationships?

Reading

If you read only one thing, read:

Wilkinson, S. (ed.) (1986) *Feminist Social Psychology: Developing theory and practice* (new edition). Milton Keynes: Open University Press.

Classics

In the very first edition of Feminism and Psychology *there are a number of useful classic articles by the like of Erica Burman, Michelle Fine, Wendy Hollway and Celia Kitzinger.*

Other useful texts

Burman, E. (ed.) (1998) *Deconstructing Feminist Psychology*. London: Sage.

Daly, M. (1978) *Gyn-ecology: The metaethics of radical feminism*. Boston, MA: Houghton Mifflin.

Dworkin, A. (1981) *Pornography: Men possessing women*. New York.

Gavey, N. (1989) Feminism, poststructuralism and discourse analysis: Contributions to a feminist psychology, *Psychology of Women Quarterly*, 13, 439–76.

Haraway, D. (1989) *Primate Visions: Gender, race and nature in the world of modern science*. London: Routledge.

Hollway, W. (1984) Gender difference and the production of subjectivity, in J. Henriques et al. (eds) *Changing the Subject*. London: Methuen.

Kitzinger, C., Wilkinson, S. and Perkins, R. (eds) (1992) Heterosexuality (special issue) *Feminism and Psychology*, 2 (3).

Ussher, J. (1989) *The Psychology of the Female Body*. London: Routledge.

Walkerdine, V. (1991) *Schoolgirl Fictions*. London: Virago.

Wilkinson, S. and Kitzinger, C. (eds) (1995) *Feminism and Discourse*. London: Sage.

Wilkinson, S. and Kitzinger, C. (eds) (1996) *Representing the Other: A feminism and psychology reader*. London: Sage.

Wood, L.A. and Rennie, H. (1994) Formulating rape, *Discourse & Society*, 5, 125–48.

Difficult but worth it

Butler, J. (1990) *Gender Trouble: Feminism and the subversion of identity*. London: Routledge.

Butler, J. (1993) *Bodies that Matter: On the discursive limits of 'sex'*. London: Routledge.

Butler, Judith (1997) *Excitable Speech: A politics of the performative*. New York: Routledge.

Haraway, D. (1991a) A cyborg manifesto: Science, technology and socialist feminism in the 1980s, in D. Haraway (1991), *Simians, Cyborgs, and Women: The reinvention of nature* (pp. 149–83). London: Free Association Books.

Part II

Resolutions and Dilemmas

Chapter 6

Subjectivity Critics

Sarah and Max have been together for fourteen years and Sarah has just left Max for another man. Max is very upset and angry – he had thought their relationship was a good one. He feels abandoned, and blames Sarah for not taking her responsibility as a mother seriously enough to keep their family together – they have two children. From Sarah's perspective, she feels both sad and guilty that Max is taking it so badly, and also slightly aggrieved – she thought that they had both agreed that there were a number of irresolvable problems with their relationship.

This is a familiar story of relationship breakdown and the trauma that often accompanies it. Note how difficult it is to even begin to characterize what is going on here without using what seem like descriptions of inner subjective states – feeling, wanting, caring. And note how using these descriptions of 'subjective states' can catapult us into the whole dynamic about who is to 'blame'. Subjectivity constructions are so much a part of our interactional currency. For Sarah and Max the whole experience seems to uncover their most intense 'inner' feelings – grief, anger, fear, guilt. But, for critical social psychologists, precisely what constitutes the private domain where, say, 'anger' appears is starting to become less straightforward (but much more interesting). As we shall discover over the course of this chapter, what seems like our most private 'inner' life can be understood in terms of history, culture and social context. Crucially, this does not mean that these things don't exist; instead they are – like everything else that 'exists' and seems 'real' – the outcome of a weave of discursive and institutional practices. This example also prefigures Edwards's discussion of emotion talk in Chapter 7. Here it is not the presence or absence of the emotional states themselves, rather the interactional *descriptions* of emotional states in relationship breakdown, that is the focus of analysis. Emotion talk will be seen to have a crucial role in how partners present themselves interactionally in terms of who is to blame, who needs to change and so on. This gives us a feel for what kind of research may be done when a postmodern perspective on subjectivity is adopted.

But why are critical social psychologists interested in something called 'subjectivity', which sounds very individual? After all, they are usually proud of their anti-individualist credentials? The answer is that they are trying to develop an account of what a person is that is different from the account in both traditional individual psychology and traditional social psychology. The term 'subjectivity' has been chosen for very specific reasons. First, it has been introduced as a direct rhetorical contrast to the more traditional notion of personality. Where personality emphasizes stable features of the person such as traits like extroversion, subjectivity emphasizes individual awareness and the weave of concepts used to understand self and world. These are seen as in continuing dynamic relation to sets of ideas and practices. Second, it makes a specific reference to post-structuralist traditions of thought, and in particular to Continental 'theories of the subject' or 'the death of the subject', most closely associated with Michel Foucault. One of the central features of this work is a concern with how the individual is produced as a subject in history and in social relations.

The issue of subjectivity is central in critical psychology; how it should be understood lies at the heart of many debates between critical psychologists. All the different perspectives covered in this book have some kind of position on subjectivity, although it is not always spelled out explicitly. In this chapter we will survey more explicitly the range of positions on subjectivity, and examine what is at stake for the different arguments. For clarity I will divide this up into two broad sections, the first on general theoretical work on subjectivity, the second on specific critical social psychological approaches to, and debates around, subjectivity.

The first section will examine whether mental terms should be seen as referents to mental states. We will move from early philosophical work by Wittgenstein, Austin and Ryle to more recent post-structuralist philosophy, focusing particularly on Foucault. This philosophical work suggests a view of the subject as decentred and fragmented, and emphasizes the practical role of psychological language. This section will also develop the discussion of psychoanalytic notions of what constitutes a self and how it comes to be gendered. As with Chapter 4 it will focus particularly on Freud, Klein and Lacan. The section will also start to consider postmodern views of subjectivity, raising issues that will be developed later in the chapter.

The second section considers approaches to subjectivity that have been developed within critical social psychology on the basis of these general philosophical and theoretical approaches. It will cover some of the classic work, including the collectively written *Changing the Subject* (Henriques et al., 1984) and the *Texts of Identity* collection edited by John Shotter and Kenneth Gergen (1989). It will also discuss some recent criticisms of social constructionist work for failing to develop a theory of the subject.

There is a lot that is tricky about the notion of subjectivity. It entails us taking a completely different view from the commonsense notions that we may harbour about each other and ourselves. Such common sense can be difficult to question, as it seems so straightforward and, well, commonsensical! We can also begin to understand some of the most complex philosophical ideas around today, ideas that have shaped contemporary notions of subjectivity.

The value of having some insight into these complex ideas and debates is that they are examining in a lot of detail the whole issue of subjectivity – what we take as the defining feature of personhood. Where do our assumptions about subjectivity come from? Where do they lead us? These are not easy questions, as is reflected in the difficult struggle that many theorists have in articulating things clearly. It pays to persevere with the reading and to try to clarify the ideas reflexively – try to relate them to your own assumptions about your 'self'. The pay-off is that this topic can be quite an eye-opener – developing your ideas here usually proves to be an exciting and liberating exercise!

Some philosophical explorations of subjectivity

This section will start by examining the relations between mental terms and mental states, between the words we say and what may be happening 'in' our minds. This will draw attention to some classic philosophical problems, with the idea that words reflect or refer to mental stuff of some kind. It will also highlight the alternative, shared by linguistic philosophy, post-structuralism and discourse analysis, that mental talk is not a description of mental worlds but a *social practice in its own right*. This will help us in understanding some of the subtle ways in which the notion of subjectivity is transformed from traditional psychological and psychoanalytic notions of persons and personality. This discussion will take us to further consideration of the work of Michel Foucault, which has been influential in the development of the issue of subjectivity in critical social psychology. His work also gives us some of the most powerful criticisms of psychology, and other 'psy-' disciplines, ever produced.

Mental terms and mental states

One of the basic issues in linguistic philosophy has been the extent to which mental terms such as 'belief' and 'intention' can be said to refer to mental states or internal entities. Gilbert Ryle and Ludwig Wittgenstein have been influential in challenging the idea that words refer to mental states. This challenge has been taken up and applied to social research by Jeff Coulter (1979, 1990) and Rom Harré (1998), and also by discursive psychologists (see Chapter 7). Rather than seeing mental terms as referents to mental states, this non-cognitive movement has preferred to see people's descriptions of mental states as part of their social practices; *mentalistic terms are part of the performance of acts*. As we shall see in Chapter 8, a further development has been that of post-structuralism, in which the idea of the self as a unified sense of awareness is similarly dismissed. Both these theoretical developments make the study of discourse, with its focus on the action-orientated nature of talk, fundamental to the study of subjectivity.

Jonathan Potter and Margaret Wetherell (1987) discuss Ryle's philosophy with respect to the term 'understanding'. They point out that although it is often thought of as a word for mental experience, Ryle shows that in practice it can be used to mark a claim to success – as in 'I finally understand what all this poststructuralism stuff is about'. However, when you are tested on your 'understanding' of this subject, it could be that you don't *really* understand it in the way that your tutor wants you to. Whatever else 'understanding' could be, one thing we can claim about it is that it is subject to *practical tests* employing criteria that are *social and public* – not exclusively internal and 'individual'.

We can also examine the term 'I'. It is often thought of as a word for the inner subject. However, Rom Harré (1989) argues that this is the *myth of self*, a myth that embodies two mistakes: (1) it treats things called mental as occurring in some inner substance and (2) it thinks that this substance is what is referred to by 'I'. Harré argues that in our Judaeo-Christian cultures 'I' is used to perform *moral* acts, in that it enables us to claim responsibility for individual choices. So in this early linguistic philosophy, and for those critical social psychologists who have drawn upon it, there has been a move to question the relationship between mental terms and mental states. This has led to the idea that psychologists do not discover psychology; instead they *produce* it. As we shall discover later in this section, this is a very Foucauldian insight. And one primary site for the production of inner life has been psychoanalysis.

Psychoanalysis and subjectivity

Psychoanalysis has already been discussed in some detail. It is necessary to extend the discussion here as a number of the recent developments in critical social psychology, covered in section two of this chapter and in Chapter 4, have tried to unite a Foucauldian account of power and social change with a psychoanalytic account of the development of the individual. But what does a psychoanalytic version of subjectivity entail?

Psychoanalysis has always focused on how the self is formed, which is one of the things that makes it so fascinating. One of the effects of psychoanalysis is to see meaning as a function of the unconscious mind and to suggest an unbridgeable gap between 'self' and 'other'. As we saw in Chapter 4, Freud's conception of the unconscious mind suggests that the unconscious develops as a result of the repression of libidinal energy by the superego, which develops anxiety about castration.

Freudian psychoanalysis, like Marxism, challenged the idea that the conscious subject comprises an individual rational decision maker. Instead individual subjectivity is understood in terms of the *irrational* workings of the 'unconscious mind'. The reasons that we give for our behaviour may be nothing more than 'rationalizations'. (Does that make them rational or irrational?)

CRITICAL DILEMMA

Note how these kinds of judgement about what is 'rational' and whether we are fundamentally irrational force us into (1) on the one hand playing 'God' – simply knowing the truth so we can decide whether something is rational or emotional; (2) on the other hand accepting that we are fundamentally 'flawed' – irrational. The view of subjectivity that this gives us is that because of some fundamental irrationality we must strive to become more rational – we are simultaneously capable and incapable of achieving knowledge. What might be the implications of accepting or rejecting this version of subjectivity?

The rationalizations that we give for our behaviour paper over the cracks of our unresolved childhood traumas. Freudian subjectivity therefore relies heavily on the repression of sexual drives into the unconscious owing to their distortion of the external world. Infants are fundamentally guilty; their selves, 'personalities', are the product of repressed desires and instincts. Freud's account of how children become social beings is essentially patriarchal – desires are usually based around possession or lack of a penis, and internalized superegos are usually in the form of a punitive father. As we have seen in Chapter 5, many feminists find this focus on the controlling power of males and their genitals particularly hard to swallow.

Kleinian subjectivities move between the sad compliance of the depressive position and the anxieties of the paranoid-schizoid position, in which our internal anxieties are projected on to the external world. More weight is given to the infant's social relations as determinants of their subjectivities, and there is more focus on the mother, rather than simply the father, as a frightening superego figure. Kleinian subjectivities are therefore more female-focused than Freudian ones.

The production of gendered selves

Traditional psychoanalysis has distinct ideas about how gendered selves are formed. For boys, the unconscious represses sexual energy due to anxiety that develops through the Oedipus complex, which means that desire for the mother results in desire to kill the father. When boys realize that girls do not have penises, they develop castration anxiety – they worry that their father may castrate them for desiring their mother. The superego represses these forbidden desires and creates the unconscious mind.

Girls feel annoyed with their mothers for not giving them a penis and they desire to be impregnated by their fathers so that they can at least have a child with a penis. This means that they switch from the initial desire for their mother that all infants have, to desire for their father. In a traditional psychoanalytic account, self and gender are formed through the process of the child's learning to repress bodily urges and desires.

DISCUSSION QUESTIONS   **Q**

Some immediately problematic features of this type of account that should alert our critical antennae are that (1) female gender is constructed negatively in terms of that which is lacking, (2) that infants' development is characterized in terms of their sexual desires and (3) heterosexuality is a foregone conclusion.

1   Why may these assumptions be problematic?
2   What would Foucault make of them?

Lacan and subjectivity

As we saw in Chapter 4, Lacan has been more successful in infiltrating critical psychological theory than Freud (see Lacan, 1989, 1992). Lacan's writing is difficult and metaphorical, but I have tried to give a feel for his claims about the production of subjectivity. In the *mirror stage*, the infant becomes aware of its own reflection and recognizes itself as an integrated and separate whole, which marks entry into the *imaginary*. However, this recognition is incomplete – a 'specular image'. In this state the pre-verbal concept of self is formed, and the pure experience of the *real* – the child's consciousness in which there is awareness only of immediate needs – is closed off forever by the formation of the ego and the unconscious mind. In this way the concept of self is formed, as well as its opposite, the 'other', both of which are bound up with an inevitable sense of loss of the real.

This development of a concept of self makes the final stage of linguistic and cognitive development possible. The loss experienced by the imaginary stage entails development of the final stage of linguistic and cognitive development – the realm of the *symbolic* – the realization of the *a priori* structure of language. Through our use of language we constantly struggle to become one with the real again, to capture experiences that are impossible to capture owing to language's inability to capture the totality of different meanings. We can never recapture the 'true' meaning of the real, so we may as well abandon the search for true meaning. Even the concept of self that we have is an illusion, as it is grounded in the misrecognition of the specular image of our 'self' that we developed in the mirror stage.

Lacan manages to bring back the Freudian focus on the penis through the idea that the phallic (essentially the real with knobs on – a realm in which there is no conception of lack) is at the heart of the semiotic system of the unconscious. Again this entails that the feminine self is defined by what it lacks. All of us desire to return to the real so that we can refrain from feeling the inevitable sense of lack that begins with the imaginary stage. But of course for women this is harder because we are defined most essentially through our lack of a penis. This seems rather pessimistic for women, yet some feminists do embrace aspects of Lacan. For a more critical feminist analysis go to Chapter 4, the section entitled 'Judith Butler and the lesbian phallus'. My preference is to bypass Lacan completely and go for a more Foucauldian take on subjectivity, our next topic.

Foucault and subjectivity

Foucault was concerned with oppressed and deviant groups – the mad, the ill, the criminal. He also produced some powerful arguments about the oppressive role of psychology and related disciplines. His central thesis is that these particular types of subjectivity are *produced*: they are the outcome of discursive practices and power relations – the power/knowledge relationship. As we saw in Chapter 3, Foucault (e.g. 1977, 1979) sees Marxist and other theories of power as overly concerned with 'sovereign power'. Sovereign power is something that can be seized and subsequently exerted by those who 'possess' it over others who do not. For Foucault there are other forms of power that are not necessarily repressive in a 'top down' way. In *The History of Sexuality*, Volume I, he argues against what he calls the 'repressive hypothesis', that is, the idea that power operates through repressing some essential aspects of subjectivity. He is critical of disciplines such as psychiatry that work on the principle that it is possible to liberate us by helping us to realize the deep truths that we have repressed. Instead he would see psychiatry itself as the source of these fundamental truths.

So Foucault gets rid of the idea that there are deep truths within us waiting to be discovered (not an easy task for many psychologists – this has become the starting point for millions of pounds of research), and argues that we should be more interested in what this type of discourse of the self might be doing, what its *function* may be. Foucault suggests that contemporary disciplinary institutions (psychiatry, medicine, psychology) both *produce* and *control* individuals through these *discourses of the self*. He is therefore concerned to expose the 'power and knowledge relations that turn human bodies into objects of knowledge'. Power operates and regulates us not through enslavement by bourgeois ideology, but ultimately through 'an affirmation of the self' (1979: 123) – the promotion of 'self'-discipline. Paradoxically, the project of liberating ourselves through realizing our 'true nature' produces us as objects of knowledge of the human sciences, furthering both their expansion and our psychological subjectification.

This can be difficult stuff to understand. Let's try and flesh it out with an example. Imagine a famous psychologist, Amanda Jones. When Amanda produces herself in her daily practices she includes intelligence as a key component. Lots of people – friends, family, teachers – have always told her how intelligent she is. She has been produced throughout her life as 'intelligent'. How is it that we all consider the same type of thing intelligent? Foucault would say that there are sets of discourses, perhaps circulating via words and images in the media and in educational institutions, about what is intelligent and what is stupid. These discourses circulate in particular cultures and historical periods, exerting their influence over how we make sense of each other and ourselves. This influence is what Foucault takes to be the idea of power/knowledge, i.e. discourses produce certain ways of making sense of what is intelligent. Which is not to say that Amanda Jones doesn't feel that she is a fundamentally intelligent person, or indeed that she wouldn't be considered intelligent in this culture at this time. Rather it is recognition of the cultural and historical influences that construct the meaning of 'intelligent'. So it means that Amanda is not intelligent in any universal or abstract ways (if such 'pure' ways can be said to exist outside the philosophy and social theory that produce them, which Foucault wouldn't agree with) but she is intelligent in ways that matter to us, and her, here and now. But despite the obvious contingency and contestability of what we take to be intelligence, it is still considered a viable topic for psychologists to study, as a thing that exists inside people's heads that can be identified with the right tests and experiments.

Foucault would say that the psychologists' scientific project is the thing that *produces* intelligence, not the supposed presence or absence of it inside anyone's head – although this in itself is a useful, and potentially oppressive, discursive practice. So the focus is on how humans are *made into* subjects possessing particular qualities. So Amanda is made into an 'intelligent person' through a set of historically and culturally contingent discourses. Of course for her (for any of us) it doesn't seem like she is the outcome of discourses, it's just who she is. As an inhabitant of Western twenty-first-century culture she is also the outcome of *individualizing* discourses, through which she will understand herself in terms of possessing a unique, private inner life comprised of other things like 'thoughts', emotions', 'motivations', 'desires', 'conflicts' and so on. This inner life, as the story goes, is always already a precursor of her 'behaviour' – the parts of her that other people can observe. Indeed, we would probably make judgements about how 'well adjusted' Amanda is by means of the idea that her behaviour demonstrates how much 'control' she has over her inner world.

Hence discourses are powerful, and this power *creates identities* for Foucault. As subjects of a particular society we become objects of a (metaphorical) penetrative gaze, which has the effect of producing, classifying, normalizing and correcting us. This is what Foucault terms 'disciplinary power', and it operates through surveillance and observation. It is important not to slip back into thinking about either power or subjectivity in the traditional way, though, when you are trying to understand this, which is why many people find it hard to understand. One way of illustrating these things more clearly is with Foucault's development of the 'panopticon' as a metaphor of power and subjectivization.

Power, subjectivity and the panopticon

Foucault suggests that mechanisms of *surveillance* have gradually taken over as a means of control, replacing the traditional 'top down' power of the sovereign over his/her subjects. Our thinking hasn't caught up, though and we still tend to think of power as something exerted upon the individual from above. Foucault uses Jeremy Bentham's plan for a new kind of prison as a metaphor that vividly illustrates this new form of disciplinary technology.

The prison consists of a large courtyard with a central tower, surrounded by cells lit up from the back, so that every action of the prisoner can be seen by the guards who are based in the central tower. 'They are like so many cages, so many small theatres, in which each actor is alone, perfectly individualized and constantly visible . . . Visibility is a trap.' (Foucault, 1977: 200). Inmates are visible to the guards but cannot in turn see their captors. Thus prisoners are led to monitor themselves, always aware that authority may be observing their actions. The operation of power is not overtly discernible to the prisoners (it does not depend on chains, threats and physical force), rather they are 'policing' themselves.

To extend Foucault's metaphor a little, we could say that *developing a preoccupation with subjectivity is a useful device for developing a docile population.*

1   Are we currently a docile population?
2   If so, whose version(s) of subjectivity might we be preoccupied with?
3   How would you confirm/refute these ideas?
4   Why should you need to?

Returning to the panopticon, it follows that, even if no guards are present, the architecture of the system is such that the institutional power relations operate as if they were. The prisoner becomes his or her own guard, is 'self'-controlled, turned in on him or her 'self'. The architecture of the panopticon also allows the controllers to be observed by another level of controllers, so there is no escape from the all-seeing eye of authority.

The deliberate exertion of power is therefore no longer necessary, having been replaced by a system of normalization that is essentially *psychological*. The incessant appeal to statistical measures and judgements about what is normal (the 'normal curve') and what is not in a given population is a very familiar story for psychologists. This subtle form of control depends on two things: (1) we must all develop a self-knowing subject; (2) we must each accept the idea that this is what we are most fundamentally. So we are here at the crux of the big problem with psychology – it *produces individualized subjectivities*. It takes sets of discourses, gestures, desires – *things that go on in the interactional domain between people*, and it turns them into *individual qualities*. If critical psychology is about anything, from a Foucauldian perspective, it should be about *the elaboration and explication of psychology's big mistake*.

People can then seek their faults within themselves; reality or truth within the person can be liberated through *confession* – a term that Foucault developed in his consideration of the social construction of sexuality. He questions the assumption that the twentieth century was the era in which sexual repression was eliminated (Foucault, 1979). This assumption relies on the premise that the Victorian era smothered the hitherto unrepressed sexuality of the time prior to the seventeenth century. Freedom could only come about by thinkers like Freud and Reich who uncovered the sexual hypocrisy inherent in that society. Talking about sex would be the key to breaking free from sexual codes. But this ignores the extent to which *talking about something also produces it as 'some thing'*. As Foucault puts it, 'What is peculiar to modern societies . . . is not that they consigned sex to a shadow existence, but that they dedicated themselves to speaking of it *ad infinitum* while exploiting it as the secret' (Foucault 1979: 35).

The paradox of freedom

One way to think about Foucault's philosophy is to see it as throwing up a set of fundamental paradoxes. These are the kinds of things that interest Derrida in Chapter 8. We think of certain things as allowing us degrees of freedom from various constraints – psychoanalysis frees us from sexual repression – but the very quest for freedom from something ends up tying us to it: *talking about ourselves as requiring freedom owing to fundamental constraints produces an 'us' that is fundamentally constrained*: hence the paradox.

Q	DISCUSSION QUESTIONS
1	How do we escape (gain *freedom* from) the paradox of freedom?
2	Aren't we now producing it as a paradox and a thing to be escaped from?
3	Does that mean there is no escape?
4	Or does it mean that it doesn't 'exist'?

Foucault shows that freedom as an idea comes about through the opposition between self and world, inner and outer. This idea then becomes something that we must strive for if we are to rid our 'selves' of contaminating influences. The claim to be liberating – giving freedom to – a population is therefore a strong one, as it meshes in with one of the fundamental concerns we may have about our 'selves'. It seems that we can gain greater freedom by ridding ourselves of various types of shackles, which as we have seen throughout this book can be produced by ideology, false consciousness, the nanny state, 'media influence' or, for psycho-analysis, various types of repression brought about through parental constraints. Only by throwing off social constraints can we get back to the real inner person and be free. But Foucault's claim would be that our *subjectivity is invented through this whole discourse of freedom/control*, and that the things we seek to be free from are thereby produced as controlling influences.

To illustrate this we can return to Amanda, our 'intelligent' psychologist. After embarking on a course of psychoanalysis, Amanda longs to be rid of the social constraints that turn her into someone purely 'rational', preoccupied by her own 'intelligence'. Instead she wants to find her 'real self' and be free. Foucault would argue that this leaves intact the notion (the discourse) that there is a real self that is submerged by social constraints, and that 'discovery' of this real self is the road to liberation. This individualist discourse is one of the ways that we invent ourselves as existing in some pure state prior to social oppression, so that this is the 'self' that we long to return to.

DISCUSSION QUESTIONS

1   Why do we need all this complicated theory to tell us about who we are?

2   If all selves are constructed, does it matter what constructions we use to build them?

3   Does it matter that psychology or psychoanalysis just assumes they are real?

4   Why do we need to learn about it all, can't we just get on with it?

In his later work Foucault embarks on a set of historical (genealogical) analyses, which allow us to see for ourselves (rather than by being guided by specific theories) how fields such as psychology and psychoanalysis often end up having the opposite effect to that which was originally intended. So perhaps Foucault's method of genealogy holds the key to understanding how we are produced through a set of paradoxes.

Genealogy

Foucault develops the method of *genealogy* as a way of displaying historical data in such a way as to show up the internal contradictions within the different fields of study. He shows the way that different fields of discourse, although presenting histories of progress and freedom, actually give birth to their own problems – constructing people as subjects of particular types while claiming to liberate them.

Foucault based his genealogical method on Nietzsche's *Genealogy of Morals* (1897). Rather than seeing morality in the Kantian sense as comprised of identifiable absolutes (the famous categorical imperative – do unto others as you would have them do unto you), Nietzsche reveals the internal contradictions of morality, showing that statements defining morality become the opposite of what they once were through morality's historical objectification of the subject.

In a similar way, in *Madness and Civilization* (1971) Foucault allows fields of discourse to contradict themselves rather than opting for a more traditional style of critique. He shows how subjectivity becomes defined within the mad–sane psychological opposition – we come to possess a psyche that is either acceptable or unacceptable to society. As we saw in the previous chapter, political power and the *status quo* are sustained by the contradictory or rhetorical nature of ideologies or discourses. The same goes for subjectivity – the paradox of freedom again: the psychological subject is invented through the very discourse that claims to hold the key to its liberation or 'cure'. So how would Foucault view the ultimate 'cure' for ailing selves?

Foucault and psychoanalytic subjectivity

Despite setting out to liberate individuals, psychoanalysis would be seen by Foucault as the site in which people's problems are created, thus giving rise to its subsequent efforts to cure those problems. Within such fields of discourse we are produced as subjects of a particular type – e.g. requiring liberation and psychological cure. So we have another paradox – like psychology, psychoanalysis produces the problems that it sets out to cure. Borrowing deconstructive insights (see Chapter 8), we could see this paradox as supplemented by oppositional structures such as freedom–control, subjective–objective, surface–depth, healthy–ill and sane–insane. This provides us with an impressive collection of tools with which to construct our subjectivities: madness is an abnormal illness lodged deep within us, over which we have no control, unless we can be cured by psychoanalysis. By Foucauldian standards, then, psychoanalysis can be seen as that which *produces* madness and psychoses, which it can then set about 'discovering' the cures for.

For Foucault, subjectivity is a rhetorical representation of some primary freedom prior to its invasion by the world. So again we have the notion of *freedom* bound up with what we take to be (and thereby produce as) our inner world. For Foucault it is through this discursive opposition between some primary 'true' subjective world and subsequent contact with the false 'external' world that subjectivity arises.

Foucault (1979) borrowed the Catholic Church's notion of *confession* as a metaphor for the technology of self that is developed by therapy. Confession, like therapy, is a practice of subjectification. It becomes a practice of subjectification through being a dialogue with another person who understands and sympathizes, and expects to hear the outcome of some inner reality or conflict. It is also a practice of subjectification through the process of 'self' examination that goes before, during and after the confession/therapy. This process involves having a dialogue with one's 'self' in which one cannot do other than construct a suffering inner self that is the object of one's 'knowledge'. Here we can start to see how knowledge, subjectivity, power and discourse all go together in Foucault's work. The process of confession/therapy is powerful in the sense that it weds us to the discourse, the knowledge, the subjectivity that goes with being a person of a particular type – it produces a 'regime of truth' that we could say exerts a power over us; it is not an authoritarian power, but it involves authority, or rather a variety of authorities and types of knowledge involved with the practices and procedures that go with having therapy. Thus it is possible to see why Foucault suggests that we think about *power* and *knowledge* as two sides of the same coin.

Free will

Foucault suggests that in order to understand subjectivity, we must refrain from imposing theories about the meaning of subjectivity on our genealogical discursive analyses. To do this would be to pre-empt and therefore contaminate the process. Subjectivity, for Foucault, is not some pre-existing entity. As we saw, one of the paradoxes of subjectivity is created by the notion of some primary freedom that is inevitably controlled or constructed by something other than itself, like social influence. Foucault does not seem to want to restore this freedom, but rather to open up subjectivity to greater scrutiny, to provide us with more space to think through how we want to produce ourselves.

The German philosopher and sociologist Jürgen Habermas (1990) has argued that it is not possible for Foucault to communicate that there is neither free will nor a self-knowing subject without presupposing his own free-willed self-knowing subject. How can Foucault say that the individual will and human subject do not exist, when the way we communicate presupposes this – the fact that 'I' am speaking gives us a relation between the 'I' and the 'non-I' – the rest of the world. Isn't the 'I' – the free consciousness – an origin to which one can refer philosophical arguments, a foundation on which to orient a genealogy?

However, for Foucault the discourse of the exercise of 'free will' – 'What do I want? What is good for me?' takes place within the existing institutional structures, for example schools, prisons, families and hospitals. The answer to this question is also constrained by this institutional context. The concern is therefore with presenting a genealogy of the modern subject as historical and cultural constructs.

To argue, as Habermas does, that Foucault cannot communicate without presupposing his own free-willed self-knowing subject is effectively to beg Foucault's questions about the genealogy of the modern subject. This is also a classical illustration of the circular reasoning that results from arguing within an overarching metanarrative. Habermas, in arguing from within the metanarrative of the free-willed self-knowing subject, is unable to renounce this notion and recognize Foucault's project as viable. Again we see the problems some theorists have with thinking outside the given notions of subjectivity. Nikolas Rose takes this difficulty as his starting point, noticing that it has become impossible for us to conceive of our own or others' personhood, or to govern others or ourselves without reference to the 'psy'-disciplines.

Rose and subjectivity

Rose has devoted considerable energy to exploring the implications of Foucauldian thinking for psychology and sociology. He argues that the 'psy'-disciplines have helped to develop our contemporary regime of subjectification. Psychology, psychiatry, educational psychology and so on are a set of institutions that produce, oversee and 'discover' particular kinds of persons. It is important to hold in mind how radical Rose's (and originally Foucault's) alternative perspective on psychology is. The idea is not that people have a pre-existing psychology that is studied by the 'psy'-disciplines; rather it is that these disciplines help establish a particular vision of what a person is. They are active managers of our psychological lives rather than passive observers.

Rose sees his project as the production of a 'genealogy of subjectification' concerned with the human being as it is thought about and understood, and the practices and techniques that go with that understanding. Individuals in a psychological sense are not prior to history but a product of history. Moreover, he draws on a metaphor of folding from the work of another important French theorist, Gilles Deleuze. He suggests that our mental life, our subjectivity, has become an 'interiority' through the 'infolding of exteriority'.

Rose likes the utility of the metaphor of folding, as folds 'incorporate without totalizing, internalize without unifying, collect together discontinuously in the form of pleats making surfaces, spaces, flows and relations' (1996: 37). Subjectivity is therefore constituted in the different practices and relations of that which can be 'enfolded' – 'anything that can acquire authority: injunctions, advice, techniques, little habits of thought and emotion, an array of routines and norms of being human' (ibid.). So subjectivity is not a unified, continuous phenomenon, although it can be thought of as 'internal'. This is a classic move in some kinds of critical social psychology, which works to place society and social relations inside the head.

Q	**DISCUSSION QUESTIONS**
1	Could the notion of 'folding' be a more elaborate way of keeping the inner/outer distinction safely separated? Read especially Rose (1996 pp. 37–8) to help you decide about this.
2	Do you think it is important to maintain this distinction?

Producing psychology

Post-structuralist and postmodern psychologists who draw upon Foucault, Derrida and Rose claim that basic psychological ideas invoking the person as an integrated centre of awareness are not *discovered* but *produced* by psychology. From this perspective, subjectivity is made up of fragmented discourses that provide us with voices to speak with and positions to speak against.

Theorists such as Donna Haraway (1991b) have drawn on this style of thinking to challenge the idea that politics ought to be based around particular *identities*. Indeed, she argues that self and identity are 'not so much resources for critical thought as obstacles to such thought' (1991b: 39). The risk of such politics is to essentialize (to make into something true and self-evident) particular categories such as woman, black, disabled, mad, which itself risks failing to see how they are a product of a complex historical process though which subjects are produced in particular institutions.

Traditionally, psychology has worked with a common Western view of the person, which sees the individual as the focal point of sets of subjective beliefs, values, desires and capacities. This association is not surprising, as psychology has developed as an institution in the West drawing on, and contributing to, this idea about people (Rose, 1989). This permeates the whole of what we like to call 'society'; the regulation of conduct is grounded upon this view of the person – the legal system, with its notions of responsibility and intent; politics, with the emphasis on individual choices and rights. This entails a fundamental separation between what we call a person and the structures and external objects that 'persons' have created, or that are simply 'real' – a term which itself usually relies on this fundamental separation between inner and outer, person and object, individual and society. Social constructionism (see Chapter 7) and various forms of postmodernism and post-structuralism provide us with ways of questioning these dualisms of subjectivity and society.

Nevertheless it is in this dualist context that we (in the West!) come to understand ourselves as psychological, as having an inner life that constitutes our unique cocktail of subjective features, and for psychologists this gives rise to particular measurable features such as identity, attitude and personality. The possession of a particular inner life or 'self' expressed through these features then allows the possibility that if we don't live in accordance with it we are somehow inauthentic, and that we can live more or less fulfilled lives according to how in/authentic we are. This is a pervasive and entrenched story about personhood that many people – critical psychologists included – find impossible to completely disentangle themselves from. As we have seen throughout this book, and as we will discover later in this chapter, it becomes important for such theorists to retain some bottom line story about selfhood.

CRITICAL DILEMMA

A fundamental critical dilemma of selfhood runs as follows. In theory, we can see the self as the object of psychological theory and knowledge, relatively easy to evaluate and doubt the existence of. But in practice, as 'individuals', we can experience the self as the very foundation of our being, or employ it as the organizing principle allowing us to make claims about, say, oppressed minorities: such selves can be less easy to make academic judgements about. In the case of minority or exploited groups it may seem dangerous and depoliticizing to doubt the existence of selves that are subject to oppression.

Ian Hacking (1995) argues that our descriptions of selves allow us to reflect upon ourselves and act. A new language of description entails a new 'human kind' – he calls this 'the looping effect of human kinds'. Hacking uses the example of trauma to illustrate this. Although 'trauma' was originally a surgeons' word for physiological wounds, over the years it has become psychologized, first with the idea that head injuries caused memory loss, and then through various permutations to Freud, and the notion that repressed memories were enough to generate hysterical symptoms. Hepburn and Brown (2001) argue for a similar psychologizing evolution for the term 'stress'.

This provides us with the vocabulary to construct disruptive events and experiences as traumatic – as damaging to some inner subjective world, perhaps even sufficient to cause 'post-traumatic stress disorder'. This new psychological vocabulary will have implications for the way we relate to our selves and each other, and so forms what Foucault would call a 'technology of the self'. Technologies refer to 'truth games' or ways of 'knowing' that people use to make sense of themselves, each other, and their environment. Technologies of the self allow people to construct 'their own bodies and souls, thoughts, conduct, and way of being, so as to transform themselves in order to attain a certain state of happiness, purity, wisdom, or perfection, or immortality' (Foucault, 1988: 18).

We can see that Foucault's work is bound up with the implications of the production of psychology. Indeed, it is one of the main sources of philosophical speculation around subjectivity, and also one of the main inspirations for critical and discursive work in psychology.

Conclusion

This section began with the problems of seeing mental terms as representations of mental states. One move in philosophy has been to focus on mental terms as parts of social practice, and we traced the implications of this for psychology's pro-duction of truths about 'the subject'. This led to Foucauldian perspectives on subjectivity – how people are made into subjects of a particular type through the discursive operation of various paradoxes and oppositions. As we saw, one of the paradoxes of subjectivity is created by the notion of some primary subjective freedom that is inevitably controlled or constructed by something external to itself – 'the social'. Foucault's response to the paradoxical nature of subjectivity is to open it up to greater scrutiny through genealogical study, allowing more space to think through how we want to produce ourselves. Another critical move has been to explore the possibilities of postmodernism and deconstruction for our under-standing of subjectivity. But the big problem with psychology (and the other 'psy'-disciplines) is that it *produces individualized subjectivities*. So, from a Foucauldian perspective, the main task for critical social psychology is to examine and bring to light this whole process, and ensure that it doesn't replicate subjectivity in traditional ways. We must keep this in mind (a practical and interactional use of mind!) in our survey of existing work on subjectivity in critical social psychology.

Critical psychology and subjectivity

Traditionally critical work in psychology has sought to embrace the subjective, with the complaint that psychology's drive for objectivity is the problem. For example, Dennis Fox and Isaak Prilleltensky (1997: 15) argue that psychologists' choices and positions can never be entirely value-free and objective, and thus critical psychologists should acknowledge the 'subjective nature' of their efforts. Similarly Michelle Fine argues that feminist psychologists 'are writing about how, not if, our subjectivities sculpt the stories that we tell and the ones that we don't' (1997: 44). So it seems that the reason why some critical social psychologists want to cham-pion subjectivity is that it is something that the 'objective' approach in psychology has ignored.

This subjective/objective split is one that Foucault and Derrida (and the more theoretically complex work that critical social psychology draws upon) would want to reject as a theoretical starting point. Indeed, as the prior section concludes, it would see this as a dangerous reintroduction of traditional notions of subjectivity.

This section will begin by discussing whether we need a 'theory of the subject' in critical social psychology, as some have argued. It will then move on to various ways of tackling aspects of subjectivity such as personality and identity, in critical work.

The subject: do we need a theory?

The answer to this question depends on what we think constitutes subjectivity. Both Marxism and psychoanalysis would find this a difficult question to answer simply. On the one hand, Marxism suggests that we do not know our own mind owing to history and class, that we suffer from false consciousness for which revolution and communism are the way to discover true being. On the other hand, psychoanalysis suggests that we do not know our own mind owing to our repression of troubling thoughts and desires into the unconscious, and that psychoanalysis is the way to discover one's true self.

A 'third hand' that we have been investigating above is the Foucauldian suggestion that we are encouraged to *produce* our own minds and selves, as well as the notion that we may need a 'cure', through various sets of regulatory discourses. Foucault's answer to the question 'What is a subject?' is that we are the outcome of discursive constitution. One site of contention for critical psychologists has thus been how far we can see subjectivity as discursively constructed, and how far down the Foucauldian subjectivity line we are prepared to go. As we shall see in the next chapter, the answer for discursive psychologists such as Potter and Edwards is 'As far as possible'.

As we saw in Chapter 4, one meeting ground for critical psychologists on the issue of subjectivity has been the work of Lacan. Lacan would see the subject as forming in terms of its distinction from the 'other' – constituted by 'mirror' type images of unattainable otherness occurring within the 'imaginary' realm. This is facilitated by language, and so it is language that structures the unconscious and its desire for the unattainable – namely self-expression and knowledge of the other. But where does all this complicated theory take us? Essentially this is a way of trying to specify the nature of subjectivity. But why does it need to be specified?

Nightingale and Cromby (1999) attempt to incorporate a 'theory of the self' into social constructionism. It is an edited collection that aims to defuse the overemphasis on language in social constructionist work like the discourse analyses of Potter and Wetherell (1987). Typical of this type of argument is the chapter by John Cromby and Penny Standen. They argue that social constructionism needs a 'notion of self thoroughly integrated into its research and practice' (1999: 141). This does not mean 'self' in the way that most discursive psychologists would view it, as a useful notion that participants employ. Instead the 'self' is recruited as an explanatory concept within social constructionist theory. For example, let's examine Cromby and Standen's version (p. 147) of discourse analysis:

> discourse analysts are easily able to differentiate between various possible responses to an accusation, such as a denial, a justification or an excuse. At the same time, they are wholly unable to even speculate as to why on a

particular occasion the response to a specific accusation was a denial, rather than a justification or an excuse . . . accepting that talk, all talk, always has a functional component, cannot exclude the possibility that on occasion it may also be expressive or representative.

The assumption here is that talk is representative *of* something – some kind of inner self, a self that drives people to deny rather than justify or excuse themselves on different occasions, and a self that we can therefore recruit in our explanations as to why people do what they do. This is a familiar story about the self that draws on the traditional Western view. But it ignores Foucault's argument that the 'self' is the *outcome* of psychological discourses; that this Western view of the self is the outcome of individualizing discourses that have been systematically supported by the psy disciplines. This isn't critical psychology – it's just more of the same.

Cromby and Standen suggest that the best illustrative example of the dangers facing a self-less social constructionism is the Human Genome Project, mapping the sequence of genomes that give the human species its distinct identity. Because social constructionism 'permits no notion of the embodied person' (1999: 151), social constructionists would be unable to convincingly argue against the biological essentialism of geneticists who give primacy to genetic make-up in the explanation of why we create the personal and social worlds that we do.

Q **DISCUSSION QUESTION**

1   Do you agree that social constructionist thought offers us a perspective on selfhood incapable of rebutting biological essentialism? Try to marshal arguments for and against each perspective.

As we saw in the previous chapter, Nikki Parker (2001) questions the notion that there is a coherent body of work that can be termed 'social constructionism' – there are many differing perspectives that claim to be drawing upon social constructionist theory. (See Chapter 7 for more discussion of social constructionism.) She suggests that Nightingale and Cromby's preservation of 'pre-discursive realities' is more of a retreat from social constructionism than a move forward to 'reconstruction'.

The issue of subjectivity is clearly a key site of contention. Often critical work in this area wants to take a more Foucauldian line and see psychoanalysis as a set of discourses rather than the truth of the human condition. However, as we have seen with Parker and Hollway in Chapter 4, such work often slips back into making individualist assumptions about what constitutes human subjectivity. We therefore need to step back and consider the terms and assumptions that constitute this debate. Section one of this chapter was designed to facilitate this. I will continue to argue throughout this book that the slide back into explanations that take traditional notions of subjectivity for granted re-import part of the problem that critical psychology arose to tackle – the idea of seeing the person as the source of their own individualized problems. The complexities of this perspective can be illustrated further with an exploration of the strengths and weaknesses of existing critical work on personality.

Personality: a psychological approach to subjectivity

One area in psychology that has extensively theorized subjectivity has been personality theory, and we have already covered a couple of psychodynamic theories (Freud and Klein) above and in Chapter 4. We also need to think about how personality has traditionally been defined, and how it has operated in mainstream psychology, before we can make sense of the critical work.

In 1937 Gordon Allport listed more than fifty distinct definitions of the term 'personality', and the list has increased since then. The simplest personality theories focus on single traits such as authoritarianism (see Chapter 3) and locus of control (indicating the extent to which people consider their lives to be under their own personal control). Personality theories are usually operationalized for experimental or correlational studies.

In the late 1940s and 1950s Hans Eysenck and his colleagues became concerned with the question of what separates one person from another. One of Eysenck's best known ideas is that of a dimension between extroversion and introversion, which now forms part of our everyday way of making sense of our 'selves' and each 'other'.

To answer the question why some people are more 'extrovert' than others, Eysenck turned to biology. He suggested that arousal is controlled by a particular bit of the brain known as the 'ascending reticular activating system'. It is a bit like a hi-fi amplifier: it can turn the volume up or down. The idea is that people in whom this chunk of the brain dampens arousal (lowers the volume) get bored easily and need to seek excitement to keep themselves aroused. On the other hand, when this bit of brain is amplifying things for someone, arousal is already pretty high. So rather than rushing out to discos to keep it up they can be quite happy sitting at home reading. (Indeed, the extra arousal of parties and socializing may be quite distasteful.)

Eysenck has had big ambitions for what this model of personality can explain. For example, he has argued that it accounts for quite a lot of social behaviour and in particular for a lot of crime and certain sorts of political views. Eysenck gives several reasons for this. The most important is that extroverts (remember, they have under-aroused brains) may turn to crime because it provides excitement and exhilaration unavailable elsewhere in their lives. It's as if you had such a poor Sony Walkman that the only thing worth listening to was heavy metal at full volume. So how do we begin to criticize this type of research?

Tod Sloan and critical approaches to personality

The critical psychologist Tod Sloan (1997: 89) suggests that any personality theory provides 'a comprehensive and integrated general psychology of motivation, development, individual differences, psychopathology and mental health, as well as an account of more specific phenomena such as dreams, creativity, aggressiveness, or social conformity'. Examples of people who have produced this kind of theory would be Eysenck, Freud, Horney, Jung, Kelly, Klein and Skinner. Sloan produces the following critique of personality and this type of personality theory.

Theorizing about personality is stifling for any society, as it maintains the *status quo* in two ways:

1   Our concepts of personality reflect the historical form of individualism that organizes how we think about ourselves and dictates how we arrange our societies. Mainstream psychology generalizes this view to all societies and all historical periods. This leads us to think that because people are always going to be the same, e.g. selfish, aggressive, we don't need to question our ideologies or change our society; we just need to change individuals.

2   Personality theories lead us to define problems as 'private matters to be solved by personal growth or self-actualization' (Sloan, 1997: 89). Most people in the world have too few resources to be concerned with personal growth. Only the privileged groups in privileged Western societies have that luxury.

It follows for Sloan that concepts of personality are *ideological constructions*, in the sense that they maintain unjust social relations.

Q   **DISCUSSION QUESTIONS**

1   We have come across the notion of the oppression of ideology in Chapter 3. Do you think that ideologies are necessarily oppressive?

2   Can they be oppressive at some times and liberating at others?

3   What is it about an ideology that could (at least potentially) produce oppressive consequences?

Sloan suggests that psychologists must make a number of theoretical choices when opting for any particular theory of personality. First they must choose a definition, for example 'A psychologist who wants to prove that personality is inherited will define it in terms that relate to temperament' (Sloan, 1997: 92). Other choices may relate to personality in terms of uniqueness, an ideal to be achieved, the quality of emotional experiences, and so on.

Second, psychologists need to draw upon theories about how personality develops. For example, different theorists may favour 'social learning, inherited temperamental factors, long term evolutionary processes, aspects of the present situation' (Sloan, 1997: 92). Each approach has its own implications for the treatment of disorders, e.g. the personality theorist who views personality as inherited will favour genetic screening over changes in social institutions. Again for

Sloan this is evidence of how the choice of personality theory serves ideological functions.

Third, personality theorists draw upon different ideas about what counts as knowledge or evidence. For example, Freudians would prove the validity of their concepts with reference to how a patient's dreams might have changed after being told the analyst's interpretation of her transference reaction. Alternatively, a cognitive psychologist would measure changes in reaction time, a phenomenologist would stress the patient's report of their experience. So *what you count as knowledge dictates the criteria by which you decide what is knowable.*

CRITICAL DILEMMA

Is there any way out of this circular form of reasoning, in which what we believe is knowable dictates the criteria by which we decide what can be known? This dilemma relates to discussions of epistemology and realism/relativism in Chapter 8.

Sloan stresses the importance of developing the discipline of critical psychology so that it is capable of identifying the ideological underpinnings of basic psychological concepts such as personality. Sloan suggests that this may eventually stop personality researchers from rushing to find their empirical justifications for concepts that they unreflectively associate with their own particular theoretical framework.

From a critical psychological perspective, personality theorists are therefore not producing anything useful to people in their everyday lives. Instead they give us a way of understanding and intervening in people's lives that replicates an individualist view of personhood – people themselves are the major source of their own problems and therefore the place we look to for solutions. This ignores the critical psychological imperative running through most of the work covered so far, that we focus on the social rather than individual factors in our explanations of what is happening. So what is the answer? Sloan's solution is to develop 'critical theories of personality'.

Critical theories of personality

We need to consider personality as part of the problem, rather than part of the solution to 'problem behaviour'. This means producing a definition of personality that focuses on 'aspects of personhood that have something to do with systematic suffering and emancipation from it', referring to 'socially produced aspects of identity and affective experience that impede self-reflection, agency, autonomy, mutuality and other capacities that characterize meaningful living' (1997: 98). This involves developing full communication between self-determining subjects.

So for Sloan the answer to the problems created by personality theorists' individualist focus is to pay more attention to individual suffering, and then look

Tod Sloan

'In my work, I have urged people to break out of individualistic and objectivistic modes of thinking about personality. What appears as a person's relatively fixed traits may actually be the frozen traces of oppressive social relations. When personality problems are reinterpreted as social in origin, we have another powerful reason to be engaged in the work of social transformation.'

Tod Sloan *is author of* Damaged Life: The crisis of the modern psyche *(1995) and editor of* Critical Psychology: Voices for change *(2000). Tod has taught psychology in the United States for twenty years and is now doing international community organizing.*

for the socially produced aspects of personality that are stopping people from engaging in clear and meaningful reflection on themselves and their lives. Factors which 'restrict capacities for self-reflection and meaningful activity . . . may be called ideological processes' (1997: 99). Sloan understands ideology as something oppressive and so personality 'is a crystallization of ideological processes . . . mainstream concepts of personality are ideological constructions to the extent that they are individualistic and asocial in character' (ibid.). Hence the proper role for psychoanalysis is to foster dialogue that is 'critical and deideologizing', because personality is an ideological construction, and a result of 'failed intrapsychic and interpersonal communication' (1997: 100).

Q	**DISCUSSION QUESTIONS**
1	How does the concept of personality restrict one's capacity for self-reflection?
2	What does it mean to say that personality is an ideological construction?
3	Is it possible to foster 'deideologized' dialogue?
4	Can you see any problems with Sloan's own assumptions about humanness?

Psychology and the postmodern subject

In Chapter 8 we will explore the efficacy of postmodernism and deconstruction for critical social psychology in some detail. One area in which these perspectives and debates have taken a particular hold is in discussions of subjectivity. For example, Ken Gergen's book the *Saturated Self* (1991) documents the breakdown and the historical contingency of features of modernist, Western, patriarchal selves. He contrasts the postmodern or saturated self with both romantic and modern selves. The romantic self is related to emotional depth and passion – mysterious and forever out of reach. By contrast the modernist self relates to rationality – it is 'reliable, self-contained and machine produced' (1991: 44–5) and hence predictable and quantifiable.

Gergen proposes that our bombardment with different forms of information technology – computers, the Internet, virtual reality, not to mention satellites which open up a multitude of perspectives from different television channels – has led to 'social saturation'. This has implications for how we construct ourselves from the myriad of new resources that are available – the self becomes much less predictable, more fragmented and decentred. This saturated self is a by-product of postmodernism. The metaphor of 'saturation' isn't meant to imply that selves are vessels waiting to be filled (that would be more of an 'empty bucket' metaphor), rather it is designed to show that, whatever a self is, it is completely saturated by culture and social life – there is no pure, untouched part of it that psychologists can get to if they only try hard enough. So it's a bit like Scotch mist – before you know it you're completely saturated.

We can see that psychology as a discipline, in common with other social science disciplines, is based upon the development of a free-willed, autonomous, self-constituting subject. For Foucault this outward appearance of freedom and autonomy is constructed through various laws, practices and texts – the social constructions or discourses that constitute us. Hence we are 'subjectivized' – these discourses constitute our subjectivity. This does not mean we are passive recipients of discourses, as there is a sense in which we participate in our own subjectivization. For example, we may come to seek only those freedoms legitimated by various laws and practices. We come to understand ourselves in the light of discourses that constitute us as autonomous and self-constituting individuals. Making sense of ourselves outside this set of discourses then becomes very difficult for us – as we saw, even critical psychologists such as Parker and especially Hollway who are familiar with Foucault's work find it difficult to completely renounce some kind of controlling constituent subjectivity (and hence 'reality', see Chapter 9) in their own theoretical/analytical work.

Traditional psychology's production of 'truths' about its subject, gleaned from the study of what are essentially ideologically produced characteristics, could from a Foucauldian perspective be seen as perpetuating the *status quo*: the lack of reflexivity about discursive constructions. Each society or culture produces its own truths discursively. Truth is therefore 'linked in a circular relation with systems of power which produce and sustain it' (Foucault, 1984: 73). Again there are links between what we take to be knowledge (the truth) and power.

Professional academic psychologists hold it as given or true that we possess a mind which mediates between individual and reality, and which functions according to 'natural principles of operation which owe nothing either to history or to society for their nature' (Shotter, 1993: 22). It follows from this view that the task for psychology is to 'discover' these principles. Shotter claims that no such 'underlying reality' of the mind can be found, and that the pursuit of such a reality leads psychologists into making some 'dangerous mistakes', which he feels mostly stem from the assumption that psychology can emulate the 'morally neutral' stance of the natural sciences. By attending to the details of humans in their transactions with one another, one reveals processes of understanding and negotiating which revolve around issues of 'care, concern . . . respect . . . justice, entitlements, etc.' (1993: 23) – for Shotter these are essentially ethical issues, and they are precisely the kind of thing that traditional experimental work overlooks. The postmodern move of deconstructing subjectivity allows us to explore these issues – but what does it mean to deconstruct subjectivity?

As we saw earlier, deconstruction clears the way for freer movement – it is not simply about the destruction or dissembling of constructions, as is often assumed. Judith Butler (1995: 49) captures this point in relation to subjectivity:

> to deconstruct the subject is not to negate or throw away the concept; on the contrary, deconstruction implies only that we suspend all commitments to that which the term 'the subject' refers, and that we consider the linguistic function it serves in the consolidation and concealment of authority.

So in Butler's terms, to gain a deconstructive understanding of the term 'femininity', say, we need to suspend our commitment to that which the term has traditionally referred to, and focus instead on *what the term is used to do*. As we saw in the previous chapter, Butler highlights the sense in which deconstruction can open up terms for redeployment, rather than simply accepting or negating them. We are still surrounded by terms like 'feminine' and 'woman' – so, rather than blindly accepting or pretending that we can simply discard them, we need to use them subversively, and to become sensitive to contexts in which they can be deployed oppressively. Rather than accepting one meaning as the defining form of femaleness, the identity around which we must mobilize, we need to become more open to the different ways that femaleness can be defined for us and by us, in different ways in different contexts, to achieve different things.

Deconstruction increases our sensitivity to the function of terms, by freeing them up to be mobilized in alternative ways, in alternative critical and political arenas. One can go on to argue that deconstruction, although invoking a radical relativization, emerges as 'compatible with a feminist commitment to emancipatory and empowerment work' (Burman, 1998: 10) or that it can be seen in some ethical sense as 'responsibility to the other' (e.g. Critchley, 1992).

Critical psychology and postmodern subjectivity

As discussed earlier, the postmodern perspective on subjectivity, which incorporates the social constructionist approach, is a move towards disrupting the neat boundaries between subjectivity and society that many social and psychological theories work with. One important early collection on the theme of more postmodern notions of subjectivity was *Texts of Identity* (1989), edited by John Shotter and Kenneth Gergen. First we will examine a classic critical text, *Changing the Subject*.

BOX 6.1   Voices of the mind

One of the powerful metaphors in recent critical psychology has been to view the mind as formed out of social processes to be made up of voices. James Wertsch (1991) has done much to popularize this idea through his use of the ideas of the Soviet literary critic Mikhail Bakhtin. Bakhtin (see Box 4.1, p. 85) suggested that even individual texts or spoken monologues turn out, on closer examination, to be made out of a weave of voices. Indeed, one of the conditions of interaction is what he calls 'heteroglossia', a weave of different styles, figures and voices. The attraction of these ideas for critical workers is its connection of individual thought with social context. It provides a way to get historical or social relations into the person and therefore a way to understand apparently individual phenomena in more social terms.

The idea of heterogeneous voices of the mind is similar to Hollway's (1989) idea of subjectivity made of discourses, which draws heavily on Foucauldian notions of discourse. It also parallels some discourse thinking, notably Potter and Wetherell's (1987) notion of people's talk being constructed of a weave of interpretative repertoires. We have already encountered Billig's (1999a) ideas in the discussion of psychoanalysis. By treating mental life in terms of arguments it highlights the conflictual, controversial issues that are often at the core of critical work.

Changing the subject with Foucault

One of the best known critical texts to incorporate Foucault's work has been *Changing the Subject* (Henriques et al., 1984, 1998). One of the key contributors was Wendy Hollway (see also 1989) whom we have already encountered in Chapter 5. Her work on the development of the discursive construction of subjectivity, and how this can be related to social structures and relationships, is particularly interesting. On the basis of her interviews with various couples, Hollway came up with four discourses that she felt were crucial for couples in their relations with one another, specifically with regard to 'making love without contraception' (MLWC):

1   Discourse of male sexual drive.
2   Have/hold discourse.
3   Permissive discourse.
4   Feminist discourse.

The primary signification of MLWC comes from the idea of romantic commitment in the have/hold discourse. Yet MLWC can also be defined as not interfering with the natural male drive – the discourse of male sexual drive. The romantic mythology of both of these discourses is rejected by the permissive discourse, and the feminist discourse problematizes major assumptions of all the other three discourses.

Hollway argues that to understand the complexity of the act and of the participant's ambivalent and finally critical response to MLWC you need to understand their positioning in all these discourses. As we saw in Chapter 4, Hollway also links these types of discourse with unconscious defence processes.

Another key contributor to *Changing the Subject* was Valerie Walkerdine. Her subsequent work has focused on the ambitious agenda of taking a post-structuralist approach to subjectivity and gender to see how they are produced through social relations and how they link in with issues of power and ideology (Walkerdine, 1986). For example, her work on mathematics (1988) focused on the way that reasoning and understanding become corrupted by gender assumptions and asymmetries at a deep level. When you learn mathematics using the story of Goldilocks and the Three Bears it becomes a way of learning about power and male authority. Further work (Walkerdine and Lucey, 1989) suggested that rather than thinking of politics as something happening in a male world of broader social institutions, it is something bound up with family relations and the local small scale economies of households: mothers, daughters and fathers.

Selves and others

One way we could define subjectivity would be in terms of that which it is not. As we saw in the previous section, this might involve invoking the *body* as oppositional and somehow separate from subjectivity. Another common opposition is to posit an 'other'. The term 'other' often refers to a person who is in some way marginal or subversive, and as such 'other'-ness has been a focus of feminist work, in which women are identified as relegated to the position of the 'other' through patriarchal domination. For example, Simone de Beauvoir (1989) suggests that 'humanity is male and man defines woman not in herself but as relative to him . . . He is the Subject, he is the Absolute – she is the Other' (p. xxii); de Beauvoir points out that this distinction between self and other is socially and historically ubiquitous. For discussion of some more contemporary feminist theories on this theme see Braidotti (1991) and Gatens (1991).

The self/other distinction has certainly been much discussed around issues of ethnicity and sexuality (Wilkinson and Kitzinger, 1996). But it is important not to see otherness as something fixed. In her discussion of sexual identity Judith Butler (1993) shows that it is always relative, and reversible. She suggests that gay and lesbian identities 'constitute themselves through the production and repudiation of a heterosexual Other' (1993: 112). In a critique of Lacanian logic, Butler suggests that the other is relative and therefore it is not useful as a fixed binary structure in our theories. By simply reinforcing such binaries we make our theories weaker and more vulnerable, and ultimately we arouse resistance in the marginalized 'other' of our binary structure.

Valerie Walkerdine

'I have been involved with what might be described as critical social psychology since the 1970s. My own work as a Ph.D. student was very influenced by two emerging developments – feminism on the one hand and European social theory (structuralism, post-structuralism) on the other. This led to a group of psychologists and sociologists starting the London-based journal Ideology and Consciousness, which was particularly involved with French feminism, Lacan, Althusser and Foucault. This work was later developed in the jointly authored book Changing the Subject: Psychology, social regulation and subjectivity (Henriques et al., 1984, second edition 1998). This work sought to introduce post-structuralism to (social) psychology and to go beyond individual–society dualism towards an understanding of subjectivity and subjectification informed by Foucault's work and by Lacanian psychoanalysis. In my own work I developed this in relation to a number of empirical and theoretical projects and became also interested in the relationship between social psychology and cultural theory. In 1997 I moved to Australia to take up a Foundation Chair in Critical Psychology and to set up the very first centre in critical psychology. This was an exciting challenge for me. As part of this I set up the International Journal of Critical Psychology and have watched critical psychology grow from something very marginalized to a powerful and diverse movement within psychology. I am most interested in understanding how we might theorize and work with subjectivity in a way that is not confined by current notions of the edges of the 'psychological', but is neither a simple addition of the social to the psychological but a radical rethinking of what that means and what a politics and theory of subjectivity might look like.'

Edward Sampson (1977) criticizes the dominant tradition of enquiry into human nature for seeking to describe individual qualities such as self, mind and personality as features that lie within the self-contained individual. In his later work Sampson (1993) suggests that the remedy for challenging this scenario is to 'celebrate the other'. Rather than seeking to understand people's true nature by isolating them from others and studying them as if they were an inert substance in a test tube we should be developing a *dialogic approach*, in which human experiences and actions are seen as essentially embedded in their own particular context. This also draws upon more postmodern ways of making sense of subjectivity.

Texts of Identity

This collection (Shotter and Gergen, 1989) explored the discursive construction of identity and selfhood, in the sense that certain culturally established texts provide us with the means of understanding our 'selves'. The critical drive of the book was in the call for psychology to embrace new and more emancipatory constructions of subjectivity. Two of the pioneers of this work have been Edward Sampson and Kenneth Gergen.

Sampson (1989) discusses how the critical theorists of the Frankfurt school construct the self as unattainable in two polarized ways. At the individualist pole there is an unattainable self, which has the autonomous individual at the centre of our ability to think, feel, act and make judgements. At the 'collectivist' pole individual selves become mechanical copies of underlying social and economic structures. Sampson suggests that what we need is a fuller exploration of the individual–society relationship, and he employs Derrida's development of deconstruction (see Chapter 8) for this task. Sampson shows that taking a deconstructive stance gives us a number of insights into the construction of the Western notion of a subject or self:

1   The notion of the subject as the centre of awareness is challenged, revealing it as the work of 'ideological practice', repressing fluidity and undecidability in favour of a fixed and transcendent centre.

2   The Western emphasis on wholeness and integration as an ideal state of personhood is challenged. The dominant (psychoanalytic) idea is of an ego organizing and integrating the competing demands, succeeding only in so far as it achieves unified wholeness. Sampson suggests that this mirrors 'theories of governance and authority within the Western world' (1989: 15). We can replace this with 'a subject who is multi-dimensional and without centre or hierarchical integration. It would give us a process and a paradox, but never a beginning or an end' (ibid.).

3   A further challenge is to the binary 'either/or' logic of identity that characterizes the Western conception of the person. Applying Derrida's supplementary logic (see Chapter 8) allows us to recognize that we are dealing not with a system of simple oppositions, but with a system of differences. Differences 'describe the relations among parts of the system' (Sampson, 1989: 16) rather than inhering in individual entities that are presumed to constitute them. Each subject is thus inextricably related to all other subjects. This means that someone who seeks to marginalize and terrorize others 'can only suffer in kind, for those others are elements of the subject's own personhood' (Sampson, 1989: 16).

Hence we have a notion of selfhood as relational, rather than autonomous, as 'a process and a paradox', as something much less identifiable and quantifiable than traditional psychology would like. Sampson wants psychology to be involved in creating this new subject, rather than simply reaffirming the old one.

Many of the contributors to *Texts of Identity* share these kinds of sentiments about the construction of selfhood and subjectivity. For example, as we saw earlier,

Harré suggests that the phenomena we investigate in a psychological study are picked out and created by the 'relevant vocabulary' (1989: 20) – they are not simply there to be discovered, rather our framework for making sense of them as 'things' colours what we think we are 'finding'.

Gergen fleshes these arguments out further, suggesting that psychologists 'possess cultural sanctions for ruling on the nature and significance of rationality, the emotions, motives, morals and the like' (1989: 78). The fundamental cognitivist epistemological assumption accepted by modern cognitive science is that knowing involves the possession and manipulation of mental representations (e.g. Fodor, 1981). The basic idea of psychology is that our talk about ourselves – about our ideas, our motives, our memories and emotions – is inductively derived from experience. Gergen reminds us that this assumption is something that Wittgenstein (1953) dispensed with quite easily, with the insight that words describing mental events are not something that can be corrected through our observations. Also Austin (1962) argued that mental talk is performative; it does not mirror some external/internal reality but is essentially part of our social processes. We are therefore not justified in seeking *referents* for mental predicates; instead we should be looking for their *consequences* in social life. Shotter (1989) and Potter and Wetherell (1987) argue the same thing. Shotter (1989) suggests that we are trapped within the text of 'possessive individualism' and that we need to focus less on 'I' and more on 'you'. Again, our current ways of making sense of ourselves are seen as part of the problem.

As we saw in Chapter 5, Celia Kitzinger (1989) argues that identities are not the private property of individuals; rather they are social constructions that can be promoted in line with the dominant social order. She argues against the 'liberal humanist ideology' that some lesbians adopt, in which personal happiness and fulfilment are valued more than the political goals of women's liberation. This reaffirms the validity of the dominant social system. We discussed the implications of a liberalist view of society in Chapter 1.

Gergen argues that we gain voice (e.g. credibility) through *conventions of warrant*. Being able to master these conventions involves understanding and enrolling mental talk – 'I know because I saw it/heard it/tasted it' and so on. Gergen suggests that 'without grasping the linguistic skills to make the inner world come to life, one ceases to become a full participant – with all the rights that may accrue – in social life' (1989: 76). Being able to elaborate a self and an inner life gives us important ways of warranting our voice. This is therefore one of the reasons why psychology has been so successful – 'the discipline's capacity to employ strong warrant to gain voice, and voice to fortify its warrant, must be viewed as an epitome of self-sustaining efficacy' (1989: 79).

Gergen concludes by asking what use psychology is if its main task seems to be this rather insular self-sustaining one. He suggests that it should be keeping up with new dialogues and discourses, developing 'innovative, invigorating and emancipatory alternatives in the construction of contemporary selves' (1989: 80).

As we saw earlier, in the discussion of postmodern subjectivity, Gergen's later work develops this, where he explores the impact of 'social saturation' on ways of making sense of selfhood and social life. Social saturation arises owing to the interactional possibilities gained from new technologies (e.g. e-mail and the Internet) and globalization. These give rise to a host of different ways of understanding ourselves and our interactions with others, disrupting traditional patterns and assumptions, and forging a 'new culture'.

Gergen (1999) develops this theme, tracing the diminishing significance of the inner subjective world with the emergence of new technologies. Both the 'romantic' (entailing characteristics of personal depth such as passion, creativity, etc.) and the 'modernist' (reasoning selves in possession of beliefs, intentions, etc.) types of self are giving way to a multiplicity of disjointed and incoherent ('microwave') relations and ways of understanding the self.

Rose (1989) develops a similar (and more overtly Foucauldian, as we saw above) kind of critique of psychology to Gergen, Sampson, Harré and Wetherell and Potter. He argues that over the last 150 years people's well-being and happiness have increasingly been constructed as dependent on 'the production and utilization of the mental capacities and propensities of individual citizens' (1989: 130). An increasingly detailed system of regulation for codifying and calculating the mental functioning of individuals has been developed. Psychology has played a major part in this, objectifying and individualizing us as 'subjects', making us 'knowable' in particular ways, so that we look to our 'selves' as the source of our problems, and search for our own 'identities'. We also seek self-fulfilment through things like 'economic advancement, family contentment, parental commitment and so on' (Rose, 1989: 130). Rose's suggestions for emancipation are simply that we need to recognize the 'practices of individualization' that govern us by encouraging us to both produce and govern our 'selves'.

Conclusion

The question of what we can or should assume about subjectivity is important for how we do critical psychology, and for what we think the issues are that need to be addressed. If we take a more Marxist perspective, like Sloan, then allowing people freedom from the external constraints of oppressive social systems seems the right direction. If we take a more Foucauldian line like many of the *Texts of Identity* contributors, we need to go more carefully, recognizing that how people are making sense of themselves, and how we are making sense of them, are both infused with historically and culturally specific discourses. It then becomes more important to think through what *function* these versions of subjectivity may serve. This brings us back to the discursive focus on the action orientation of language, which the following chapter explores.

Application and intervention

How can a social constructionist version of subjectivity help people in real world situations? Can we use it to develop a new language of the self? Would we want to? Maybe the problem lies in having too many ways of specifying a self as an object of knowledge. In this sense what we need is to set about examining the implications of different versions of the self in everyday situations and contexts. In terms of application and practice, this suggests close examination of people's everyday activities in talk, and text (cf the following chapter, on discursive critics). To give an example, I am developing a project (with Jonathan Potter) that examines interaction in the NSPCC Helpline, and one of the focuses of this will be on different subjectivity constructions (see also Hepburn, 2000a) and the function that these have in the everyday business of the call. These findings will feed back into counsellors' training materials, providing a detailed resource for understanding different types of call. We also need to understand the limitations that different versions of reality and knowledge place on our understanding of what a subject can be, and this will be explored further in Chapter 9.

Conclusion

Throughout this chapter I hope to have given some sense of how the issue of subjectivity is an important one for critical social psychologists. We began with the problem of seeing mental terms as representations of mental states, which led to Foucauldian perspectives on how people are made into subjects of particular types, a key resource for this being various paradoxes and oppositions. It was argued that Foucault is an important figure for critical social psychologists, giving us a strong criticism of the 'psy'-disciplines as the producers of subjectivity in the Western world. It follows that we will run into problems if we simply slide back into traditional notions of subjectivity, as some critical social psychologists have been tempted to do. In Chapter 9 we will draw upon the epistemological arguments developed in Chapter 8 to explain how realist arguments provide a gap that some fixed notion of subjectivity is produced to fill.

In the second section we have reviewed a set of critical work that has focused in specifically on subjectivity. This has covered debates on whether critical psychology needs a 'theory of the subject', Sloan's fascinating work on personality, and some more postmodern versions of subjectivity from the contributors to the classic *Texts of Identity* collection. Throughout there has been concern to step back from making definitive statements or building-in unexamined assumptions about what subjectivity 'is' in any theoretical sense. It has been suggested that a more critical and subversive move would be to look at what different versions of subjectivity can achieve both within and outside psychology. This is something that the discursive critics in the following chapter can help us with.

But are we any nearer to understanding what a self is, or what we have become? According to deconstruction, to suggest a pre-existing, identifiable, measurable or in any other way concrete subject is futile. But that does not mean there is no such thing as a self. We cannot simply dismiss objects or selves because they fail to match up to the realist objectivist standards of how things must 'exist' or not. A self is like every other 'thing' – it is discoverable only in the moment of undecidability, and there is no being outside that moment. This means that no object (person, thing) can exist 'for itself', separate from every other object. Any theory that tries to develop selfhood outside this moment can only become hopelessly mechanistic, weighed down by causal stories about the nature of reality and selfhood. We can think through the problems caused by such simple stories in Chapter 8, on postmodernism.

Practical exercises

1   Look for an old diary or personal piece of writing of your own. Look for a description of something intimate (the start of a relationship, say). Try to view the words and style of writing as historically developed discourses. How does it affect your understanding of the event?

2   Go to the library and choose the earliest and the most recent textbook on abnormal or clinical psychology that you can find. Compare the definitions of well known 'mental illnesses'. Look for things that appear in the earlier one but not the most recent and vice versa. Think about these changes in terms of Foucault's theory.

3   Make a list of the various places where official records are kept about you (university, doctor, etc.). What kind of surveillance do they allow? Think how these different forms are part of your understanding of what you are. Try to identify some of the ways in which these forms of surveillance affect how you act.

B The best thing about subjectivity research

We are presented with new and often liberating ways of understanding ourselves and others.

W The worst thing about subjectivity research

The inevitable slippage into seeing subjectivity as the cause, rather than the outcome, of human action.

Where next?

A more comprehensive integration of post-structuralist theory and discursive psychological methodology into critical work.

Reading

If you read only one thing, read

Wetherell, M. and Maybin, J. (1996) The distributed self: A social constructionist perspective, in R. Stevens (ed.) *Understanding the Self*, pp. 219–65. London: Sage.

This is clear, constructionist and critical. Draws upon anthropological and sociological research.

Classics

Henriques, J., Hollway, W., Irwin, C., Venn, C. and Walkerdine, V. (1984, 1998) *Changing the Subject: Psychology, social regulation and subjectivity.* London: Methuen.

Hollway, W. (1989) *Subjectivity and Method in Psychology: Gender, meaning and science.* London: Sage.

Also useful

Gergen, K.J. (1991) *The Saturated Self: Dilemmas of identity in contemporary life.* New York: Basic Books.

Harré, R. (1998) *The Singular Self: An introduction to the psychology of personhood.* London: Sage.

Shotter, J. and Gergen, K.J. (eds) (1989) *Texts of Identity.* London: Sage.

Difficult but worth it

Rose, N. (1996) *Inventing Ourselves: Psychology, power and personhood.* Cambridge: Cambridge University Press. **Rose has done most to apply a Foucaudian perspective to modern psychology.**

Chapter 7

Discourse Critics

When US President George W. Bush was Governor of Texas one of the things he had to do was look at pieces of paper. A video of him doing this would not have been very interesting to watch. We would see a middle-aged man wearing a dark suit and leafing through documents. Images, movements, gross behaviours do not catch much of what is going on here. A psychology based on observing this would be extremely impoverished. To understand what is going on it is vital to understand the words. And, crucially, to understand that Bush's words were not merely an abstract commentary – they were *performing acts*. In fact Bush was considering documents proposing that incarcerated and convicted murderers should not be killed. As governor he had the authority to suspend their execution, to stop them being strapped to a gurney and injected with poison – but he let them go ahead, and in unprecedented numbers.

This is an extreme case. Nevertheless, it reminds us of the important point that words are the primary way in which we perform actions, and these actions may have profound consequences. This reminder is particularly relevant for traditional social psychologists because, for the last thirty years at least, they have emphasized that something called cognition is the fundamental motor of what people do, and that what people do is behaviour (as though that made it somehow more objective or scientific!). Discourse work in social psychology comes in a range of different flavours and has focused on very different topics. Nevertheless, in terms of the broad narrative running through the book, it can be understood as an attempt to socialize psychology by considering what were traditionally seen as inner, personal, cognitive notions in terms of their location in broader social practices. For example, how can we understand 'memory' as part of a legal performance of a defence in court, or how can we understand 'attitudes' in terms of their position in broad debates about controversial topics?

Discourse workers have done more than highlight an important topic for social psychologists to study. They have proposed a completely different analytic approach from the experiments and questionnaires common in mainstream North American research. They have also proposed a complete rethink of the terms that social psychologists use to understand what people do. And often they take a very different approach to epistemological issues of knowledge and truth.

BOX 7.1　Foucault and discursive psychology

Parker (most definitively in 1997b) has made a number of claims about the need for a more Foucauldian version of discursive psychology, and this distinction has been picked up by subsequent literature in critical psychology (e.g. Willig, 1999). Taking the (now rather dated) focus on 'function, construction and variability' of Potter and Wetherell's (1987) original work, Parker suggests more 'Foucauldian' replacements of 'power', 'constitution' and 'contradiction'. The Loughborough school of discursive psychology (which includes Potter, Edwards, Billig and Antaki) is accused of being more 'conservative', at times even embracing 'reductionism, essentialism and quantification' (Parker, 1997b: 294), making it more acceptable to traditional social psychology than his more 'radical' Foucauldian version of discursive psychology. This argument is not supported by any examples of discursive analysis, so it is difficult to evaluate the claims to analytical superiority. Also Parker's claims to be adopting a Foucauldian perspective are challenged elsewhere in this book, e.g. Chapter 4.

This chapter will focus on three connected themes, illustrating them with examples from published analytical research. First, it will describe the critique of individual psychology and the move to a discursive psychology. Second, it will cover work on discourse and fact construction. This will highlight the close relation of discourse work to social constructionism. Third, it will cover work on broader systems of discourse and their political implications. Let us start at the most basic level with the idea of an inner psychology itself.

Discourse, psychology and the individual

Individualist and cognitivist assumptions are wired very deep into psychology. The focus on individuals and their inner life of thoughts and memories, their faculties for information processing, and their evolutionary heritage of hot emotions and cool reasoning, has been treated as indispensable. In previous chapters we have seen a number of ways in which individualism has been questioned. Discursive psychology has drawn on the philosophy of the later Wittgenstein, on ethnomethodology, and on elements of Foucauldian thinking, to develop an alternative to this individualism and cognitivism. But these have been combined with direct studies of people's activities. In this section we will focus on the discursive respecification of memory and emotion. Let us start with an example that illustrates these features in the context of an analysis of US political hearings.

Lynch and Bogen (and Clinton) and the spectacle of history

One of the features of US political life is the regular occurrence of high-profile judicial hearings. The Watergate hearings led to President Nixon's resignation; the Iran-Contra hearings focused in particular on the role of Oliver North in providing covert funds for the right wing Contra guerrillas; President Clinton's grand jury inquisition involved his being questioned about lying and inappropriate sexual relations. Michael Lynch and David Bogen (1996) were particularly interested in the way notions of remembering were used in these hearings. For example, they note that Oliver North answered 'I don't remember' so many times during the Iran-Contra hearings that the words came to be called the Contra mantra.

The 'don't remember' response has the virtue of defeating what McHoul (1987) calls the binary logic of yes/no questions. The problem with such questions is that either option can lead to further trouble. While a 'yes' can imply guilt a denial can suggest dissembling when contradictory evidence is produced. Not remembering is neither agreement nor denial. Rather than stay with Lynch and Bogen's materials, let us take a more recent example from President Clinton's grand jury testimony.

Bill Clinton's phone call

Clinton has been asked about a phone call to his 'lover' Monica Lewinsky on a particular day. The issue at stake (although not spelled out here) is her reported anger and its possible causes. Could it be because Clinton had asked her to lie in an impending court case that both of them are involved in? This is how Clinton replies.

> (12.0)
> Mister Wisenberg ((C raises an index finger at
> Q)) I remember that she came in to visit that
> day, (0.5) I remember that she was very upset.
> (2.5)
> I don't recall whether I talked to her on the
> phone before she came in to visit, (.) but I
> may well have.= I'm no- not denying that I did.
> I just don't recall that.

Clinton is on camera throughout the testimony. In the twelve seconds following the difficult questioning he locks his hands together as if praying, frowns, purses his lips and stares at the table. Non-vocal activity like this is ambiguous. We may see him in desperate trouble, groping for some way of managing this killer question. But equally we may see him as trying really hard to be co-operative and 'searching his memory' for the required information that would anyway be innocuous. Whatever the openness of the visual image, his reply builds the picture of someone trying his best to remember. It acts out the listing of items recovered from a search by looking back at the camera, addressing his interrogator directly and raising a finger to underline his points. What he lists has already been established as a public record – that Lewinsky visited and that she was upset.

Now note how he manages the contentious phone call. He doesn't *recall* talking to her, but he *may* have. He is not denying it. This beautifully evades the binary logic. He does not accept that he talked to her on the phone. If he did, the interrogator may come back directly with a question about what was said during the call, presenting yet another possibility of incrimination. Nor does he deny talking to Monica on the phone. Such a denial may be contradicted by a public record or testimony. Clinton is able to avoid both these dangerous options by his claim, and theatrical display, of not recalling.

Note also that the effectiveness of this approach to questions is dependent on its plausibility. People *do* have difficulty recalling things. For someone to remember one phone call out of very many *may* not be surprising. Moreover the less memorable the event the less likely it is to be remembered; if this call has not been remembered then it is unlikely to have contained consequential and incriminating interaction. The beauty of it is that Clinton is doing just what anyone would who was trying his or her best to recall and failing, in the face of hostile and insinuating questioning. Its rhetorical effectiveness is precisely that it may not be rhetorical!

Discursive psychology, cognition and action

Let us sum up the main points that the Clinton example illustrates. First, remembering and non-remembering are practices done in discourse. That is not to say that nothing is going on in Clinton's head, that chemical reactions, neurons and so on are not involved. The point is that the practice of remembering and forgetting is a public and social one.

Second, this example shows the way remembering is evaluated not through comparing input with output as in a traditional cognitive psychological memory experiment, but via normative criteria that are brought into play locally, managed rhetorically, and are open to contest.

Third, there is no simple objective record against which a remembering or failure to recall can be compared. Outside the world of the laboratory, where researchers can use their unlimited definitional authority to specify the nature of the input, there are only versions that can be more or less telling or open to doubt (Edwards & Potter, 1992).

More generally, this example shows that there are two distinct approaches to memory. Psychology has been dominated by the traditional cognitive approach that compares input with output. This has offered some interesting observations about capacities and competences. However, its relation to memory as a social practice in courts, relationship disputes and school classrooms is complex and, as yet, not well understood. Discursive psychology takes a very different approach. It considers how memory, remembering, failures to recall and so on appear in practical settings. It considers the way versions are built up as plausible versions of the past, or dismissed as mistakes or lies.

Just in case memory seems to be a rather soft case to illustrate a discursive approach to psychological phenomena, let us take a further example: emotions.

Edwards and emotion

It is difficult to resist the idea that emotions are things that emerge within us. We think of them as linked in to physiology and, sometimes, as things that burst through cultural restrictions as a legacy of a more primitive animal past. Psychology degrees endlessly talk of the sympathetic nervous system and its ability to generate a surge of emotion that triggers the famous fight–flight response. However, a number of researchers have started to work up a very different image. This image does not take emotion as something underlying discourse, and separate from discourse, but as something that is managed and made accountable in discourse. Emotion is invoked, described, displayed for the purposes of actions. Rom Harré (1986) and Richard Buttny (1993) have made important contributions, but we will concentrate here on the more recent work done by Derek Edwards (1997, 1999).

Edwards has two rhetorical targets. On the one hand, there is the ethological, universalist idea of people, whatever their culture, sharing the same basic set of emotions. Although this notion dates back at least to Darwin, it has been more recently popularized by Paul Ekman (1992). On the other, there is a cognitive psychology of emotions, developed by researchers such as Anna Wierzbicka (1995). This considers emotions in terms of abstract models that build on universal conceptual primitives such as 'good' and 'bad'. (We will not consider the technical details here!)

Edwards raises a major concern with various styles of cross-cultural research into emotions. Their problem is that rather than being open to difference in emotions they invariably start with English categories. That is, if you are doing cross-cultural work on emotions it is very difficult to avoid looking for anger, sadness and so on. This means that typical English emotion terms are treated as the kind of thing that emotion *is*, and the problem is to look for *it* – emotion – cross culturally. Indeed, when we look at emotion in this way we can start to question whether the very *category* 'emotion' is part of the problem. Edwards notes that the category of emotion is a recent arrival even in English:

> the English word *emotion* has only recently acquired its current status as a *superordinate* category under which other words such as *anger*, *indignation*, *jealousy*, and *surprise* can be grouped together. As a historically modern concept (at least in English), the word *emotion* starts to look a dubious category under which to group all the ways that other cultures (including our own, in other times) talk about feelings, reactions, attitudinal judgments (if we can use all *these* terms), and related matters.
>
> (1997: 196)

He is here highlighting the ethnocentric basis of studies which take a variety of possible notions that are given priority in other cultures, and make them all subordinate to the English category of emotion.

Although Edwards's critique is important, it is only a move on the way to building a very different account of, um, emotion (see how I am caught up in the ethnocentric problems that Edwards highlights: I am writing this book in English and framing things using the English word). What Edwards proposes is an approach that does not start from a technical vocabulary of emotion terms, or from the idea that emotions are related to cognitive models. Instead he demonstrates the virtue of considering the way emotions enter into actual practices through being described, avowed and displayed. He is here starting from the fundamental discursive psychological idea that *words, categories and so on are there for what you do with them*. To understand emotion the thing to do is not to consider it in the abstract but to look at emotion in its home environment. And studies of emotion here find an extraordinary flexibility and rhetorical development that is almost entirely absent from the traditional studies.

Let us take one of Edwards's examples. He has been studying material from relationship counselling sessions. As you would expect, the passions of relationship trauma, which are both reported and enacted in the sessions, provide a productive hunting ground for the emotion researcher. This example comes from the first session with a couple Edwards calls Jeff and Mary. They have been asked by the counsellor why they have come for counselling in the first place. This is part of Mary's answer.

> *Mary* (. . .) so that's when I decided to (.) you know
> to tell him. (1.0) U::m (1.0) and then::, (.)
> obviously you went through your a:ngry stage,
> didn't you?
> (.)
> Ve:ry upset obviously, .hh an:d uh, (0.6)
> we: started ar:guing a lot, an:d (0.6)
> just drifted awa:y.

In this extract Mary reports her telling Jeff about having an 'affair' with another man and Jeff's reaction. Edwards beautifully dissects the way in which Mary is able to construct and deflect blame in this passage. And blame here is not just an abstract moral matter – important though that may be – but also a consequential, practical matter with respect to who needs counselling and who needs to change.

First, note the way that Mary describes Jeff's reaction as *emotional* rather than as a damning rational condemnation of Mary's actions and character. And by characterizing the emotions as 'obvious' and a 'stage' she presents them as understandable, conventional and appearing in the proper place. Second, note the way an understandable 'angry stage' sets up something that Mary exploits – Jeff's anger is continuing beyond its appropriate place, and this is getting in the way of progress. It is this continuation of anger beyond its proper time rather than her original affair that has started to be the problem for counselling.

Edwards is here pointing out the kinds of business that emotion categories can perform:

> Emotions and cognitions (and the differences between them) are not just sitting there, inside Jeff's head and actions, waiting to be reported on. 'Anger' and 'upset' are *descriptions* that, first and easily missable, can be used to

BOX 7.2   The context debate

One of the most high-profile debates at the intersection of discourse work, conversation analysis and critical psychology has concerned the role of context in analysis. Put at its crudest, the debate hinges on whether analysis should start from an existing idea of the context of a particular interaction or should start from material available in the interaction itself. The conversation analyst Emanuel Schegloff (1992) has highlighted two problems with traditional ways of considering interaction to be determined by its context.

The first is the problem of relevance. Given the highly varied ways in which context and identity can be formulated, which formulation is relevant? Are two people interacting in a hairdresser's an expert and a client, two friends, two women, a black worker and a white client?

The second problem is the consequentiality of the context. What is it about the room, say, or the West, that has consequences?

Schegloff argues that these problems are profound and difficult to manage. His approach is to do analysis. If we have good records of interaction, we can consider how context is *made* relevant, described, orientated to, and so on, by the participants. And we can consider what is consequential in terms of the patterning of activities. One of his observations is that analysis of this kind may highlight the *lack* of consequence of obvious features of context.

Schegloff was invited to develop a version of this argument for the journal *Discourse & Society*. In *Whose Text? Whose context?* (1997) he raised the issue of how far critical researchers were imposing their concerns on inter-action. He took the issue of gender and interruption and suggested, through analysing some examples, that some of the claims about interruption being gender-related (men interrupt more) were questionable.

This article sparked vigorous debate. Margaret Wetherell (1998) responded by suggesting an alternative way of seeing the relevance of gender in a set of materials. They ended up disagreeing on some analytic points (see Schegloff, 1998). Michael Billig (1999b, 1999c) has vigorously attacked Schegloff's views and the broader conversation analytic take on interaction; Schegloff has responded equally vigorously (1999a, b). Both make telling points. Articles by Speer and Potter (2000) and Stokoe and Smithson (2001) take the debate forward through analysis of heterosexism and gender.

Overall, although some of the heat has been a distraction, the debate has raised fundamental issues about what is involved in doing analysis that are broadly relevant to critical researchers. Most discursive psychologists admire and emulate the analytical rigour of conversation analysis, while being concerned to flesh out 'broader' constructionist concerns (the production of 'relationship counselling', critiques of cognitivism and racism, adult–child relations) with detailed analytical examples. This blurs the artificial separated boundaries between 'micro' and 'macro' in analysis.

construct reactions as reactions, and *as* emotional ones, rather than, say, as something like coming to a view or an opinion.

(1997: 172)

It is through looking at these categories as they appear in these practical situations that we start to understand their role and the way they can provide particular rhetorical oppositions. It captures just the stuff that is missed from the abstract cognitive modelling and cross-cultural studies of the 'perception' of emotions in faces.

DISCUSSION QUESTIONS

1   Is this going to be all there is to cognition and emotion?
2   Will there be 'nothing' left after a full-scale study has considered the way the terms for mental objects in traditional psychology are analysed for their role in social practices?
3   Do we need to change our everyday views of cognition and emotion?

Emotion, rhetoric and discursive flexibility

Edwards suggests that whatever semantic and conceptual features there may be to emotions, and whatever similarities there may be between these things in different cultures, what is crucial is the flexible potential of emotion terms. They can be worked up in different ways to do different things. Indeed, the flexibility and rhetorical potential of emotion terms make them ideal for performing a range of actions, for making one's actions accountable. Edwards (1997: 194) offers a variety of possible ways in which emotion terms can figure in interaction as a start-point for study. Here are some examples:

1   Emotions contrast with cognition. Actions and words can be constructed as expressions of feelings rather than of thoughts or opinions.
2   Emotions can be irrational or rational. Although emotions can be countered to thought-out responses, they can also be treated as rational and appropriate.
3   Emotions can be driven by events or dispositions. They may be responses to things that happen that anyone would have; or they can be characteristic features of the way individuals act.
4   Emotions can be controllable or can be passive reactions. Feelings can be expressed or acted out, or can flood through the person beyond their control.
5   Emotions can be natural or moral. They can be presented as something that is automatic and bodily (the evolutionary heritage again) or as righteous judgements on actions and events.

It is important to emphasize that these are not simply statements 'about' emotion; rather they are listing different things that can be *done* with emotion terms *in interaction*. The point here is to lock the study of emotion into a study of human practices in counselling and courtrooms and other practical settings. Rather than moving to abstraction and universalism, this approach stays with the specifics of emotions and their local deployment.

More broadly, in terms of critical social psychology, the problem with etho-logical and cognitive notions of emotion is that they encourage a static determinist notion of human action. They make it seem very resistant to change, and thereby encourage a conservative, fatalist approach to life. These more traditional con-structions of emotion also imply that explanations of action need to consider *features of individuals*, as do programmes for change, rather than seeing actions in relation to broader social and political arrangements.

Just as with the notion of memory, a very different perspective comes from taking *practices* rather than *cognition* as primary. We move away from seeing emotions as inner objects that influence behaviour and are perceived by looking inwards, to seeing them instead as public, social entities that have a role in getting things done. Moreover, by focusing on practices as discursive psychology does, we get away from the abstract, technical concerns of psychologists and start to consider issues that arise as important for people in the settings in which they live their lives. Hence discursive psychology is an important resource for critical social psychology.

Discourse and construction

Up to now we have been concerned with the way discourse work provides a counter to more traditional individualist forms of psychology by focusing on the way psychology is public and social, and how it is constructed and used in practices. Another fundamental interest in discourse work is fact construction. How are versions of people, events and social relations put together to make them seem literal and factual? And what are these versions used for? For example, how can a version of the role of the royal family in British society be produced to appear both obvious and sensible? Before discussing this work it is worth commenting on some different ways in which constructionism has been understood in psychology.

Constructing reality

Constructionism, constructivism, social constructivism, sociological construction-ism – there is actually a rather complicated terrain of different positions with very similar names but rather different ways of treating reality and subjectivity. Indeed, a description of social constructionism in its broadest sense, as a perspec-tive wherein people are seen as produced (constructed) through social interaction (rather than through genetic programming and biological maturation) is an adequate description for most areas of social psychology. Ken Gergen (1999) usefully distinguishes a number of different traditions. The most relevant are the following.

Constructivism has been used in psychology to describe the work of thinkers such as Jean Piaget and George Kelly. There is a strong emphasis on the constructions as something mental (like images or pictures) produced through interaction with objects or some features of the external world.

Social constructivism has been used for work where the constructions are something mental, as with constructivism, but they are generated as much through social relations and conversation as through interaction with objects. Lev Vygotsky and Jerome Bruner are key exponents of this perspective. Another variant of social constructivism comes in the form of social representations theory, developed by Serge Moscovici. Its emphasis is on mental representations and how these are used to construct reality.

Social constructionism is distinct again for giving discourse a central role in the construction of self and the world. In social psychology it has been developed in particular by thinkers such as Rom Harré (Harré & Gillet, 1994), John Shotter (1993) and Gergen himself. Gergen (1994) usefully highlights some basic assumptions for a social constructionist science. These include the following:

1   The terms we use to describe ourselves and our worlds are not dictated by their objects.
2   The terms through which we understand the world and ourselves are social artefacts, produced over historical time through exchanges between people within cultures.
3   Any account of the world or self is sustained not by its objective validity but by social processes.
4   Language derives its significance in human affairs from the way it functions within relationships.

Discursive psychology takes a broadly constructionist position, although its roots are rather different, lying within the sociology of scientific knowledge (e.g. Woolgar, 1988 and see box 2.1, p. 26) and non-foundational philosophy (e.g. Rorty, 1989). Some of these ideas will be covered more fully in the next chapter.

Construction in discursive psychology

Jonathan Potter (1996a) has clarified the role of constructionism in discourse work. He starts with the observation that constructionism can be understood as a practical position. Rather than searching for a fundamental philosophical justification, the idea of discourse *constructing* the world rather than *reflecting* it is much more productive in research terms. Reflection is a metaphor (the mirror metaphor, following Rorty, 1980) that makes descriptions passive; they merely reflect the world and they can even stand in for the world. Construction, however, suggests activity. Descriptions are doing things; they are parts of practices and they are inextricable from history and conflict. For Potter, this is the start-point of the analytic perspective of discursive psychology.

Discursive psychologists have found it useful to distinguish two levels of construction:

John Shotter

*'All my work – which, incidentally, is better called, I now think, "social ecology"
(Shotter, 1984) rather than 'social constructionism' (Shotter, 1993a, b) – has been
dominated by one negative theme and two positive concepts. The negative theme
(taken from Wittgenstein's, 1953, later philosophy) is that, whatever concepts we
take to be intellectually basic in our studies, we must always look beyond them, to
their grounding in a larger, dynamic network, that engendered by the relations
between our social and natural activities and their surroundings. The two positive
concepts, which interlock, are living spontaneity and joint action (initially taken
from Luria, 1961, and Vygotsky, 1962). Everything we later do, deliberately and
voluntarily, as socially responsible individuals has its origins in what we do
spontaneously as living beings, in dialogical response to the activities of the others
and othernesses around us. Recently, this has led to a study of the work of
Voloshinov, and Bakhtin.*

1 First, we examine the way discourse *itself* is constructed: how are words,
   idioms, metaphors, accounts, stories and so on put together in the course of
   interaction? For example, how is a description manufactured to present
   something we have done as orderly and unproblematic? We are all fantas-
   tically skilled builders of descriptions, having spent our lives learning how to
   do it. Part of the art of discourse analysis is to reveal the complicated work
   that goes into this effortless building.

2 The second level of construction looks at the way versions of the *world* are
   constructed in discourse. How does someone assemble a picture of her/his
   inner life, or of the way society operates, or of characteristics of members of a
   minority group, in order to do something in interaction?

The general point is that descriptions are construct*ed* (how are accounts
built?) and construct*ive* (how do accounts build the world?). These different
constructions are not there by accident. Discourse researchers have focused on the
way constructions are used in different practices. For example, when we considered
Mary's description of Jeff's 'angry stage' earlier in the chapter we were interested in
the way it constructed problems as lying within Jeff. This is not just a moral
construction – who is right and who is wrong in this relationship. The description
also has a *practical* upshot. It contributes to making Jeff the focus of counselling,
and the one who has to change his life. It is a general feature of discursive
psychology that it treats constructions (the building of accounts, the building of
the world) as *orientated to action*.

It is the role of descriptions *in action* that the mirror metaphor misses. Research that considers language as important for how accurately it mirrors the world is focused on issues of truth and falsity or, to put it another way, on the relation between the description and what is described. For discursive psychologists, however, accuracy is often beside the point. (Indeed, accuracy is itself a troubling and contested notion.) Different descriptions are often equally accurate – it is what they are *doing* that is significant. The different constructions underpin different actions. Constructionism in discursive psychology encourages us to consider these differences and the actions they underpin.

Facts and the dilemma of stake

One of the reasons why descriptions are important in interaction has been highlighted by Derek Edwards and Jonathan Potter (1992). They note that, when they are communicating with one another, speakers and writers are caught in a *dilemma of stake*. What this means is that when a speaker is describing something (e.g. 'It's raining outside') there is always the possibility of taking that description as *either* saying something about the thing that is described (wonderful British weather) *or* saying something about the speaker (does the speaker want me to get the washing in?). It is a generic feature of interaction that speakers can treat others as saying what they do because of their stake in what is being claimed. For example, I am writing this in the middle of a general election campaign. It is characteristic that when a politician such as William Hague (former leader of the Conservative Party) makes claims about his beliefs, about the economy or about a 'flood of bogus asylum seekers' his claims are treated by media commentators and other politicians as a product of his stake in marketing the Conservative Party's policy and dealing with its weaknesses.

Rather than being something aberrant and a feature of general elections, Edwards and Potter suggest, this dilemma of stake is something that pervades our interaction with others. It may be less dramatic, but we inspect what other people say for how it may be related to their stake in what is said. Did they pay me that compliment to butter me up? Was that offer an attempt to influence me? Did they mention their car problems because they wanted a lift? Although this possibility is always there we do not have to think that way at all times as if we live in a world of cynical manipulators. The point about a dilemma is that it can have two poles. We can also treat as straightforward and sincere people whose descriptions are merely telling it how it is. Moreover, we are not passive victims of this dilemma. We can construct our descriptions in ways that manage the dilemma. We can make them seem separate from us and from our interests, and we can do things that disguise or counter our interests.

Again, this is not necessarily cynical or manipulative. In one way or another we learn to manage these things as we grow up as conversationalists. Discursive psychologists have identified a number of techniques through which descriptions are made to seem solid and independent of the speaker and thereby manage the dilemma of stake. Let us consider some of these, taking a particular example of talking about strange or paranormal experiences.

Jonathan Potter

'I have spent much of my academic life attempting to develop an alternative to mainstream experimental social cognition. Discursive psychology is concerned with people's practices and how they are understood and organized. Its focus is on action, *situated in* interaction, *and given sense through the* categories, formulations *and* orientation *of participants. Practices understood in this way have virtually been ignored by cognitivist work (Potter, 2000). I find the richness and subtlety of interaction fascinating to study and its sophistication often contrasts with impoverished strictures of psychological 'experts'. I am also excited by the possibility of showing that what seems solid and timeless is, in fact, contingent and constructed. One of the challenges of critical work is to develop ways of doing research (rather than theorizing or moralizing) that can do justice to critical concerns.*

Making the extraordinary real

Robin Wooffitt (1992) has done a wonderful study of the way people tell stories about extraordinary events such as ghosts, poltergeists, flying saucers and other mystic events. His interest in these things is not just because of their intrinsic fascination – although it is hard not to be entertained by his material. It is also because it is an enormously rich arena for studying fact construction. The beauty of talk about ghosts is that in most situations people tend to be sceptical. If we want to look at fact construction then descriptions of ghosts and flying saucers are a good starting place. In effect, the less the surface plausibility of some description the more work that has to go into managing the dilemma of stake, thereby making it factual rather than fanciful. Ghost talk brings fact construction out into the open.

Wooffitt identifies a number of common features of accounts of extra-ordinary events. They tend to start in the same way and they often have particular elements in them. From a discursive psychologist's point of view these features can be seen as ways of managing the very sharp dilemma of stake that arises when telling extraordinary tales.

Indirect references in openings

Let's take an example (this is not one of Wooffitt's) and consider just one of these elements. The speaker in the following extract is describing seeing a UFO. This is how they start their story.

Um::, (2.0)

i:t wasn't okay the first bit wasn't really an <u>abduction</u>

it was a °it was just a° (1.0)

well I saw it (.) a I saw a <u>UFO</u>

°or whatever spaceship or whatever you wanna call it°

and err it was when I was living in South Africa

and I guess at the time

I °was about thirteen or something like that° (.)

and em(.)I was at boarding school

Wooffitt notes that paranormal accounts typically start with a number of regular features. For instance, they often start with an oblique reference to the phenomenon that is to be talked about. If they are going to talk about a poltergeist, they do not start by describing it as that, but usually use some more indirect description such as 'the weird thing' or simply 'it'. Why is this? Because easy familiarity with the technical terms may give the impression that they were the sort of person who believes in poltergeists or flying saucers – the sort of person who wants to see them, who will imagine them when they're not there, and who will interpret the flimsiest evidence as proof of their existence. The oblique reference is a subtle way of managing issues of stake.

What is nice about the example above is that we can see this dilemma played out in the talk. The speaker uses the technical and explicit term UFO right at the start. This is not what you would expect on Wooffitt's analysis because of the way it positions the speaker as a believer. Yet what happens immediately is that the speaker repairs what he was saying to something looser: 'or whatever' (lovely description, 'whatever', suggesting indifference to the actual term 'UFO') followed by 'spaceship or whatever [again!] you wanna call it'. Contrary to how one might imagine descriptions work, the speaker starts from a clear and certain term and repackages it as loose and uncertain. Wooffitt's account of what is going on explains why this should happen.

Let us take a further feature of Wooffitt's analysis to develop this way of thinking about how accounts are made factual as they are delivered.

I was just doing X . . .

One of the common features of the way people tell stories of extraordinary events is that they often deliver them as a contrast to something ordinary. For example, Harvey Sacks (1992) noted that when people told stories of President Kennedy's assassination a common description would go: 'At first I thought a car had back-fired, and then I realized that the President had been shot.' There may be a number of reasons for describing things in this way (and think of the enormously wide range of possible alternatives), but one of them is to highlight the specialness by contrasting it with the mundane.

Wooffitt develops this way of thinking about accounts of paranormal experiences by considering them in terms of categories. One of the problems with telling stories about strange events is that you may be categorized as a 'loony' who believes in impossible things, or someone weirdly credulous. In terms of the dilemma of stake the account risks being treated as being about the speaker and her/his stake and interests, rather than as a straightforward description of an event. How do speakers manage this dilemma? One way is to build their membership of an alternative category that does not have this problem. The ideal contrast with 'loony believer in the impossible' is 'ordinary, everyday person'. This helps explain why our assassination witness describes things as they do; they present their first thought as the mundane thought that anyone might have.

Wooffitt notes that when describing paranormal events people use descriptive forms that emphasize their thoughts or their actions. Let's take an example with an action focus. The basic form that these take is:

> I was just doing X [where X is a mundane thing]
> when Y [where Y is an extraordinary thing]

This mundane action works against the idea that they are a 'crank' or 'loony' hoping or expecting something weird to happen. The following is from a little later in the same UFO story we started above. I have marked the X and Y on the account.

it was probably(.) it was probably urr about half past	
eight in the evening(.)	
and I was walking acr- like down the <u>sports</u> track (.)	
listening to my <u>walkman</u>	←X
just °I don't know what I was doing	
but I was just listening to my walkman	←X
and whatever else kinda thing°	
I was just walking down the sports track (.)	←X
and err (.) ↑<u>basically</u>	
in my school there was a big <u>hall</u>	
and on top of the hall was a big clock to:wer	
(1.5)	
and err (.)	
so I was walking (.)	
walking towards that (.) °part of the school°	←X
an:d then something just caught my eye (.)	
and (.) I looked up	
(1.0) and err (0.5)	
what I saw I cou- I couldn't really see an outline (0.2)	
but um: it was just some:thing (.) floatin in the air	←Y
(1.0)	
and (.) it's what I believed to be (.) a °UfO↓°	←Y
and it was (1.0)	
li:*ke it had ↑<u>lights</u> <u>going</u> <u>around</u> <u>it</u>	
in err sort of err (.) circular pattern	

This example is a good illustration of Wooffitt's claims. We can see the speaker repeatedly producing mundane descriptions, with a variety of repairs and versions ('listening to my walkman', 'whatever else', 'just walking down the sports track'). He does not merely describe mundane actions and then move on; he reiterates the mundane actions just before describing the extraordinary thing, a UFO. This shows the speaker orientating to the importance of this X/Y structure in constructing the description. He reiterates his ordinariness just prior to describing the UFO, just when there might be an issue about whether he was imagining, wanting, fantasizing about aliens.

Rhetorics of reality

Potter (1996a) reviews a range of different procedures for constructing factuality and managing the dilemma of stake. These are rhetorical procedures for establishing what is said as credible and independent of the speaker. By simplifying a bit, they can be thought of as a kind of 'reality production kit', but beware of trying to identify them in isolation from each other – vivid description, for example, may provide category entitlement and collaboration simultaneously, and as we saw above, oblique reference was also a way of managing stake.

Reality production kit

1   *Category entitlement* Construct your talk as coming from a category that is credible or knowledgeable in a way that is relevant to the claim. The X/Y format above does this just when it is needed.

2   *Stake inoculation* Construct your talk as coming from someone whose stake in that talk is counter to what you would expect when making the claim. 'I used to be sceptical, but experience of [the death penalty/ workers' co-operatives/alien abduction/etc.] leads me to think . . .'

3   *Corroboration and consensus* Construct your description as corroborated by an independent witness (preferably from an appropriate category) and/or something that everyone agrees on 'Two or three other people started to look scared . . .'

4   *Active voicing* Use quotations and reports of thoughts to present the views and impressions of others as corroborating, or to show the vivid or unexpected nature of what is described. 'Karen turned to me and said, "What the hell's that?"'

5   *Vivid description* Make your description rich with vivid detail, careful observation and things that 'in themselves' would not be surprising. Vivid description invokes a powerful category: witness.

6   *Systematic vagueness* You may need to be systematically vague about features of descriptions that do not add up or which draw attention to your stake and interest in the claims you are making.

Script and dispositions in the construction of order

Constructing versions is not just about establishing the solidity of things beyond talk (through using talk in the right way). It is about establishing the nature of that solidity. One of the issues often fundamental in human affairs is the issue of how much action flows from the nature of a particular individual, or how much it follows social or external patterns. This issue was highlighted as fundamental in traditional attribution theory, but it has been reworked in discursive psychology. The interest there is in the way actions or events are constructed as scripted in some way, following rules or orderly and stable patterns or constructed as a product of unique or special dispositions, beliefs or personal characteristics. Such 'attributions' are, of course, bound up with issues of blame and have very different upshots.

Derek Edwards (1994, 1997) has developed the key thinking in this area. He shows the way 'script formulations' are used to generate order, and the business that this can do. Let's take one of Edwards's simpler examples. The following comes from an editorial in the British tabloid newspaper, *The Sun*. It appeared the day after the funeral of Princess Diana at which her brother, Earl Spencer, had made an impassioned speech attacking the papers for hounding her to her death.

> ***Don't blame the press***
> ***The* Sun *says***
>
> In the depths of his grief, Diana's brother is entitled to be bitter about her death . . . At such a harrowing time, we can understand his emotional outburst.
>
> (*The Sun*, 1 September 1997, p. 10)

We can see here a fantastic mix of emotion construction and scripting. Note the way emotion terms are here used to suggest irrationality – 'bitter', 'depths of grief', 'emotional outburst'. We have already noted that possibility above. Yet there is something even more interesting here. The emotions are constructed as scripted: grief *leading* to bitterness, harrowing time *leading* to emotional outburst. These relations are not argued for; they are treated as obvious and unproblematic – part of the script of everyday life.

The effect of this is to make Earl Spencer's words just what you would expect from someone (anyone) in his situation. The beauty of this from the newspaper's point of view is that it both sympathizes with him and discounts what he has said. He has said just the kind of emotional, bitter things that people do at times like this, to be sympathized with but not taken too seriously. The emotion and scripting together are a double whammy – they discursively neutralize his powerful attack on the press.

Construction, contingency and ideology

Discourse work is often criticized for not being critical enough. How does this detailed work on texts relate to a critical agenda? Discourse work on fact construction and the production of versions of reality are critical in two important ways:

1   First, they are a major part of the critique of mainstream social cognition work. As we saw in Chapter 2, social cognition sets up a contrast between outside and inside, between world and mind, where the business for social psychology to explain is the information processing of people's perception input from that world. This is what Edwards and Potter (1992) call the *perceptual cognitivism* of traditional psychology. Discursive work inverts and reworks this perceptual cognitivism. It emphasizes the way versions of world and mind are constructed, and established as factual, and as having particular orderly features, for practical purposes. It takes psychology out of the head and leaves it where it started: as a set of concerns that are relevant to different practices – cross-examination, counselling, complaining. It opens psychology to the, er, 'real world' concerns in all their complexity!

2   Second, discursive work is critical in a broader sense. Its constructionist approach emphasizes contingency. That is, it emphasizes the way versions of society and social organizations of classes, ethnic groups and gender can be considered as contingent constructions that are put together in such a way as to relate to practices or problems. This is in the tradition of classic studies of ideology that ask how social relations are legitimated and made to seem necessary, timeless and obvious. It is this latter strand of critical work that we will focus on.

Rhetoric and ideological dilemmas

We have already encountered the Marxist notion of ideology in Chapter 3, and indicated some of its limitations. One of the achievements of discourse work by figures such as Michael Billig, Derek Edwards, Jonathan Potter and Margaret Wetherell has been to develop and rework notions of ideology. They are not disagreeing with the central aim of studies of ideology, which is to understand how issues of meaning are involved in sustaining relations of domination (although the image of domination has a slightly quaint, slightly pre-Foucauldian feel to it). Rather they are disagreeing with the story of how ideology works. We have already encountered these ideas briefly in Chapter 3; here we will be looking at them in more detail. Let us start with the idea of ideological dilemmas and then consider the two most ambitious and realized studies of discourse in this tradition: *Mapping the Language of Racism and Talking of the Royal Family.*

Ideological dilemmas

The notion of ideological dilemmas was a collective product of Loughborough's Discourse and Rhetoric Group (Michael Billig, Susan Condor, Derek Edwards, Mike Gane, David Middleton, and Alan Radley when it was written). They noted that in studies of ideology it is common to distinguish *lived ideology*, which is part of the commonsense or everyday practices of a culture, and *intellectual ideology*, which is crystallized in the works of key thinkers – liberals such as Adam Smith, say (discussed in the 'Capitalism' section of Chapter 3). One of the things that both conceptions of ideology share is the importance of consistency. Ideology is treated as effective in so far as it hangs together in a consistent system. This is the point that the notion of ideological dilemmas was designed to contest.

The suggestion is that consistency is far from crucial: to be effective in practical settings, it is contradictions and tensions that are crucial. This was the conclusion in Chapter 5 in the discussion of sexism and the legitimation of gender inequalities. But let's take education as an example. The authors note that it is customary to distinguish two sorts of educational ideology. One is 'traditional', and focuses on learning set outcomes, and following rules; the other is 'progressive', and focuses on bringing out the pupils' own potentials and skills, allowing them to come to their own understandings of the world. Although these have been seen as opposed in educational debates and political discussion of the future of schooling, the insight of this approach is that in practical situations the two ideologies are bound up together in a dilemmatic relation. Teachers work with both ideas of education as they manage classes and try to achieve particular outcomes for pupils.

This is seen in Derek Edwards and Neil Mercer's (1987) study of the management of school lessons. They worked with video recordings of young pupils (eight- and nine-year-olds) in science classes. They identified in some detail a range of interactional devices used to lead pupils to a specific outcome while presenting the arrival at those outcomes as an achievement of the pupils themselves. They call this process by which teachers use actions and gestures to generate desired outcomes 'cued elicitation'; some of the major techniques are summarized below.

Cued elicitation

1   Use gestural cues and demonstrations while asking questions to indicate correct answers.

2   Control the flow of conversation – such as who is allowed to speak and when, and about what.

3   Use silence to mark non-acceptance or the inadequacy of a pupil's contribution.

4   Ignore or sidetrack unwelcome suggestions.

5   Take up and encourage welcome suggestions.

6   Introduce 'new' knowledge as if it were already known – and therefore not open to question.

7   Paraphrase pupils' contributions to bring them closer to the intended meaning.

8   Over-interpret observed events to make them seem to confirm what should be the case.

9   Summarize what has been done or 'discovered', in a way that reconstructs and alters its meaning.

(Modified from Billig et al., 1988: 54)

The general point is that concern with control and outcome, and with realizing the learner's potential and self-discovery, is fundamental to the practice of this kind of teaching. Neither ideology drives the practice on its own. Rather, it is the combination of the two in practice that sustains what is going on. And the combination of the two enables very different tasks to be achieved. The use of cued elicitation generates the specific outcomes that are inscribed in the curriculum, in learning targets, exam answers and so on, while at the same time allowing the practice to be constructed as pupil-centred and progressive. What appear to be tensions and contradictions when the ideology is considered in the abstract serve as strengths when it works in practice. We have already seen this in operation in Chapter 5, where we discussed the way unequal egalitarians play off assertions of equality against the constraints of real world practice to undermine moves for gender equality.

Let us see how this kind of thinking develops in one of the major discourse studies in social psychology, a study which is also one of the most ambitious in developing a critical theme.

Mapping the language of racism

Margaret Wetherell and Jonathan Potter's (1992) study of racism in New Zealand provided a radical contrast to both the sociology and the social psychology of racism available at that time. The sociological approach considered racism as a feature of conflicts between large-scale social groups. It typically drew on modified forms of Marxist thinking where racial conflict was understood as patterned on, or developed from, broader class conflict. The notion of ideology used by this socio-logical approach emphasized the development of false consciousness (see Chapter 3) that covered over real conflicts between minority and powerful groups, replacing them with false images that promote conflict between minority groups. For example, the shared class interests of working class blacks and whites might be submerged in a mythology of cultural difference and competition for jobs (Miles, 1989).

We have already discussed social psychological approaches to racism in Chapters 2 and 3. The classic authoritarian personality study (see Chapter 3) combined a Marxist account of social relations with a psychoanalytic account of personality development. Crucially, this study saw racism as, at least in part, a form of projected hostility resulting from particular forms of early parenting (Adorno et al., 1950). In contrast, social cognition approaches to racism focus on faulty infor-mation processing that results from the kinds of short cuts that generally make information processing more efficient, for example, short cuts that exaggerate similarities within groups and differences between groups (Hamilton & Troiler, 1986).

Discourse work on racism makes some fundamentally different assumptions from these approaches. Three can be picked out as particularly important.

1   It treats all versions of the world as constructions and focuses on what is done with those constructions rather than concerning itself with questions of truth and falsity. This allows it to avoid the danger of traditional work on stereo-types, which often ended up studying minority group characteristics to assess their truth, ultimately following the agenda of racism rather than subverting it.

2   It focuses on discursive resources rather than cognitive processes, and in particular the way resources are drawn on to legitimate inequality and exploitation. This moves the focus on to practices rather than features of individuals, and on to broader features of ideology rather than errors of processing.

3   It picks up from the 'ideological dilemmas' perspective in treating the fragmentation and variation of discursive resources as a potentially powerful feature rather than expecting ideologies to have conceptual order and rigidity.

Wetherell and Potter studied the talk of white majority group members who were mainly middle class professionals such as social workers, bankers, doctors and teachers. Mostly this talk was from open-ended or conversational interviews, although it was backed up by newspaper articles and reports of parliamentary debates. These people had often escaped the scrutiny of researchers on racism who had focused more on working class bigots or extremists who fit the traditional authoritarian picture; for these researchers racism has not been seen as a problem for 'people like us'. Yet people like us are involved in potentially the most important consequences of racism, as they control intakes to professions, dispense resources, have the power to label and exclude individuals, and are instrumental in the running of basic institutions of policing, employment and law making. They are also the people most able to disguise or discount racism. Often this involves the ability to provide articulate justifications for policies that have racist effects or cover injustices and inequalities.

In this case the issues at stake were often conflicts between the white majority groups of European origin (described by the Maoris as Pakehas) and indigenous groups of Maoris and Polynesian Islanders. These often concerned rights to land, inequalities of employment and political representation. Put simply, this study shows how majority-group Pakehas manage a fundamental dilemma. On the one hand, they do not wish to support policies that will makes their lives more complicated, will involve them in abandoning resources or privileges or lead to potentially threatening social change. On the other, they do not want to be heard as racist or bigoted, particularly when being interviewed by a sympathetic and liberal-seeming social researcher. The research is about how they manage this dilemma through the flexible and practical use of a range of symbolic and discursive resources.

Wetherell and Potter pick out a number of themes in their analysis of this material. Let us briefly take two to illustrate their general approach and some of their conclusions.

Mapping racism (1) Constructing social groups

One of the features that became apparent when Wetherell and Potter looked closely at the talk of these Pakeha majority group members was the variety of ways in which the nature of social groups was constructed. Traditional race discourse was easy to find in the material; that is, talk about innate intelligence, traits carried 'in the blood', skin colour, purity and so on. Yet it was not the principal way in which this talk was organized. It existed there as a kind of residual sediment, appearing at the edges of the talk, but not bound up with its main themes. Much more common was talk of culture.

When the Pakeha participants in this research talked about group relations, the situation of Maoris in New Zealand culture was the main building block. However, it was not a single building material; there were two principal forms of brick. First, there was culture-as-heritage, a repertoire of terms and metaphors used to build culture as an archaic heritage that must be treasured and protected from the rigours of the 'modern world'. Second, there was culture-as-therapy, a different repertoire of terms and metaphors used to build culture as a psychological require-ment for Maori well-being.

These repertoires were extremely user-friendly in late twentieth century New Zealand, and probably in other westernized countries as well. They probably still are. They seem to display a sensitivity to difference that is related to social relations rather than innate propensities. They are also relatively free of connotations of eugenics or bigotry. Yet this friendliness is part of what makes them usable for more politically problematic or racist tasks. Part of their power comes precisely from the fact that they do not have to be whispered, or kept discreet.

These constructions appeared in interview talk, newspaper articles and parliamentary debates, but often in ways that work insidiously against Maori and Polynesian political aspirations. For example, the culture-as-heritage repertoire could be used to freeze a social group into a particular position by separating 'cultural' actions from the 'modern world' of politics. In this study Pakeha parti-cipants rarely constructed their own group as having a culture – it had politics, nation and society. Maoris were the ones with culture.

The culture-as-therapy repertoire was equally pervasive, but used in rather different ways. It was used, for example, to represent young urban Maoris as deficient as *Maoris*. And it was also used to reduce Maori protests about sovereignty and land rights to the level of psychology. The protests become a consequence of difficulties with cultural identity rather than legitimate action against continuing injustice.

The important point is that although these discourses of culture can be publicly spoken and heard as positive, they can also be used to do some of the things that traditional racist discourses do. They can maintain the idea of natural or fundamental differences between groups, and they foreground in-group explana-tions of inequality rather than intergroup ones.

Mapping racism (2) Practical politics

We saw above that Billig et al.'s (1988) discussion of ideological dilemmas empha-sized that the power of ideology often flows from its fragmentary and dilemmatic organization. Another key idea is that of a *rhetorical commonplace*. Michael Billig (1987) notes that in any culture, at any time in history, certain phrases or sayings have a familiar and taken-for-granted quality. Often they seem proverbial or idio-matic. Such commonplaces form an assumed conversational currency. Wetherell &

BOX 7.3   Greenspeak

Green issues of pollution, genetically modified (GM) crops, reusable resources have been relatively slow to come to prominence for critical social psychologists. Given their world significance, and the relevance of a range of social psychological issues, this lack of attention is disappointing.

Some important headway has been made. Michael Michael (1996 and see box 3.1, p. 64) has studied some of the constructions of risk from 'natural' and 'artificial' radiation in the environment. Philip Macnaghten (1993) studied the way notions of nature and wilderness were understood in a planning enquiry for the placing of a new landfill site.

One of the most sustained treatments comes from Rom Harré, Jens Brockmeir and Peter Mülhaüsler (1999) in their study of 'greenspeak'. They were particularly interested in the way 'the environment' is constructed as an object, and the various uses that are made of these constructions. For example, they compared the way a British Nuclear Fuels brochure and a classic environmentalist text construct their positions as reasonable, both drawing on scientific constructions, and both implicitly recruiting the readers as sensible people like us.

Potter drew on these ideas when focusing on the way political discourse about race was organized in their material.

They noted that in the broad political discourse of newspaper articles, interviews and parliamentary debates, a small number of claims or arguments were repeatedly drawn on. Indeed, they could be formulated as a set of maxims.

Maxims of practical politics

1   Resources should be used productively and in a cost-effective manner.
2   Nobody should be compelled.
3   Everybody should be treated equally.
4   You can't turn the clock back.
5   Present generations cannot be blamed for the mistakes of past generations.
6   Injustices should be righted.
7   Everybody can succeed if they try hard enough.
8   Minority opinion shouldn't carry more weight than majority opinion.
9   We've got to live in the twentieth century.
10   You've got to be practical.

These statements are unexceptional and familiar – they have a taken-for-granted feel that is characteristic of mundane politics. Taking each statement individually, who could disagree that it is important to be practical, that history moves forward, that injustice and inequality are wrong? They can be seen as a summary of an area of folk wisdom.

Wetherell & Potter's interest was in how the maxims were used in practice. Note the way this list embodies some basic tensions. For example, while some of the maxims emphasize individual rights (2, 3, 6, 8) others emphasize practical considerations (1, 7, 9, 10). From a traditional position on ideology we might think that this weakened the effect of the maxims, which seem to be having a quiet war with each other. But the insights of ideological dilemmas lead us to expect that these tensions will make the maxims more powerful. The tensions provide rhetorical flexibility and argumentative power. One of the ways in which the maxims are flexibly used is in arguments against radical social change and Maori advancement in particular.

Take the contentious issue of teaching the Maori language in schools. Should Maori be available to all? Should it be a compulsory school subject? The maxims can be flexibly bought to bear on such suggestions. They could be attacked on grounds of principle (nobody should be compelled) or they could be attacked as unpractical and unsuited to the modern world (we've got to live in the twentieth century, you've got to be practical). Both these critical routes are constructed out of political commonplaces and therefore not immediately recognizable as having racist motivations. Moreover, such negative motives could be further concealed by stressing a personal desire to learn the Maori language, or claiming it would be nice to have as an optional extra in schools. Here is an example:

Wetherell . . . this Taha Maori programme, is it? What is it actually?
Kenwood A::h well you know I hope when I retire that I will learn the Maori language, I think it (.) I want to learn it you know because I think I have to learn it, but I'd like to, but I think it's they (.) unfortunate with these Te Kohanga Reo [a Maori language teaching programme] situations, is that, you know, they're sort of forcing Maoris and peop- (.) forcing Maori children to learn Maori language, well I can see it has no value in our education system. Now they'll straight away say that our system is wrong. But um er er you know as far as the Maori language is concerned, singing and that sort of thing and on the marae, it has its place. But in a Western world it has no place at all.

(Wetherell & Potter, 1992: 188–89)

This example shows the way the practical political resources of a culture can be mobilized to stop moves towards minority group advancement and the righting of past wrongs. The power of these resources is that they are clothed in the caring ethics of liberalism and common sense. They enable speakers to display themselves as concerned yet aware of the pressures of 'living in the modern world'. They are justifiable and, indeed, sayable, in a way that traditional forms of racism are not.

Wetherell and Potter's study shows how these justifications are put together, how they are assembled from various discursive resources, and the procedures for assembly. In doing so it highlights the difficulty for anyone wishing to combat arguments having these racist uses when they are couched in rhetorical common-places. Attacking these commonplaces directly risks appearing to attack common sense itself! The concern with common sense and political legitimacy is also central to Michael Billig's (1992) work on ideology and the royal family.

CRITICAL DILEMMA

Does this approach to racism place too much emphasis on the resources used to construct racism and the role of this kind of talk in sustaining social relations? Is there therefore a danger that individuals will appear to be less accountable for their racist claims? Or perhaps that is a good thing?

Talking of the Royal Family

Michael Billig's *Talking of the Royal Family* is one of the most ambitious critical works in the area of discourse and rhetoric. The study used over sixty group interviews with sets of family members from a range of social backgrounds. The interviews were done in a conversational manner to allow speakers the flexibility to construct the world in their own words, as well as to argue with one another and, sometimes, themselves. The royal family was a topic that was chosen because of its centrality and its legitimacy, and because, at the time of the research, there was a massive weight of public opinion in favour of the royal family and its continued place as the centrepiece of the British state.

The study attempted to show how members of different families draw on, and reproduce, notions of privilege, equality, nationality and morality when being interviewed about the royal family and its role in their lives and the life of the nation. Most broadly it documented the ways in which a weave of contradictory and dilemmatic notions were drawn on in practical settings, to cover over inequalities and legitimate current social arrangements. Billig suggests that the participants in the study are performing 'acts of settlement' in their talk: 'commonsense talk about royalty settles ordinary people down into their place within the imagined national community' (1992: 23). At the same time he shows the way that the participants' talk had a 'double-declaiming' character: 'as people make claims about the royal family, justifying its position of privilege, so they [are] making claims about the desirability of their own unprivileged lives' (1992: 23). Let us consider two of the themes in this work to illustrate its claims and the style of argument.

Talking royalty (1) The tourist argument

One of the major themes in the study concerned talk about the so-called 'tourist argument'. Arguments of this kind have been common in public opinion research, with respondents suggesting that abolishing the monarchy would be bad for the tourist industry and that this industry compensates financially the cost of the monarchy. Billig notes that the tourist argument is used as a rhetorical counter to economic criticisms of the monarchy. Hardheaded cynicism about the financial cost of the monarchy could be answered with a hardheaded cynical response in terms of tourist pounds. Billig builds his argument using quotations from his interviews:

> The mother was complaining about royal expense and extravagance. Her arguments elicited counter-economics from her son: 'I think it's good for the country and I think it brings a lot of trade in, it brings a lot of tourism' . . . 'The government's not going to stop it, it's bringing in billions and that's my reasoning, why I don't mind really.' Again, monarchy was the major tourist attraction: 'It's our biggest tourist draw . . . without that we've got nothing . . . there's nothing to top it, nothing to compare with the monarchy.'
>
> (1992: 40)

Billig's point is that these arguments have a dilemmatic structure – the one counters the other. The tourist argument is a powerful antidote to the economic critique. But he also notes that part of its success is its status as a rhetorical commonplace. The economic calculations are never performed; they are simply asserted and assumed to be correct. His participants talked of thousands, or billions of pounds, or a lot of money – they didn't cite statistics or address the complexity of the calculation to be done.

In fact, in the unusual cases where the economic argument was questioned, supporters of royalty would not continue with the economic justification, but hastily move away from rational, financial justification to emphasize nationalistic considerations. A critic of monarchy tried to undermine his mother's economic arguments:

> The first time he tried to interject the economic doubt ('its difficult to get the figures'), his voice was swamped by the combined effort of the rest of the family. He could hardly make his doubt heard in between talk of Buckingham Palace, the Japanese, the Americans. The Royal Family, including 'the old Queen Mother', were ambassadors '*all* over the world', said the mother. She turned to dismiss the economic argument, reversing its value: '*That's priceless I think*'.
>
> (Billig, 1992: 44)

Again, we can see the value of a rhetorical analysis here. We can see how the arguments are fluidly organized so that as one argument (economic) hits trouble another (nationalist) is developed.

Billig also notes that the opposition of these two arguments should not be overestimated. While nationalist ideas about the monarch as the central symbol of the state may seem to be contradicted by the economic rationalism of tourism and sightseeing, the economic argument is about national economics, not about household budgets or minimum wages. As Billig elegantly puts it:

nationality and rationality are not arranged into a neat ideological ordering, with the former residing at a deeper level than the latter. The tourist argument is not merely a surface rationalization for underlying nationalism, for the economics are already national, and nationality already seems rational. Rationality has been nationalized, even as nationality is being rationalized.

(1992: 45)

Talking royalty (2) Credit, debt and the just world

Another important theme in the analysis is the way the relative status of royals and commoners is maintained in these people's talk. They were able to give many reasons for being envious: the opportunities the royal enjoyed, their good life, their servants and palaces, being exempted from shopping, dusting and washing clothes, their incomparably greater wealth and so on. Billig suggests that they are reading into the royal life the counter to discontents in their own. Worries about money can be set against the royal wealth; concerns about job security can be contrasted by formulating the privileges of the royal job born into for life. This double-declaiming is pervasive in the material.

The envy is contained. It does not develop into a full-blown critique of royal privilege. In Billig's terminology, the credits of royal privilege are countered by a commonsensical debit. Although royalty do not know what it is like to get up at six in the morning and do a hard graft job, their life is not without hardship. One of the participants said that the royals could not relax in the evening with their feet up in front of the television as they might 'have to go out to a banquet'; another said that 'it must be hard doing what they are doing' and 'they have to go to film premieres and spend hours shaking hands'. Living the life of a royal was described as a 'hollow existence'. As Billig puts it:

> As the columns of credits and debits are summed, so the accounts are settled to arrive at the conclusion that there is a 'just-world', at least so far as royals and commoners are concerned.
>
> (1992: 124)

Ultimately Billig offers insight into the way the privilege and hereditary principles of monarchy are sustained as a central part of the state. His view of ideology and common sense as fragmented helps explain how trouble and conflict are rhetorically settled, and how the political *status quo* is perpetuated. The challenge it implicitly lays down is to find new ways of effecting social change that will not simply get fractionated in the shifting kaleidoscope of commonsense political reasoning.

Critiques of discourse and rhetoric

Although discourse and rhetoric research is a relatively new development, it has attracted its fair share of critiques from different groups of researchers with different concerns. Three examples will indicate some of the issues:

1   Traditional social psychologists, predictably, are doubtful of the methodo-
     logical rigour of the approach. Where are the control groups, randomization
     and statistical analysis? Isn't it possible to imagine alternative interpretations
     of materials? Isn't it just describing interaction rather than identifying its
     causes? For this kind of critique see Abrams and Hogg (1990) and the papers
     in Conway (1992), including responses from Edwards, Middleton and Potter
     (1992a, b).

2   For some critical social psychologists the problem with discourse work is that
     it is focused on discourse and not on more 'material' things like the self,
     bodies and social classes. For this kind of critique see Parker (1990, and
     response from Potter et al., 1990) and Nightingale and Cromby (1999; and
     critical commentary by N. Parker, 2001; see also Carla Willig's box below).

3   From a different perspective, some conversation analysts are concerned that
     the focus on people's abstract talk in interviews is not easy to relate to actual
     practices in particular settings. Widdicombe and Wooffitt (1995) discuss
     these kinds of criticism. There has also been a general move in contemporary
     discourse work towards collecting conversational non-interview data. Some
     papers in Carla Willig's collection (1999) illustrate this idea.

Carla Willig

*'For me, critical psychology is a process rather than a product. It involves the
continual questioning of the assumptions upon which our own and others' work is
based. This means that critical psychology is always in motion. It also means that
I feel a little trapped in this box. I do believe that critical psychology should have
something to say about the relationship between discourse and materiality, and
that we need to look at what makes certain constructions of reality possible. This is
important because such a focus allows us to think about what needs to be done in
order to change those constructions of reality which we experience as oppressive or
limiting.'*

Application

Discourse work has a number of practical and critical roles. First, as was noted
briefly in Chapter 3, it provides a way of thinking about ideology and its role in
sustaining particular social relations. In so far as the exposé of the operation of
ideological dilemmas and the weave of maxims of practical politics allow better
understanding of how social organizations are sustained, this ought to be a
powerful resource for social psychologists who wish to question the *status quo*. To
put it another way, anyone who wishes to promote social change in basic

institutions or question the legitimacy of social arrangements will be better armed with an understanding of the fragmentary and dilemmatic nature of ideology and the kinds of discourse repertoire that are used to keep things settled as they are. For example, anyone aiming to engage practically with the problems of nationalism and how they can be tackled would be well advised to read Michael Billig's (1995) analysis of how nationalism is threaded through the little words and rituals of everyday interaction.

Second, much of the impact, actual and potential, of discourse work comes from its critique of traditional ways of doing psychology. Discourse work has provided some of the most rigorous and thoroughgoing critiques of the methods psychology uses, the ways its theories are sustained, and the way notions of individuality are built into methods and theory at a very deep level.

Third, discourse work is also increasingly moving to consider interaction in institutional settings. Recent examples include studies of relationship counselling, of police interrogation and of calls to abuse help lines. (I am myself researching calls to the NSPCC child protection help line.) There is a prospect that this work may provide help in training as well as a greater understanding of what is going on in these settings.

Conclusion

Discourse work is less than twenty years old, and is evolving fast. It has made a major impact in Britain, continental Europe, Australia and New Zealand. It has yet to make much impact on the mainstream tradition of North American social psychology. However, that is partly because of the conservative approach to methods taken in the main journals and teaching institutions in North America. So far the main response to the critical issues raised has been to ignore them and hope they will go away, rather like the response to the crisis in social psychology of the 1970s (see Chapter 2). So many people, and so many institutions, have so much invested in the traditional methods and theories that it is hard to shift them. Yet when change does start to happen – as it undoubtedly must – then it could be quite swift.

B The best thing about discursive psychology

Discourse work places a fundamental emphasis on people as they live their lives, acting and interacting with one another. Its critiques are rooted in an appreciation of people's own approach to things rather than in abstract categories or statistical laws. In Billig's (1994) terms it offers a *populated* psychology.

W The worst thing about discursive psychology

It's hard, and it's difficult to learn to do. Badly done discourse analysis (like any other type of badly done analysis) is really bad!

Where next?

More sophisticated studies of psychology in practice, such as in therapy talk, with more applied studies that feed back into everyday practices. North American social cognition – storm the gates!

Practical exercises

1   Look for a television programme that has unedited chunks of non-scripted interaction. Some piece of 'reality TV' or a fly-on-the-wall documentary. Something with a lot of 'human interest' would be ideal (the breakdown of a marriage, contestants being ejected from *Big Brother*). Video it and go through the video looking for references to (a) memory; (b) emotion. Now read the first section of this chapter again and remind yourself of the way discursive psychologists have treated these terms as practical resources for performing actions. Now look at your examples and try to pick out some of the things that these words might be doing. For example, why are people describing themselves as having precisely these feelings? How does that relate to justifying what they have done or paving the way for future action?

2   Ask around friends and family to find someone who has had a strange or paranormal experience. You will find that a surprising number of people have if you ask them. Ask if they would mind being tape-recorded talking about it for a training exercise. Record them telling the whole story. Now transcribe the story as carefully as possible. (It will look a bit like the transcript in this chapter.) Now re-read the description of Wooffitt's study of paranormal accounts. Look at the opening of the account. Does it have the indirectness that Wooffitt found? Now look at the body of the account. Can you see X/Y constructions as strange or paranormal elements are introduced? Now take the reality construction kit from page 181. Go through it trying to identify at least one example of each element of the kit in your account. (Note that the use of these reality constructions will depend on the interaction – if you are a rabid ufologist who spends his time talking about Roswell the story teller is unlikely to treat you as a sceptical recipient; embellishment will be the order of the day!)

3   This exercise will take a bit of time, but it is worth it. Its aim is to start to identify some of the commonplaces of contemporary practical politics. It can be done live but a video recorder would help a lot. Collect a week's worth of news, current affairs programmes and panel discussion programmes. The most useful are the kind of programmes where a panel of opposing politicians are asked questions by a studio audience (e.g. *Question Time* in the United Kingdom). Review the discussion of the maxims of practical politics on pages 187–190. Now start to identify maxims from your material. Some of them will

be the same as those identified by Wetherell and Potter; others may be more specific or newer. How do you identify a maxim? It is something that is treated as not up for dispute. While other questioners may dispute aspects of the claim, the maxim will not be disputed. Often maxims appear at the end of a point to finish it off with a summary that sounds a bit like a proverb: 'So, you must move into the modern world here.' List these maxims as a table.

Reading

If you read only one thing, read:

Wetherell, M., Taylor, T. and Yates, S.J. (2001) *Discourse Theory and Practice: A reader*. London: Sage. **An excellent collection of classics (going beyond the confines of psychology) with some really clear contextualizing chapters.**

Classics

Billig, M. (1991) *Ideologies and Beliefs*. London: Sage.
Billig, M. (1992) *Talking of the Royal Family*. London: Routledge.
Billig, M. (1996) *Arguing and Thinking: A rhetorical approach to social psychology*, second edition. Cambridge: Cambridge University Press.
Edwards, D. (1997) *Discourse and Cognition*. London and Beverly Hills, CA: Sage.
Edwards, D. and Potter, J. (1992) *Discursive Psychology*. London: Sage.
Potter, J. (1996) *Representing Reality: Discourse, rhetoric and social construction*. London: Sage.
Potter, J. and Wetherell, M. (1987) *Discourse and Social Psychology: Beyond attitudes and behaviour*. London: Sage.
Wetherell, M. and Potter, J. (1992) *Mapping the Language of Racism: Discourse and the legitimation of exploitation*. Brighton: Harvester Wheatsheaf.
Wooffitt, R. (1992) *Telling Tales of the Unexpected: The organization of factual discourse*. London: Harvester Wheatsheaf.

Also useful

Conway, M. (ed.) (1992) Developments and debates in the study of human memory, *The Psychologist*, 5, 493–61. **A set of responses to discourse work by mainstream psychologists.**
Hook, D. (2001) Discourse, knowledge, materiality, history: Foucault and discourse analysis, *Theory & Psychology*, 11, 521–47. **For a critique of this work from a strict Foucauldian perspective see:**
Wood, L.A. and Kroger, R.O. (2000) *Doing Discourse Analysis: Methods for studying action in talk and text*. London: Sage. **Despite the methodological focus it provides an up-to-date summary of quite a lot of material.**

Difficult but worth it

Edwards, D. and Potter, J. (1993) Language and causation: A discursive action model of description and attribution. *Psychological Review*, 100, 23–41.

Chapter 8

Postmodern Critics

Here's an interesting story, taken from the film *Memento*, directed by Christopher Nolan. Leonard is an insurance investigator, whose memory has been impaired following a head injury he sustained after intervening in (what seemed like) a fatal attack on his wife. Leonard wants revenge for his wife's murder but his head injury appears to leave him unable to remember anything for more than a few minutes. He makes sense of his life by taking pictures of things with a Polaroid camera and scribbling notes on the pictures – these things stand in for his 'memories'. When he thinks he has discovered a 'fact' he has it tattooed on his body. Indeed, the main fact that gives his whole life direction and meaning is tattooed backwards across his chest 'John G raped and murdered my wife' – his life's one main 'truth' is readable only by looking in the mirror. It's not hard to find links with Lacan's mirror stage here.

The story itself is told backwards, forcing the viewer to see things in the same way as Leonard probably does – in small two-minute bursts that we have to try and piece together. Like Leonard, we form hypotheses as we go along about what is going on and who the heroes and villains are, only to have them falsified by what happens next (i.e. what happened in the previous two minutes). But the big problem for Leonard in organizing his life around revenge is that if ever he does succeed in exacting it he will forget. This leaves him open to exploitation by those who can understand and take advantage of his condition. The main way they can do so is by leading him to 'believe' that certain things are 'facts'. The result is a film that weaves together a set of stories into a coherent (enough) narrative, where we are left guessing what the 'real facts' are ourselves.

Memento provides us with some interesting ways into understanding post-modernism, because postmodernism messes up simple organizing stories of truth and reason. It adopts a perspective on the 'facts', on knowledge and on subjectivity that doesn't see these things as functioning in one way, for all people, for all time. Facts are no longer seen as unified and explainable, or locatable as distinct self-evident entities. Indeed, for Leonard it is precisely the presence of the 'facts' tattooed on his body that *creates* the problems and violence in his life. In the postmodern condition, state control is diversified, and transient social movements prevent any easy characterization of what the 'political' may be. The facts cannot be unproblematically 'represented' or 'discovered', knowledge is multiple, fragmented and indeterminate, and people are seen not as bounded, unique individuals, but as decentred, fragmented social constructions. Some postmodern writers, e.g. Jameson (1988, 1991) see the subject as schizophrenic – splintered apart from its 'unique individuality' much as Leonard appears to be.

By way of highlighting the utility (or futility) of postmodernism for critical psychology, this chapter will do three things. The next section will begin with a discussion of the problems around defining what postmodernism 'is'. It will move on to provide an overview of the development of some of the key epistemological notions of post-structuralism and postmodernism, mainly through a brief examination of key aspects of the work of Jean-François Lyotard and Jacques Derrida. Two key areas of interest in this work will be the development of a more sophisticated understanding of both language and claims to knowledge than modernism alone has given us.

The following section will review work in critical psychology that has used the title 'postmodern' or 'deconstruction'. Obviously there are a wide range of different arguments and issues here. However, the focus will be on the way postmodern and deconstructive thinking changes notions of the subject of knowledge, and what counts as 'social' and 'critical'.

The third section will explore the relation between broad epistemological arguments about realism and relativism that have arisen in critical social psychology and different kinds of critical practice. Part of the aim will be to provide an accessible overview of the debate, and part will be to explore some of the tensions and reflexive ironies in current critical work and its various arguments for philosophical legitimacy. A number of the issues introduced in this chapter are picked up and developed further in the final chapter.

For those trained solely in psychology this will probably be the most difficult chapter to identify with. I have endeavoured to keep discussion at an introductory level, but most of the theorists and debates covered are complicated, and may require careful and repeated reading and discussion.

Postmodern theories

The last few decades have seen some radical developments in philosophy and social theory. Much of this research could come under the umbrella term 'postmodernism', and the first part of this section aims to provide at least a working definition of what is meant by this notoriously slippery term. The following sub-section elucidates this further through the work of Lyotard, and this leads to a discussion of the possibility of 'postmodern politics'. The final section explores Derrida's work, providing some context through an examination of Ferdinand de Saussure's development of structuralism, and Derrida's post-structuralist developments of that.

What is postmodernism? Problems of definition

Most written work on postmodernism begins with some statement about the impracticality of defining what it is in any coherent or factual way. Although it is a term that appears in a wide variety of disciplines – architecture, film, literature, philosophy, music, art, social sciences and even technology – it has emerged as an academic line of study only since the 1980s. One way of understanding post-modernism is to set it in the context of the 'modern' that it is post-ing (literally 'arriving after').

Modernity is generally characterized as a historical period incorporating the Enlightenment faith in progress and reason. Modernity's accompanying narrative is that if we build our theories on basic foundations of reason, we will move towards universally applicable truths. The two competing political systems of state control that go with modernity are generally recognized as socialism and liberal democracy.

However, the tendency to see postmodernism in terms of a coherent histori-cal movement from modernism to postmodernism can be confusing, because from its own perspective there is no such thing. Indeed, feminist critiques of history as male-orientated highlight a central postmodern idea that history is a fiction (often a horror story!) that we all live in.

Judith Butler suggests that postmodernism is often invoked as a catch-all term for approaches which *subvert* important modernist tasks, like 'the effort to shore up primary processes, to establish in advance that any theory of politics requires a subject' (1995: 35). The term has often been used in critical and feminist psychology texts in a similar way to warn of the dangers of abandoning politics by abandoning the subject (as discussed in Chapter 6), or the real, or some such kind of grounding (e.g. Burman, 1990; Sampson, 1990; Gill, 1995; Parker, 1998; Nightingale and Cromby, 1999). Here postmodernism is seen as dangerous and apolitical, because the only way to represent human suffering or real world events is through retaining some fixed notion of reality and/or subjectivity, which post-modernism doesn't allow.

However, there are many different versions of postmodernism. For example, within critical social psychology there is a gentler, more friendly and inspiring postmodernism, which emerges from theorists such as Ken Gergen (e.g. 1994). Gergen suggests that we must understand postmodernism not as just another 'totalitarian discourse' but rather as 'an invitation to reflexivity' (1994: 414) – a way of seeing realities, and selves, as local, provisional and political (see box, p. 20). Foucault (1984) also contemplates the term 'postmodern'; he suggests that we should think of it as a general 'ethos' – a set of discourses and practices – rather than a historical era.

Postmodern enquiry focuses on 'local and narrative knowledge, on acceptance of the openness of practical knowledge, on the study of heterogeneous, linguistic and qualitative knowledge of the everyday world, and on validation through practice' (Kvale 1992: 51). There is a focus away from theorizing the interior of the individual, e.g. through cognitive mechanisms or consciousness, to the individual's relations in society and the implications of those relations on behaviour. The postmodern question would be not 'Is this statement true or false?' but rather 'What makes this statement legitimate?' and also 'What function does it serve?'

By way of further explicating what is meant by postmodernism, we will explore the development of the notions of post-structuralism and postmodernism,

Ken Gergen

'My involvement with critical work in social psychology has spanned over three decades. By and large, such work is not appreciated within the field more generally, so life in the critical groves can be quite difficult. Yet such work is essential not only to the vitality of social psychology, but in terms of its relation to society more generally. The critical channel is one of the few means by which voices from outside the discipline can be heard – voices of minorities, the voiceless, the marginalized and as well voices from other disciplines – anthropology, sociology, cultural studies and the like. I also feel that in the long run we must learn how to expand our genres of discourse so that we may go beyond critique. This genre in itself is limited, and not necessarily optimal for future building within the field or the society.'

starting briefly with the work of Frederic Jameson, and moving on to Jean-François Lyotard and Jacques Derrida in more detail.

Lyotard's work can be usefully, though cautiously, set in the context of Jameson's, in the sense that Jameson, like Marx, sees economic forms of organization as primary; he sees capitalism in terms of stages. We are now in the late or 'third stage' of capitalism, so postmodernism can be directly linked with this particular economic organization. Jameson argues that 'realism, modernism, postmodernism are the cultural levels of market capitalism, monopoly capitalism, and multinational capitalism' (Best and Kellner, 1991: 185). Postmodernism is a 'cultural logic' in dialectical relation with the economic arrangements of the market.

For Jameson, postmodernism becomes the logical conclusion to Marx's commodity reification (Jameson, 1992: 11), as it is simply about celebrating the 'signifier'. (See the discussion of post/structuralism below to help you make more sense of this.) Postmodernism is all about surfaces – it destroys the opportunity of depth as it relies on images that are separated from the things they refer to – the 'signified'. We glorify surface images that can have no meaning aside from their value as commodities.

Jameson's version of postmodernism takes Marxist theory as its starting point. It is seen in cultural terms, and is linked with economic organization. Our culture may be more diverse and technologically sophisticated than that of Marx's day, but it is still based on capitalism – it presents an intensification of the logic of capitalism. However, postmodernism is radically different in that it opposes the central feature of Marxist theory – its historical emancipatory narrative. Thus there is a tension between seeing postmodernism as on the one hand linked in with economic organization and, on the other, taking on board the radical epistemological developments that it brings. Jameson deals with this tension in various ways, but one postmodern theorist whom I find to be clearer on the role of narrative and epistemology is Lyotard.

Lyotard and the postmodern condition

Lyotard's ideas developed through his book *The Postmodern Condition: A report on knowledge* (1984). It was a report commissioned by the Canadian province of Quebec to investigate the way knowledge is being made sense of in the face of the new microelectronic technologies. (Lyotard's final report was probably the last thing they were expecting!) Lyotard argues that these knowledge industries are now driving our society, replacing the Marxist and modernist modes of production. But again we need to be clear about what is meant by 'modernism'. For Lyotard (1984: xxiii) it is a term that is used to:

> designate any science that legitimates itself with reference to . . . an explicit appeal to some grand narrative, such as the dialectics of Spirit, the hermeneutics of meaning, the emancipation of the rational or working subject, or the creation of wealth.

For Lyotard, the main problems with modernity arise from two of its distinguishing features: the requirement of a metanarrative and the need to have a communicable representation of reality. The failure of modernist scientific knowledge and rationality to achieve the status of an overarching methodology, and the consequent 'incredulity towards metanarratives' and the 'crisis of representation', have led to growing dissatisfaction with modernism out of which has sprung 'the postmodern condition' (Lyotard, 1984).

Metanarratives are organizing stories or narratives that create a unification of ideas and methodologies which may be used to understand all aspects of the social world. For example, in political/social institutions, there are 'unitary systems' based on an overarching idea, grounded in a metanarrative, of what constitutes a 'good' or 'just' life. Enlightenment myths presuppose that true emancipation can be achieved only through the application of rationality to communicable ideas. Metanarratives are overarching theories of modernism that have organized industrial society. Such metanarratives include Marxism, with its story of emancipation from capitalism, and science, with its story of emancipation through objectivity. For Lyotard, multiple 'little narratives' have now replaced these metanarratives.

Modernists such as Habermas (1990) have developed these ideas, seeking emancipation in a universal consensus, created through rational communication and dialectic. One of the key ideas to be taken from Lyotard's work is the issue of how operating with a metanarrative, a fixed point of reference, leads one to *legitimate one's argument with reference to this metanarrative*, such that it seems that one has some *pre-discursive realm* (something fixed, self-evidently true or real) to appeal to as a way of grounding one's argument.

Lyotard holds that the distinguishing features of modernism – metanarratives and the representation/reality dialectic – have acted as forces that are *insensitive to differences*, and consequently are *repressive and exclusionary* forces. In particular, political structures are notably maladapted to the eclectic and fragmentary nature of the postmodern condition, and many other different groups and value systems become marginalized as a result. Modernism incorporates and organizes a desire for certain legitimating criteria. These certainties create a 'violence to the other' through the marginalization of certain sectors of the population, (e.g. women, children, ethnic minorities), leading to their consequent powerlessness.

This is an important point that we will return to later, which allows theorists with postmodern leanings to organize a defence against the notion that post-modern thought is apolitical. One Lyotard-inspired line of argument would be that the violence of certainty operates defensively, transparently, as a power that can be used without even calling it such. It follows that postmodern analysis, in being sensitive to the ways that metanarratives close off alternative versions of the person or the world, can give us the tools we need to challenge the big stories that organize our lives. A postmodern analysis can also show us the ways in which traditional rationalist representations of reality suppress the emergence of their own discursive power.

Lyotard applies Wittgenstein's (1953) idea of language games. Wittgenstein viewed language as a series of games, organized by their own rules. He rejects the correspondence view of language, in which our language mirrors the world in some way. Instead the world exists for us through language; our linguistic concepts define our experience of it. Lyotard picked up on this idea, suggesting that science is a language game that denies the relevance of a wide range of other games. Scientific knowledge involves the use of the 'denotative game', which focuses on distinguishing between true and false knowledge. It may also employ the 'technical game', which distinguishes between what is efficient and inefficient, and the 'prescriptive game', which focuses on what is just or unjust.

There are plenty of examples of this in psychology, where the analogies and metaphors of computers are used to make sense of the workings of the 'mind' and 'cognitive processing', as well as social psychological phenomena (e.g. Cantor and Mischel, 1979; Nisbett and Ross, 1990). Lyotard would suggest that what makes such accounts plausible is their ability to link in with other language games which scientists themselves may not be aware of. While scientists would claim, in line with the denotative game, that the distinction between what is true and false is the only one at work, instead what really gives their accounts plausibility is the way they slot in with common sense – other language games. The identification of suppressed language games can therefore be of immense benefit to critical researchers in disrupting the domination of the denotative game. There are interesting parallels here with the findings of those working in the sociology of scientific knowledge (see Box 2.1 on the sociology of scientific knowledge).

For those interested in Lyotard's subsequent work it has developed from here, looking at how the multiple 'little narratives' that have replaced metanarratives in the postmodern condition legitimate themselves without the modernist recourse to metanarratives (e.g. Lyotard, 1989).

Postmodern politics?

Critiques of a postmodern politics often assume that political action and social change can be sustained only through the operation of some given truth or metanarrative, the perceived problem with postmodernism being often that it involves taking a critical stance towards certainties. For example, 'the flight from foundationalism, and the suspicion against claims of truth, is at the same time a flight from politics' (Baumann, 1992: 5).

The general call from a range of positions critical to postmodernism is for a watered down version in which it is possible to identify fixed points of reference, or self-referential metanarratives, which give us the criteria to assert, for instance (as we saw in Chapter 5), that there are such things as 'women', and that we therefore have a unified identity around which to mobilize (e.g. Gill, 1995). We shall return to these complex debates, but for now one way of steering a course through them, and so clarifying our critical aims and targets, is to consider aspects of Jacques Derrida's development of deconstruction.

Derrida and deconstruction

Critical psychologists' appropriation of the term 'deconstruction' has up to now claimed that it can be emancipatory only if defined in technical ways and incorporated into a 'committed' programme (e.g. see Burman, 1990; Parker et al., 1995). Other writers such as Sampson (1989) and, outside critical psychology, Eagleton (1981) and Critchley (1992), have seen deconstruction as emancipatory in itself. Elsewhere (Hepburn, 1999a) I have argued against loose appropriations of the term, and the next section provides a summary firstly of what can be said about deconstruction, and secondly how it has been applied in critical social psychology.

Deconstruction has been central to the development of postmodern and post-structuralist thought. Any approach that is critical or defensive of postmodernism would do well to understand the implications of deconstruction, both for politics and for analysis. So what exactly is deconstruction? Derrida would resist answering this type of question: 'All sentences of the type "Deconstruction is X" or "Deconstruction is not X" *a priori* miss the point' (1983: 275). So no answer there, then. A better way of describing deconstruction would be as a *critical orientation towards asking* 'What is X?' Derrida seeks to deconstruct any text that equates truth with presence or *logos*, which privileges the voice over writing, and which debases forms of otherness. As Geoffrey Bennington, the renowned Derrida scholar and translator warns, Derrida's work 'demands a delicacy of reading which is all but unmanageable . . . But in spite of its undeniable difficulty, Derrida's work is in fact quite susceptible of reasoned exposition *up to a point*, beyond which something 'undecidable' begins to happen' (Bennington, 2000: 7, emphasis in original). So I think if we can get some 'reasoned exposition' here we'll be doing well!

Many works in critical social psychology have utilized the term 'deconstruction', although it often appears in the title and is subsequently ignored in the text! This reflects both the huge impact that Derrida's work has had all over the social sciences (deconstruction has become a 'buzz word') and also the difficulty that many researchers have in fully applying Derrida's work to their own. This section provides a brief overview of Derrida's writing, highlighting aspects that are of particular interest to critical and discursive psychologies, with their focus on the role of language in the construction of subjectivities and realities. (For more details on Derrida's work and on its relation to critical and discursive psychology see Hepburn, 1999a.)

Saussure and structuralism, Derrida and post-structuralism

Derrida's work can be set in the context of Saussure's 'semiology', which challenges the representational view of meaning – the modernist idea that our language needs to reflect the realities that the rational mind observes. Structuralism is therefore best conceived in the context of humanism, an influential school of thought for psychology. Humanism assumes:

1   The real world is discoverable.
2   It can be described through language.
3   Language is the outcome of individual intentions and meanings – it can express some essential self.
4   This self is the centre of meaning and creativity.

By contrast, structuralism argues:

1   Any thought or intention is achieved through language.
2   Meaning arises through structures of language rather than individual experience.
3   The structure of language replaces the self as the centre of meaning, and hence;
4   The structure of language produces realities and selves for us.

Saussure (1974), generally acknowledged as one of the foremost structuralist thinkers, simply replaced objects in the world with *signs*, and divided the sign into sound image, or *signifier* (e.g. the noises I make to form the word 'breakfast') and concept, or *signified* (the muesli and cup of tea that I'm referring to). An important insight that Saussure gives us is that *the relation between signified and signifier is arbitrary* – every language is free to produce its own relationships between sound images and ideas (*le petit dejeuner, el desayuno*, etc.). The identity of a sign, its meaning, is determined not by its essential properties – its muesli-ness and cup-of-tea-ness – but by the *differences that distinguish it from every other sign*. It doesn't make sense on its own outside our systems of meaning.

This means that there is no reality to ground our claims that is outside our systems of signification – a point similar to the one Lyotard was making earlier, that operating with metanarratives leads one to legitimate one's argument with reference to that metanarrative, such that it seems that one has some *pre-discursive realm* to appeal to as a way of grounding one's argument.

For Saussure, language is a system of signs (words and concepts) that exists independently of what people say. We can say something only with the words we have available, which were around long before we were. This does not mean that meaning is historically determined; we can creatively synthesize meanings. Rather the meaning of a sign depends on its differences from all other signs. What we mean by what we say depends not on any inner subjective states or processes, but rather on the system of signs that surrounds us in this context at this time. West (1996) suggests that, by abstracting from subjectivity, structuralists aimed to demonstrate their scientific objectivity. At the same time they emphasized 'the distinctive properties of systems as wholes, which are more than the sum of their parts' (1996: 166), thereby distancing themselves from some of the more reductive analytic excesses of science. One of Derrida's criticisms of Saussure is that despite this move to 'objectivity', and despite the subject being inscribed in the play of differences, the sign is still seen as a mental representation. In psychology, *Gestalt* psychologists supported structuralism.

Derrida and post/structuralism

These structuralist insights give us a powerful critique of the whole tradition of Western metaphysical thought (see box opposite for an explanation of meta-physics), which has often taken the identity of the sign as an unproblematic 'given'. Derrida agrees with the structuralist view that meanings are worked up by the system of signs that surrounds us. The only way of securing meaning is as relative to something else rather than relative to reality: each word or concept carries within it all other words and concepts that are different from it.

However, Derrida takes things a step further with his development of deconstruction. Drawing on his extensive work in philosophy, he suggests that any system of thought seems to posit some kind of centre or *logos* – for humanism it is the self, for structuralism it is the structure of language, for Freud it will be the unconscious, for Marx the relations of production, for different types of religion it will be different types of god, and so on.

This organization of thought both produces and disguises the ways that certain meanings take on more importance than others. Derrida suggests that in order to *reify* a meaning – to posit it as some superior representation of reality through the logic and structure of metaphysics – the different concepts that help shape its meaning are going to be subordinated. This subordination of certain terms gives the *appearance* of some originary meaning or *logos* (see *logocentrism* below): hierarchical binary oppositions privilege the 'presence' or centre.

One side of an opposition does not exist in its own right, although it is set up as if it did by the metaphysical binary structure and logic. And this encourages the forgetting of its reliance on its opposite. For example, freedom does not make sense in a particular context without, say, being related to oppression (or in a different context it might be determinism, imprisonment and so on). Instead, each word differs from, is evaluated against, and also incorporates its opposite in a fluid and contextual sense, and this realization marks one of the major differences between Saussure and Derrida, between structuralism and post-structuralism.

BOX 8.1   Metaphysics

What is metaphysics? The form of this question is to ascertain what something 'is'. And this 'is' is metaphysics. Defined as a theory of existence, the quest of metaphysics is to claim what can be said to simply exist – *a priori*. It is therefore *ontological* – it searches for *a priori* being – the essence of being. Metaphysics is therefore the metaphysics of *presence* (what Derrida terms logocentrism) – the self-evident presence of *a priori* existence or *transcendental signifieds* (God, consciousness, truth, good, spirit, love and so on – similar to Lyotard's meta-narratives). The whole history of metaphysics has been dominated by the presupposition of the existence of the pure transcendental signified, uncon-taminated by empirico-historical culture. Derrida's work demonstrates that the transcendental ideality of signified concepts is impossible. He does so by writing in a quasi-transcendental manner (this makes his written work sound different from other philosophy) and through the introduction of quasi-concepts – *différance*, the trace, proto-writing and so on.

Although Saussure treats the relation between signifier and signified as arbitrary, he also treats that relationship as stable: it is where meaning can be made present. In Derrida's view, this fails to acknowledge the 'play' between signifiers, and he suggests that in order to escape the closures of metaphysical language we should think of language in terms of its *function* – referring to an endless play of sign substitutions – rather than its mere presence.

Logocentrism

For Derrida, metaphysics constructs things on the unquestioned value of *presence*. To attempt to disrupt this order is an incredibly complex task. Geoffrey Bennington attempts to outline what is at stake:

> The metaphysics of presence thinks in two (logical and often historical) moments; presence first, of the world to a gaze, of a consciousness to its own inspection, of a meaning to a mind, of life to itself, of a breast to a mouth; absence next – the world veiled, consciousness astray, non-sense, death, debauchery, language, weaning. By thinking the second moment as derived with respect to the first, one returns, if only in thought, the complex to the simple, the secondary to the primary, the contingent to the necessary. This is the very order of reason and meaning, of the *logos*, and one does not escape it as easily as seem to think those who quickly invoke the unconscious or matter . . . , madness . . . or even the other . . .
>
> (Bennington and Derrida, 1993: 17–18)

Derrida's deconstructions are a way of disrupting *logocentrism*. The term derives from the Greek word *logos*, where this denotes any kind of transcendental signified such as logic, reason, God, etc. – a bottom line reality which transcends human judgement, which is available to us as a resource for making our human and therefore 'flawed' judgements legitimate. Logocentrism is the impulse to invoke some such ultimate authority as a foundation for all thought, language and action. It is through the operation of binary oppositions in hierarchical relation (e.g. God–man, spiritual–physical, male–female) that this authority can be invoked and the establishing of foundations for knowledge gets done. This is because one term (e.g. God, male) is grounded in the *logos* and so has clearer access to the truth, to the full presence of meaning, whereas the other is seen as lacking or corrupting of the truth as organized by the *logos*. This produces a rhetoric of metaphysical *decidability* – a rhetoric of the fixity of signified meaning, of pure uncontaminated transcendence. Derrida sees his job as that of demonstrating the *impossibility* of pure uncontaminated meaning – the impossibility of timeless truths. He does this through marking the *undecidability* of meaning through a set of 'undecidables' – quasi-concepts that illustrate the impossibility of the transcendental signifieds colonizing logocentrism. The problem is that this type of logocentric thought is so pervasive as to be impossible to escape completely. A particular type of logo-centrism that relates to Derrida's deconstruction of the speech–writing binary is phonocentrism (Derrida, 1976). As we shall see, this is especially relevant to critical and discursive psychological concerns.

Phonocentrism

Because we have a distinction between inside and outside, between the world and our ideas about the world, it seems to us that when we speak we have more direct access to this presence of meaning. There is no gap between seeing the word and understanding it, as there is with writing – we can see written words without necessarily understanding them. We don't seem to first hear and then understand our voices; rather, hearing and understanding ourselves seem to be the same thing. Derrida (1982c) calls this the system of *s'entendre parler*, to hear/understand oneself speak. Signifiers do not seem to be external to us when we speak, so our speech can be viewed as the point where signified and signifier appear fused, along with inside–outside, individual–society, mind–body.

This moment of spoken clarity serves as a fixed reference point which allows us to posit distinctions, and by referring to this moment we can treat these distinctions as hierarchical oppositions, one term reflecting the *logos*, as *phone* (speech) or presence, the other denoting writing or absence. Speech 'is the unique experience of the signified producing itself spontaneously, from within the self' (Derrida, 1976: 20). We therefore have the illusion of constant meaning through the direct presence of a 'thought' expressed by the 'self' in speech.

For Saussure the existence of this moment of *s'entendre parler* means that writing is secondary to the full presence of meaning in speech. Saussure wants an 'inner system' of language that is expressed in speech. Although developing the idea that concepts can't exist independently from their expression, Saussure's conceptualization of the distinction between speech, the signified, and writing, the signifier, constructs the relation between the two as no longer arbitrary. Speech becomes the reality which writing represents.

Derrida's deconstruction of the speech/writing hierarchy therefore reverses the initial hierarchy, making writing the condition of the possibility of speech, while at the same time *reinscribing the newly privileged term* – i.e. writing. For Derrida, then, there is a sense in which Saussure's text, like all texts dogged by logocentrism, already contains within it the tools for its own deconstruction, tools such as 'the absence of positive terms and the action of difference' (Gane, 1989: 69).

Hence deconstruction is not a pre-formulated technique or method which can be *applied* to texts. Instead it highlights aspects of the text (these can be what Derrida terms 'undecidables' – the supplement, *différance*, the trace and so on) that a logocentric system forgets or cannot deal with, and which therefore disrupt its order and logic when introduced.

A deconstruction shows how the marginalized 'half' of a binary can be given priority over the dominant half, allowing meaning to emerge from the 'undecidables'. To oversimplify, the principle of uncertainty is embraced in that either/or binary logic is replaced by the 'logic of supplementarity' (Derrida, 1976), which has a both/and, neither/nor construction. The pharmakon is *both* poison and cure; *différance* refers to both difference and deferral, both conceptuality and the possibility of non-conceptuality; 'The supplement is neither a presence nor an absence. No ontology can think its operation' (Derrida, 1976: 314). Derrida's introduction of the logic of supplementarity subverts the binary logic that organizes our constructions in logocentric ways. By displacing the system of oppositions Derrida shows that there is *no neutral and transcendent meaning of any term* – including the subordinated one that is initially reversed in the process of deconstruction.

Conclusion

In summary, for Saussure and structuralism meaning is an effect of a linguistic system of differences; and this presents two main problems. First, the need to treat some meanings as simply self-evident or 'present' is antithetical to Saussure's own thesis on the arbitrariness of the sign. Second, to describe meaning as simply emerging from linguistic relations in an utterance does not account for the function of language: the same utterance with the same linguistic differences can nevertheless be *doing* several different things.

Derrida wants to avoid having the centred modes of thinking – such as phonocentrism and logocentrism – which arise from operating with metaphysical certainties. The critique of these two areas of thought seems to be the central project of deconstruction. Deconstruction of phonocentrism provides a critique of truth as centred within autonomous individuals, as evidenced by the speech/ writing argument outlined above, so it is especially relevant to the development of understanding in critical and discursive psychologies. This arises from the wider project of the deconstruction of logocentrism, which provides a critique of Enlightenment rationality and the universal political principles that arise from it.

Logocentrism organizes an inescapable positing of foundations and certainties. Treating deconstruction as a relativist position in which 'anything goes' will therefore not account for deconstruction as a *response* to the endless positing of foundations. We are unable to escape or stand outside logocentric thought from some privileged position. Recognizing this, deconstruction urges us to develop greater sensitivity to the ways that reality and truth – in psychology concerning the mind, or humanness, or the physical world – become constructed. It is not simply a question of identifying hierarchies and overturning them. Instead we recognize the importance of focusing on the function of language, and the violence of operating with preordained 'facts' (as we also discover in the film *Memento*), making the subversion of claims to truth and realism into an ethical and political move.

From Derrida's work we learn that meaning is created through the subordination of signs through binary logic, encouraging the forgetting of the reliance of a term on its opposite. Deconstruction of logocentrism involves challenging the authority of meanings that are reified in this way. Despite these arguments, and the widespread adoption of the term 'deconstruction' in critical work in psychology, deconstruction is routinely characterized by the practice of overturning hierarchies and the labelling of a Derridean deconstruction as a step too far – it is relativist (though Derrida doesn't like the term), and so apolitical. This is the topic I now turn to.

Postmodernism, deconstruction and critical social psychology

This section will focus on the ways that critical psychologists have taken up both postmodernism and deconstruction. We will begin with an exploration of the ways in which deconstruction has been ab/used, highlighting the omissions of a range of deconstructive notions (which are sometimes deliberate and well flagged, e.g. Parker et al., 1995), and so illustrating the value of certain sidelined features of deconstructive practice.

Deconstruction and critical social psychology

The general argument will be that most critical accounts stick with a polarized version of deconstruction that omits the subversive and intrinsically postmodern 'undecidability' discussed earlier. The importance of taking a deeply committed critical stance towards oppressive uses of psychology is not being contested here; rather the problem is with criticisms of deconstruction using polarized terms. Ian Parker (1988) begins his 'deconstruction' of an extract from a script of *The Archers* radio programme in promising mode – with a disruption of the speech–writing polarity that organizes a preference for 'real' conversation by many social researchers. However, he reinstates this same hierarchical polarity when he concludes that 'the pity is that a deconstruction would not necessarily lead to a progressive type of action research if it was applied to real explanations given by real people' (1988: 198).

Deconstruction is often positioned as the opposite of construction: it is taken simply to refer to 'breaking things down' – the unravelling of a text's assumptions and the overturning of hierarchies. For example, Parker and Shotter claim in their introduction to *Deconstructing Social Psychology* that a Derridean deconstruction exists 'just to unravel hidden assumptions and to uncover repressed meanings' (1990: 4). And even Edward Sampson (1989, 1990) who is widely supportive of the emancipatory possibilities of deconstruction, characterizes its aim as being to 'deconstruct the prevailing conception of the person and so reveal its political underside' (1990: 118–19).

A related ab/use of a Derridean deconstruction builds upon this reading of deconstruction as merely overturning hierarchies or binaries. The claimed problem is its inability to provide the grounding for a political position. For example, what Parker and Shotter call for are approaches such as feminism and psychoanalysis, which 'afford a space for the exploration of an "other" in a more radical sense than a mere polar contrary' (1990: 4). Kenneth Gergen (1997) contrasts a deconstructive movement with something that can provide a more 'generative' basis for change, again implying that deconstruction is useful for dismantling rather than regenerating texts. In earlier work, however, Gergen displays more comprehensive insights into Derrida's work – see for example his discussion of the 'supplementary action' necessary for an utterance to gain meaning (1994: 264–67). In general, though, a major area of Derridean deconstruction is left unaddressed in critical work in psychology, namely the critical and subversive impact of undecidable terms.

Erica Burman similarly omits major aspects of deconstructive practice when she suggests that it is linked with the 'identity politics' of one of the less sophisticated aspects of feminism, which leads to 'an individualization and depoliticization of experience with a corresponding shift from questions of oppression to questions of identity' (1990: 212). She also claims that 'deconstruction is fundamentally committed to a liberal pluralism which . . . paralyses political motivation' (1990: 214–15). Again these claims about the political implications of deconstruction rely on its construction as simply overturning hierarchies, and as merely invoking a kind of liberal plurality of 'anything goes' types of interpretative analysis. This polarizes deconstruction: either it is something concrete or it could be anything, and if it is the latter we are paralysed, unable to act politically. This falls victim to the same kind of binary logic that a Derridean deconstruction was developed to disrupt. Similar limitations beset Burman's discussion of *différance*, where she claims that the 'methodology' of 'difference (with 'differance') . . . is to adopt the devalued term of the opposition it identifies to highlight the metaphysical dynamic of its construction . . . the principal danger with deconstruction is that difference may become a substitute rather than a starting point for resistance' (1990: 214). Again deconstruction is treated merely as a focus on oppositions and differences, so that we need to impose our own 'starting points' or foundations for political action.

As Bennington argues:

> The absence of a unitary horizon of meaning for the process of reading does not commit Derrida to the recommendation of meaninglessness, nor does it entail the equivalence in value of all different readings (rather the singularity of each), and indeed demands the most rigorous textual evidence for readings proposed: but it does argue that no one reading will ever be able to claim to have exhausted the textual resources available in the text being read.
>
> (2000: 11)

This type of debate echoes the style of arguments between realists and relativists in critical and discursive psychology below, and is something that seems to be endlessly misunderstood by those advocating a realist or critical realist approach in critical psychology.

It can be argued that by leaving unread the complexities of undecidable terms, critical psychologists reject aspects of deconstruction that could provide them with a powerful tool – a way of subverting metaphysical foundations without putting other foundations in their place. To develop discourses less concerned with developing regimes of truth, more open and careful about their own modalities of writing, is surely a *precondition* for resistance.

In an interview in *Radical Philosophy*, when questioned as to whether deconstruction entails an 'ethico-political responsibility', Derrida replies:

> Asking oneself questions, including ones about the questions that are imposed on us or taught to us as being the 'right' questions to ask, even questioning the *question form* of critique, and not only questioning, but thinking through the commitment, the stake, through which a given question is engaged: perhaps this is a prior responsibility, and a precondition of commitment. On its own it is not enough of course; but it has never impeded or retarded commitment – quite the reverse.
>
> (1994b: 40)

In the face of an endless logocentric positing of foundations, Derrida claims we should never be content to have reached some bottom-line truth or reality – even as we are engaged in committed political action. One of the main themes running through the preceding discussion of Derrida's work has been the idea that one must work from within existing logocentric language in order to deconstruct it. This requires us to attend closely to the function of language and the way that realities are constructed as such, through the text's own structure and logic. We also need to develop ways of thinking and accounting for metaphysical foundations without replicating the violence of metaphysical exclusions. In this sense deconstruction can have a profound effect on political thinking and decision making. As Derrida often repeats – a decision that was determined by some prior reality or political theory would not be a decision, but merely the administration of a programme. Decisions occur in a situation of undecidability – they are not given but rather they are taken.

BOX 8.2   Textuality and tectonics

One of the most thoroughgoing attempts at social psychology in a post-modern voice comes from Beryl Curt (1994). Unlike much postmodern work in social psychology, which develops arguments about postmodern thinkers such as Derrida and Lyotard, and considers the merits of deconstruction, say, as a practice, Curt attempts to *do* postmodernism. That is, the form of the writing is as much part of the argument as the topic. Indeed, the author is part of the argument: Curt herself does not exist but is an amalgam of a group of 'devoted amanuenses'. This device is used to raise issues about authorial control, about the academic market place, and the social and heterogeneous nature of individuals.

The book is organized into conventional chapters, but they are broken up by the interventions of an 'interrupter' and 'personal' responses from the (unreal) Beryl herself. She is concerned to contribute to the 'climate of problematization' in social psychology left by the crisis and the various critiques that have developed through interdisciplinary boundaries opening up. In line with her general focus on heterogeneity, the concern with tectonics is a concern with the relations between texts, the contours or topography that bound texts, the conditions of plausibility of texts, and the dynamics of textuality. These ideas are developed in discussions of topics such as jealousy in relationships and the rights of children.

Despite their reservations about these undecidable features, critical psychologists such as Parker and Burman propose the adoption of deconstruction as a critical method, as witness their long list of books with 'deconstruction' in the title. For example, Jonathan Potter and Margaret Wetherell (1987) are censured for watering deconstruction down in order to fit it into the prevailing paradigms of ethnomethodology and linguistics. Burman suggests that they make it more difficult to 'bring the full force of these [deconstructive] critiques to bear on the practice of psychology' (1990: 216). The implication is that by focusing on language and what it achieves, rather than what it represents, Potter and Wetherell are making a political stance more difficult for critical psychology. This chapter develops an opposing view: that by rejecting the view of language as descriptive or representative of some reality – a *central feature* of the deconstruction that Burman claims to adopt – we can develop critical psychology further. This point is developed in the chapter on discursive psychology.

The key to understanding Burman's acceptance/rejection of deconstruction is to see that she is starting from a polarized and undeconstructed representation–reality binary. She warns us not to 'tackle the representation at the expense of engaging with the political reality . . . focusing on a politics of subjectivity can lead to a celebration of difference rather than a galvanizing into action' (1990: 218). Again there is a polarizing of the issue into binaries of reality–representation. This introduces closure in the sense that for Burman the 'reality' of political action cannot be achieved simultaneously with the celebration of difference, which the unsettling and subversion of a Derridean deconstruction instigates. So Burman's position is that deconstruction is fine up to a point, but as critical psychologists we are presented with the simple choice of either becoming lost in an endless play of differences *or* galvanizing ourselves into action. It is simply legislated in this kind of critical work (as we saw in Chapter 5) that if we take deconstruction or relativism too far we shall lose sight of political 'realities'. To reiterate, the problem is not Burman's emphasis on the importance of taking a deeply committed critical stance towards oppressive uses of psychology; it is with criticisms of deconstruction using undeconstructed and polarized terms. As Derrida argued earlier, deconstruction facilitates commitment; it is an important task for those who claim 'ethico-political responsibility'.

Thus far this section has argued that critical psychologists have spotted the radical potential of deconstruction, but have not fully exploited it. It is suggested that deconstruction can provide a resource (as opposed to a definitive answer) for critical psychology and constructionism by showing how we can come to uncritically recognize aspects of ourselves and our 'realities' as not constructed – as simply providing their own grounds for legitimation – through the operation of transcendental signifiers.

Deconstruction has a tendency to *relativize* – to demonstrate that the fixity invoked by a text is organized by its own structural features, its own economy of signification (e.g. binary logic) rather than through reference to some extra-discursive 'reality'. Deconstruction therefore subverts metaphysics (see box above) by introducing terms that its 'either/or' binary logic cannot deal with. As with Lyotard's work, there is a drive against self-legitimating claims to certainty or reality. The argument is that any text contains within it the potential for its own subversion. That subversion involves our suspension of commitment to the meaning of a term, to be replaced by sensitivity to the way that the meaning is constructed *in situ*, and also an exploration of the function that this particular construction may serve. It is this radical subversion and uncertainty, so characteristic of postmodernism, which critical social psychologists have found troubling.

As we have seen, postmodernism, relativism and deconstruction often give rise to complaints about abandoning the subject of psychology, or the reality of human suffering. From a deconstructive perspective, rather than getting caught in self-referential questioning about whether the subject or the real exist, we can ask, What do such warnings about postmodernism achieve? To position postmodern claims as non-political? Is there such a thing as a non-political claim? Perhaps such claims serve to position their own claims as 'properly political', to warrant specific types of political action over others. This may allow important political action but *we should be clear about the basis of that action*. Claims such as 'postmodernism is running rampant without political direction' (Simons and Billig, 1994) can be motivated only by an implicit commitment to a certain kind of politics.

Tomás Ibáñez

'It is probably too late for me to get rid of some bad habits, I just don't see how I could work and think without trying to be constantly critical. Maybe this is why I enjoy questioning (may we say deconstructing?) much more than answering (may we say constructing?). I am afraid that my main contribution to critical social psychology is simply to help opening spaces where younger colleagues can work outside any kind of mainstream pressures, and to try to persuade them that staying for too long on a given position is quite bad for intellectual health. Critical analysis of postmodernity, without going back into modern ethos, seems to me a politically relevant concern to be developed in present times.'

Conclusion

This section has argued for a more thorough and scholarly discussion of deconstruction and postmodernism than has been present in critical social psychology thus far, illustrating the value of certain sidelined features of deconstructive practice. The tendency in critical work has been to see postmodernism and deconstruction as apolitical and therefore useful only in some watered-down form. However, I have argued here that deconstruction allows radical insights into language, knowledge and meaning that provide us with strong critical tools, while also questioning traditional notions of 'critical'.

In Chapter 6 there is a discussion of one possible way for critical psychology to pursue this subversive agenda through the development of a deconstructive understanding of subjectivity. Similarly in Chapter 7 the development of discursive psychology was cited as one way of building a psychology more concerned with people and their everyday concerns. However, there has been a section of research in critical social psychology which claims that any approach that adopts a relativist perspective is politically paralysed, and it is to these arguments that we now turn.

Postmodern knowledge and the realism/relativism debate

The realism/relativism issue is a thorny one for critical psychologists, as evidenced in arguments between the various contributors to Ibáñez and Íñiguez (1997). The realist position typically characterizes relativist research as 'apolitical' (e.g. Parker, 1997b), and calls for various 'groundings', notably a 'theory of the subject' (e.g. Spears, 1997). There are parallels here with critical psychologists' dismissal of the 'undecidable' aspects of deconstruction discussed earlier. As a way through these arguments, this section will begin with a further examination of the relation between knowledge and subjectivity.

Lupicinio Íñiguez

'"Critical social psychology" is just a label like any other. The name we use is not important – remember that that category has been called other things: "new social psychology", "alternative social psychology", "social psychology as critique" or "radical social psychology", for instance. From my point of view, the name is less important than the practice. The critical look serves to identify the production of compromised knowledge done within the fuzzy borders of academically institutionalized "social psychology".

Despite the different labels we always find recognizably similar perspectives and a rebellious spirit of problematization. In my view, "Critial Social Psychology" can be seen as a consequent of a continuous questioning and critique of the production of knowledge. In that sense "critical social psychology" shares most of the characteristics of constructionism (and many other approaches, like the sociology of scientific knowledge). It does so in a number of ways: at an ontological level it takes on the "constructionist turn". At an epistemiological level it is non-fundamentalist, questioning even the very notion of "epistemology". At a methodological level it shares with constructionism the "interpretative and linguistic turn", and finally, at a political level, it engages with emancipatory and social transformative practices. Also, "critical social psychology" participates in the project of permeabilization of all the social and human sciences, which can be seen as a magma impregnating every place and bend of this generic field.

Nevertheless it is an approach looking to the past. Thinking to the future, I see "critical social psychology": (1) in a permanent state of problematization, attentive to any change produced in the general area of human and social sciences and, also, contributing to it; (2) continuing in radical opposition to any kind of despotic or authoritarian thinking; (3) criticizing any form of individualistic thinking; (4) committing itself to, and collaborating with, any social and political processes of change; (5) contributing to the elimination of frontiers between theoretical and methodological, or between natural and social.'

The subject of knowledge

Psychology grew out of the 'accepted wisdom' of traditional philosophical notions, which centred around issues of 'knowledge' – what can be known, how we know what we know, the nature of truth, logic, reason, and so on. In philosophy this usually entails that the reference point of knowledge is the knower – how can we be sure that our 'representations' of 'reality' are accurate? It seems that formulating how 'knowledge' is to proceed commonly involves two polarized ideas – the (external) real and the (internal) representation of it. This realist way of making sense of knowledge or enquiry creates a requirement for a method of examining the real that is not 'biased' by our possibly inaccurate internal notions about what the real is. As discussed in Chapter 6, realism creates a requirement for a 'subject' that is fundamentally biased and flawed, until it apprehends the real. Realism therefore requires strategies that will promote objectivity, that disregard subjective accounts, which simply display the real independence and objectivity of the researcher. We can then begin to 'describe' the world as it is. Such descriptions need to be true and certain representations of reality. Disciplines such as the natural sciences have developed rhetorical strategies capable of mapping out what this reality may be, and, in relation to people, sociology, economics and politics have developed as a way of 'describing' the kinds of social structures that exist.

Conversely, if we want to develop enquiry into the knower, the internal states of the person, we need strategies that isolate parts of that knower from the confounding variables of the external world. We can then begin to document the true physiological and psychological make-up of all humans. Disciplines such as psychology and psychiatry, medicine and human biology, have developed as a way of achieving these types of goal.

According to this polarized (what Derrida would term logocentric) view we need methods that allow us true knowledge of what exists at either end of the dichotomy. We generally think of science as an umbrella term for this mode of enquiry, and of empiricism and positivism (see Chapter 1) as appropriate analytic strategies.

As we saw in Chapter 2, social psychology has also developed from within these philosophical dichotomies of inner–outer, individual–society, subjective–objective. Its aim is usually to document how the outside gets inside, how the social affects the individual, or to document the cognitive information processing responsible for 'social behaviour'. The focus on cognition and the adoption of traditional scientific methods and assumptions picks up on the general develop-ment of thought from within the limited binary structure.

However, more recent philosophical thought (e.g. Derrida, Foucault, Butler, Haraway, Lyotard, all covered throughout this book) has moved away from this dichotomized notion of how knowledge proceeds. One accessible introduction to the kinds of change that have taken place is Richard Rorty's work. He suggests that the empiricist–positivist programme in philosophy still mistakenly believes in the mind as mirror, the 'glassy essence' which can reflect objective reality. (We came across this metaphor in Chapter 6.) Rorty claims that 'Without the notion of mind as mirror, the notion of knowledge as accuracy of representation would not have suggested itself' (1980: 12). So the dichotomy we started with – between the external and the internal – has shaped our whole way of making sense of things in the Western world. The dichotomy, by virtue of its deceptive 'either/or' structure and logic, sends us off on false trails, in pursuit of goals that make sense only if we accept these basic premises. As we saw in our discussion of Lyotard's work above, to work with fixed stories about the way the world is (metanarratives) entails that our accounts must legitimate themselves with reference to those big stories. We become locked into a self-referential circle of legitimation.

So what is the alternative? In Chapter 5 we covered the realism–relativism arguments as they apply to feminism. Here it was found that those arguing a realist perspective are missing a vital strand in the relativist's perspective – the issue of making judgements. From a realist perspective, making judgements inevitably involves recourse to some objective referent exterior to the interaction in which the judgment is made. However, from the relativist perspective (as adopted by some of the discursive critics in Chapter 7) all our descriptions involve inter-pretation, which in turn involves some kind of linguistic community. All judge-ments are made from within these communities. There is nothing more to truth and reality than the historical and social consensus operating from within a linguistic culture. This is what Rorty would term a hermeneutic circle, and we cannot escape from it. As pragmatists we should repress the urge for 'the search for some final vocabulary which can somehow be known in advance to be the common core, the truth of all other vocabularies which might be advanced in its place' (Rorty, 1980: 390).

This also maps on to the discursive psychological critique – that our elabor-ate psychological procedures for deciding what term conveys what experience are misguided, as they occur divorced from actual practices – ahead of time, as if there were general ways of matching internal to external. Our judgements are relative to the context in which we utter them – the language, the culture, the other people present, the previous utterance.

This relates to the debates around conversation analysis (CA) covered in Chapter 7 – essentially the CA idea taken up by Edwards and Potter is that we do not need recourse to external realities to analyse talk. Instead we need to focus on what is displayed as relevant in the conversation – for those speakers in that context, assuming the prior self-evident existence of neither a particular type of speaker nor a particular type of context. Rorty makes a similar point:

> If we see knowing not as having an essence, to be described by scientists or philosophers, but rather as a right, by current standards, to believe, then we are well on the way to seeing *conversation* as the ultimate context within which knowledge is to be understood. Our focus shifts from the relation between human beings and the objects of their inquiry to the relation between alter-native standards of justification, and from there to the actual changes in those standards that make up intellectual history.
>
> (1980: 389–90 emphasis in original)

It is unlikely that Rorty means conversation in the mundane, everyday CA sense, more in terms of some abstract notion of dialogue, or a dialogue between different philosophical perspectives.

To a large degree, then, it is impossible to say what is known in any absolute sense. To assume, as we do, that we are moving ever forward, from the unknown to the known, is therefore an illusion – we move from one dialogue to the next, what we 'know' is relative to the dialogue and its context. Perhaps our 'standards of justification' become more sophisticated (or just more complicated?) along the way.

In his later work Rorty develops this point:

> there is nothing deep down inside us except what we have put there ourselves, no criterion that we have not created in the course of creating a practice, no standard of rationality that is not an appeal to such a criterion, no rigorous argumentation that is not obedience to our own conventions.
>
> (1982: xiii)

From the traditional scientific perspective, the scientific paradigm is the only dialogue that counts when it comes to knowledge. Rorty's response is to suggest that there are many dialogues, with many changing rules. Their truths and realities are all culturally and historically relative. This is close to the position adopted by those advocating relativism in critical social psychology.

Exploring relativism

Edwards et al. (1995) discuss how objections to relativist arguments often introduce a 'bottom line' that limits what may be treated as 'mere' social construction. Edwards et al. discuss two related kinds of bottom line arguments. First there is the 'furniture' move, in which tables and chairs can be constructed (with the appropriate thump) as 'the reality that *cannot* be denied' (p. 26). Secondly death, suffering and oppression are invoked as 'the reality that *should not* be denied' (ibid.). This section will explore both these moves and will then provide a general discussion of the relativist potential for commitment.

Furniture

Edwards et al. (1995) argue that furniture arguments are themselves rhetorical, despite being designed to be above rhetoric. They question the idea that table thumping can prove not only one particular table's continuing existence but also the existence of all other tables. Just like any argument, the reality of furniture is constructed and deployed to particular effect in particular contexts. That tables and chairs 'exist' is certainly a feature of common sense (as may be the existence of God for some), but this cannot serve as a demonstration of their reality.

Relativism therefore argues that there are no reality-producing claims that are immune from examination. What it is that makes a furniture argument work so convincingly for many people is precisely what makes it interesting to a relativist analysis – it is an illustration of the workings of 'consensual common sense'.

Death

When the death argument is invoked, the relativist is often accused of an irresponsible lack of interest in the realities of death. Perhaps one of the most vociferous critics of relativism, and exponent of the 'death argument', has been Ian Parker:

> In one particularly pernicious example, 'discursive psychologists' have analysed the way in which references to the Holocaust function as part of a bottom-line argument against relativism . . . [in doing so they] undermine the truth claims of those who refer to the Holocaust as a real and historical event.
>
> (1997b: 297)

However, this critique, which appears regularly in Parker's work, does not capture the sense of, or even specifically address, the argument as it was originally put:

> Claims for the unreality of the Holocaust are, like all preposterous claims, like all claims of any sort, examinable for how they are constructed and deployed. Realism is no more secure than relativism in making sure the good guys win, nor even in defining who the good guys are – except according to some specific realist assumptions that place such issues outside of argument . . . There is no contradiction between being a relativist and being *some*body, a member of a particular culture, having commitments, beliefs, and a commonsense notion of reality.
>
> (Edwards et al., 1995: 35)

For the relativist there is no option but to engage with consensus, argument and common sense, even about how the 'realities' of death are constructed. This does not mean that 'anything goes', that there are suddenly no values or meanings. Jonathan Potter argues, 'Anything goes is an *extraordinarily* realist claim' (1998: 34). Instead meanings and values – what 'goes' and what 'doesn't go' – are precisely what are in dispute, the things that we can study as well as argue about and either challenge or defend. Analysing how our culture works does not mean we can suddenly step outside it and not have some kind of position. Analysing what talk is doing does not mean we can pretend that our own talk is not itself rhetorical, or above this process of analysis.

Kenneth Gergen also criticizes Parker for using Nazism as the primary example of why we should be anti-relativist. He suggests that Nazism can be traced to the more general Western historical context in which groups are able to silence opposing voices through asserting certain 'truths' about their own group, and hence asserting their own moral superiority (1994: 113). Bronwyn Davies also suggests that realist claims about relativists' lack of commitment rely on weak evidence – 'vague reference to specific unnamed others who are incapable of commitment' (1998: 136). She asserts that, for her and the teachers and students she has worked with, an understanding of the inherently constructive nature of self and reality has enabled rather than inhibited action and commitment.

The realist therefore has no privileged access to the moral high ground; in fact by advocating claims that attempt to hide their own rhetorically constructed character, and that are not open to examination, realism 'can be argued to operate *against* truth as much as for it, just like censorship, ignorance and deception' (Edwards et al., 1995). To engage with relativism is not to reject commonsense reality, as the quotation above demonstrates. Rather it is to reject the idea that this common sense must not be open to enquiry.

DISCUSSION QUESTIONS

1   If all truth is relative, by what criteria can we understand the truth in any situation?

2   Is it just what everyone decides at any one time?

3   What more could there be to it than that?

Relativist commitment

A common objection to relativism is that everyone's views must be treated as equally valid. This develops into the criticism that relativist research is 'apolitical' (Parker, 1997b) and requires various types of 'grounding', notably a 'theory of the subject' (e.g. Spears, 1997) or a proper psychological notion of agency (Burr, 1995, 1998; Madill and Doherty, 1994). However, as argued above, rather than *rejecting* the possibility of justifications for particular views, these are precisely the things that relativism *insists* upon. Edwards et al. quote Barbara Herrnstein Smith: 'The idea that relativism makes one's moral or political life easy is an especially absurd fantasy of objectivist thought' (Smith, 1988: 166).

The relativist claim is that because it is a matter of dispute as to where the line should be drawn between what is simply and objectively real, and what is constructed as real, the only assurance we have is in constant vigilance. Moreover if anything is or can be 'simply real', it surely has nothing to fear from such scrutiny. To insist on protecting one's 'truths' from examination is deeply conservative, and more appropriate to religious than social scientific enquiry.

So is relativism a position that we should adopt? This is a tricky issue, because as Smith (1988: 150 ff.) notes, usually the 'relativism' under discussion is an invention of 'objectivists' – those who seek objective reality. If we cannot abandon this truth-seeking enterprise, any relativist statements seem like denials of reality, which seem to lead us into various kinds of anarchy and chaos. It is important to note, however, that *these predictions emanate from a realist perspective*. From a relativist and postmodern 'perspective' this is *circular reasoning* – for example, we start with the premise that we need the real in order to make sense of things, and this leads to the conclusion that without the real there is no way of deciding between sense and nonsense. These are precisely the kinds of self-

Ros Gill

'For me, the critical in critical social psychology refers both to a political project and an epistemological stance. To be critical, psychology must start from a position that interrogates rather than accepts existing power relations, inequalities and injustices, and is committed to challenging them. But it must also be wary of orthodoxy, of all attempts to close down debate, and must take up a critical reflective stance in relation to its own knowledge production. To stay alive, vibrant and critical, critical psychology must resist becoming exclusionary and must resist promoting itself as The Way.

In my own work I've been asking rather "old-fashioned" questions about ideology – questions like "How do enduring inequalities come to be perceived as natural and inevitable" – and trying to reformulate them in discursive, social constructionist terms. I've also been attempting to think about what form political critique can take in these "post" times in which everything has been said before, and irony hungrily devours protest.

Or is this statement just an example of the familiar "critical move" – a powerful rhetorical step . . .'

referential metanarratives that Lyotard (1984) claims we become increasingly incredulous of.

Perhaps the most important thing for critical and analytical work is to be alive to different possible interpretations and arguments from those prescribed by our own methods, as Ibáñez (see box, p. 215) argues above.

CRITICAL DILEMMA

Discursive psychologists sometimes claim to be 'understanding the way the world works' or 'discovering commonsense practices' (cf. Edwards, 1997). On the other hand they draw attention to the way such claims retain their status as stories, rather than as timeless, factual accounts, usually by drawing on Malcolm Ashmore's (1989) work on reflexivity (see box in Chapter 9). Is the appeal to reflexive awareness of the contingency of our own versions enough to provide us with a strong critical perspective? Or is discursive psychology uncritical in some basic sense, as many critical psychologists argue?

Conclusion

This section has tried to clear up some of the common misconceptions about the relativism that is endemic to most postmodern stances:

1   Relativism does not mean 'anything goes'.
2   It is possible to 'take a position' and 'make judgements' while adopting a relativist epistemology.
3   The relativist has no option but to engage with consensus, argument and common sense, even about how the 'realities' of death are constructed. This does not mean that there are suddenly no values or meanings.
4   To engage with relativism is not to reject commonsense reality. Rather it is to reject the idea that this common sense must not be open to enquiry.
5   Opening one's ideas up to enquiry provides a firmer, rather than a weaker, basis for adopting a critical/political stance.

Application _____

Perhaps from a postmodern perspective there needs to be a more thorough interrogation of what it means to make a difference in the world. One possible site of intervention could be in examining the way certainties and truths can exert a controlling and repressive influence. From a discursive perspective we know that speakers need to conceal the arbitrary nature of their claims to truth in order to 'know' or 'speak' the truth. But how is this concealment achieved? It is not a deliberate subjective act; people do not set out to conceal their own concealment. Perhaps one way in which postmodernism can be applied is in looking at precisely how the truth is spoken, how facts are constructed, how realities and subjectivities are made concrete.

Another possible consequence of postmodernism would be a much more rigorous exploration and challenge of what we mean by application. It would be the basis of a critique of critical application, if you like. One of the dilemmas of existing 'applied' critical work in psychology can be illustrated through a consideration of the jointly authored book *Psychology Discourse Practice* (Burman et al., 1996). The authors, some academic psychologists, and some practitioners, describe a recurring tension between *regulation* and *resistance*. It often seems in this type of practical 'political' (often drawing on Marxist tropes) style of work that regulation is given a negative evaluation in contrast to the positive evaluation given to resistance. Psychology provides the regulatory practices that must be resisted.

This relates to a larger problem, namely the lack of conceptual clarity in theorizing the difference between structuralist and post-structuralist positions on the role of language. This in turn relates to how language is related to (or supposedly representative of) 'realities' such as lived or subjective experience. In *Psychology Discourse Practice* the 'dialogical we', while situating themselves within post-structuralism, want to retain a 'realist suspicion of social constructionist work' as they address 'different gradients of materiality of those extra-(and/or) discursive practices' (Burman et al., 1996: 196–7).

This focus on reality and materiality is antithetical to the 'deconstructive' stance that *Psychology Discourse Practice* claims to adopt. As a consequence the book struggles to address in any integrated way what is most oppressive and authoritarian about certain discourses (which Derrida developed the term 'deconstruction' to subvert), namely their claims to represent some pre-discursive reality or *logos*.

The insistence on the 'extra-discursive' tends to obfuscate the critical potential of this kind of work, creating confusion about what might count for critical and poststructuralist work in psychology. We are therefore often taken from regulation to resistance only to slide back again into the regulatory practices of discourses that appeal to extra-discursive truths, which themselves close down possibilities for further multiple perspectives to be aired, and hence possibilities of further resistance.

Conclusion

We started this chapter with some concerns about defining postmodernism. Perhaps a more fruitful line will be to turn postmodernism in on itself and ask instead what it *does*, which is to provide a critique of some of modernism's most cherished and fundamental themes:

1   The self is an individual knowable entity.
2   A rational and unbiased self gives us 'scientific' ways of knowing.
3   In order to be objective and unbiased our language must reflect the realities that the rational self observes.
4   By rationally reflecting on reality we are provided with timeless truths that will advance human progress.
5   All human practices and features can be scientifically (neutrally and objectively) analysed.

Many of these modernist themes help to co-ordinate traditional individualist work throughout the whole field of psychology, and as such they are often jealously guarded as if it were ridiculous to question them. Postmodernism certainly stirs up trouble, which is one of the reasons why theoretical sophistication and informed argument are needed.

The first main section of this chapter highlighted aspects of Jameson, Lyotard and Derrida's writing which allow some insights into the complexities of their work, but which also speak (or write) to the concerns of critical and discursive psychologists. As we saw, Jameson borrows heavily from Marx's focus on economic organization, which created problems in terms of the epistemological focus of postmodernism. Lyotard gave us more insight into epistemology through the discussion of the role of metanarratives and the self-referential and exclusionary work they do. Derrida's work was set in the context of Saussure's, highlighting differences and tensions between structuralism and post-structuralism.

For Derrida 'subjective' categories like 'intention' need to be simultaneously used and disabled. This disruptive focus is something that critical psychology needs to take more seriously. We need to emphasize the supplementary nature of psychological phenomena (e.g. Hepburn, 2000a) – to recognize that they are not complete in themselves, that their presence is characterized by an absence, that they are always already dependent on non-presence – the movement of *différance*. Psychological phenomena have no origins – they are constituted by a non-origin – the trace.

Like discursive psychology (see Chapter 7) deconstruction shares a distaste for relying on speakers' intentions to gauge the accuracy of meanings: this leads discursive psychologists to focus on the identification of conventional procedures for doing things with words, as a way of disrupting the presence of meaning organized by logocentrism. This suggests that the focus on the role of language and meaning in constructing realities is particularly salient for the development of critical work in psychology. What we cannot escape in logocentrism is an endless positing of foundations and realities, and if we cannot escape it our only option is to work within it, to attend closely to the function of language and the ways in which the violations and exclusions are brought about through the construction of realities. This means that a strong focus for critical psychology can be the identification of the ways in which persons, identities, subjectivities, and other psychological 'realities', are constructed in order to be recognizable as not constructed.

In general deconstruction requires us to use language itself as a way of questioning its own basis of meaning. If we see language as having material substance, the problems we perceive will be like those of the cartoon character who stands on the area s/he is sawing around, removing the foundations needed to support them. Instead if we reject this view, and see language as discourse, if we can cease constructing language in terms of presence, and see it rather in terms of its *function* – as a play between signifiers rather than the *representation* of the signified – then problems organized by the realism–representation duality dissolve. We can then see language in terms of what it does, what it achieves, and see meaning as shifting its function for particular purposes. This focus on language and the subversion of transcendental signifiers also entails that deconstruction need not be confined to classical philosophical texts, but can be introduced into more mundane contexts and discursive practices, e.g. in areas like critical psychology which are focused on reform – of prisons, education, health care and so on.

If deconstruction can help us to identify the horizons of thinking which produce demarcations about 'reality' or what it is to be a person, we have a powerful resource for challenging such essentialist constructions. Deconstruction also allows the development of discourses that are more reflexive about their own modalities of writing. It is therefore an important contributor to the development of discursive and critical psychologies, some of which have already begun to integrate a 'relativist' perspective.

Relativism in discursive psychology functions in similar ways to deconstruction, in that it sees the continual subversion of claims to truth about the mind or the physical world as a prerequisite for making informed analytical or theoretical judgements about the social life. To posit a realm that lies beyond this type of questioning (what Derrida would term logocentrism) is precisely the type of move that keeps oppressive practices alive.

B The best thing about postmodernism

Postmodernism gives us striking new ways of understanding knowledge, where we proceed from a situation where knowledge comes without foundations. We can also develop novel ways of connecting 'persons' with 'social organizations'. The postmodern emphasis on undecidability will help prevent critical social psychology from developing into orthodoxy (see Billig's box in Chapter 2 and Gill's box, this chapter).

W The worst thing about postmodernism

Francis Fukuyama (see Chapter 3).

Where next?

I would like to see more engagement with some Marxist insights about work, economics and collective organization. The danger of postmodernism is that the insights about signification and difference draw attention away from more mundane, but equally important, concerns about poverty and work.

Practical exercises _____

1   One of the themes in postmodernism is distortion of time and space as a consequence of new technology. Communication across long distances is instantaneous; people do not have to be close by to keep in touch with one another. List the various forms of communication that you use with your friends and acquaintances. Keep a diary of your interaction. What proportion is face-to-face and what proportion is electronic (phone, sms, email, etc.)?

2   Go to the Web and take a look at some personal Web sites (preferably people you know). Think about the way these sites construct them as people. What do pages emphasize? What kinds of things do they leave out?

3   'See this!' (Bangs on the table) 'You're not saying this is a social construction, are you?' Use the discussion of realism and relativism in this chapter to consider some of the rhetorical business done by this form of argument. What is the response of Edwards et al. (1995)?

Reading _____

If you read only one thing, read:

Gergen, K.J. (1999) *An Invitation to Social Construction*. London: Sage. ***Especially chapters 7 and 8.***

Classics

Edwards, D., Ashmore, M. and Potter, J. (1995) Death and furniture: The rhetoric, politics, and theology of bottom line arguments against relativism. *History of the Human Sciences*, 8 (2), 25–49. ***Entertaining and challenging; still generating controversy.***

Gergen, K.J. (1991) *The Saturated Self: Dilemmas of identity in contemporary life*. New York: Basic Books.

Also useful

Curt, B.C. (1994) *Textuality and Tectonics: Troubling social and psychological science*. Buckingham: Open University Press.

Gergen, K.J. (1992) Toward a postmodern psychology, in S. Kvale (ed.), *Psychology and Postmodernism*, pp. 17–31. London and Beverly Hills, CA: Sage.

Hepburn, A. (1999) Derrida and psychology: Ab/uses of deconstruction in critical and discursive psychologies. *Theory and Psychology*, 9 (5), 641–667.

Kvale, S. (ed.) (1992) *Psychology and Postmodernism*. London and Beverly Hills, CA: Sage.

Parker, I. (ed.) (1998) *Social Constructionism, Discourse and Realism*. London: Sage. ***Especially the chapters by Burr, Potter and Davies.***

Difficult but worth it

Rorty, R. (1989) *Contingency, Irony, and Solidarity*. Cambridge: Cambridge University Press.

Chapter 9

Integration and Subversions

One of the primary aims of this book has been to clarify the terms with which criticism and argumentation get done in critical social psychology. This brings us back to where we started in Chapter 1, where we examined the different theories of knowledge, society and subjectivity that critical social psychologists can adopt. We will review these *critical assumptions* in the first section of this chapter. This involves developing themes relating to society, knowledge and the subject as they have occurred throughout the book. The second section will spotlight *critical practice*, drawing on themes developed right through the book and particularly in the sections on application near the end of each chapter. A third section will discuss *critical evaluations*, taking each chapter in turn and producing some of my own critical evaluations of different perspectives in the different areas. My position in these debates leans towards postmodern and discursive work. A concluding section explores prospects for the future – where should critical social psychology go next? What is the best case/worst case scenario for the future?

Critical assumptions

In Chapter 1 we noted three areas that are important for critical work: writing society, knowledge and the subject in critical social psychology. One of the aims of this book has been to highlight the way critical work is dependent on a series of operational assumptions about these three areas that are not always made explicit, so throughout we have interrogated critical social psychology for its assumptions about:

1   How *society* works, and how it can be changed.
2   How *knowledge* is justified and made factual, and how it can be changed.
3   How the *subject* and personhood are made sense of, and what the implications of such understandings might be.

We have here three broad sets of assumptions organizing critical work: assumptions regarding theories of society, knowledge and the individual. Over the course of the book we have discovered that these assumptions are not free-standing – taking a position on one entails having a corresponding position on the others. Let us examine the symbiotic nature of subjectivity, society and knowledge in more detail.

The co-dependence of subjectivity, reality and knowledge

Part I of this book aimed to document the different ways that critical research has grappled with the problem of the relation between 'Mind and Society'. For the social cognition critics in Chapter 2, society is the separated 'outside' that needs to be processed in order to get 'inside'. This outside is usually divided into social groups of various types that somehow trigger subjective psychological processes. Marxist critics are similar, in that they see social and economic structures (another type of 'outside') as in some ways fixed and causal. This leads people to depart from their true selves (the fixed inner aspects are affected or produced by the fixed outer aspects) so that they become alienated.

This binary structure of outside–inside is evidence that some version of realism underpins this type of research. This forces our theories into a metaphysical either/or kind of state, as Derrida would suggest, where some kind of dominant and causal relationship exists between the two 'sides'. Perhaps ideas about the mind, or subjective states of some kind, are inextricably linked with views about reality – society or objective states of some kind. And perhaps these both link with views about knowledge, and how we can know the things we know.

In Part II, 'Resolutions and Dilemmas', there are some serious attempts to resolve or problematize the mind–society issue. Some of the subjectivity critics in Chapter 6 develop a notion of subjectivity that constructs it out of social and culturally specific ways of making sense of things. This meshes with the discursive perspective of Chapter 7 and the postmodern perspective in Chapter 8. On this view, whatever a person, self or mind is, it is something produced in and through interaction. It is a product rather than a source. To take some given aspect of subjectivity as the starting point of our theories is therefore to miss this important part of subjectivity completely and, worse, to send us spiralling down into an individualist culture where people become the source of their own problems. In Chapter 6, Foucault allowed us to develop a strong critique of psychology – it produces *individualized subjectivities* by taking things that go on in the interactional domain between people, and making them into individual qualities. We concluded that one of critical social psychology's aims should be to uncover this major problem with traditional psychology. Ironically, as we have seen, many critical social psychologists want to retain (or are forced into retaining through their realist project) some notion of the individual subject, thereby replicating psychology's big mistake.

One thing we can draw from our discussions about discursive critics in Chapter 7 and postmodern critics in Chapter 8, particularly with respect to debates around realism and relativism, is that if reality simply exists in some form or other outside our ways of describing it, then that forces subjectivity and knowledge to *become* particular types of thing. For example, we have knowledge if we can tap into the 'real' – things that just self-evidently exist – but we then need to posit an inner subjective world that can be in the right state to allow us to make sense of it. Theoretically there is a co-dependent relationship between subjectivity, reality and knowledge: changing or accepting a view about one implies changing or accepting views of the other.

This relationship also became an issue earlier in Chapters 3 and 4, with the discussions around what makes psychoanalysis an attractive option for critical social psychologists. It was suggested that Marxism leaves a gap that psychoanalysis can fill, as it is able to provide explanations about why people continue to participate in oppressive institutions and practices. Because there are some things that we can simply take to exist – like economic conditions – it follows that these things will have implications for subjectivity and knowledge. Sure enough, Marx predicts that knowledge – in the form of the ideological superstructure – must always lag behind the economic 'base'. Similarly if people do not recognize this there is something flawed about their subjective states; they are operating with false consciousness.

Complementary to this Marxist view, and unlike traditional psychology, psychoanalysis has a view of the person as fundamentally 'irrational', driven by 'emotions' and 'desires', therefore allowing us to explain what it is that makes subjectivity flawed enough to believe that oppressive ways of living are acceptable, rendering us unable to make sense of our own oppression. This in turn explains how it is that we can repeat behaviours that have negative outcomes, and how we become resistant to social change (while simultaneously producing the need for 'personal' change).

This meshing with Marxist themes, combined with its opposition to the traditional experimental approach in psychology and its strong explanatory features, makes psychoanalysis attractive to critical social psychologists. However, the problem is that psychoanalysis assumes misogynist sexual norms and familial roles and responsibilities. It also takes subjectivity and the way it has developed as an explanatory resource for human action. This takes it a million miles away from the concerns of critical social psychology. Not surprisingly there were tensions in the work of those critical social psychologists seeking to incorporate some form of psychoanalytic perspective.

This strikes at the heart of what critical social psychology is for or about. One of the strongest themes throughout all the work presented here has been the anti-individualist theme. Virtually all the problems identified by critical social psychologists have revolved around the problems associated with traditional work that views individuals as in some sense the source of their own problems. For example, in Chapter 2 the focus on identity was a running theme – each new perspective sought a more sophisticated solution to the problem of focusing on the individual and identity issues. The move was towards increasingly social constructionist or discursive positions on identity, from Tajfel through to Reicher and Hopkins. We ended up with a brief summary of the work of Antaki and Widdicombe, who want to completely respecify identity along discursive lines, seeing it as something we do, rather than as something we are.

Applying the idea of society, subjectivity and knowledge as co-dependent notions rather than separate categories, we can see that the individual is forced into 'becoming' something separate when reality is seen as something knowable and fixed. Because what we know (reality) and how we know it (objective knowledge or science) are in some sense fixed or fixable, that leaves the knower as a passive recipient and container of that which can be known. Perhaps this helps to explain how so much of social cognition research still relies on rather old-fashioned views of science as capable of capturing reality and progressing knowledge using the right types of experiment.

Derrida's call for undecidability can be seen as one of the ways of disrupting this state of affairs. In Chapter 8 we discussed the idea of deconstruction as a *response* to the endless positing of foundations – of fixed notions of the world or the mind. This is what Derrida means by logocentrism – the centring of our ways of understanding things around some fixed point of 'truth' or 'reality'. If, as Derrida seems to suggest, we are unable to escape or stand outside logocentric thought, we need to develop greater sensitivity to the ways that reality and truth – in psychology concerning the mind, or humanness, or the physical world – become constructed.

As we saw in Chapter 7, this has been one of the focuses of discursive work, and, in contrast to the tensions created by Marxism and psychoanalysis, discursive critics give us a different way of making sense of subjective categories such as 'emotion' and 'desire'. Rather than fundamental features of subjectivity that drive our actions, they can be viewed as the *outcome* of human action. Emotions and other supposedly inner features are useful *practices* that can achieve many things in talk and interaction. This view implies and draws upon a more relativist version of knowledge and reality.

Subjectivity and reality are two sides of the same coin – to have fixed ideas about one is to imply fixed ideas about the other. If there are some things that we can know for sure because they simply exist out there in the world, then we need only to apply the right methods, and bypass the human frailties that prevent us from seeing and knowing the 'truth' – i.e. become more 'objective'. On this realist view the implication for our understanding of subjectivity is that it will be comprised of biases and passive elements that simply need to observe and describe the world the way it is, rather than act on and interpret things (including the subject itself) in different ways in different contexts. Having a view about reality implies having a view about subjectivity. This is why debates about realism and relativism keep cropping up in critical social psychology, and why it is important to think the different assumptions through carefully.

From a relativist, discursive or postmodern perspective on knowledge, these versions of subjectivity are interesting for what they can achieve in different contexts. Rather than simply buying into them we need to understand what function they have. What do we gain as a culture by seeing subjectivity as flawed and passive and the world as preordained? Is this always the most productive way of constructing things? What particular ways of relating to one another does it prescribe? As we've seen throughout this book, a reflexive (see box) awareness of the kinds of version available to us, and what function they might serve, is necessary.

BOX 9.1   Reflexivity

It is possible to identify 3 kinds of reflexivity:

Classical

Usually employed by more traditional psychological approaches, e.g. personal construct theory. The idea here is that any theory ought to be able to explain its own construction and origins. So for example Skinnerians would be criticized on the grounds that stimulus–response theorists don't explain how their theories came into being. So the solution to problems of reflexivity is that you had better make sure that your theory can explain itself.

Confessional

Here the authors of the research consider their own social and psychological perspectives – their interests, motives and history – resulting in a kind of confessional story. This move to reflexively consider the impact of one's own social position has been popular with many critical social psychologists. The *solution* to problems of reflexivity is simply to fess up!

Epistemic

In Malcolm Ashmore's *Reflexive Thesis* (1989) he is interested in how we understand the texts through which facts are constructed. For example, in an account of social history that employs analysis of fact construction to criticize social processes, he asks about the way in which *those* accounts are constructed. There are a couple of different ways of solving problems of reflexivity here; Ashmore's *solution* would be to suggest that there is no solution, so it is interesting to look at the whole process of fact construction and reflexivity. One way of doing this is to develop new or alternative literary forms in our academic work; Ashmore employs a number of these – an encyclopaedia, a fake lecture, a double text, dialogue and various ironies and parodies.

     CRITICAL DILEMMA

Reflexivity shows us the importance of the situated-ness of knowledge production and of how knowledge is produced as such.

> Malcolm Ashmore
>
> How did I get here?

However, the playful breaches of conventional forms of academic writing that this gives rise to have been criticized for detracting from serious debate about language and reality, e.g. 'This seems a bit daft to me' (Parker, 1998: 43). Do you agree? Under what circumstances is reflexivity important?

BOX 9.1   Continued

This use of alternative literary forms has the effect of drawing attention to various textual conventions, to textuality itself, and the way it works on a number of different levels at once. There are parallels with Derrida's work here – for example, Derrida's use of terms under erasure and his attention to tropes and constructions.

Foucault's work provides us with a vision that similarly unites the three board areas of critical assumptions – subjectivity, knowledge and society. He does this through his reading of history as a discontinuity of power relations – a reading that has radical implications for our understanding of subjectivity. Foucault speaks of a 'circular process' (Foucault, 1977: 224) of disciplinary 'power-knowledge', where practices of power and relations of power are bound up with the production of knowledge: the knowledge of individuals. In this way, the 'individual' is not the cause, but rather the effect, of power. But insofar as it is the effect, it is also the transportation of power:

> The individual is an effect of power, and at the same time, or precisely to the extent to which it is that effect, it is the element of its articulation. The individual which power has constituted is at the same time its vehicle.
>
> (Foucault, 1980: 98)

Thus, unlike Marx, no-body owns power, for power functions through a series of disciplinary practices, which constitute individuals *as* individuals; they individualize – subjectivize – individuals. Hence the term 'subjectivity' in critical social psychology often refers to this more Foucauldian notion, replacing traditional psychology's notions of 'personality' and suchlike.

So for Foucault power produces knowledge, and such a production is in turn a form of power that can 'create' the individual as an object of knowledge. In this way, the birth of the 'individual' – humanity itself – is fairly recent and is related to the birth of the human sciences, which take the individual human subject as the possible object of knowledge and thus produce a 'norm' of what it is to be an 'individual'.

So this shows us how power, subjectivity and knowledge can be interlinked. How does this relate to events in society – to writing of a history of the present? In Foucault's words:

> I would like to write the history of this prison, with all the political investments of the body that it gathers together in its closed architecture. Why? Simply because I am interested in the past? No, if one means by that writing

a history of the past in terms of the present. Yes, if one means writing the history of the present.

(1980: 30–1)

Writing a history of the present thus becomes analogous to the genealogical project of writing an 'effective history' (Foucault, 1984b), in which one is attentive to the dispersal of events that constitute that which is closest and the most localized in the production of knowledge.

Thus for Foucault there are certain studiable objects of power-knowledge – madness, criminality, and sexuality – which cannot be studied in a top-down way, but rather must be studied in a bottom-up way. This entails that the analysis is one of localized knowledges (Foucault, 1980: 85), meaning knowledge (of 'individuals') that is produced through the rituals, exercises, and techniques of disciplinary power relations through which a person is produced as a particular type of individual. In this way, a genealogy would provide the basis for transgressing the limits of our present by revealing the way in which such localized knowledge constitutes the very foundation of the current beliefs of modernity that we are closest to (mainly, that there is *a priori* an individual at the origin of practices as the cause rather than effect of power).

Writing the history of the present therefore means to transgress the modern world-view of the individual-as-origin – the world-view of modernity itself. Indeed, it is to transgress the concept of 'man' (*sic*) as such: 'As the archaeology of our thought easily shows, man is an invention of recent date. And one perhaps nearing its end' (Foucault, 1970: 387).

However, although Foucault thinks that we can transgress the limits of the present, and thus transgress our present concept of the 'individual', he does not think that we can transcend power-knowledge as such, because as we move from one epoch to the next, we move to another epoch of power relations. For Foucault, that there is no origin of power requires that there is no teleology of power: there is only the dispersion of micro-powers that constitute us in various ways. And writing the history of the present, writing an effective history, is the archaeological-genealogical demonstration that, today, in the discontinuity of power relations, *we are not ourselves*. We are ourselves only on condition that we are not ourselves: we are 'individual' on the basis that we are not *primordially* 'individual' – we have been produced as such through a series of disciplinary power practices which themselves are only a couple of centuries old. We have been produced through disciplinary power, and we therefore have the power to re-produce ourselves through an analysis of those displinary practices that have made us what we take ourselves to be; and *only through such an analysis* can we produce a critical and non-dogmatic approach to our ethical and political relations with each other.

Thus critical psychology can take three main points from these dicussions of Foucault's work:

1   As 'individuals' we are the outcome of historically contingent disciplinary power practices – we are fundamentally not ourselves.

2   Analysing those disciplinary relations and practices will allow us to undertake a radical re-production of our 'selves'.
3   Power is bound up with relations and practices that produce 'knowledge' of 'individuals' – the subjective, the real, and the knowledge we take on board about each of these things are co-dependent.

In Chapter 3 we developed a Foucauldian critique of Marx, in which subjectivity and ideology are simply the *effects* of the historical conditions of possibility of our knowledge and the procedures that produce it. This suggests that we should understand how we are situated by the theories and procedures for producing knowledge about subjectivity and reality that we have. This is why a particular focus of this book has been to set out the different theories and assumptions that make up what we have historically come to term critical social psychology as clearly as possible – this in itself can be seen as an empowering move. But as Chapter 1 pointed out, the real test for CSP is whether it can be applied to real world situations. The following section explores the issue of application in more detail.

Critical practice

This section explores the kind of critical practice that different critical social psychologists (could) propose. Traditionally in psychology any piece of research that studies people in real world settings, rather than in the ubiquitous laboratory, has been termed 'applied'. However, in critical social psychology there is more focus on practical interventions, and what is taken to be appropriate critical practice depends on the basic assumptions made, and on the way objects of criticism have been identified.

But practical intervention is far from easy, and what constitutes a problem requiring intervention is often tricky. As we saw in Chapter 3, Francis Fukuyama's vision of the triumph of free market economics over Marxism is something that even anti-foundationalist thinkers like Derrida are arguing against, weighing in on the side of Marx. Free-market economies the world over are pretty problematic – homelessness, environmental pollution, burdens of national debt, health care difficulties, ethnocentrism and xenophobia are rife. And what are we to make of the violent nationalist conflicts in post-communist countries? How will political, critical and practical researchers tackle these problems in the twenty-first century? Who will have the responsibility for asking/answering these questions?

If we are sympathetic at least to the spirit of Marx, the future of critical social psychology lies in thinking through and acting to address social problems and oppression. If it seems that we can understand more clearly than others the nature of social problems, we have a responsibility to act. But how do we go about it? From our different discussions of application throughout the book it is possible to identify five major styles of critical intervention for future development:

1   *Social interventions and changes in public policy.* This has been a traditional aim in social psychology, particularly in its North American social cognition guise. The overall goal of social cognition research appears to be the development of well supported theories through rigorous scientific testing. However, in Chapter 2 we questioned how far such work could be applicable when the focus is on individual features of people. The goal must be to develop critical work along less individualist lines, which could feed in to public information campaigns, changes in penal policy, and so on. Feminist critics have been particularly successful in this style of intervention.

2   *Rhetorical intervention.* The basis for intervention here is at a discursive and ideological level, offering resources for criticizing established constructions of the world and unpacking their procedures for legitimation. Discursive and rhetorical research is particularly useful for this style of intervention. There is an emphasis on ideology, where social change is brought about through looking at the role of ideas in legitimating particular (e.g. capitalist) types of social organization, and in hiding social conflicts. For example, in Chapter 3 we examined Billig et al.'s (1988) argument that the common sense of everyday talking and arguing is organized around dilemmas, which are ideological in the sense that they relate to broader societal concerns with authority, legitimation and social organization. We then become interested in examining everyday practices that are sustainable through discourse.

3   *Intervening in psychology.* A number of different critical approaches treat the discipline of psychology itself as part of the problem and have developed a range of more or less thoroughgoing critiques. Their proposals range from altering its individualist and cognitivist bias, to identifying its complicity with dominant political or cultural values, to closing it down altogether. Most of the chapters in this book have provided various types of criticism of individualism in psychology. Perhaps the most developed of these critiques come from discursive critics, who advocate a wholesale discursive respecification of cognitive terms previously assumed to be features of inner life.

4   *Practical interventions.* Here the view of psychological practice is of aligning with oppressed and marginalized groups, or relatively powerless service users, to develop their own critiques and to empower them against established psychological practices. In Chapter 5 Warner (1996) and Heenan (1996), arguing from a feminist perspective, want to help service users to resist 'normalizing practices' in conventional psychotherapy. In Chapter 4 examples of applied work by Parker et al. and Harper (1995) also show the possibilities of this type of applied research. Each of the chapters in Willig (1999) tries to identify how discourse analytic research can provide practical recommendations.

5   *Postmodern intervention.* The basis of intervention from research into social practice here is in the very grounding of commonsense understandings of social processes, knowledge and the self. At the same time, it provokes reflexive (Box 9.1) issues about the nature of critical practice and the forms of

critical writing. In many sections covering application, problems arose due to a lack of conceptual clarity, often with the term 'deconstruction'. There is a tendency to introduce the 'real' into applied work, as it is considered important as a grounding for making claims about the oppression and suffering of minority groups. In Chapter 8 it was suggested that one possible site of intervention could be to examine the way certainties and truths exert a controlling and repressive influence. Postmodernism can be applied by looking at precisely how the truth is spoken, how facts are constructed, how realities and subjectivities are made concrete. This constructionist endeavour is something that Potter (1996) has been developing and the resulting discursive psychological approach is being developed in many real world situations, such as AIDS counselling (Peräkylä, 1995), eating practices (Wiggins, in press) and my own research into the NSPCC help line (Hepburn, 2001).

As these different strategies show, there are many potential ways to intervene as critical social psychologists, and it is important not to see practical intervention as somehow separate from theoretical development. If either is going to be any use it needs to rely on the other. This makes communication between different types of critical social psychologist of primary importance. However, we are left with a dilemma.

CRITICAL DILEMMA

If mind, society and knowledge are all linked together theoretically – versions of one implicate versions of the other – it would seem that critical social psychologists who mix realist versions of knowledge with more relativist versions of subjectivity are producing confused and inconsistent theories. However, in practice, as we discovered in Chapter 7, people employ ideological dilemmas to good rhetorical effect. Does this mean that we are all getting away with messy arguments in real life? Should we be telling our participants off for being inconsistent? Or celebrating the plurality of perspectives that they have available? Perhaps this relates to what we think the relationship is between 'abstract theories' and 'everyday talk'. Should we construct these as separate categories? What is gained by such a construction? What are the implications of respecifying mind, society and knowledge as discursive practices – things that we do with our talk? Does this mean that inconsistencies are OK?

Critical evaluations

This section aims to take each area of critical social psychology in turn and produce some critical evaluation. This kind of critical evaluation is important, as it is the debates to be had *between* different areas of critical social psychology that give it much of its character. It is done in the spirit of provoking further ideas and debates.

Social cognition

In Chapter 2 we covered a range of social psychological literature from early research by Sherif, Zimbardo and Milgram to later crisis-inspired European social cognition. It was suggested that each perspective provides a more sophisticated solution to the problem of focusing on the individual in social psychology. But why should the focus on individuals be a problem? Surely psychology is all about individuals, and the job of social psychology is therefore to look at individuals in their social context?

But there is a problem, and it relates to the strongly anti-individualist perspective of Marxism. One of the central features of Marxism is the notion that one's class position will determine the social consciousness, or ways of understanding, of its members. A particularly good way of maintaining inequalities and controlling people is to make sure they see their impoverished circumstances as arising not from changeable social structures but rather from unchangeable individual features. And if we take this on board, psychology becomes part of some oppressive social practices, as many, notably Ian Parker, have been arguing. By narrowing things down to individual features psychology encourages and legitimates the idea that people's problems emerge from somewhere within them. This kind of critique has inspired the development of discursive and postmodern critics, where subjectivity is dissolved or respecified.

So how does this relate to social cognition? In our earlier criticisms of self-categorization theory (one of contemporary social cognition's more developed forms) Reicher and Hopkins rightly criticized the lack of thought that goes into 'context'. Rather than look at people's practices in everyday life, self-categorization theorists supply participants with ready-made vignettes about context. Because self-categorization theory treats category definitions as merely the cognitive reflection of social reality, it misses the sense in which participants can re/create different contexts. However, Reicher and Hopkins believe that we need to take account of the 'fact' that people have 'agency' – free will – to create new social contexts, and to interpret existing contexts in different ways.

Even here, at the cutting edge of social cognition research, where efforts are being made to combine elements of radical constructionist and discursive work, there is a reluctance to let go of some element of individuality as part of our basic explanatory framework. People can 'choose' to create and define the world in different ways, and this is an important internal process that we need to take account of. This is just what we are like – we can't deny it.

However, this does not answer the Edwards (1991) style of critique, which argues that 'categories are for talking'. Rather than being evidence of subjective states or structures – 'just what we are like' – categories are revealed as a useful part of participants' everyday practices. Similarly in Chapter 7 Wetherell and Potter's

(1992) work on racism and practical politics showed how participants employ a weave of contradictory maxims and tropes – again, this goes beyond what Reicher and Hopkins suggest.

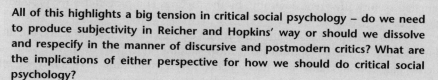

CRITICAL DILEMMA

All of this highlights a big tension in critical social psychology – do we need to produce subjectivity in Reicher and Hopkins' way or should we dissolve and respecify in the manner of discursive and postmodern critics? What are the implications of either perspective for how we should do critical social psychology?

Marxist critics

In Chapter 3 we examined the philosophical, economic and historical features of Marxist theory, which set the scene for a discussion of power, ideology and subjectivity. These are concepts close to many critical social psychologists' hearts, because if we can document the effects of power on people, often through some notion of ideological or discursive influence, we are in a better position to facilitate social change – to help people to realize the ways in which they are oppressed. For Marx people have no control over their lives. Our creative abilities are transformed into capital for the elite few. We become alienated from our 'true being', and focus on earning money and accumulating possessions, defining ourselves in terms of these belongings, little realizing that this will contribute to our continued alienation.

This is nothing less than mass exploitation, and we don't realize it is happening because we can't see how our motives, intentions and actions are conditioned by objective structural causes imposed by those in authority – we are suffering from false consciousness. We have internalized the ideology of the ruling class. This allows the ruling class to maintain their favoured social order without having to try – it seems to us like the natural order of things, rather than something tied to the institutional practices and agendas of the dominant group. Ideologies become circulated only if they support existing social relations or promote appropriate class interests. This means that any new philosophical, psychological or sociological ideas, or political groups, will have no impact upon society in terms of social change unless they support the existing economic and social order.

As always when describing these types of Marxist ideas I have mixed feelings. On the one hand it seems inspirational and in some ways right. On the other hand it seems clunky and out of date, which is why more up-to-date thinkers such as Foucault and Derrida were wheeled into the discussion in Chapter 3. We can make Foucault speak to Marx on the issue of power. For Foucault the Marxist notions of power are insufficient, as they focus on single entities such as 'bourgeoisie' versus 'proletariat' at the expense of more local and provisional configurations of power relations. Power does not simply operate from the top down, and so class domination alone is not an effective guide to understanding power relations.

Foucault would also argue that subjectivity and ideology are simply the effects of the historical conditions of possibility of our knowledge and the procedures that produce it, so we should be seeking to understand how we are situated historically (genealogically) by the theories and procedures for producing the knowledge that we have.

From Derrida we learnt the importance of keeping the spirit of Marx, but also introducing a more sophisticated understanding not just of power, but of democracy, politics and law. Recognizing the tensions and revisability of our judgements and choices becomes fundamental to developing a richer, more sensitive democracy, which is why we need deconstruction. If we can develop a more sensitive democracy then it becomes more of a two-way process, and even if Marx is right, we will be less 'determined' and oppressed by the ideologies of those in authority.

CRITICAL DILEMMA

This underlines another tension in critical social psychology. Are oppressive social structures simply *there* as part of reality, as Marxist-inspired critical social psychologists would want to argue? Or are they locally constructed in everyday practices, as more Foucauldian and discursive-inspired critical social psychologists maintain? What are the implications of adopting either perspective?

My preference is for a more Foucauldian take, as I feel that taking fixed points of reference about the 'real' corners us into taking fixed points of reference about subjectivity and knowledge (as argued in section one above). And for me this would lead to explanations of power and oppression in terms of fixed points in subjectivity – motives, interests and intentions of individuals or groups, which brings us back to precisely the types of individualism that Marx himself sought to reject.

But the questions for Marxists remain: why do people participate in their own oppression? Why can't they see the chains that bind them? We have seen that many critical psychologists have turned to psychoanalysis to answer this question.

Psychoanalytic critics

Psychoanalysis has been set up in this book as something that bridges a gap left by Marxism, the question of why people can't see their own oppression for what it is. As we discovered in our review of classic Freudian and Kleinian psychoanalysis, the types of stories psychoanalysis can tell about the psyche – denial, repression, displacement and so on – are very useful in this respect. People act irrationally owing to psychic sedimentation caused by their historical and biological context. It was suggested in the first section of this chapter that this desire to theorize subjectivity goes hand in hand with assumptions about the nature of reality and knowledge. If we have fixed points for one then we are forced into theorizing fixed points for the others.

This problem was highlighted in our discussion of Wendy Hollway's work. It was suggested that by putting subjectivity into centre stage a strong critical tool is lost – the action-orientated nature of language. When subjectivity is pinned down into something specific, language can be taken as a simple representation of these inner states: this was identified as one of the problems in Hollway and Jefferson's (2000) work.

Michael Billig usually provides a more thorough integration of contemporary notions of language, rhetoric, power and discourse; however, even his theorizing about the unconscious is unclear. It seems that Billig is not totally happy with the idea of a thoroughly discursive respecification of the unconscious, as that would implicate a more relativist notion of knowledge and reality. As we have seen, critical social psychologists who aim for fixity in terms of reality and knowledge are pushed back into having fixity in their notions of subjectivity.

I think this is a dangerous direction for critical social psychology to travel in, as it moves us backwards into talking about theories of subjectivity, people's inner states and so on as *explanatory theories of human action*. For me psychoanalysis is problematic in many ways – it is individualist: by theorizing fixed notions of subjectivity it sediments social and cultural phenomena into fixed aspects of people such as gender; in its classic form it is misogynist and dangerous. In sum I prefer Parker's position (minus the critical realist spin!), which suggests that we need to be aware of psychoanalytic notions in order to make sense of the potentially oppressive, individualizing and authoritarian aspects of discourses that surround and construct us. However, it seems difficult to produce psychoanalytic insights into social problems without invoking culturally and historically crystallized features of the word, the world or the person – in a Foucauldian sense we are in danger of producing the very thing we want to complain about. For this reason I tend to think critical social psychology would be better off without psychoanalysis.

Feminist critics

Chapter 5 began with the intention of persuading people that feminism is still a viable enterprise. In the past so many of my students have objected to the idea of learning about feminist psychology. It seems to capture something unpleasant for people. The irony is that if most contemporary Western students could be transported back forty (even twenty) years I'm sure they would be shocked at the differences in gender politics and relations. We've come a long way, and it is largely thanks to feminists pushing for various social reforms and policies, for changes in labour relations and even in everyday personal relations between partners, peers and family members. But the same will probably be true of students forty years hence – if they were transported back to the present, my bet is that they would be equally shocked at the gender inequalities in our supposedly more civilized Western cultures.

But given that many gender inequalities are written into the fabric of everyday life, and therefore often seem invisible, how are we to notice and study them as social scientists? Chapter 5 examined some early feminist discourse research that sought to do just this. By operating with a non-essentialist notion of gender, the research was able to highlight participants' versions of gender relations that were made to seem natural and obvious. This illustrates the value of the points made in section one above: by taking a more discursive and less essentialist view of subjectivity, reality and knowledge, we are able to highlight taken-for-granted ways of making sense of things that would otherwise seem just 'natural' or part of reality.

In a similar way, the heterosexism and embodiment debates covered in Chapter 5 bring to the fore assumptions about heterosexuality and biological explanations as the norm in Western culture – it shows how ingrained they are both in psychology as an institution and in other social practices. However, while there has been a gradual move towards more post-structuralist, discursive anti-essentialist positions in research around gender, embodiment and heterosexism, most of the feminists (e.g. Gill, Kitzinger, Wilkinson) operating in this area would not want to line up with a totally relativist perspective on knowledge.

The anti-relativist arguments put forward by feminists were also examined in Chapter 5, and their limitations were documented. While this may still leave many feminists (even social constructionist and 'discursive' ones) uncomfortable with the idea that they should adopt a relativist perspective, it is important to point out that better arguments are needed to justify this. Without the relativism of a strong constructionist position, you are left as a researcher with the difficult job of arguing for, and providing evidence of, non-constructionist realities. As argued above, this also has the knock-on effect of implicating more fixed views of subjectivity. Some may feel that this is a price worth paying in order to ground their commitment, but that is a strange argument – it misunderstands the difficulties that a realist perspective presents for the idea of commitment, as it binds us to particular versions of reality, subjectivity and knowledge as the 'right' ones. Of course this provides rhetorical grounding for our 'committed' stance, but it also introduces inflexibility. Feminist critical research is generally about challenging these types of fixity, and pointing out the damage that inflexible constructions of gender can do. Its attempts to deal with the many contingencies, arguments and agendas that go with doing feminist and critical research is something that has made it such a fascinating area of study.

Subjectivity critics

In Chapter 6 we examined the issue of subjectivity, and the different ways that critical social psychology has taken it up as an issue. Much has already been said on this topic – throughout the book subjectivity has been highlighted as an important feature of critical work, and also as something that links up theoretically with notions of reality and knowledge. Throughout I have argued for a more Foucauldian perspective on subjectivity – looking at how people are made into subjects of a particular type through the discursive operation of various paradoxes and oppositions. As we saw, one of the paradoxes of subjectivity is created by the notion of some primary subjective freedom that is inevitably controlled or constructed by something external to itself – 'the social'. On this view, what we need to do is to somehow regain our 'real' and 'authentic' selves. For Freud and other psychoanalysts the answer is to have lots of psychoanalysis – change the subjective structures. For Marx the answer is revolution – we need to replace capitalism with communism, change the social structures. This makes Marxism preferable for critical social psychology simply because it does not take the individual as the defining force. If we take a more Marxist perspective on subjectivity (like Sloan), then giving people freedom from the external constraints of oppressive social systems seems the right direction for critical social psychology.

However, Foucault's work leads us to question this simple story of freedom from social constraints. He shows how subjectivity can be seen as the *outcome* (rather than the source, as many critical social psychologists assume) of different sets of discursive resources, oppositions and paradoxes. Psychology and other psy- disciplines are instrumental in producing versions of the subjective world. Foucault's response to this type of production is to examine its development through genealogical study. I think this is the most liberating perspective, allowing us more space to think through how we want to produce ourselves. If we take a more Foucauldian line on subjectivity, as many of the *Texts of Identity* contributors claim to do, then recognizing how subjectivities are the outcome of historically and culturally specific discursive constructions, and how these versions of subjectivity operate, becomes the most important thing.

In Chapter 6 we also discussed the difficulties of making judgements about what is 'rational' and whether subjectivity is fundamentally 'irrational'. As the argument in this chapter suggests, it is a problem only for those who assume that there is something self-evidently 'real' that we must strive to discover. We begin in a state of ignorance – our fundamental irrationality – so we must strive to become more rational. The view of people generally that this gives us is problematic yet widespread – people are irrational, fundamentally flawed, in need of correct instruction. We must instil the truth into them. To know the truth is to be in a position of power and control over those who do not. We can start to see Foucault's point – that truth, power, knowledge and subjectivity are all interlinked, and that making people into subjects of a particular type is an effect of power. It is a theoretical practice that links in with the theoretical assumption that we need fixed notions of reality. These things are possible at the level of theory, but they also produce power relations and have broad implications for social and institutional practices.

One important development for critical and subversive studies of subjectivity has therefore been to stand back from making theoretical pronouncements about the non/existence of subjectivity, and to look instead at what different versions of subjectivity can *achieve* both within and outside psychology, and this is a project that discursive psychologists have been engaged with for some time.

Discursive critics

In the section above on critical practice we ended with an interesting dilemma for the practice of discursive psychology. What use is being able to look at the way people construct issues in inconsistent and dilemmatic ways, and looking at what those constructions are doing in different contexts? Why do we need to know the different ways that people make things factual in everyday talk? There is so much human suffering in the world, and there are so many oppressive practices, surely critical social psychologists should just get on with the job of changing things?

But the big question for activists seeking change, for complex philosophical theorists, or just for Joanna Bloggs next door, is how do we find things out about the world? Do we just observe and assume that we can identify what is going on in any particular context? Do we ask people, and if so whose version of events do we prioritize? These questions relate to a bigger issue about what can be known prior to conducting our analyses (at whatever level) of the social world (whatever that is). Normally in everyday interaction we have to take some things as basic and simply knowable – if asked, many people would certainly agree that some things are obviously real and self-evident. But one of the main findings of discursive psychology has been that in our practices of everyday interaction we don't *treat* anything – even a basic thing like mind, self, reality or knowledge – as though it were fixed. It is precisely the dilemmatic features and action-orientated nature of people's talk that give it such rhetorical power. Stories and accounts about the nature of reality don't quite match up with everyday practice.

In some ways the issue facing discursive psychologists is similar to the issue facing scientists – how to minimize the potentially confusing effects of everyday assumptions. For example, to study memory, we need to set aside all our well worn assumptions about what memory is. Two major assumptions would probably be that memory is something residing inside people's heads, and related to this, that what people say is evidence of some inner state, like memory. If we ditch these assumptions (and there are probably lots more that we haven't ditched, but let's do what we can!) then we need to look at what people actually say about memory in everyday interaction, how it gets used as a resource, and what people are doing with their talk about memory. This is what discursive psychologists such as Edwards and Potter have done.

Discursive psychology provides a strong critical tool, in that it criticizes psychology's built-in assumptions that simply draw upon and reinforce everyday assumptions about memories and emotions. It also gives us a way of studying these hitherto 'inner' psychological phenomena differently: we can study them as social practices – useful devices for doing things in talk. In contrast to Marxist-inspired critical social research, the focus is on understanding practices rather than ideologies. There are also some interesting contrasts with postmodern critical social psychologists, who tend to focus more on theories than on practices.

Postmodern critics

If the real exists, it needs to be represented clearly and accurately, and whatever else 'knowledge' can be, it has to be something that mirrors the real. Language becomes something that reflects categories in the real world, rather than constructing them. Whatever subjectivity is, it has to be something that can understand the real when it encounters it, and so accumulate knowledge – it needs the capacity for accurate perception, memory and cognition. For critical social psychologists who adopt some form of realist epistemology, there are therefore problems in letting go of traditional psychological notions of subjectivity and society.

Philosophers such as Lyotard, Foucault and Derrida have given us a strong set of arguments against this story (or ideology, discourse, metanarrative – take your pick!), and a variety of postmodern critical social psychologists such as Gergen have imported these stories into psychology.

For Lyotard reality is constructed through metanarratives – stories that rely on their own internal logic for validation. How do we know what knowledge is? It is that which mirrors the real. How do we know what the real is? Because we (those of us with brilliant enough 'minds') have accumulated the knowledge. The story of the real relies on its own logic to verify it, so is not so objective after all.

For Derrida the traditional stories of reality involve centred modes of thinking – such as phonocentrism and logocentrism. These give rise to binary logic – *either* real *or* pretend, either true or false, either male or female – and one 'side' of the opposition gains its positive value at the expense of the other. We need to develop deconstruction as a way of destabilizing and subverting these stories and the universal political and moral principles that arise from them. Deconstruction involves challenging the authority of meanings that are reified in this way.

Many of our avowed ways of making sense of things would seek to destroy uncertainty and ambiguity. However, as we saw from our discursive critics, most of the things we say are contradictory and ambiguous, especially when we are trying to be persuasive. Derrida's work shows that even philosophical work relies on uncertainties – they are precisely the things that allow philosophers to appear certain. This places uncertainty where postmodernists would suggest it belongs – at the heart of all human theories and action.

It was argued that the widespread adoption of the term 'deconstruction' in critical work in psychology has watered it down into being simply about taking things apart or criticizing. It's not surprising that the main arguments for this 'practical deconstruction' have come from Ian Parker, who wants to retain some notion of the 'real' in critical work. Strong versions of postmodernism, deconstruction and social constructionism are seen as apolitical, relativist and therefore unable to make moral and political judgements and commitments.

However, those adopting the stronger discursive and postmodern perspective have repeatedly stressed that these arguments don't work. Even early work in discourse analysis, such as that covered in Chapter 5, showed that the force of a political perspective does not rely on its internal coherence, or its representation of some reality. Rather it was the weave of contradictory accounts that sustained the *status quo*. Indeed, if there is no self-evident reality that we can simply be guided to, then as relativists all we have left are arguments, commitments and judgements. And if we are not hampered by the idea that some things are just self-evidently true, we are in a much stronger position to join in with these arguments, commitments and judgements – indeed, they are all the relativist has, so they assume a much *greater* importance. Although the realist position would be that relativists blithely (and dangerously) ignore real things like tables and chairs, the contrary is true: to engage with relativism is not to reject commonsense reality but to reject the idea that it cannot be open to enquiry. My position is that engaging with the relativism of a strong postmodern perspective provides us with a stronger rather than a weaker basis for doing critical social psychology.

Conclusion: looking to the future

There are certain general things that one could suggest for the advancement of critical social psychology as a discipline. Perhaps most important is the development of scholarly engagement with arguments combined with a healthy dose of postmodern reflexivity. In the past there has been a great deal of critical social critique that doesn't quite make it: things are wrong because they do not accord with the basic (often political) assumptions adopted by a particular perspective; things are not argued for, they are simply assumed or stated. This makes critical social psychology no better than the unexamined assumptions of traditional psychology.

As we have seen, things are not so simple – often one's critical objects depend on the set of critical assumptions and *theories of subjectivity, society and knowledge* that one adopts. A disappointment of critical work thus far is that there has been too much 'political' critique, point scoring and posturing, and not enough *scholarly engagement* with different arguments. Throughout this book I have tried to set out the arguments from each position as clearly as possible. The rest depends on the reader, and how much reading they are prepared to do!

This relates to the second recommendation for greater *reflexivity*, which means understanding the extent to which the positions we speak from arise out of a whole set of assumptions about society, subjectivity and knowledge. As we have seen, some critical social psychologists would see this as a postmodern relativist move, which puts us in a weak political or critical position. I have argued that realizing the contingency of one's own perspective builds a stronger, rather than a weaker, position.

The third recommendation is for greater *optimism* and *opportunity*. Critical social psychology is an exciting area of academic work, genuinely interdisciplinary, posing real challenges to the *status quo*. It forces on us questions normally avoided in social psychology – questions of application, questions about our relation to other social science disciplines, and questions about our relation to morality and politics. The tensions between different theories and perspectives are what make it a productive and exciting enterprise. While I am carving a path through it with this book, I hope I have also accurately represented opposing arguments so that different types of work can inspire different readers in different ways. As a discipline I think critical social psychology ought to be at the forefront of social psychological research.

Let me end by picking up some important issues raised by people who have contributed comments on the nature of critical work. Ken Gergen (p. 201) asks us to consider how we can go beyond critique to focus on future-building within both social psychology and society. This raises an acute dilemma for someone who has just produced a book-length discussion of critical social psychology. However, if critical social psychology is something that can provide stepping stones towards change, and away from certain entrenched psychological orthodoxies, I hope that it can contribute to the future-building that Ken desires.

Both Mick Billig (p. 41) and Ros Gill (p. 222) pick up the issue of orthodoxy. Is the risk of producing a text on critical social psychology that it will establish its own orthodoxy? Again, I can see the risk. However, I see the dilemma rather differently. One of the points that I have been concerned to tackle in writing this book has been the implicit assumptions underlying much current critical work. There is a kind of orthodoxy or, at least, a set of orthodoxies, as things stand. I have offered my own judgements of positions and ideas, but in order to make them explicit, rather than in the hope that everyone will agree. What I hope is that by making some of the underlying assumptions explicit and tracing the different theoretical strands that underpin this work it will be possible to make new and perhaps different choices.

Practical exercise

1   Look through the text and the author index of this book. What do the names suggest about the nationality and gender of the critical social psychologists discussed? Think of this pattern in terms of Moghaddam's thesis of the three worlds of psychology. How is critical work distributed?

2   Choose a well known North American social psychology textbook (e.g. Myers or Baron and Byrne). Look through the contents in detail and think about what should be retained in the light of critical social psychology. Now consider what sorts of topics you think should be added to it. Produce a new contents list.

3   Where is critical psychology going? Sketch out one or more possible futures for fifteen years' time. What will be its most important feature? What will its relation to traditional social psychology be?

Criticial resources

Books

In addition to the specific works suggested at the end of chapters, there are a number of books that cover critical social psychology at different levels and with varying degrees of focus on social psychology rather than psychology in general. At the time of writing there are two single-author works on the topic published, and one is in preparation:

Gough, B. and McFadden, M. (2001) *Critical Social Psychology*. London: Routledge.

Wexler, P. (1983) *Critical Social Psychology*. Boston MA: Routledge & Kegan Paul.

Widdicombe, S. (forthcoming) *Critical Social Psychology*. Buckingham: Open University Press.

Three collections of papers have been published:

Ibáñez, T. and Íñiguez, L. (eds) (1997) *Critical Social Psychology*. London: Sage. **This is a high-quality collection of papers by key figures in the field. It would be an excellent work to tackle after reading this one.**

Fox, D. and Prilleltensky, I. (eds) (1997) *Critical Psychology: An introduction*. London: Sage. **This is another high-quality collection, although it has rather less of a social psychology focus.**

Sloan, T. (ed.) (2000) *Critical Psychology: Voices for change*. London: Macmillan. **This is a forum for various psychologists from different countries to offer views on how psychology can be transformed. It is strong on providing different international perspectives. The focus is largely social.**

Journals

Two journals have recently started with an explicitly critical focus. The *International Journal of Critical Psychology* is edited by Valerie Walkerdine of the University of Western Sydney. The *Annual Review of Critical Psychology* is edited by Ian Parker of Manchester Metropolitan University. Apart from these specific titles other journals are important for critical work. *Feminism & Psychology* has provided a central forum for critical feminist work for more than a decade. *Theory & Psychology* publishes a broad spread of work, but critical voices are prominently represented. *Discourse & Society* has established itself as the foremost journal for critical work from a discourse perspective. There is also a web-based journal: *Radical Psychology: A journal of psychology, politics and radicalism*. This can be found through www.yorku.ca/faculty/academic/danaa/

Web sites

Web sites come and go. However, the excellent Rad Psy Net (at www.uis.edu/~radpsy) is a first stop for links to other critical sites.

References

Abrams, D. and Hogg, M. (1990) The context of discourse: let's not throw out the baby with the bathwater. *Philosophical Psychology*, 3, 219–25.

Abrams, D. and Hogg, M. (1999) *Social Identity and Social Cognition*. Oxford: Blackwell.

Adorno, T.W., Frenkel-Brunswik, E., Levinson, D.J. and Sanford, R.N. (1950) *The Authoritarian Personality*. New York: Harper & Row.

Alcoff, L. (1988) Cultural feminism versus post-structuralism: the identity crisis in feminist theory, *Signs: Journal of Women in Culture and Society*, 13.3, 405–36.

Allport, G.W. (1937). *Personality: A psychological interpretation*. New York: Holt, Reinhart & Winston.

Allport, G.W. (1954) *The Nature of Prejudice*. Cambridge and Reading, MA: Addison-Wesley.

Allport, G.W. (1985) The historical background of social psychology. In G. Lindzey and E. Aronson (eds), *Handbook of Social Psychology*, third edition (I, pp. 1–46). New York: Random House.

Althusser, L. (1971) *For Marx*. London: Allen Lane.

Antaki, C. (1994) *Explaining and Arguing: The social organization of accounts*. London and Beverly Hills, CA: Sage.

Antaki, C. (1998) Identity-ascriptions in their time and place: 'Fagin' and 'The Terminally Dim'. In C. Antaki and S. Widdicombe (eds), *Identities in Talk*. London: Sage.

Antaki, C. and Widdicombe, S. (1998) Identity as an achievement and as a tool. In C. Antaki and S. Widdicombe (eds), *Identities in Talk*. London: Sage.

Armistead, N. (1974) Experience in everyday life. In N. Armistead (ed.), *Reconstructing Social Psychology*. Harmondsworth: Penguin.

Aron, A. and Aron, E. (1989) *The Heart of Social Psychology*, second edition. Lexington, MA: Lexington Books.

Ashmore, M. (1989) *The Reflexive Thesis: Wrighting sociology of scientific knowledge*. Chicago: University of Chicago Press.

Ashmore, M., Myers, G. and Potter, J. (1994) Discourse, rhetoric and reflexivity: Seven days in the library. In S. Jasanoff, G. Markle, T. Pinch and J. Petersen (eds), *Handbook of Science, Technology and Society* (pp. 321–42). London: Sage.

Augoustinos, M. (1999) Ideology, false consciousness and psychology, special issue of *Theory and Psychology*, 9, 295–392.

Augoustinos, M. and Reynold, K. (2001) *Understanding Prejudice, Racism and Social Conflict*. London: Sage.

Augoustinos, M. and Walker, I. (1995) *Social Cognition: An integrated introduction*. London: Sage.

Austin, J.L. (1962) *How To Do Things with Words*. Oxford: Clarendon Press.

Bahktin, J.L. (1981) *The Dialogic Imagination*. Austin, TX: University of Texas Press.

Baron, R.A. and Byrne, D. (2003) *Social Psychology*. Boston: Allyn and Bacon.

Baumann, Z. (1992) *Intimations of Postmodernity*. London: Routledge.

Baumeister, R.F. (1995) Self and identity: an introduction. In A. Tesser (ed.), *Advanced Social Psychology* (pp. 51–98). New York: McGraw-Hill.

Beasley, C. (1999) *What is Feminism? An Introduction to Feminist Theory*. London: Sage.

Bem, S.L. (1974) The measurement of psychological androgyny. *Journal of Consulting and Clinical Psychology*, 42, 115–62.

Bennington, G. (2000) *Interrupting Derrida*. London: Routledge.

Bennington, G. and Derrida, J. (1993) *Jacques Derrida*. Chicago: University of Chicago Press.

Best, S. and Kellner, D. (1991) *Postmodem Theory. Critical Interrogations*. New York: Guildford Press.

Bhaskar, R. (1975) *A Realist Theory of Science*. Brighton: Harvester.

Bhaskar, R. (1989) *Reclaiming Reality: A critical introduction to contemporary philosophy*. London: Verso.

Bhavnani, K-K. (1993) Talking racism and the editing of women's studies. In D. Richardson and V. Robinson (eds), *Introducing Women's Studies: Feminist theory and practice* (pp. 27–48). London: Macmillan.

Bhavnani, K-K. and Phoenix, A. (eds) (1994) *Shifting Identities, Shifting Racisms: A feminism and psychology reader*. London: Sage.

Billig, M. (1976) *Social Psychology and Intergroup Relations*. London: Academic Press.

Billig, M. (1978) *Fascists: A social psychological view of the National Front*. London: Academic Press.

Billig, M. (1982) *Ideology and Social Psychology*. Oxford: Basil Blackwell.

Billig, M. (1985) Prejudice, categorization and particularization: From a perceptual to a rhetorical approach. *European Journal of Social Psychology*, 15, 79–103.

Billig, M. (1987) *Arguing and Thinking: A rhetorical approach to social psychology*. Cambridge: Cambridge University Press.

Billig, M. (1991) *Ideologies and Beliefs*. London: Sage.

Billig, M. (1992) *Talking of the Royal Family*. London: Routledge.

Billig, M. (1994) Repopulating the depopulated pages of social psychology. *Theory and Psychology*, 4, 307–35.

Billig, M. (1995) *Banal Nationalism*. London: Sage.

Billig, M. (1997a) Freud and Dora: Repressing an oppressed identity, *Theory, Culture and Society*, 14, 29–55.

Billig, M. (1997b) The dialogic unconscious: Psychoanalysis, discursive psychology and the nature of repression. *British Journal of Social Psychology*, 36, 139–59.

Billig, M. (1999a) *Freudian Repression: Conversation creating the unconscious*. Cambridge: Cambridge University Press.

Billig, M. (1999b) Whose terms? Whose ordinariness? Rhetoric and ideology in conversation analysis, *Discourse and Society*, 10, 543–58.

Billig, M. (1999c) Conversation analysis and the claims of naivety, *Discourse and Society*, 10, 572–76.

Billig, M., and Tajfel, H. (1973) Social categorisation and similarity in intergroup behaviour. *European Journal of Social Psychology*, 3 (4), 447–60.

Billig, M., Condor, S., Edwards, D., Gane, M., Middleton, D.J. and Radley, A.R. (1988) *Ideological Dilemmas: A social psychology of everyday thinking*. London: Sage.

Bly, R. ([1990] 1991) *Iron John: A book about men*. Shaftesbury, Dorset: Element Books.

Bonss, W. (1984) Critical theory and empirical social research. Introduction to E. Fromm, *The Working Class in Weimar Germany*. Warwick: Berg.

Braidotti, R. (1991) *Patterns of Dissonance: A study of women in contemporary philosophy*. London: Routledge.

Brennan, T. (ed.) (1989). *Between Feminism and Psychoanalysis*. London: Routledge.

Brown, R. (1996) *Group Processes*. Oxford: Blackwell.

Bruins, J.J. and Wilke, H.A.M. (1993) Upward power tendencies in a hierarchy: Power distance theory versus bureaucratic rule. *European Journal of Social Psychology*, 23, 239–54. Buckingham: Open University Press.

Burkitt, I. (1991) *Social Selves: Theories of the social formation of personality*. London: Sage.

Burkitt, I. (1999) *Bodies of Thought*. London: Sage.

Burman, E. (1990) Differing with deconstruction: A feminist critique. In I. Parker and J. Shotter (eds), *Deconstructing Social Psychology* (pp. 208–220). London: Routledge.

Burman, E. (1991) What discourse is not, *Philosophical Psychology*, 4, 325–43.

Burman, E. (ed.) (1998) *Deconstructing Feminist Psychology*. London: Sage.

Burman, E., Aitken, G., Alldred, P., Allwood, R., Billington, T., Goldberg, B., Gordo-López, A.J., Heenan, C., Marks, D. and Warner, S. (1996) *Psychology Discourse Practice: From regulation to resistance*. London: Taylor and Francis.

Burr, V. (1995) *An Introduction to Social Constructionism*. London: Routledge

Burr, V. (1998) Overview: Realism, relativism, social constructionism and discourse. In I. Parker (ed.), *Social Constructionism, Discourse and Realism* (pp. 13–27). London: Sage.

Burr, V. (1999) The extra-discursive in social constructionism. In D. Nightingale and J. Cromby (eds), *Social Constructionist Psychology: A critical analysis of theory and practice* (pp. 113–26). Buckingham: Open University Press.

Burr, V. and Butt, T. (2000) Psychological distress and postmodern thought. In D. Fee (ed.), *Pathology and the Postmodern: Mental illness as discourse and experience*. London: Sage.

Butler, J. (1990a) 'Performative Acts and Gender Constitution: An Essay in Phenomenology and Feminist Theory'. In S. Case (ed.), *Performing Feminisms: Feminist Critical Theory and Theatre* (pp. 270–82). Baltimore: John Hopkins University Press.

Butler, J. (1990b) *Gender Trouble: Feminism and the subversion of identity*. London: Routledge.

Butler, J. (1992) Contingent foundation: feminism and the question of 'postmodernism'. In J. Butler and J.W. Scott (eds), *Feminists Theorize the Political*. London: Routledge.

Butler, J. (1993) *Bodies that Matter: On the discursive limits of 'sex'*. London: Routledge.

Butler, J. (1995) 'Contingent foundations: feminism and the question of postmodernism'. In S. Benhabib, J. Butler, D. Cornell and N. Fraser, *Feminist Contentions: A political exchange* (pp. 34–56). London: Routledge.

Butler, J. (1997) *Excitable Speech: A Politics of the Performative*. New York: Routledge.

Buttny, R. (1993) *Social Accountability in Communication*. London: Sage.

Callon, M. and Latour, B. (1981) Unscrewing the big Leviathan. In K.D. Knorr-Cetina and M. Mulkay (eds), *Advances in Social Theory and Methodology* (pp. 275–303). London: Routledge & Kegan Paul.

Cantor, N. and Mischel, W. (1979) Prototypes in person perception. In L. Berkowitz (ed.), *Advances in Experimental Social Psychology*. New York: Academic Press.

Cartwright, D. (1979) Contemporary social psychology in historical perspective. *Social Psychology Quarterly*, 1, 82–93.

Center for Democratic Studies (1996) *Promise Keepers: The third wave of the American right, a special report*. November: 1–18.

Chalmers, A. (1992) *What is this Thing Called Science?: An assessment of the nature and status of science and its methods*, second edition. Milton Keynes: Open University Press.

Cixous, Hélène (1986) The Laugh of the Medusa. In H. Adams and L. Searle (eds), *Critical Theory Since 1965*. Tallahassee: University Presses of Florida.

Clark, K.B. and Clark, M.P. (1947) Racial Identification and Preference in Negro Children. In T.M. Newcombe and E.L. Hartley (eds), *Readings in Social Psychology* (pp. 169–78). New York: Holt.

Coates, L, Bavelas, J.B. and Gibson, J. (1994) Anomalous language in sexual assault trial judgements, *Discourse & Society*, 5, 189–206.

Collins, H.M. (1985) *Changing Order: Replication and induction in scientific practice*. London: Sage.

Conway, M.A. (ed.) (1992) Developments and debates in the study of human memory. *The Psychologist*, 5, 439–55.

Coulter, J. (1979) *The Social Construction of Mind: Studies in ethnomethodology and linguistic philosophy*. London: Macmillan.

Coulter, J. (1990) *Mind in Action*. Oxford: Polity.

Coyle, A. and Kitzinger, C. (2002) *Lesbian and Gay Psychology*. Oxford: Blackwell.

Critchley, S. (1992) *The Ethics of Deconstruction*. Oxford: Blackwell.

Cromby, J. and Nightingale, D.J. (1999) What's wrong with social constructionism? in D.J. Nightingale and J. Cromby (eds), *Social Constructionist Psychology: A critical analysis of theory and practice* (pp. 1–19). Buckingham: Open University Press.

Cromby, J. and Standen, P. (1999) Taking our selves seriously, in D. Nightingale and J. Cromby (eds) (1999), *Social Constructionist Psychology: A critical analysis of theory and practice* (pp. 141–56). Buckingham: Open University Press.

Curt, B.C. (1994) *Textuality and Tectonics: Troubling social and psychological science*. Buckingham, UK and Philadelphia, PA: Open University Press.

Daly, M. (1978) *Gyn-ecology: The metaethics of radical feminism*. Boston, MA: Houghton Mifflin.

Daly, M. (1998) *Quintessence . . . Realizing the Archaic Future: A radical elemental feminist manifesto*. London: The Women's Press Ltd.

Davies, B. (1994) *Poststructuralist Theory and Classroom Practice*. Geelong, Australia: Deakin University Press.

Davies, B. (1998) Psychology's subject: A commentary on the relativism/realism debate, in I. Parker (ed.), *Social Constructionism, Discourse and Realism* (pp. 133–47). London: Sage.

Davies, M. (1995) *Childhood Sexual Abuse and the Construction of Identity: Healing Sylvia*. London: Taylor and Francis.

de Beauvoir, S. (1989) *The Second Sex*. New York: Vintage.

de Saussure, F. (1974) *Course in General Linguistics*. London: Fontana.

Derrida, J. (1976) *Of Grammatology*. Baltimore: Johns Hopkins University Press.

Derrida, J. (1977a) Signature event context. *Glyph*, I, 172–97.

Derrida, J. (1977b) Limited Inc. abc. . . *Glyph*, II, 162–254.

Derrida, J. (1978) *Writing and Difference*. (Trans. Alan Bass). London: Routledge & Kegan Paul.

Derrida, J. (1982a) White mythology: Metaphor in the text of philosophy, in J. Derrida, *Margins of Philosophy* (pp. 207–272). Hemel Hempstead: Harvester/Wheatsheaf.

Derrida, J. (1982b) Différance, in *Margins of Philosophy* (pp. 1–27). Hemel Hempstead: Harvester Wheatsheaf.

Derrida, J. (1982c) Signature Event Context, in *Margins of Philosophy* (pp. 307–30). Hemel Hempstead: Harvester Wheatsheaf.

Derrida, J. (1983) Letter to a Japanese Friend, in P. Kamuf (ed.), (1991), *A Derrida Reader: Between the blinds*. Hemel Hempstead: Harvester Wheatsheaf.

Derrida, J. (1994a) *Specters of Marx: The state of the debt, the work of mourning and the new international*. London, New York: Routledge.

Derrida, J. (1994b) The Deconstruction of Actuality, an Interview with Jacques Derrida, *Radical Philosophy*, 68, 28–41.

Donzelot, J. (1980) *The Policing of Families*. London: Hutchinson.

Drew, P. (1992) Contested evidence in courtroom cross-examination: The case of a trial for rape, in P. Drew and J. Heritage (eds), *Talk at Work: Interaction in institutional settings* (pp. 470–521). Cambridge: Cambridge University Press.

Dreyfus, H.L. and Rabinow, P. (1982) *Michel Foucault: Beyond structuralism and hermeneutics*. London: Harvester/Wheatsheaf.

Dworkin, A. (1981) *Pornography: Men possessing women*. London: Womens Press.

Eagleton, T. (1981) Marxism and deconstruction, *Contemporary Literature*, 5 (3), 271–91.

Edley, N. and Weatherell, M.S. (1997) Jockeying for position: The construction of masculine identities, *Discourse and Society*, 8, 203–17.

Edwards, D. (1991) Categories are for talking: On the cognitive and discursive bases of categorization, *Theory and Psychology*, 1 (4), 515–42.

Edwards, D. (1994) Script formulations: A study of event descriptions in conversation, *Journal of Language and Social Psychology*, 13 (3), 211–47.

Edwards, D. (1995) Two to tango: Script formulations, dispositions, and rhetorical symmetry in relationship troubles talk, *Research on Language and Social Interaction*, 28, 319–50.

Edwards, D. (1997) *Discourse and Cognition*. London: Sage.

Edwards, D. (1999) Emotion discourse, *Culture & Psychology*, 5 (3), 271–91.

Edwards, D. and Mercer, N.M. (1987) *Common Knowledge: The development of understanding in the classroom*. London: Routledge.

Edwards, D. and Potter, J. (1992) *Discursive Psychology*. London: Sage.

Edwards, D. and Potter, J. (1993) Language and causation: A discursive action model of description and attribution, *Psychological Review*, 100 (1), 23–41.

Edwards, D., Ashmore, M. and Potter, J. (1995) Death and furniture: The rhetoric, politics, and theology of bottom line arguments against relativism, *History of the Human Sciences*, 8 (2), 25–49.

Edwards, D., Middleton, D. and Potter, J. (1992a) Remembering as a discursive phenomenon, *The Psychologist*, 15, 441–6.

Edwards, D., Middleton, D. and Potter, J. (1992b) Remembering, reconstruction and rhetoric: A rejoinder, *The Psychologist*, 15, 453–5.

Ekman, P. (1992) Are there basic emotions? *Psychological Review*, 99 (3), 550–53.

Ellemers, N., Doosje, B., Van Knippenberg, A. and Wilke, H. (1992) Status protection in high status minority groups, *European Journal of Social Psychology*, 22: 123–40.

Elliott, G. (1987) *Althusser: The detour of theory*. London: Verso.

Elliott, G. (ed.) (1994) *Althusser: A critical reader*. Oxford: Blackwell.

Evans, G. (1993) Cognitive models of class structure and explanation of social outcomes, *European Journal of Social Psychology*, 23: 445–64.

Evans, T. (1994) Reclaiming your manhood, in B. Bright (ed.), *Seven Promises of a Promise Keeper* (pp. 75–89). Colorado Springs: Focus on the Family.

Evans, T. (1996) *No More Excuses: Be the man God made you to be*. Wheaton, Ill.: Crossway Books.

Fee, D. (ed.) (2000) *Pathology and the Postmodern: Mental illness as discourse and experience*. London: Sage.

Feyeraband, P.K. (1975) *Against Method*. London: New Left Books.

Fiske, S.T. and Taylor, S.E. (1991) *Social Cognition*, second edition. New York: McGraw-Hill.

Fodor, J.A. (1981) *Representations: Philosophical essays on the foundations of cognitive science*. Cambridge: MIT Press.

Foucault, M. (1967) *Madness and Civilisation: A history of insanity in the age of reason*. London: Tavistock.

Foucault, M. (1970) *The Order of Things*. London: Tavistock.

Foucault, M. (1971) Orders of discourse, *Social Science Information*, 10, 7–30.

Foucault, M. (1972) *The Archaeology of Knowledge*. London: Tavistock.

Foucault, M. (1977) *Discipline and Punish: The birth of the prison*. Sheridan, A. (Trans.). London: Penguin.

Foucault, M. (1979) *The History of Sexuality, Volume 1: An introduction*. Harmondsworth, UK: Penguin.

Foucault, M. (1980) Two lectures, in *Power/Knowledge: Selected interviews and other writings 1972–1977*. Gordon, C., Marshall, L., Mepham, J. and Soper, K. (trans.). London: Harvester Wheatsheaf.

Foucault, M. (1982) Afterword: The subject and power, in H.L. Dreyfus and P. Rabinow, *Michel Foucault: Beyond structuralism and hermeneutics*. Brighton: Harvester.

Foucault, M. (1984a) What is Enlightenment? in P. Rabinow, *The Foucault Reader*. London: Penguin.

Foucault, M. (1984b) Nietzsche, Genealogy, History, in P. Rabinow, *The Foucault Reader*. London: Penguin.

Foucault, M. (1986) Disciplinary power and subjection, in S. Lukes (ed.), *Power*. Oxford: Basil Blackwell.

Foucault, M. (1986) *The Use of Pleasure: The history of sexuality, Volume 2*. London: Viking.

Foucault, M. (1988) Technologies of the Self, in L.H. Martin and P. Hutton (eds), *Technologies of the Self: A seminar with Michel Foucault* (pp. 16–49). Amherst, Mass.: University of Massachusetts Press.

Fox, D. and Prilleltensky, I. (1997) *Critical Psychology, an Introduction*. London: Sage.

Fraser, N. and Nicholson, L. (1988) Social criticism without philosophy: An encounter between feminism and postmodernism, in A. Ross (ed.), *Universal Abandon? The politics of postmodernism*. Minneapolis: University of Minnesota Press.

Freud, S. (1927) *The Ego and the Id*. London: Hogarth.

Freud, S. (1936) *The Problem of Anxiety*. New York: Norton.

Freud, S. (1955) *Standard Edition of the Complete Psychological Works of Sigmund Freud*, ed. J. Strachey, 24 vols. London: Hogarth Press.

Frohmann, L. (1998) Constituting power in sexual assault cases: Prosecutorial strategies for victim management, *Social Problems*, 45, 393–407.

Frosh, S. (1987) *The Politics of Psychoanalysis: An introduction to Freudian and post-Freudian theory*. London: Macmillan.

Frosh, S. (1994) *Sexual Difference: Masculinity and psychoanalysis*. London: Routledge.

Fukuyama, F. (1992) *The End of History and the Last Man*. London: Hamish Hamilton.

Fuss, D. (ed.) (1991) *Inside/Out: Lesbian theories, gay theories*. London: Routledge.

Gallop, J. (1982) *Feminism and Psychoanalysis: The daughter's seduction*. London: Macmillan.

Gallop. J. (1986) 'Keys to Dora', in C. Bernheimer and C. Kahane (eds), *In Dora's Case*. London: Virago.

Gane, M. (1989) Textual theory: Derrida, in M. Gane (ed.), *Ideological Representation and Power in Social Relations*. London: Routledge.

Gatens, M. (1991) *Feminism and Philosophy: Perspectives on difference and equality*. Cambridge: Polity Press.

Gavey, N. (1989) Feminism, poststructuralism and discourse analysis: contributions to a feminist psychology, *Psychology of Women Quarterly*, 13, 439–76.

Gergen, K.J. (1973) Social psychology as history, *Journal of Personality and Social Psychology*, 26, 309–20.

Gergen, K.J. (1989) Warranting voice and the elaboration of the self, in J. Shotter and K.J. Gergen (eds), *Texts of Identity* (pp. 70–81). London and Beverley Hills, CA: Sage.

Gergen, K.J. (1991) *The Saturated Self: Dilemmas of identity in contemporary life*. New York: Basic Books.

Gergen, K.J. (1992) Toward a postmodern psychology, in S. Kvale (ed.), *Psychology and Postmodernism* (pp. 17–31). London and Beverly Hills, CA: Sage.

Gergen, K.J. (1994) *Realities and Relationships: Soundings in social construction*. Cambridge, MA: Harvard University Press.

Gergen, K.J. (1997) On the Poly/tics of Postmodern Psychology, *Theory and Psychology*, 7 (1), 31–6.

Gergen, K.J. (1999) *An Invitation to Social Construction*. London: Sage.

Gilbert, G.N. and Mulkay, M. (1984) *Opening Pandora's Box: A sociological analysis of scientists' discourse*. Cambridge: Cambridge University Press.

Gill, R. (1993) Justifying injustice: Broadcasters' accounts on inequality in radio, in E. Burman and I. Parker (eds), *Discourse Analytic Research: Repertoires and readings of texts in action* (pp. 75–93). London: Routledge.

Gill, R. (1995) Relativism, reflexivity and politics: Interrogating discourse analysis from a feminist perspective, in S. Wilkinson and C. Kitzinger (eds), *Feminism and Discourse: Psychological perspectives* (pp. 165–87). London: Sage.

Gill, R. (1996) Discourse analysis: Methodological aspects, in J.E. Richardson (ed.), *Handbook of Qualitative Research Methods for Psychology and the Social Sciences* (pp. 141–59). Leicester: British Psychological Society.

Gilligan, C. (1982) *In a Different Voice: Psychological theory and women's development*. Cambridge, MA: Harvard University Press.

Goffman, E. (1971) *Asylums*. Harmondsworth: Penguin.

Gough, B. and McFadden, M. (2001) *Critical Social Psychology*. London: Routledge.

Habermas, J. (1990) *Moral Consciousness and Communicative Action*. Cambridge, MA: MIT Press.

Hacking, I. (1995) *Rewriting the Soul: Multiple personality and the sciences of memory*. Princeton: Princeton University Press.

Hamilton, D.L. (ed.) (1981) *Cognitive Processes in Stereotyping and Intergroup Behaviour*. Hillsdale, NJ: Lawrence Erlbaum.

Hamilton, D.L. and Trolier, T. (1986) Stereotypes and stereotyping: An overview of the cognitive approach, in J.F. Dovidio and S.L. Gaertner (eds), *Prejudice, Discrimination and Racism* (pp. 165–201). Orlando: Academic Press.

Haraway, D. (1984) Primatology is politics by other means, in R.Bleier (ed.), *Feminist Approaches to Science* (pp. 77–118). London: Pergamon.

Haraway, D. (1989) *Primate Visions: Gender, race and nature in the world of modern science*. London: Routledge.

Haraway, D. (1991a) A cyborg manifesto: Science, technology and socialist feminism in the 1980s, in D. Haraway (1991), *Simians, Cyborgs, and Women: The reinvention of nature* (pp. 149–83). London: Free Association Books.

Haraway, D. (1991b) *Simians, Cyborgs, and Women: The reinvention of nature*. London: Free Association Books.

Haraway, D. (1992) When Man^{TM} is on the menu, in J. Crary and S. Kwinter (eds), *Incorporations* (pp. 104–21). New York: Zone Books.

Hare-Mustin, R.T. and Maracek, J. (1997) Abnormal and clinical psychology: The politics of madness, in D. Fox and I. Prilleltensky (eds), *Critical Psychology, an Introduction* (pp. 104–21). London: Sage.

Harper, D.J. (1995) Discourse analysis and 'mental health', *Journal of Mental Health*, 4, 347–57.

Harré, R. (1989) Language games and the texts of identity, in J. Shotter and K.J. Gergen (eds), *Texts of Identity* (pp. 20–35). London and Beverly Hills, CA: Sage.

Harré, R. (1998) *The Singular Self: An introduction to the psychology of personhood*. London: Sage.

Harré, R. (ed.) (1986) *The Social Construction of Emotions*. Oxford: Blackwell.

Harré, R. and Gillett, G. (1994) *The Discursive Mind*. London: Sage.

Harré, R. and Secord, P.F. (1972) *The Explanation of Social Behaviour*. Oxford: Blackwell.

Harré, R., Brockmeir, J. and Mülhäusler, P. (1999) *Greenspeak*. London: Sage.

Harvey, D. (1989) *The Condition of Postmodernity*. Oxford: Basil Blackwell.

Heenan, C. (1996) Feminist therapy and its discontents, in E. Burman, P. Alldred, R. Allwood, T. Billington, B. Goldberg, A.J. Gordo-López, C. Heenan, D. Marks and S. Warner, *Psychology Discourse Practice: From regulation to resistance* (pp. 55–73). London: Taylor and Francis.

Henriques, J. (1998) Social psychology and the politics of racism, in J. Henriques et al. (eds), *Changing the Subject*. London: Routledge.

Henriques, J., Hollway, W., Irwin, C., Venn, C. and Walkerdine, V. (1984 & 1998) *Changing the subject: Psychology, social regulation and subjectivity*. London: Methuen.

Hepburn, A. (1997) Teachers and secondary school bullying: a postmodern discourse analysis. *Discourse and Society*, 8, 27–49.

Hepburn, A. (1999a) Derrida and Psychology: Deconstruction and its ab/uses in critical and discursive psychologies, *Theory and Psychology*, 9 (5), 641–67.

Hepburn, A. (1999b) Postmodernity and the politics of feminist psychology, *Radical Psychology*, 1 (2), http://www.yorku.ca/faculty/academic/danaa/hepburn.html

Hepburn, A (2000a) Power lines: Derrida, discursive psychology, and the management of accusations of teacher bullying, *British Journal of Social Psychology*, 39 (4), 605–28.

Hepburn, A. (2000b) On the alleged incompatibility between feminism and relativism, *Feminism and Psychology*, 10 (1), 91–106.

Hepburn, A. (2001) Building a helping psychology: discursive psychology and institutional interaction, National Communication Association Conference, Atlanta, November.

Hepburn, A. (2002) Figuring gender in teachers' talk about school bullying, in P. McIlvenny (ed.), *Talking Gender and Sexuality* (pp. 263–88). Amsterdam: Benjamin.

Hepburn, A. and Brown, S.J. (2001) Teacher stress and the management of accountability, *Human Relations*, 54 (6), 531–55.

Heritage, J.C. (1984) *Garfinkel and Ethnomethodology*. Cambridge: Polity.

Heritage, J.C. (1995) Conversation analysis: Methodological aspects, in U. Quasthoff (ed.), *Aspects of Oral Communication* (pp. 391–418). Berlin and New York: De Gruyter.

Herzlich, C. (1973) *Health and Illness: A social psychological analysis*. London: Academic Press.

Hewstone, M., Johnstone, L. and Aird, P. (1992) Cognitive models of stereotype change: (2) Perceptions of homogenous and heterogenous groups, *European Journal of Social Psychology*, 12, 235–50.

Hinshelwood, R.D. (1983) Projective identification and Marx's concept of Man, *International Review of Psycho-Analysis*, 10, 221–6.

Hogan, R.T. and Emler, N.P. (1978) The biases in contemporary social psychology, *Social Research*, 45, 478–534.

Hogg, M.A. and Abrams, D. (1990) Social motivation, self-esteem and social identity, in D. Abrams and M.A. Hogg (eds), *Social Identity Theory: Constructive and critical advances* (pp. 28–47). Hemel Hempstead: Harvester Wheatsheaf.

Hollway, W. (1983) Heterosexual sex, power and desire for the other, in S. Cartledge and

J. Ryan (eds), *Sex and Love: New thoughts on old contradictions* (pp. 108–34). London: Women's Press.

Hollway, W. (1984 and 1998) Gender difference and the production of subjectivity, in J. Henriques et al. (eds), *Changing the Subject* (pp. 227–64). London: Methuen.

Hollway, W. (1989) *Subjectivity and Method in Psychology: Gender, meaning and science.* London: Sage.

Hollway, W. (ed.) (1997) *Mothering and Ambivalence.* London: Routledge.

Hollway, W. and Jefferson, T. (2000) *Doing Qualitative Research Differently.* London: Sage.

Hook, D. (2001) Discourse, knowledge, materiality, history: Foucault and discourse analysis, *Theory and Psychology*, II, 521–47.

Horkheimer, M., Fromm, E. and Marcuse, H. (1936) *Studien über Autorität und Familie.* Paris: Felix Alcan.

Humm, M. (1996) Feminist theory, in A. Kuper and J. Kuper (eds), *The Social Sciences Enclopedia*, second edition (pp. 296–7). London: Routledge.

Ibáñez, T. and Íñiguez, L. (eds) (1997) *Critical Social Psychology.* London: Sage.

Ingleby, D. (1985) Professionals and socialisers: the 'psy-complex', *Research in Law, Deviance and Control*, 7: 79–109.

Irigaray, L. (1985) *This Sex which is Not One.* Ithaca, New York: Cornell University Press.

Israel, J. and Tajfel, H. (eds) (1972) *The Context of Social Psychology.* London: Academic Press.

Jameson, F. (1988) The politics of theory: ideological positions in the postmodern debate', in *The Ideologies of Theory, Essays, 1971–1986:* Vol. 2 *The Syntax of History* (pp. 214–46). London: Routledge.

Jameson, F. (1991) *Postmodernism, Or, The Cultural Logic of Late Capitalism.* Durham: Duke University Press.

Jameson, F. (1992) *Signatures of the Visible.* London: Routledge.

Jodelet, D. (1991) *Madness and Social Representations.* London: Harvester/Wheatsheaf.

Jones, E.E. (1985) Major developments in social psychology in the last five decades, in G. Lindzey and E. Aronson (eds), *Handbook of Social Psychology*, third edition 1 (pp. 47–107). New York: Random House.

Kamuf, P. (1982) Replacing feminist criticism, *Diacritics*, 12, 42–7.

Kidder, L. and Fine, M. (1997) Qualitative Inquiry in Psychology: a Radical Tradition, in D. Fox and I. Prilleltensky, *Critical Psychology, an Introduction* (pp. 34–50). London: Sage.

Kitzinger, C. (1987) *The Social Construction of Lesbianism.* London and Beverly Hills, CA: Sage.

Kitzinger, C. (1989) The regulation of lesbian identities: Liberal humanism as an ideology of social control, in J. Shotter and K.J. Gergen (eds), *Texts of Identity* (pp. 82–99). London and Beverley Hills, CA: Sage.

Kitzinger, C. (1994a) Experiential authority and heterosexuality, in G. Griffin (ed.), *Changing Our Lives: Doing women's studies* (pp. 7–31). London: Pluto Press.

Kitzinger, C. (1994b) The spoken word: Listening to a different voice: Celia Kitzinger interviews Carol Gilligan, *Feminism and Psychology*, 4, 408–19.

Kitzinger, C. (1995) Social constructionism: Implications for lesbian and gay psychology, in A.R. D'Angelli and C.J. Patterson (eds), *Lesbian, Gay and Bisexual*

Identities over the Lifespan: Psychological perspectives (pp. 149–73). New York: Oxford University Press.

Kitzinger, C. (1996) Speaking of oppression: psychology, politics, and the language of power', in E.D. Rothblum and L.A. Bond (eds), *Preventing Heterosexism and Homophobia* (pp. 3–19). Thousand Oaks, CA: Sage.

Kitzinger, C. (1997) Lesbian and gay psychology: a critical analysis, in D. Fox and I. Prilleltensky (eds), *Critical Psychology: An introduction* (pp. 202–16). London: Sage.

Kitzinger, C., Wilkinson, S. and Perkins, R. (eds) (1992) Heterosexuality [Special Issue]. *Feminism and Psychology*, 2 (3). London: Sage.

Klein, M. (1932) *The Psychoanalysis of Children*. London: Hogarth Press.

Klein, M. (1946) Notes on some schizoid mechanisms, in J. Mitchell (ed.) (1986) *The Selected Melanie Klein*. Harmondsworth: Penguin.

Knorr Cetina, K. (1995) *Epistemic Cultures: How scientists make sense*. Chicago: Indiana University Press.

Kolominsky, Y. (1991) Soviet psychology today. Invited address by Vice-President, Soviet Psychological Society, Hope College.

Kristeva, J. (1980) *Desire in Language: A semiotic approach to literature and art*. Oxford: Blackwell.

Kuhn, T.S. (1962) *The Structure of Scientific Revolutions*, second edition. Chicago: University of Chicago Press.

Kvale, S. (ed.) (1992) *Psychology and Postmodernism*. London and Beverly Hills, CA: Sage.

Lacan, J. (1949) The mirror stage as formative of the function of the I as revealed in psychoanalytic experience. Reprinted in J. Lacan, *Ecrits*. pp. 1–7. Trans. A. Sheridan. London: Tavistock.

Lacan, J. (1977) *Ecrits: A selection*. Trans A. Sheridan. London: Tavistock.

Lacan, J. (1989) *Speech and Language in Psychoanalysis*. Trans. Anthony Wilden. Baltimore: Johns Hopkins UP.

Lacan, J. (1992) *The Ethics of Psychoanalysis*. London: Routledge.

Langer, M. (1989) *From Vienna to Managua: Journey of a psychoanalyst*. London: Free Association Books.

Lash, S. and Urry, J. (1987) *The End of Organised Capitalism*. Cambridge: Polity.

Latour, B. and Woolgar, S. (1986) *Laboratory Life: The construction of scientific facts*, second edition. Princeton: Princeton University Press.

Lynch, M. and Bogen, D. (1996) *The Spectacle of History: Speech, text and memory of the Iran-Contra hearings*. Durham, NC: Duke University Press.

Lyotard, J-F. (1984) *The Postmodern Condition: A report on knowledge*. Manchester, UK: Manchester University Press.

Lyotard, J-F. (1989) *The Differend*. Minneapolis: University of Minnesota Press.

MacMartin, C. (2002) (Un)reasonable doubt? The invocation of children's consent in sexual abuse trial judgments, *Discourse and Society*, 13 (1), 9–40.

Macnaghten, P. (1993) Discourses of nature: Argumentation and power, in E. Burman and I. Parker (eds), *Discourse Analytic Research: Repertoires and readings of texts in action* (pp. 52–72). London: Routledge.

Madill, A. and Docherty, K. (1994) So you did what you wanted then: Discourse analysis, personal agency, and psychotherapy, *Journal of Community and Applied Social Psychology*, 4, 261–73.

Malson, H. (1998) *The Thin Woman: Feminism, post-structuralism and the social psychology of anorexia nervosa*. London: Routledge.

Manstead, A.S.R. and Hewstone, M. (eds) (1995) *The Blackwell Encyclopedia of Social Psychology*. Oxford: Blackwell.

Marcuse, H. (1955) *Eros and Civilisation: A philosophical inquiry into Freud*. Boston: Beacon.

Markova, I. (2000) Amedee or how to get rid of it: Social representations from a dialogical perspective, *Culture and Psychology*, 6, 419–60.

Marshall, H. and Wetherell, M. (1989) Talking about career and gender identities: A discourse analysis perspective, in S. Skevington and D. Baker (eds), *The Social Identity of Women* (pp. 106–130). London: Sage.

Marx, K. and Engels, F. (1964) *The German Ideology*. Moscow: Progress.

Marx, K. and Engels, F. (1965) *Selected Correspondence*. Moscow: Progress.

Marx, K. (1972) *Critique of the Gotha Programme*. Peking: Foreign Languages Press.

Matoesian, G.W. (1993) *Reproducing Rape: Domination through talk in the courtroom*. Oxford: Blackwell.

McGuire, W.J. (1973) The Yin and Yang of progress in social psychology: Seven Koan, *Journal of Personality and Social Psychology*, 26, 446–57.

McHoul, A.W. (1987) Why there are no guarantees for interrogators, *Journal of Pragmatics*, 11, 455–71.

McHoul, A. and Grace, W. (1993) *A Foucault Primer: Discourse, power and the subject*. London: UCL Press.

McLellan, D. (1975) *Marx*. London: Fontana.

McLellan, D. (1986) *Ideology*. Milton Keynes: Open University Press.

Michael, M. (1996a) *Constructing Identities: The social, the nonhuman and change*. London: Sage.

Michael, M. (1996b) Pick a utopia, any utopia: How to be critical in critical social psychology, in I. Parker and R. Spears (eds), *Psychology and Society: Radical theory and practice* (pp. 141–53). London: Pluto Press.

Middleton, D. and Edwards, D. (eds) (1990) *Collective Remembering*. London: Sage.

Miles, R. (1989) *Racism*. London: Routledge.

Milgram, S. (1963) Behavioural study of obedience, *Journal of Abnormal and Social Psychology*, 67, 371–78.

Milgram, S. (1965) Some conditions of obedience and disobedience to authority, *Human Relations*, 18, 57–76.

Miller, A.G. (1986) *The Obedience Experiments: A case study of controversy in social science*. New York: Praeger.

Miller, L.J. (2000) The poverty of truth-seeking: postmodernism, discourse analysis and critical feminism, *Theory & Psychology*, 10 (3), 313–52.

Millett, K. (1971) *Sexual Politics*. New York: Avon Books.

Minsky, R. (1992) Lacan, in H. Crowley and S. Himmelweit (eds), *Knowing Women: Feminism and knowledge* (pp. 81–119). Cambridge: Polity Press.

Mitchell, J. (1974) *Psychoanalysis and Feminism*. Harmondsworth: Penguin.

Moghaddam, F.M. (1987) Psychology in the third world: As reflected by the 'crisis' in social psychology and the move towards indigenous third world psychology, *American Psychologist*, 47, 912–20.

Moghaddam, F.M. (1990) Modulative and generative orientations in psychology: Implications for psychology in the third world, *Journal of Social Issues*, 56, 21–41.

Moghaddam, F.M. and Taylor, D.M. (1986) What constitutes an 'appropriate psychology' for the developing world? *International Journal of Psychology*, 21, 253–67.

Moi, T. (1985) *Sexual/Textual Politics*. London: Methuen.

Moi, T. (1986) Representation of patriarchy: Sexuality and patriarchy in Freud's Dora, in C. Bernheimer and C. Kahane (eds), *In Dora's Case* (pp. 78–97). London: Virago.

Moscovici, S. (1972) Society and theory in social psychology, in J. Israel and H. Tajfel (eds), *The Context of Social Psychology* (pp. 17–68) London: Academic Press.

Moscovici, S. (1976) *La psychoanalyse: Son image et son public*. Revised edition. Paris: Presses Universitaires de France.

Mulkay, M. (1991) *Sociology of Science: A sociological pilgrimage*. Milton Keynes: Open University Press.

Myers, D.G. (1993) *Social Psychology*, fourth edition. New York: McGraw-Hill.

National NOW Times (1996) *Promise Keepers: A real challenge from the right*. 1–16.

Nicholson, L. (1990) *Feminism/Postmodernism*. London: Routledge.

Nightingale, D.J. and Cromby, J. (eds) (1999) *Social Constructionist Psychology: A critical analysis of theory and practice*. Buckingham: Open University Press.

Nisbett, R. and Ross, L. (1990) *Human Inference: Strategies and shortcomings of human judgement*. Englewood Cliffs, NJ: Prentice-Hall.

Oakes, P.J. (1987) The salience of social categories, in J.C. Turner, M.A. Hogg, P.J. Oakes, S.D. Reicher and M.S. Wetherell, *Rediscovering the Social Group: A self-categorisation theory* (pp. 117–41). Oxford: Blackwell.

Oakes, P.J., Haslam, S.A. and Turner, J.C. (1994) *Stereotyping and Social Reality*. Oxford: Blackwell.

Oakes, P.J., Turner, J.C. and Haslam, S.A. (1991) Perceiving people as group members: The role of fit in the salience of social categorisations, *British Journal of Social Psychology*, 30, 125–44.

Operario, D. and Fiske, S.T. (1999) Integrating social identity and social cognition: A framework for bridging diverse perspectives, in D. Abrams and M.A. Hogg (eds), *Social Identity and Social Cognition* (pp. 26–54). Oxford: Blackwell.

Orne, M.T. (1969) Demand characteristics and the concept of quasi-controls, in R. Rosenthal and R.L. Rosnow (eds), *Artifact in Behavioural Research* (pp. 143–79). New York: Academic Press.

Pancer, S.M. (1997) Social Psychology: The crisis continues, in D. Fox and I. Prilleltensky (eds), *Critical Psychology: An introduction* (pp. 150–65). London: Sage.

Parker, I. (1988) Deconstructing accounts, in C. Antaki (ed.), *Analysing Everyday Explanation: A casebook of methods*. London: Sage.

Parker, I. (1989a) Discourse and power, in J. Shotter and K. Gergen (eds), *Texts of Identity*. London: Sage.

Parker, I. (1989b) *The Crisis in Modern Social Psychology – and how to end it*. London: Routledge.

Parker, I. (1997a) *Psychoanalytic Culture: Psychoanalytic discourse in Western society*. London: Sage.

Parker, I. (1997b) Discursive psychology, in D. Fox and I. Prilleltensky (eds), *Critical Psychology: An introduction* (pp. 284–98). London: Sage.

Parker, I. (1997c) The unconscious state of social psychology, in T. Ibáñez and L. Íñiguez (eds), *Critical Social Psychology* (pp. 157–69). London: Sage.

Parker, I. (1997d) Discourse analysis and psychoanalysis, *British Journal of Social Psychology*, 36, 479–95.

Parker, I. (ed.) (1998) *Social Constructionism, Discourse and Realism*. London: Sage.

Parker, I. (ed.) (1999) *Deconstructing Psychotherapy*. London: Sage.

Parker, I. and Burman, E. (1993) Against discursive imperialism, empiricism, and constructionism: Thirty-two problems with discourse analysis, in E. Burman and I. Parker (eds), *Discourse Analytic Research: Repertoires and readings of texts in action* (pp. 155–72) London: Routledge.

Parker, I. and Shotter, J. (1990) *Deconstructing Social Psychology*. London: Routledge.

Parker, I. and Spears, R. (eds) (1996) *Psychology and Society: Radical theory and practice*. London: Pluto Press.

Parker, I., Georgaca, E., Harper, D., McLaughlin, T. and Stowell-Smith, M. (1995) *Deconstructing Psychopathology*. London: Sage.

Parker, N. (2001) Social constructionist psychology: Is there something missing? *International Journal of Critical Psychology*, 2, 169–76.

Pepitone, A. (1976) Toward a normative and comparative biocultural social psychology, *Journal of Personality and Social Psychology*, 34, 641–53.

Peräkylä, A. (1995) *AIDS Counselling: Institutional interaction and clinical practice*. Cambridge: Cambridge University Press.

Poster, M. (1979) *Sartre's Marxism*. London: Pluto.

Potter, J. (1996a) *Representing Reality: Discourse, rhetoric and social construction*. London: Sage.

Potter, J. (1996b) Discourse analysis and constructionist approaches: Theoretical background, in J.E. Richardson (ed.), *Handbook of Qualitative Research Methods for Psychology and the Social Sciences* (pp. 125–41). Leicester: British Psychological Society.

Potter, J. (1998) Fragments in the realisation of relativism, in I. Parker (ed.), *Social Constructionsim, Discourse and Realism* (pp. 27–47). London: Sage.

Potter, J. (2000) Post cognitivist psychology, *Theory and Psychology*, 10, 31–7.

Potter, J. (2001) Wittgenstein and Austin, in M. Wetherell, S. Taylor and S. Yates (eds), *Discourse Theory and Practice* (pp. 39–46). London: Sage.

Potter, J. and Edwards, D. (1999) Social representations and discursive psychology, *Culture & Psychology*, 5, 445–56.

Potter, J. and Mulkay, M. (1985) Scientists' interview talk: Interviews as a technique for revealing participants' interpretative practices, in M. Brenner, J. Brown and D. Canter (eds), *The Research Interview: Uses and approaches* (pp. 247–71). London: Academic Press.

Potter, J. and Reicher, S. (1987) Discourses of community and conflict: The organization of social categories in accounts of a 'riot', *British Journal of Social Psychology*, 26, 25–40.

Potter, J. and Wetherell, M. (1987) *Discourse and Social Psychology: Beyond attitudes and behaviour*. London: Sage.

Potter, J. and Wetherell, M. (1994) Analyzing discourse, in A. Bryman and B. Burgess (eds), *Analyzing Qualitative Data*. London: Routledge.

Potter, J, Edwards, D., & Ashmore, M. (1999) Regulating criticism: some comments on an argumentative complex, *History of the Human Sciences*, 12, 79–88. (This is reprinted in I. Parker (ed.) (2002), *Critical Theoretical Psychology*. London: Palgrave.)

Potter, J., Wetherell, M., Gill, R. and Edwards, D. (1990) Discourse – noun, verb or social practice? *Philosophical Psychology*, 3, 205–17.

Rabbie, J.M. and Horwitz, M. (1988) Categories versus groups as explanatory concepts in intergroup relations, *European Journal of Social Psychology*, 18, 117–23.

Read, A.J. (1996) Marxist history, in A. Kuper and J. Kuper (eds), The Social Science Encyclopedia, second edition (pp. 509–11). London: Routledge.

Reich, J.W. (1981) An historical analysis of the field, in L. Bickman (ed.), *Applied Social Psychology Annual* (pp. 45–70). Beverly Hills, CA: Sage.

Reicher, S. (1984) Social influence in the crowd: Attitudinal and behavioural effects of deindividuation in conditions of high and low group salience, *British Journal of Social Psychology*, 23, 341–50.

Reicher, S. (1987) Crowd behaviour as collective action, in J. Turner, M. Hogg, P. Oakes, S. Reicher and M. Wetherell, *Rediscovering the Social Group*. Oxford: Blackwell.

Reicher, S. (1996) The reactionary practice of radical psychology, in I. Parker and R. Spears (eds), *Psychology and Society: Radical theory and practice* (pp. 230–41). London: Pluto.

Reicher, S. (1997) Laying the ground for a common critical psychology, in T. Ibáñez and L. Íñiguez (eds) (1997) *Critical Social Psychology*. London: Sage.

Reicher, S. and Hopkins, N. (2001) *Self and Nation*. London: Sage.

Ricoeur, P. (1970) *Freud and Philosophy: An essay on interpretation*. New Haven, CT: Yale University Press.

Ring, K. (1967) Experimental social psychology: some sober questions about some frivolous values, *Journal of Experimental Social Psychology*, 3, 113–23.

Robinson, P. (ed) Social Groups and Identities: Developing the legacy of Henri Tajfel. London: Butterworth Heinemann.

Roiser, M. and Willig, C. (1996) Marxism, the Frankfurt School, and working-class psychology, in I. Parker and R. Spears (eds), *Psychology and Society: Radical theory and practice* (pp. 50–64). London: Pluto Press.

Romme, M. and Escher, S. (eds) (1993) *Accepting Voices*. London: MIND.

Rorty, R. (1980) *Philosophy and the Mirror of Nature*. Princeton, NJ: Princeton University Press.

Rorty, R. (1982) *Consequences of Pragmatism: (Essays: 1972–1980)*. Minneapolis: University of Minnesota Press.

Rorty, R. (1989) *Contingency, Irony, and Solidarity*. Cambridge: Cambridge University Press.

Rose, N. (1985) *The Psychological Complex*. London: Routledge & Kegan Paul.

Rose, N. (1989) *Governing the Soul*. London: Routledge.

Rose, N. (1990) Psychology as a 'social' science, in I. Parker and J. Shotter (eds), *Deconstructing Social Psychology* (pp. 103–15). London: Routledge.

Rose, N. (1996) *Inventing Ourselves: Psychology, power and personhood*. Cambridge: Cambridge University Press.

Rosenthal, R. (1969) Interpersonal expectations: Effects of the experimenter's hypothesis, in R. Rosenthal and R.L. Rosnow (eds), *Artefact in Behavioural Research* (pp. 181–277). New York: Academic Press.

Sacks, H. (1992) *Lectures on Conversation.* Vols. I & II, edited by G. Jefferson. Oxford: Basil Blackwell.

Sampson, E.E. (1977) Psychology and the American ideal, *Journal of Personality and Social Psychology*, 35, 767–82.

Sampson, E.E. (1983) Deconstructing psychology's subject, *Journal of Mind and Behaviour*, 4, 135–64.

Sampson, E.E. (1989) The deconstruction of the self, in J. Shotter and K. Gergen (eds), *Texts of Identity* (pp. 1–20). London: Sage.

Sampson, E.E. (1990) Social psychology and social control, in I. Parker and J. Shotter (eds), *Deconstructing Social Psychology* (pp. 117–26). London: Routledge.

Sampson, E.E. (1993) *Celebrating the Other: A dialogic account of human nature.* Hemel Hempstead, UK: Harvester/Wheatsheaf.

Sampson, E.E. (1998) Establishing embodiment in psychology, in H.J. Stam (ed.), *The Body in Psychology* (pp. 30–53). London: Sage.

Sayers, J. (1990) Psychoanalytic feminism: deconstructing power in theory and therapy, in I. Parker and J. Shotter (eds), *Deconstructing Social Psychology* (pp. 196–208). London: Routledge.

Schegloff, E.A. (1999a) 'Schegloff's texts' as 'Billig's data': A critical reply, *Discourse and Society*, 10, 558–72.

Schegloff, E.A. (1999b) Naivete vs sophistication or discipline vs self-indulgence: A rejoinder to Billig, *Discourse and Society*, 10 (4), 577–82.

Schegloff, E.A. (1992) On talk and its institutional occasions, in P. Drew and J. Heritage (eds), *Talk at Work: Interaction in institutional settings* (pp. 101–34). Cambridge: Cambridge University Press.

Schegloff, E.A. (1997) Whose text? Whose context? *Discourse and Society*, 8, 165–87.

Schegloff, E.A. (1998) Reply to Wetherell, *Discourse & Society*, 9, 413–16.

Sears, D.O. (1986) College sophomores in the laboratory: Influences of a narrow database on social psychology's view of human nature, *Journal of Personality and Social Psychology*, 51, 515–30.

Sève, L. (1974) *Man in Marxist theory, and the Psychology of Personality.* Sussex: Harvester Press.

Sherif, M. (1966) *In Common Predicament: Social psychology of intergroup conflict and cooperation.* Boston, MA: Houghton Mifflin.

Shotter, J. (1989) Social accountability and the social construction of 'you', in J. Shotter and K.J. Gergen (eds), *Texts of Identity* (pp. 133–51). London: Sage.

Shotter, J. (1993) *Conversational realities: Constructing life through language.* London: Sage.

Shotter, J. and Gergen, K.J. (eds) (1989) *Texts of Identity.* London: Sage.

Silverman, I. (1977) Why social psychology fails, *Canadian Psychological Review*, 18, 353–58.

Sim, S. (1999) *Derrida and the End of History.* Cambridge: Icon Books Ltd.

Simon, B. (1993) On the asymmetry in the cognitive construal of ingroup and outgroup: a model of egocentric social categorization. *European Journal of Social Psychology*, 23, 131–48.

Simons, H. and Billig, M. (1994) *After Postmodernism: Restructuring ideology critique.* London: Sage.

Sloan, T. (1995) *Damaged Life: The crisis of the modern psyche.* London: Routledge.

Sloan, T. (1997) Theories of personality: Ideology and beyond, in D. Fox and I. Prilleltensky (eds), *Critical Psychology: An Introduction* (pp. 87–104). London: Sage.

Sloan, T. (2000) *Critical Psychology: Voices for change.* London: Palgrave.

Smith, B.H. (1988) *Contingencies of Value: Alternative perspectives for critical theory.* Cambridge, MA: Harvard University Press.

Smith, B.H. (1997) *Belief and Resistance: Dynamics of contemporary intellectual controversy.* Cambridge, MA: Harvard University Press.

Smith, M.B. (1972) Is experimental social psychology advancing? *Journal of Experimental Social Psychology*, 8, 86–96.

Spears, R. (1995) Social categorisation, in A.S.R. Manstead and M. Hewstone (eds), *The Blackwell Encyclopedia of Social Pschology* (pp. 530–35). Oxford: Blackwell.

Spears, R. (1997) Introduction, in T. Ibáñez and I. Íñiguez (eds), *Critical Social Psychology.* London: Sage.

Speer, S. and Potter, J. (2000) The management of heterosexist talk: Conversational resources and prejudiced claims, in P. McIlvenny (ed.), *Talking Gender and Sexuality.* Amsterdam: Benjamin.

Speer, S.A. and Potter, J. (2002) Judith Butler, discursive psychology, and the politics of conversation, in P. McIlvenny (ed.), *Talking Gender and Sexuality: Identities, agencies and desires in interaction.* Amsterdam: John Benjamins.

Squire, C. (1989) *Significant Differences: Feminism in psychology.* London: Routledge.

Squire, C. (1995) Pragmatism, extravagance and feminist discourse, in S. Wilkinson and C. Kitzinger (eds), *Feminism and Discourse* (pp. 145–65). London: Sage.

Steiner, I.D. (1974) Whatever happened to the group in social psychology? *Journal of Experimental Social Psychology*, 10, 94–108.

Stokoe, L. and Smithson, J. (2001) Making gender relevant: Conversation analysis and gender categories in interaction, *Discourse & Society*, 12, 217–44.

Tajfel, H. (1972) Experiments in a vacuum, in J. Israel and H. Tajfel (eds), *The Context of Social Psychology* (pp. 69–119). London: Academic Press.

Tajfel, H. (1978) *Differentiation Between Social Groups: Studies in the social psychology of intergroup relations.* London: Academic Press.

Tajfel, H. (1982) *Social Identity and Intergroup Relations.* Cambridge: Cambridge University Press.

Tajfel, H. and Turner, J.C. (1979) The social identity theory of intergroup behaviour, in W.G. Austin and S. Worchel (eds), *The Social Psychology of Intergroup Relations* (pp. 7–24). Chicago, IL: Nelson-Hall.

Tajfel, H., Flament, C., Billig, M.G. and Bundy, R.P. (1971) Social categorisation and intergroup behaviour, *European Journal of Social Psychology*, 1, 149–78.

Thompson, J.B. (1984) *Studies in the Theory of Ideology.* Cambridge: Polity.

Thompson, J.B. (1990) *Ideology and Modern Culture.* Cambridge: Polity.

Turner, J.C. (1975) Social comparison and social identity: Some prospects for intergroup behaviour, *European Journal of Social Psychology*, 5, 149–78.

Turner, J.C. (1985) Social categorization and the self concept: A social-cognitive theory of group behaviour, in E.J. Lawler (ed.), *Advances in Group Processes: Theory and research* (2 pp. 77–122). Greenwich CT: JAI Press.

Turner, J.C. (1995) *Social Influence*. Milton Keynes: Open University Press.

Turner, J.C. (1995) Self-categorisation theory, in A.S.R. Manstead and M. Hewstone (eds), *The Blackwell Encyclopedia of Social Pschology* (pp. 502–4). Oxford: Blackwell.

Turner, J.C., Hogg, M., Oakes, P., Reicher, S. and Wetherell, M. (1987) *Rediscovering the Social Group*. Oxford: Blackwell.

Unger, R. and Crawford, R. (1992) *Women and Gender: A feminist psychology*. New York: McGraw Hill.

Ussher, J. (1989) *The Psychology of the Female Body*. London: Routledge.

Ussher, J. (1991) *Women's Madness: Misogyny or mental illness?* Hemel Hempstead: Harvester Wheatsheaf.

Ussher, J. (1997) *Fantasies of Femininity: Reframing the boundaries of sex*. London: Penguin.

Ussher, J. (2000) Women's Madness: A material-discursive-intrapsychic approach, in D. Fee (ed.), *Pathology and the Postmodern: Mental illness as discourse and experience* (pp. 207–31). London: Sage.

Van Dijk, T.A. (ed.) (1985) *Handbook of Discourse Analysis. Vols. 1–4*. London: Academic Press.

Vygotsky, L.S. (1962) *Thought and Language*. Cambridge, MA: MIT Press.

Wagner, W., Duveen, G., Thermel, M. and Verma, J. (1999) The modernization of tradition: Thinking about madness in Patna, India, *Culture & Psychology*, 5, 413–45.

Walkerdine, V. (1986) Post-structuralist theory and everyday social practices: The family and the school, in S. Wilkinson (ed.), *Feminist Social Psychology: Developing Theory and Practice* (pp. 57–76). Milton Keynes: Open University Press.

Walkerdine, V. (1988) *The Mastery of Reason: Cognitive development and the production of rationality*. London: Routledge.

Walkerdine, V. (1991) *Schoolgirl Fictions*. London: Virago.

Walkerdine, V. and Lucey, H. (1989) *Democracy in the Kitchen*. London: Virago.

Warner, S. (1996) Special women, special places: Women and high security mental hospitals, in E. Burman, P. Alldred, R. Allwood, T. Billington, B. Goldberg, A.J. Gordo-López, C. Heenan, D. Marks and S. Warner, *Psychology Discourse Practice: From regulation to resistance* (pp. 96–104). London: Taylor and Francis.

Wertsch, J.V. (1991) *Voices of the Mind: A sociocultural approach to mediated action*. Hemel Hempstead, UK: Harvester/Wheatsheaf.

West, D. (1996) *An Introduction to Continental Philosophy*. Cambridge: Polity.

Wetherell, M. (1995) Romantic discourse and feminist analysis: Interrogating investment, power and desire, in S. Wilkinson and C. Kitzinger (eds), *Feminism and Discourse: Psychological perspectives* (pp. 128–45). London: Sage.

Wetherell, M. (1996a) Fear of fat: Interpretative repertoires and ideological dilemmas, in J. Maybin and N. Mercer (eds), *Using English: From conversation to canon* (pp. 76–89). London: Routledge.

Wetherell, M. (1996b) Constructing social identities: The individual/social binary in Henri Tajfel's social psychology, in P. Robinson (ed.), *Social Groups and Identities* (pp. 269–85). Oxford: Butterworth Heinemann.

Wetherell, M. (1998) Positioning and interpretative repertoires: Conversation analysis and post-structuralism in dialogue, *Discourse and Society*, 9, 387–412.

Wetherell, M. and Maybin, J. (1996) The distributed self: A social constructionist perspective, in R. Stevens (ed.), *Understanding the Self* (pp. 219–65). London: Sage.

Wetherell, M. and Potter, J. (1992) *Mapping the Language of Racism: Discourse and the legitimation of exploitation*. Brighton: Harvester/Wheatsheaf, New York: Columbia University Press.

Wetherell, M., Stiven, H. and Potter, J. (1987) Unequal egalitarianism: a preliminary study of discourses concerning gender and employment opportunities, *British Journal of Social Psychology*, 26, 59–71.

Wexler, P. (1983) *Critical Social Psychology*. Boston, MA: Routledge and Kegan Paul.

Widdicombe, S. (in press) *Critical Social Psychology*. Buckingham: Open University Press.

Widdicombe, S. and Wooffitt, R. (1995) *The Language of Youth Subcultures: Social identity in action*. Hemel Hempstead, UK: Harvester/Wheatsheaf.

Wierzbicka, A. (1995) Emotion and facial expression: A semantic perspective, *Culture and Psychology*, 1 (2), 227–58.

Wiggins, S. (in press) Talking with your mouth full: 'Mmm's and the embodiment of pleasure, *Research on Language and Social Interaction*.

Wiggins, S., Potter, J. and Wildsmith, A. (2001) Eating your words: Discursive psychology and the reconstruction of eating practices, *Journal of Health Psychology*, 6, 5–15.

Wilkinson, S. (ed.) (1986) *Feminist Social Psychology: Developing theory and practice*. Milton Keynes: Open University Press.

Wilkinson, S. (1997) Prioritizing the political: Feminist psychology, in T. Ibáñez and L. Íñiguez (eds), *Critical Social Psychology* (pp. 179–85). London: Sage.

Wilkinson, S. and Kitzinger, C. (eds) (1993) *Heterosexuality: A Feminism and Psychology Reader*. London: Sage.

Wilkinson, S. and Kitzinger, C. (eds) (1995) *Feminism and Discourse*. London: Sage.

Wilkinson, S. and Kitzinger, C. (eds) (1996) *Representing the Other: A feminism and psychology reader*. London: Sage.

Willig, C. (ed.) (1999) *Applied Discourse Analysis: social and psychological interventions*. Buckingham: Open University Press.

Wilig, C. (2000) A discourse-dynamic approach to the study of subjectivity in health psychology, *Theory & Psychology*, 10, 547–70.

Wittgenstein (1953) *Philosophical Investigations*. Oxford: Blackwell.

Wood, L.A. and Rennie, H. (1994) Formulating rape, *Discourse & Society*, 5, 125–48.

Wooffitt, R. (1992) *Telling Tales of the Unexpected: The organization of factual discourse*. London: Harvester/Wheatsheaf.

Woolgar, S. (1988) *Science: The very idea*. Chichester: Ellis Horwood/London: Tavistock.

Wowk, M. (1984) Blame allocation: Sex and gender in a murder interrogation, *Women's Studies International Forum*, 7, 75–82.

Yardley, L. (1997) Introducing material-discursive approaches to health and illness, in L. Yardley (ed.), *Material Discourses of Health and Illness*. London: Routledge.

Zaleznik, A. (1996) Psychoanalysis, in A. Kuper and J. Kuper (eds), *The Social Science Encyclopedia*, second edition (pp. 684–7). London and New York: Routledge.

Zimbardo, P.G. (1972) Pathology of imprisonment, *Transactional/Society*, 4–8 (a).

Zimbardo, P.G. (1971) The psychological power and pathology of imprisonment. A statement prepared for the US House of Representatives Committee on the Judiciary, Subcommittee No. 3: Hearings on Prison Reform, San Francisco, CA., October 25.

Žižek, S. (1998) Psychoanalysis in post-Marxism: The case of Alan Badiou, *The South Atlantic Quarterly*, 2, 235–63.

Index

Abrams, D. 32, 193
Adorno, T.W. 53, 54, 55, 185
Aird, P. 39
Aitken, G. 223–4
Alcoff, L. 118
Alldred, P., 223–4
Allport, G.W. 20–21, 25, 151
Allwood, R., 223–4
Althusser, L. 53
Antaki, C. 41, 167, 230
Armistead, N. 27
Aron, A. 22
Aron, E. 22
Asch, S. 22, 44
Ashmore, M. 8, 9, 80, 117, 123, 219, 220,
    221, 222, 226, 227, 232
Augoustinos, M. 29, 35, 43, 44, 45, 61,
    69
Austin, J.L. 28, 120, 134, 161
Ab/normal 84
Actor network theory 64
Agency, *see* freedom
AIDS counselling 236
Alienation, *see* Marxism
Androgyny 101, 112
Anthropology 5
Anti-Semitism 86
Anything goes 9, 82, 123, 223
    see also relativism
Application 29, 41–2, 66–7, 93–5, 122, 128,
    162–3, 235–7
    see also critical practice
Asylum seekers 19
Attitudes 104–5
Attribution theory 182
Authoritarian personality, *see* Frankfurt
    School
Authority 22, 216

Bakhtin, M.M. 84, 85
Baron, R.A. 247
Baumann, Z. 204
Baumeister, R.F. 43
Bavelas, J.B. 124
Beasley, C. 100
Beauvoir, S. de 158
Bem, S.L. 101
Benjamin, W. 53
Bennington, G. 204, 207, 212
Best, S. 201
Bhaskar, R. 8
Bhavnani, K-K. 100, 101
Billig, M. 2, 11, 14, 33, 39–40, 41, 44, 45, 55,
    56, 60, 66, 69, 71, 79 84–87, 96, 106,
    157, 167, 172, 183, 184, 187, 190–2,
    194, 196, 215, 226, 236, 241, 247
Billington, T., 223–4
Bly, R. 80–81
Bogen, D. 168
Bonss, W. 54
Bradbury, M. 11, 13
Braidotti, R. 158
Brennan, T. 86, 96
Brockmeir, J. 188
Brown, R. 35
Brown, S.J. 147
Bruins, J.J. 39
Bruner, J. 175
Bundy, R.P. 33
Burkitt, I. 114, 116
Burman, E. 59, 82, 84, 122, 123, 126, 130,
    156, 199, 204, 211, 213–4, 223–4
Burr, V. 83–4, 114, 116, 221, 227
Bush, G.W. 166
Butt, T. 83–4
Butler, J. 14, 90, 92, 96, 110–11, 114–15,
    117, 118, 120–1, 130, 156, 158, 200, 217
Buttny, R. 170

Byrne, D. 247
Biology 14, 116, 150, 217
Binary oppositions, *see* Derrida,
    deconstruction
Bodies 111–16
    And eating 116–17
    Anorexia nervosa 112–13
    Cyborg manifesto 115–16
    Embodiment 114, 150
    Gendered 14, 110, 115
    Mind/body split 112, 114
    Women's bodies 111–14
    see also feminism, heterosexism, sexuality

Callon, M. 64
Cantor, N. 203
Cartwright, D. 27
Center for Democratic Studies 98
Chalmers, A. 10
Cixous, Hélène 90
Clark, K.B. 20, 45
Clark, M.P. 20, 45
Coates, L. 124
Collins, H.M. 25
Comte, A. 7
Condor, S. 56, 66, 106, 183, 184, 236
Conway, M. 193, 196
Coulter, J. 135
Coyle, A. 109
Crawford, R. 99
Critchley, S. 156, 204
Cromby, J. 116, 117, 149–150, 193, 199
Curt, B.C. 213, 227
Capitalism 7, 46, 47, 49–51, 61, 65, 183, 201,
    243
    Anti-capitalism 40
    see also Marxism
Cartesian dualism 112, 114
Categorisation and particularisation 40
Children's rights 213
Circular reasoning, *see* moral superiority
Class, *see* social class
Cognition 166, 169, 195, 203
    And emotion 173
    Cognitive miser 10, 32
    Cognitive processes 185
    Cognitivism 19, 40–41, 60–61, 167
    Perceptual cognitivism 183
    Traditional approach 32, 36, 39
    see also social cognition, information
        processing, memory
Commodity reification, *see* Marxism
Communism 46, 49, 243
Conflict 68
    see also Marxism, Groups, social class

Conformity 22–3
Constructionism 15, 30, 216
    see also social constructionism
Constructivism 175
Contact Hypothesis 20
Context debate, the 172
Conversation 84–6
    And context 172, 218
    Conversation analysis 109, 218–9
Crisis in social psychology 12, 24–30
Crime 25
    Criminal, the 64–5
Critical realism 8, 122, 241
    see also Bhaskar, Parker, realism,
        relativism
Critical practice 228, 235–7
    Practical intervention 235–6, 237
    see also application
Critical social psychology
    And orthodoxy 41, 222, 247
    Assumptions of 5–11, 228–235
    Critical evaluation of 228, 237–246
    Definition 1
    Recommendations for the future 246–7
Critical theory, *see* Frankfurt School
Criticism/critique 1–3, 201, 212, 215, 216,
    222
Crowds 38
    see also groups, Reicher, S.
Culture 5, 187
    Culture-as-heritage 187
    Culture-as-therapy 187
    see also interpretative repertoires

Daly, M. 98, 102, 130
Davies, B. 126, 220, 227
Davies, M. 124
Deleuze, G. 146
Derrida, J. 11, 15, 61, 92, 110, 120, 199, 201,
    204–10, 224, 225, 226, 229, 231, 235,
    245
    And Marx 65–6, 69, 239–40
    see also deconstruction
Doherty, K. 221
Donzelot, J. 89
Doosje, B., 39
Drew, P. 124
Dreyfus, H.L. 91
Durkheim, E. 31
Duveen, G., 31
Dworkin, A. 102, 114, 130
Death and furniture 209–211
    see also realism, relativism
Death of the subject 11
    see also postmodernism, subjectivity

Deconstruction 15, 65, 81, 90, 114, 118, 121, 124, 156, 160, 163, 204–15, 224, 225, 231, 236, 245
  And feminism 121, 206
  And CSP 210
  Binary oppositions 79, 92, 93, 114, 158, 207–8
  Différance 209, 211, 225
  Double movement 121
  Either/or logic 92, 160, 206, 210, 214, 217–8, 245
  Iterability 110, 215
  Logocentrism 90, 206, 207–8, 209–210, 212, 217, 225, 226, 231, 245
  Of the self/subject 60, 156
  Phonocentrism 208–9, 245
  'Practical' deconstruction 47, 66, 93, 245
  Presence/absence 207, 225
  Quasi-transcendental 207
  Speech/writing argument 208–9
  Supplement, the 160, 209
  Trace, the 225
  Undecideability 204, 208–9, 210, 212, 215
  see also Derrida, metaphysics, post-structuralism, structuralism
Deindividuation 22
Democracy 66, 240
Dialectic 48
Diana, Princess of Wales 182
Discourse 56, 57, 61–5, 157, 166–197
  Analysis 106, 166–197, 245
  And construction 174–183
  And embodiment 116–17
  And psychoanalysis 90
  And the individual 167–174
  'extra/pre-discursive', the 83, 115, 116, 202, 224
  individualising 140
  see also cognition, discursive psychology, Foucault, ideology, language
Discrimination 19
Discursive psychology 2, 3, 15, 39, 40, 86, 111, 124, 149, 169, 175–8, 215, 222, 225, 230, 231, 236, 238, 243–4
  and construction 175–7
  and Foucault 167
  and paranormal accounts 178–181
  and practices 174, 183
  as critical 182–3
  dilemma of stake 177, 181
  fact construction 177, 178–181
  reality production kit 181
  script formulations 182
  Stake and interest 124

  Stake inoculation 181
  View of subjectivity 11, 14
  see also cognition, discourse, emotion, memory

Eagleton, T. 204
Edley, N. 81
Edwards, D. 8, 9, 31, 40–41, 56, 66, 80, 106, 117, 123, 149, 167, 169, 170–4, 183, 184–5, 193, 196, 218, 219, 220, 221, 222, 226, 227, 236, 238, 244
Ekman, P. 170
El Saadawi 111
Ellemers, N., 39
Elliott, G. 53
Emler, N. P. 25
Engels, F. 49
Escher, S. 94
Evans, G. 39
Evans, T. 98
Eysenck, H. 151
Education
  Ideologies of 184–5
  Cued elicitation 184
Embodiment, *see* bodies
Emotion 170–4, 182, 244
  see also cognition
Empiricism 8, 9, 79, 126, 217
  see also positivism, science, methodology
Enlightenment 79, 210
  Myths of 202
Environment, the, *see* Green issues
Epistemology, *see* knowledge
Ethnomethodology 167
Experiments 7, 25–27
  Criticisms of 27, 44, 60, 169, 230
  see also empiricism, science, methodology

Fairbairn, W.R.D. 73
Fee, D. 83
Feyerabend, P.K. 25
Fine, M. 130, 148
Fiske, S.T. 10, 19
Flament, C. 33
Fodor, J.A. 161
Foucault, M. 11, 13, 28, 47, 56, 57, 80, 82, 118, 138–145, 155, 164, 183, 229, 233–5, 241, 245
  And interlinking of power, subjectivity and knowledge 233–5
  And Marx 13, 61–65, 67, 138, 233, 239–40
  And postmodernism 82, 200
  And subjectivity 83, 90, 138–145, 233 243

And psychoanalysis/psychiatry 90–1, 137, 139, 144
And sexuality 115, 120, 141
Confession 141, 144
Disciplinary power 140, 233, 234
Geneaology/history 91, 143, 145, 233, 234, 243
Panopticon 140–1
Sovereign power 139
Technology of the self 147–8
see also discourse, discursive psychology, Marxism, power
Fox, D. 51, 56, 57, 148, 248
Fraser, N. 119
Frenkel-Brunswik, E. 54, 55, 185
Freud, S. 11, 12, 14, 54, 71–2, 84–6, 87, 92, 96, 115, 136–7, 243
Frohmann, L. 124
Fromm, E. 53, 54, 79
Frosh, S. 73, 86, 96
Fukuyama, F. 65, 226, 235
Fuss, D. 120
Facts 7, 26, 177
see also discursive psychology
Fascism 53, 55
Feminism 2, 3, 59, 86, 98–130, 211, 236, 241–2
And ethnicity 100
And social intervention 236
Commitment 125–6
Definitions of 99–100
Influence 126–7
Jouissance 91
L'écriture feminine 91
Liberal 100, 118
Marxist 100
Misogyny 95
Patriarchy 72, 88, 90, 101, 102, 108
Phallogocentrism 90
Political 122–3
Postmodern 100, 115, 117–121
Post-structuralist 112, 117
Psychoanalytic 90–91, 100
Radical 100 Rape 124
see also bodies, gender, heterosexism, knowledge, lesbianism, power, relativism, sexism, sexuality
Frankfurt School, The 53–5, 160
Critical theory 53–4
Authoritarian personality 54–5
Freedom 143, 155, 206, 243
Free will/agency 144, 145, 155, 238

Gallop, J. 86
Gane, M. 56, 66, 106, 183, 184, 209, 236

Gatens, M. 158
Gavey, N. 127
Georgaca, E 79, 93–5, 204, 210, 236
Gergen, K.J. 8, 27, 28, 81, 114, 117, 134, 154–5, 160, 161–2, 165, 174, 175, 200, 201, 211, 220, 227, 245, 246–7
Gergen, M. 126
Gibson, J. 124
Gilbert, G. N.
Gill, R. 105–6, 122, 126, 193, 200, 204, 222, 226, 242, 246
Gillett, G. 175
Gilligan, C. 101, 123, 126
Goffman, E. 21
Goldberg, B., 223–4
Gordo-López, A.J., 223–4
Gough, B. 248
Grace, W. 52
Gramsci, A. 51
Greenaway, P. 87
Gender 3, 14, 90, 92, 99, 101, 102 111, 112, 116, 119, 120, 137, 158, 183, 242
And interruption 172
As performance 114–15, 120–1
Inequalities 103–7, 108
Roles 96
see also feminism, heterosexism, bodies
Genealogy, *see* Foucault
Gestalt psychologists 206
Green issues 188
Ecology struggles 52
Groups 10, 19, 30, 32–7, 39
Conflict 20–2, 186
Influence 67 Majority 186
Minimal group paradigm 33, 34
Minority 32, 46, 185
Relations 20
Processes 6, 22–3, 46

Habermas, J. 145, 202
Hacking, I. 147
Hague, W. 177
Hamilton, D.L. 32, 185
Haraway, D. 59, 115–16, 130, 146, 217
Hare-Mustin, R.T. 84
Harper, D.J. 79, 93–5, 204, 210, 236
Harré, R. 8, 27, 28, 135, 136, 161, 162, 165, 175, 188
Harvey, D. 7
Haslam, S.A. 38
Hayes, B.K.
Heenan, C., 128, 223–4, 236
Hegel, G.W.F. 48
Henriques, J., 28, 40, 89, 97, 134, 157, 165

Hepburn, A. 92, 122, 124–5, 147, 163, 204, 205, 227
Heritage, J.C. 56
Herzlich, C. 31
Hewstone, M., 32, 39
Hinshelwood, R.D. 59
Hogan, R.T. 25
Hogg, M.A. 32, 36, 193
Hollway, W. 11, 14, 71, 72, 74–8, 86, 89–90, 97, 130, 134, 150, 157–8, 165, 241
Hook, D. 196
Hopkins, N. 6, 34, 37, 38–9, 41, 44, 230, 238–9
Horkheimer, M. 53, 54
Horwitz, M. 34
Humm, M. 99
Hearing voices network 94
Hegemony 51, 63
  Definition 51
  Heterosexual 115
  see also Marxism
Hermeneutic circle 218
Heteroglossia, see Bakhtin
Heterosexism 14, 16, 59, 107–111, 120, 172, 242
  Heterosexist talk 110–111
  Heterosexual other 158
  Homophobia 107
Holocaust 22, 220
Humanism 80, 87, 119
  Assumptions 205
  Bourgeois 79
  Liberal 108, 118
  Vs structuralism 205
  see also individualism

Ibáñez, T. 215, 222, 248
Ingleby, D. 80
Iñiguez, L. 216, 248
Irigaray, L. 90, 119
Irwin, C., 28, 89, 97, 134, 157, 165
Israel, J. 32
Identity 39, 41, 119, 230
  see also social identity theory
Ideology 13, 15, 29, 34, 46, 48–9, 51–3 55–7, 80, 82, 102, 106, 109, 139, 143, 152–154, 183, 222, 236, 240, 244
  Ideology and Consciousness 159
  And discourse 56, 61–3
  Critique 80
  Intellectual 183–4
  Liberal humanist 108
  Lived 183–4
  see also Marxism

Ideological dilemmas 14, 47, 56, 66, 106, 109, 183–5, 236, 237
  Talking of the Royal Family 190–3
Inequality 16, 19, 222
Individual, the 7, 10, 12, 13
Individual/social 6, 13, 25, 40, 43, 89, 208, 217
  see also binary oppositions
Individualism 25, 29, 30, 60–61, 95, 224
  Criticism of 25, 30, 79–80, 216, 236, 238, 240, 241
  see also Marxism, subjectivity
Information processing 10, 19, 25, 32, 39, 60, 183, 203
  see also cognition
Information technology 7, 155, 226
Intelligence 139
Intentions 63
Inter-disciplinarity 201, 216, 246
Interpretative repertoires 103, 112
  Of culture 187
Interviews 3
Iron John 80–1, 82
  see also masculinity

Jameson, F. 15, 82, 199, 201, 224
Jefferson, T. 76–8
Jodelet, D. 31
Johnstone, L. 39
Jones, E.E. 29
Jung, C.G. 80
Jealousy 213
Just world, the 192

Kamuf, P. 118–19
Kant, I. 143
Kellner, D. 201
Kelly, G. 175
Kitzinger, C., 10, 14, 107–109, 118, 122, 123, 126, 129, 130, 158, 161, 242
Klein, M. 11, 12, 14, 59, 71–4, 80, 92, 96
Knorr Cetina, K. 25
Kolominsky, Y. 43
Kristeva, J. 119
Kroger, R.O. 196
Kuhn, T.S. 25
Kvale, S. 200, 227
Knowledge 7–10, 14, 136, 224, 226, 228–235
  Epistemology 14, 15, 121, 125, 153, 166, 216, 222 199
  see also empiricism, Foucault, positivism, postmodernism, realism, relativism, science

Knowledge, subjectivity and society 15
   Interdependence between 217, 229–235,
     237, 243

Lacan, J. 11, 14, 82, 87–92, 96, 110 149, 158
   And subjectivity 138
   Imaginary, the (mirror stage) 87–8, 149
   Symbolic, the 87–8, 92
   Real, the 87–8, 91
   Phallus, the 88
   Law of the father 88
   Problems with 90
Langer, M. 59
Lash, S. 7
Latour, B. 64
Lawson, H. and Appignanesi, L.
LeBon, G. 38
Levinson, D.J. 54, 55, 185
Lucey, H. 158
Luria, A.L. 176
Lynch, M. 168
Lyotard, J.F. 9, 11, 15, 81, 199, 201, 202–3,
     214, 217, 218, 224, 245
Laboratory studies 22, 34–5, 42
   see also experiments, methodology,
     positivism
Language 7, 29, 91, 205–7, 223, 224, 225,
     233, 244–5
   Action-orientated 163, 176–7, 244
   Constructive role 83, 84–6
   Games (Wittgenstein) 203
   Philosophy of 135–6
   Pre-linguistic 88
   see also structuralism and post-
     structuralism
Lesbianism 14, 108–9
   Gay affirmative research 108, 118
   Lesbian and gay issues 10, 107–111, 127
   Lesbian phallus 90, 110, 113, 120, 138
   Queer theory 120
   see also gender, feminism
Liberalism 6, 7, 189
   Liberal pluralism 122
   see also society, humanism
Logocentrism, *see* deconstruction

MacMartin, C. 124
Macnagten, P. 188
Madill, A. 221
Malson, H. 112–13, 117, 118
Manstead, A.S.R. and Hewstone, M.
Maracek, J. 84
Marcuse, H. 53, 54, 79
Markova, I. 31
Marks, D. 223–4

Marshall, H. 35–6
Marx, K. 12, 43, 46–67, 224, 229, 235, 243
   see also Marxism
Matoesian, G.W. 124
Maybin, J. 164
McFadden, M. 248
McGarty, C.
McGuire, W.J. 27
McHoul, A. 52, 168
McLellan, D. 52, 55
McLaughlin, T. 79, 93–5, 204, 210, 236
McRae, N. 32
Mercer, N.M. 56, 184–5
Michael, M. 60, 64, 68, 69, 188
Middleton, D. 56, 66, 106, 183, 184, 193, 236
Miles, R. 185
Milgram, S. 23–4, 44, 238
Miller, A.G. 24
Millett, K. 100, 102
Minsky, R. 88
Mischel, W. 203
Mitchell, J. 86
Moghaddam, F.M. 42–3, 247
Moi, T. 86
Moscovici, S. 24, 29–30, 31, 32, 42, 45, 46,
     175
Mühlhäusler, P. 188
Mulkay, M. 25
Myers, D.G. 6, 23, 247
Marxism 1, 3, 4, 6, 7, 8, 12, 13, 42, 46–67,
     149, 202, 230, 231, 237, 239–40, 243
   Alienation 47, 50, 239
   And psychology 46, 237
   And society 6, 25
   Anti-individualism 13, 237
   Class, *see also* social class 52, 62, 67, 237,
     239–40
   Commodity fetishism/reification 60, 201
   Dialectical materialism 48
   Economic base 48–9, 52–3, 67
   False consciousness 51, 54, 57, 61, 149, 239
   Hegemony 51
   Historical materialism 48, 58, 68
   Ideological superstructure 48–9, 52–3, 239
   Ideology 51–2, 240
   Labour theory of value 49–50
   Materialism vs idealism 51
   Mode of production 48
   Power 50
   Problems with 52–4
   Revolution 50, 55, 63, 243
   Subjectivity 52
   Utopia 60, 68–9
   see also Foucault, ideology, power,
     psychoanalysis, postmodernism

Masculinity 80–1, 86, 98
Memory 22, 168–9, 195, 244
   Traditional approach 32
   see also discursive psychology, cognition
Metanarrative, see postmodernism
Metaphysics 206–7
Methodology
   Methodological critique 25–7
   Quantification 9
   see also science, positivism and
      empiricism
Mind
   And society 12, 14, 229
   As mirror 217–18
   see also cognition, individual/social,
      subjectivity
Modernity 7, 9, 200, 201, 234
Monarchy, criticism of 190–3
Moral superiority, see self-referentiality

National NOW Times 98
Neitzsche, F. 143
Nicholson, L. 119
Nightingale, D. J. 116, 117, 149, 193,
   200
Nisbett, R. 203
Narrative 94, 116, 202, 203
   see also metanarrative
Nationalism 16, 39 Banal 2, 193
Neutrality 5
Nolan, C. 198
NSPCC Helpline 163, 193

Oakes, P.J., 36, 38
Operario, D. 29
Orne, M.T. 27
Obedience 23–4
Object relations theory 72–6
   Depressive position 74
   Infant development 72, 73
   Paranoid schizoid position 74
   Projective identification 73
   Separation/engulfment 73
   see also psychoanalysis, Klein, Hollway
Oppositions 15
Oppression 19
Other, the 158, 207, 211
   Self/other 158

Pancer, S. M. 25, 29
Parker, I. 8, 11, 14, 39, 46, 47, 58–61, 69, 71,
   72, 79–83, 93–5, 96, 114, 122, 150, 167,
   193, 200, 204, 210–11, 213, 215, 227,
   232, 238, 241, 245
Parker, N. 117, 150, 193

Peffer, R.
Pepitone, A. 25
Peräkylä, A. 237
Perkins, R. 107, 122, 130
Phoenix, A. 100
Piaget, J. 175
Poster, M. 53
Potter, J. 8, 9, 28, 31, 40, 64, 80, 103–5, 107,
   111, 112, 116, 117, 123, 124, 135, 149,
   157, 161, 162, 163, 167, 169, 172,
   175–8, 183, 185–190, 193, 196, 213,
   218, 219, 220, 221, 226, 227, 237,
   238–9, 244
Prilleltensky, I. 51, 56, 148, 248
Paedophiles 70
Paradoxes 15, 142
   Of freedom 142
   see also subjectivity
Paranormal 178–181, 195
   see also discursive psychology
Patriarchy, see Feminism
Personality 22, 134, 151–4
   Critical approach to 151–4
   see also subjectivity
Phenomenology 83
Politics and the political 1, 6, 7, 123, 212,
   214, 223, 234, 240, 244–5, 246
   Maxims of practical politics 188–9, 195
   see also Foucault, postmodernism, power
Positivism 7–8, 9, 10, 26, 52, 80, 217
   see also science, knowledge, empiricism
Postmodernism 2, 4, 12, 15, 198–227, 238,
   244–6
   and critical social psychology 210–23
   and economics 201
   And Marxism 226
   And politics 200, 203, 204, 211–212,
      213–14, 221–3, 245–6
   And post/structuralism 205–10
   And psychoanalysis 81–3
   And society 7
   Approach to knowledge 9–10, 198, 202–3,
      215–23, 245
   Approach to subjectivity 11, 15, 198,
      217–19, 224–6, 245, 246
   Definitions 199–202
   Intervention 236–7
   Metanarrative 9, 96, 119, 202–4, 207,
      245
   Problems with 81–2, 200
   Theories of 199–210
   Uncertainty 245
   see also feminism, deconstruction,
      knowledge, metaphysics, post-
      structuralism, Foucault, Lyotard

Post-structuralism 14, 58, 60, 61, 81, 199,
    200, 223
    And deconstruction 206–7
    And psychoanalysis 87–92
    Contrasted with structuralism 206, 223,
        225
    see also deconstruction, feminism,
        postmodernism, structuralism
Power 13, 50, 61, 82, 88, 93–4, 106, 121, 235
    Foucault contra Marx 61–65, 82, 235,
        239–40
    Power/knowledge 144, 233–5, 243
    Power relations 6, 13, 51, 56, 63, 83, 100,
        222, 235
    see also Foucault, ideology, Marxism
Practical intervention, *see* critical practice
Prejudice 3, 20, 32
Promise keepers 98, 102, 107, 112
Psychology's big mistake 141
Psy-complex 80, 145–6
    see also Foucault, Parker, Rose
Psychoanalysis 1, 3–4, 10, 12, 13, 14, 31,
        70–95, 119, 122, 136–8, 149, 211, 230,
        231, 240–241
    And Marxism 53, 54, 58–9, 66, 70, 80,
        82–3, 136
    Death instinct 54, 72
    Introjection 75–6
    Libido 31
    Oedipus complex 72, 88, 92, 115
    Projection 70, 75–6, 185
    Repression 31, 71, 84–6, 240
    see also Freud, Klein, Lacan, object relations
        theory, postmodernism, unconscious
Punishment 22

Qualitative studies 13
    Q methods 108
    see also methodology, experiments,
        positivism

Rabbie, J.M. 34
Rabinow, P. 91
Radley, A. 56, 66, 106, 183, 184, 236
Read, A.J. 49
Reich, J. W. 29
Reicher, S. 6, 22, 34, 36, 37, 38–9, 41, 44,
        230, 238–9
Rennie, H. 124, 130
Reynold, K. 35
Ricoeur, P. 72
Ring, K. 25
Robinson, P. 45
Roiser, M. 54, 55, 69
Romme, M. 94

Rorty, R. 175, 217–19, 227
Rose, N. 64, 80, 145–6, 162, 165
Rosenthal, R. 27
Ross, L. 203
Ryle, G. 134, 135
Racism 16, 19, 20–21, 32, 35, 40, 172, 183
    Repertoires of 185–7
    Practical politics 187–190
Realism 8, 66, 201, 219–224
    Objectivism 124, 163, 221
    Vs relativism 6, 15, 59–60, 115, 122–7 153,
        199, 215–223, 231, 245–6
    see also critical realism, discourse,
        knowledge, relativism, social
        constructionism
Realistic conflict theory 21, 33
Reality claims, *see* circular reasoning
Reality production kit 181
Reality/representation 225
Reality TV 195
Reductionism 30
Reflexivity 200, 231, 232, 236–7
    And alternative literary forms 232
    see also Ashmore, relativism, science
Relationship counselling 171–3, 176
Relativism 9, 59, 210, 214, 215–223, 231,
    And commitment 220, 221–222
    And feminism 122–7, 218, 242
    see also realism
Rhetoric 4, 14, 40, 106, 173, 183–193, 219,
        221, 222, 244
    Kaleidoscope of commonsense 192
    Rhetorical commonplace 187–190
    Rhetorical intervention 236
    see also Billig, discourse, ideology
Robber's Cave study 21

Sacks, H. 179
Sampson, E. E. 25, 60, 116, 159, 160, 200,
        204, 211
Sanford, R.N. 54 , 55, 185
Sartre, J.-P. 53
Saussure, F. de 87, 205–6, 207, 208–9, 225
Sayers, J. 86, 96
Schegloff, E. A. 172
Sears, D. O. 42
Secord, P. F. 27, 28
Sève, L. 58
Sherif, M. 21, 33, 44, 45, 238
Shotter, J. 134, 155–6, 160, 165, 175, 176,
        211
Silverman, I. 27
Sim, S.
Simon, B. 39
Simons, H. 214

Sloan, T 56, 58, 151–4, 162, 163, 243, 248
Smith, A. 49, 183
Smith, B.H. 9, 123, 124, 221
Smith, M.B.
Smithson, J. 172
Spears, R. 32, 58–61, 215
Speer, S. 107, 111, 172
Squire, C. 94, 96, 119, 127
Standen, P. 149–150
Steiner, I.D. 25
Stiven, H. 103–5
Stokoe, L. 172
Stowell-Smith, M. 79, 93–5, 204, 210, 236
Science 25–7
    As language game 203
    Scientific method 7, 46, 108
    Scientific rationality 9, 46
    Sociology of scientific knowledge 26, 64, 116, 125, 203, 216
Self categorisation theory 36–9, 238
    Criticism of 37–9
Self-referentiality, see reality claims
Sexism 3, 15, 32, 103–7
Sexuality 91, 120
    see also bodies, heterosexuality, Foucault
Signifier-signified, see structuralism
Skinnerians 232
Social change 1, 4, 6, 16, 22, 32, 216, 225
Social class 3, 4, 6, 13, 52, 62
    Class conflict 13, 67
    see also Marxism, Foucault
Social cognition 10, 19–45, 46, 166, 183, 236, 237
    Criticisms of 39–41, 195, 236
Social constructionism 2, 15, 59–60, 108, 117, 124–7, 147, 149, 162, 174–5, 222, 223
    constructivism 175
    social constructivism 175
Social identity theory 32, 33–6, 44
    Criticism of 34–6
    see also Groups, experiments
Social psychology
    European vs North American 30, 31
    see also social cognition
Social representations theory 31, 175
Social structures 13, 243
    Reality of 240
Society 5–7, 29, 228–235
    Liberal 6, 25, 108
    Relation to subjectivity and knowledge, see knowledge
    see also Marxism and postmodernism
Sociology 7

Sociology of scientific knowledge, see science
Stalinism 55
Stanford prison experiment 21
Stress 147
Structuralism 110, 205–6, 209
    Signifier/signified 205–6, 225
    Signifying systems 110, 201, 214
    Speech-writing distinction 208–9
    Vs humanism 205
    see also post-structuralism, Saussure
Subject, the
    As schizophrenic 199
    Death of 134
    Desire as 'truth' of 91
    Theory of 15, 134, 149
Subjective/objective split 148, 206
Subjectivity 4, 10–11, 14, 15, 92, 94 133–165, 228–235, 240, 241, 242–3
    and critical psychology 148, 242–3
    And reality 8
    As paradoxical 142, 148, 160, 243
    Dialogic 159
    Discursive 11
    Gendered 115
    Philosophy of 135–148
    Production of 16
    Psychoanalytic 11, 47, 86
    Social cognitive 10
    Relation to knowledge and society, see knowledge
    see also deconstruction, Foucault, postmodernism
Symbolism 5, 29, 30

Tajfel, H. 24, 29, 30, 32, 33, 34, 39, 41, 42, 45, 230
Taylor, S.E. 10, 19
Thermel, M. 31
Thompson, J.B. 55–6, 69
Trolier, T. 185
Turner, J.C. 33, 34, 36–9, 41
Textuality 15, 213, 232
    And reflexivity 232
    And tectonics 213
    Nothing outside the text 124, 212
    Textual idealism 124–5
Therapy 81, 144
    And postmodernism 83–4
    Constructionist 84
    Deconstructive 93

Unger, R. 99
Urry, J. 7
Ussher, J. 113–14, 130
Uncertainty, see postmodernism

Unconscious 11, 71, 72, 73, 87, 89, 119, 136, 207
  Dialogic 84–7
  see psychoanalysis
US politics 168–9
  Watergate 168
  Iran-Contra hearings 168
  Nixon 168
  Oliver North 168
  Bill Clinton's grand jury inquisition 168–9
  Kennedy assassination 179

Van Knippenberg, A. 39
Venn, C., 28, 89, 97, 134, 157, 165
Verma, J. 31
Voloshinov, V.N. 176
Vygotsky, L.S. 59, 175, 176
Voices of the mind 157
  see also Bakhtin

Wagner, W., 31
Walker, I. 29, 35, 43, 45
Walkerdine, V. 28, 89, 97, 126, 130, 134, 157, 158, 159, 165, 248
Warner, S. 128, 223–4, 236
Wertsch, J.V. 157
West, D. 49, 50, 51, 53, 54, 206

Wetherell, M. 35–6, 40, 44, 45, 81, 103–5 112, 127, 129, 135, 157, 161, 164, 167, 172, 183, 185–190, 193, 196, 213, 238–9
Wexler, P. 248
Widdicombe, S. 41, 193, 230
Wierzbicka, A. 170
Wiggins, S. 116–17, 236
Wildsmith, A. 116
Wilke, H.A.M. 39
Wilkinson, S. 99, 100, 101, 102, 103, 122, 123, 130, 158, 242
Willig, C. 54, 55, 69, 114, 167, 193, 236
Winnicott, D.W. 73
Wittgenstein, L. 28, 134, 135, 161, 167, 176, 202
Wood, L.A. 124, 130, 196
Wooffitt, R. 178–181, 193, 195, 196
Woolgar, S. 25, 125, 175
Wowk, M. 124
Websites 226, 248
World War 2 20, 22, 30, 33

Yardley, L. 113

Zaleznik, A.
Zimbardo, P.G. 21–22, 238
Žižek, S. 53